MW00857140

THE ESSENTIAL SCHOOL
COUNSELOR IN A CHANGING SOCIETY

This book is dedicated to Cameron, Jackson, Ryan, Mia, and Allison, who have enriched my life

THE ESSENTIAL SCHOOL COUNSELOR IN A CHANGING SOCIETY

Jeannine R. Studer

University of Tennessee, Knoxville

Los Angeles | London | New Delhi
Singapore | Washington DC

Los Angeles | London | New Delhi
Singapore | Washington DC

FOR INFORMATION:

SAGE Publications, Inc.
2455 Teller Road
Thousand Oaks, California 91320
E-mail: order@sagepub.com

SAGE Publications Ltd.
1 Oliver's Yard
55 City Road
London EC1Y 1SP
United Kingdom

SAGE Publications India Pvt. Ltd.
B 1/I 1 Mohan Cooperative Industrial Area
Mathura Road, New Delhi 110 044
India

SAGE Publications Asia-Pacific Pte. Ltd.
3 Church Street
#10-04 Samsung Hub
Singapore 049483

Acquisitions Editor: Kassie Graves
Associate Editor: Eve Oettinger
Assistant Editor: Lauren Habib
Editorial Assistant: Elizabeth Luizzi
Production Editor: Stephanie Palermini
Copy Editor: Kate Macomber Stern
Typesetter: C&M Digitals (P) Ltd.
Proofreader: Penelope Sippel
Indexer: Jean Casalegno
Cover Designer: Michael Dubowe
Marketing Manager: Shari Countryman

Copyright © 2015 by SAGE Publications, Inc.

All rights reserved. No part of this book may be reproduced or utilized in any form or by any means, electronic or mechanical, including photocopying, recording, or by any information storage and retrieval system, without permission in writing from the publisher.

Printed in the United States of America

Library of Congress Cataloging-in-Publication Data

Studer, Jeannine R.

The essential school counselor in a changing society / Jeannine R. Studer, University of Tennessee, Knoxville.

pages cm
Includes bibliographical references and index.

ISBN 978-1-4522-5746-4 (pbk. : alk. paper)
ISBN 978-1-4833-1245-3 (web pdf) 1. Educational counseling. I. Title.

LB1027.5.S85313 2015
371.4'22—dc23   2013038067

This book is printed on acid-free paper.

14 15 16 17 18 10 9 8 7 6 5 4 3 2 1

BRIEF CONTENTS

Detailed Contents

Chapter 3 Comprehensive, Developmental School Counseling Programs 87

Michael Bundy

PREFACE

School system seeking motivated, passionate individual who is flexible, has an exceptional ability to communicate, knowledge of collaboration through networking, and inordinate stamina to deal with the myriad job demands. Individuals seeking a school counseling position must have indepth knowledge of the school environment, extraordinary ability to teach classroom guidance lessons while maintaining classroom management, and outstanding individual and group counseling skills to work with students on academic, vocational, and personal/social concerns. Consultation skills, awareness of developmental stages of growth, and ability to advocate for change while demonstrating effectiveness of interventions are additional skills required for this position. The successful candidate must also have the skills to lead a comprehensive, developmental school counseling program while bringing about systemic change in which all students are able to access equal educational opportunities.

An enthusiastic, dedicated school counselor who advocates for the students with whom he/she works is one of the most vital, exciting, exhausting, life-altering positions in the school. As the invented job description illustrates in the example above, the school counselor has multiple roles to play in which a variety of skills and knowledge are necessary. As you begin your journey to enter the school counselor profession, consider your reasons for choosing this profession and the skills you possess that will assist you in successfully working with the many stakeholders who have a mutual interest in the development of school-age youth. The profession of school counseling is one that can be overwhelming, and emotionally and physically strenuous as we listen to students' struggles, hear stories of gruesome living conditions, and try to understand how youth are able to cope despite deplorable life situations. It can also be one of the most rewarding professions when we are able to see that our work with students has contributed to new skill development and knowledge that have led to well-adjusted, confident adults. For an example of how you are able to be a powerful force in each student's life, read the following incident as relayed by an elementary school counselor.

A professional school counselor reminisced about one of his male 5th grade students, who faced difficult conditions but was eventually able to learn resiliency skills to achieve personal goals. The counselor explained that this young student lived with his single mother in a rough section of the small, rural town. The town had some gang activity with daily violence that caused the young man to develop anger issues, resulting in physical fights nearly every day. The counselor clarified that the student stated he did not like to fight but felt that if he did not stand up for himself, the situation would be worse because others would view him as a "wimp" and an easy target. The counselor listened empathically and explained to the student that although he lived in a tough setting, he had the choice of being a student while he was in school. This youth's intelligence helped him meet his academic goals and during games of chess that the counselor used as a counseling strategy to engage the 5th grader, the counselor continually reinforced the boy's progress toward his goals. By the end of the school year the student grew academically and socially due to the interest and time the school counselor invested in him.

The information in this book is intended to provide a comprehensive understanding of the role of the professional school counselor in a wide range of settings. The chapters are written to address the Council for Accreditation of Counseling and Related Educational Programs (CACREP) 2009 standards for school counseling in the foundation, counseling prevention, and intervention, diversity and advocacy, assessment, research and evaluation, academic development, collaboration and consultation, and leadership domains. Throughout this book I have addressed the knowledge, skills, and practices for each of the standards for school counselor trainees, in order to develop a greater understanding of the school counselor's role and what successful practice in a school setting entails. Each domain and standard is

CACREP

indicated by a marginal icon within the various chapters through a didactic discussion, case studies, activities designed for K-12 students, and conceptual application activities to facilitate knowledge of self and the profession. In addition to the information included in this text, a companion website supplements these materials.

The increasing diversity of our education system is a reflection of how our school population has changed over the decades. School counselors are instrumental in contributing to a safe, respectful school environment with a culture of appreciation for differences. In addition, social justice principles serve as a basis for designing, implementing, and evaluating strategies, programs, and policies to promote egalitarian practice. As school counselors, we strive to ensure that all students have access to opportunities that enhance academic, vocational, social, and personal success. Too often school counseling students are educated about multiculturalism and social justice in individual courses with little understanding of how these areas are infused in all aspects of our professional obligations. Therefore, I have addressed these issues throughout each of the chapters, integrating relevant concepts with theories and ideas applicable to the school counselor's profession.

For School Counselors-in-Training: As you read the materials in this book, take time to read and reflect on your reasons for entering the school counseling profession. Did you choose this profession because you had a school counselor who was instrumental in helping you improve your grades or assisting with your post-secondary plans? Perhaps this person was significant in supporting you when you were having difficulties in your personal life. Did you choose this profession because you wish you had had someone in your school who was able to provide the help you needed during troubled times in your life? These are exciting times to be a source of support in the schools and make a difference in the lives of preK–12 students in various capacities. The *conceptual application activities* included throughout the book are designed to promote a greater understanding of yourself and the profession. *Student activities* in the chapters are provided to assist you in applying theory as you work with school-age youth.

Your education does not end when you leave your training program. This is just the foundation for the skills and knowledge you will need to work with youth in the 21st century. Be aware that as a novice school counselor, you will be asked to perform the same tasks with the wisdom that experienced practitioners enjoy. This expectation may seem unreasonable, but nevertheless there is a belief that you will leave your training program with the same skills and knowledge as those who have been in the profession for many years. Don't hesitate to consult with your experienced colleagues, join your professional organizations, read counseling literature, take a leadership position to advocate for our profession, and most important of all, take care of yourself as you enter this inspiring, yet exhausting profession.

For Counselor Educators. The materials in this book provide foundational information for students entering the school counseling specialty area. The chapters were written by school counselors for school counselors-in-training and contain practical advice, case studies, self-reflection activities, resources, student activities, and valuable websites. Several chapters were written to supplement some of the free-standing courses in the counseling curriculum with the intention of specifically applying concepts that are school-specific. For instance, *Chapter 5—The School Counselor as a Group Leader and Facilitator* is not intended to replace a course on group work, but rather to provide school counselor trainees specific group concepts that relate to a school setting. Likewise, *Chapter 8—The School Counselor and Career Counseling,* supports the knowledge of school counselors-in-training through in-depth discussions of school-related career activities, websites, and resources.

This book is divided into three sections: "Foundations of School Counseling," "Counseling, Intervention, and Prevention," and "Enhancing Academics through a Positive School Culture." A description of the chapters in each section follows.

SECTION I. FOUNDATIONS OF SCHOOL COUNSELING

Pearl Buck wrote, "if you want to understand today, you have to search yesterday." School counselors who are preparing to work with school-age youth have knowledge of the school counselor pioneers who paved the path for school counseling in the 21st century. As you read chapter 1 you will find that some of the same challenges our predecessors confronted are still troubling the profession today, although the American School Counselor Association (ASCA) has taken significant steps in supporting school counselors at all levels. The chapters in this section provide an integrated base for the roles and responsibilities of the school counselor and the movements that led to the profession it is today.

Chapter 1—From Guidance Worker to Professional School Counselor

Chapter 2—The School Counselor and Ethical and Legal Issues

Chapter 3—Comprehensive and Developmental School Counseling Programs

Chapter 4—The School Counselor's Role in Assessment and Research

Chapter 1 From Guidance Worker to Professional School Counselor

In this chapter the history of the school counseling profession, with attention to the early school counselor pioneers and counselor identity, is discussed. The characteristics of effective counselors, credentialing, professional organizations, state models, and predictions for the future of school counseling are examined.

Chapter 2 The School Counselor and Ethical and Legal Issues

School counselors often have difficulty making professional decisions, particularly when legal and ethical issues collide. A decision-making model is provided in this chapter with attention to moral decision-making principles. The ASCA ethical standards are summarized and applied to vignettes that relate to each of the standards.

Chapter 3 Comprehensive and Developmental School Counseling Programs

Michael Bundy

This chapter is written to supplement the information within the ASCA National Model—3rd edition (2012). The foundation, management, delivery services, and accountability components, in addition to the integral themes of advocacy, leadership, collaboration, and systemic change are discussed.

Chapter 4 The School Counselor's Role in Assessment and Research

The importance of accountability in the schools including program, school counselor competencies and assessment, and the use of needs assessments to determine program goals are highlighted in this chapter. Action-based research and other evidence-based strategies for assessing program effectiveness are also summarized.

SECTION II. COUNSELING, INTERVENTION, AND PREVENTION

Vocational guidance was the catalyst behind the school counseling profession, and throughout the ensuing years career planning and development remain a critical component of the school counselor's role. Throughout the decades school-age youth brought personal and social issues into the school environment, and school counselors responded to these concerns through group, individual, and crisis counseling to mediate the negative influences that impact personal growth and learning.

Chapter 5—The School Counselor as a Group Leader and Facilitator

Chapter 6—Individual Counseling in the School Environment

Chapter 7—The School Counselor's Role in Crisis Counseling

Chapter 8—The School Counselor and Career Counseling

Chapter 5 The School Counselor as a Group Leader and Facilitator

Tara Jungersen & Carolyn Berger

School counselors provide group counseling in the school milieu. The authors of this chapter provide an overview of group work in schools with specific strategies and considerations for implementing groups.

Chapter 6 Individual Counseling in the School Environment

The school counselor has the skills and training to provide individual counseling to school-age youth. Motivational interviewing is viewed as a "front-loaded" intervention used with all theoretical approaches. Popular common counseling theories counselors adapt in school settings are summarized in addition to the use of creative arts in counseling.

Chapter 7 The School Counselor's Role in Crisis Counseling

The various types of crises are examined as are the various cognitive, emotional, and behavioral responses to these events. A crisis intervention model that school counselors are able to implement for work with youth in crisis is summarized. In addition, specific crises such as youth living in poverty, child abuse and neglect, substance use and abuse, homelessness, youth who self-harm, bullying, and suicidal ideation are discussed.

Chapter 8 The School Counselor and Career Counseling

Aaron H. Oberman

In this chapter school counselor roles and responsibilities related to careers are discussed and sample activities and websites for use with K-12 youth are given. In addition, this chapter contains suggestions for writing letters of recommendations as well as career planning strategies to use with diverse students and their families. Finally, a glimpse of future career trends is offered with attention to the impact of technology.

SECTION III. ENHANCING ACADEMICS THROUGH A POSITIVE SCHOOL CULTURE

The school counselor is an integral part of the academic mission of the school, and a collaborative partner in creating a safe, trusting academic environment for all students to develop to their fullest extent. The effective school counselor has an awareness of child and adolescents' developmental stages, needs, and tasks. A multiculturally aware school counselor has a responsibility to self-assess awareness, knowledge, and skills to assist all youth and their families. Advocating for diverse youth and their needs in addition to collaborating and consulting with stakeholders provides an enriched, respectful academic culture that enhances the development of students regardless of differences.

Chapter 9 The School Counselor's Role in Academic Achievement

Deborah Buchanan

This chapter provides an overview of the school system including the culture and climate, professional learning communities, and improving academic achievement through guidance delivery. Learning styles, classroom management, developing lesson plans, and peer programs are discussed.

Chapter 10 Developmental and Multicultural Issues of School-Age Youth

Developmental theories guide school counselors as they work with diverse students. Attention is given to students with special needs, English-language learners, students who are gifted, those with mental health disorders and disabilities, and students who are a sexual minority.

Chapter 11 The School Counselor as an Advocate and Leader

Advocacy and leadership are essential school counselor tasks to reach all students and their families. Advocacy models, characteristics of effective leaders, and strategies for communicating with school principals about the vital role of the school counselor are included in this chapter.

Chapter 12 The School Counselor as Consultant and Collaborator

In this chapter the various consultative models and collaborative strategies, including Response to Intervention and School-wide Positive Behavioral Intervention and Supports, are discussed with attention to multiculturalism. In addition, working with families of students with special needs, grandparents raising their grandchildren, and working with military families are summarized.

ACKNOWLEDGMENTS

I am grateful to numerous individuals who have been instrumental in the development of this book. First of all, I would like to acknowledge Carolyn Berger, Mike Bundy, Debbie Buchanan, Tara Jungersen, and Aaron Oberman, who offered time, energy, and expertise in writing their chapters.

I am also appreciative of Kassie Graves, senior acquisitions editor, Elizabeth Luizzi, and Eve Oettinger for their assistance in providing information, feedback, and help in the preparation of this book, and their sense of humor in listening to my dog snore during a phone conference. I would also like to acknowledge Kate Stern for her thoughful copyediting and sense of humor, and Stephanie Palermini, production editor, for her assistance with this project.

A special thank you to the following school counselors, who provided me with rich, real-life incidents they encountered as school counselors. Your experiences provide actual examples of how the classroom concepts relate to the meaningful school counselor position. I value your dedication to our profession and helping students of all ages succeed. The list of individuals follows: Beverly Anderson, Elishia Jones Basner, Sarah Bast, Betty Anne Domm, Sharon Earley, Vicki Hill, Amy Kroninger, Amy Marshall, Brittany Pollard, Andrew Phillips, Natasha Self-Dorow, Linda Treadwell, Vicki Van Ness, and Mary Webster. Finally, thanks to my husband, Jim, who played many games of golf while I worked on this book, and Maggie, my Cavalier King Charles Spaniel, who spent many hours underneath my desk.

SECTION I

FOUNDATIONS OF SCHOOL COUNSELING

Chapter 1

FROM GUIDANCE WORKER TO PROFESSIONAL SCHOOL COUNSELOR

CACREP

CACREP OUTCOME

FOUNDATIONS

A. *Knowledge*

    1. Knows history, philosophy, and trends in school counseling and educational systems.

    4. Knows professional organizations, preparation standards, and credentials that are relevant to the practice of school counseling.

B. *Skills and Practices*

    2. Demonstrates the ability to articulate, model, and advocate for an appropriate school counselor identity and program.

COUNSELING, PREVENTION, AND INTERVENTION

D. *Skills and Practices*

    1. Demonstrates self-awareness, sensitivity to others, and the skills needed to relate to diverse individuals, groups, and classrooms.

    5. Demonstrates the ability to recognize his or her limitations as a school counselor and to seek supervision or refer clients when appropriate.

Counseling reached its "adolescence" in the early 1960s and achieved a central perspective and direction. . . . The counseling profession is now being deluged by numerous forces calling for a more mature response than in an adolescent period . . . the central issue for the counseling profession today—that is, how do we best maintain hard-fought gains while moving further up the ladder of development? (Aubrey, 1983 p. 78.)

The profession of school counseling is one that has a relatively short history compared to many other occupations. It is also one that is often misunderstood, despite the American School Counselor Association's (ASCA) efforts to define and advocate for the profession of school counseling. The ASCA (n.d.) states, "Professional school counselors have a minimum of a master's degree in school counseling, meet the state certification/licensure standards, and abide by the laws of the states in which they are employed" (para. 2).

Yet we come in contact with individuals known as "credit counselors" and "weight loss counselors"; there is even a "car counselor" talk show that I recently listened to on the radio. Although these various occupations are important, many of these occupations do not require a college degree. The education and training of licensed professional counselors, and more specifically school counselors, may appear to be diluted by the use of the term 'counselor' for these other occupations. To assist in thinking about your career as a school counselor, complete Conceptual Application Exercise 1.1.

CONCEPTUAL APPLICATION EXERCISE 1.1

1. When you think of the school counselor you had when you were in school, what were some of the tasks this professional performed? What were some of the activities that your elementary school counselor performed? Middle school counselor? High school counselor?

2. Interview three different people and ask them how they would describe the role of the school counselor. Share your responses with your classmates.

No doubt, you have received different opinions from each of the individuals you interviewed from the activity above. From these responses, are you able to explain the reasons that the school counselor is such a difficult profession to describe? Do these responses give you any insight as to how the profession evolved from its inception in the early part of the twentieth century to where it is today? In the section below, read how guidance workers evolved into what are now known as ***professional school counselors***. Note the historical trends that have influenced this profession and the tasks our predecessors assumed compared with the tasks that school counselors perform today. Vocational trends, individual and group counseling, testing, accountability, organizational structure, credentialing, and the formation of our school counseling professional organization, the American School Counselor Association (ASCA), are trends that have impacted our profession. These are discussed in the next section to assist in your understanding of how the profession has grown to what it is today. A summary of state school counseling programs and models, national and state credentials and requirements, counselor identity, and characteristics of successful school counselors are included, followed by predictions for the school counseling profession.

BOX 1.1 REFLECTIONS FROM THE PROFESSION

Counselors were asked to give their answers to what they believe is the most important part of their role as a school counselor. Answers include:

- Relationships, relationships, relationships. I believe showing students, families, and school staff my desire to help and encourage students every day is the basis of my job, which I love more and more the older I get!Sharon Earley, elementary school counselor
- The most important thing about my role as a school counselor is that I have the opportunity to make a difference in a child's life every day. Even though I may never know if I have had an impact, I realize that for some children, I am an important resource that is absent in every other area of his or her life. Betty Anne Domm
- Relationship with the kids. It's the foundation for all of the advocacy, change, and support I can offer them or the larger school community. Helping kids grow starts at knowing who they are; even the most resistant parent or teacher can tell the difference between "doing my job" and genuinely, honestly knowing his/her child and trying to give the student the best you can offer. Amy Marshall

---

A HISTORICAL PERSPECTIVE

The Industrial Revolution is credited as the catalyst behind the school counseling profession. About 1890, the United States shifted from a rural to an urban society. Factories were built and families moved to urban areas for the new occupations that were created (Herr, 2001), with a large number of immigrants entering our nation in search of better opportunities. With the rapid proliferation of industries, occupations emerged that had never existed before, which created a need to prepare workers for a changing, uncertain workplace. Yet adverse social circumstances accompanied industrialization, such as indentured child servitude and child labor. It was not uncommon for children to work 12–14 hours a day under dangerous, deplorable conditions and subjected to harsh forms of punishment by their employers. Many reformists lobbied for the abolishment of child labor, but regardless of these efforts employers preferred to hire child laborers because they were more manageable and cheaper. Some parents supported child labor because they believed this form of work built character and a work ethic, not to mention the income their children brought home (Solomon-McCarthy, 2012).

Photo 1.1   Children During the Industrial Revolution

Source: © duncan1890/iStockphoto.com

Vocational Guidance

In the early 1900s compulsory education laws were passed that took youth out of factories, off the streets, and put them into the educational setting (Katz, 1976). Teachers were unprepared for this influx of students who were far different from those they had taught in previous years. There was also recognition that students needed to be prepared for the wide range of occupations which were rapidly emerging. In response, teachers were given the task of fulfilling a role of "guidance worker," a role that included a list of duties for which the teachers received no training, no additional pay, and no relief from regular classroom duties (Gysbers, 2001).

At this time Meyer Bloomfield, a leader in the vocational guidance movement, concerned that no one was guiding and evaluating students as they transitioned to work, advised students and their parents to give thought to future careers. In addition, he recognized the importance of providing occupational information to teachers who agreed to assist students with their vocational development. Therefore, 117 teachers were trained in vocational guidance techniques (Free Online Library, n.d.) but were still expected to perform their regular teaching obligations.

With various political, economic, and social issues emerging, different perspectives regarding the term "guidance" surfaced with a variety of questions. Was guidance in schools a way to prepare and assist students with educational and vocational decisions? For vocational selection? Or should guidance address concerns in all aspects of life? (Gysbers, 2001).

Jesse B. Davis is regarded as being America's first school counselor, due to his implementation of a systematic guidance program in Grand Rapids, Michigan (Pope, 2009) in the early 1900s. Davis infused guidance lessons on such topics as interpersonal communication, character development, and vocational interests into the English curriculum. Interestingly, when Davis was asked to present his work at a conference, he was "ruled out of order at first when he began to tell of using English classes for guidance. Apparently few had envisioned the possibilities through curriculum studies" (Brewer, 1942, p. 139, as cited in Pope, 2009; Zytowski, 2001). Others supported this vision and approach. As stated in the *New York Times* (1912), "The demand for a practical course of moral instruction in the public schools, and particularly in the high school, has been urgent for many years" (para. 13).

Eli Weaver and Anna Y. Reed were also instrumental in infusing guidance into the school curriculum. Weaver believed that students needed advice and guidance before entering the workforce. As a part of the work experience, he organized guidance services for boys in New York City by placing these city boys on farms to work during the summer months. Anna Reed believed that since business personnel were successful, schools should emphasize the money making potential of entering business, a concept to which she believed students would be able to relate.

Despite the efforts of these early pioneers, Frank Parsons is regarded as the "father of vocational guidance" (Zytowski, 2001). Parsons was concerned about people entering the workforce without adequate training and was a firm believer that schools needed to teach more than academics.

BOX 1.2 BIOGRAPHY OF FRANK PARSONS

Frank Parsons was born in 1854, in Mount Holly, New Jersey, entering Cornell University at the age of 16. He became a civil engineer and later worked as a laborer for a mill. After this, he taught and supervised an art program (Davis, 1969, as cited in Gummere, 1988). From there, he went to law school, where he crammed three years of law classes into one year of study. This experience resulted in illness and damaged eyes, and to recover he spent 3 years in New Mexico. After his recovery he practiced law in Boston but did not enjoy it. He turned to writing, and one of his best known books, *Choosing a Vocation*, was posthumously published. In this book he describes a career decision-making model that includes three steps:

- Self-understanding of aptitudes, skills, and interests
- Knowledge of requirements for different types of work
- Congruence of self-understanding and work requirements for job satisfaction (true reasoning)

During the early 1920s, there was a greater emphasis on educational guidance with less attention to vocational guidance. As stated by Brewer (1918, as cited in Gysbers, 2001), educational guidance was anything that "had to do with instruction or with learning . . . as a conscious effort to assist in the intellectual growth of an individual." The Great Depression in the 1930s meant a scarcity of funds for guidance programs regardless of focus.

In 1946 the Vocational Education Act (also known as the George-Barden Act) and the passage of the National Defense Education Act (NDEA) in 1958 played important roles in highlighting the vocational aspect of guidance. The George-Barden Act provided funding for the selection and training of individuals to maintain a vocational guidance program (Barrett, 1948) and was amended in 1963 to provide greater flexibility in vocational programs.

In 1957, the launching of the Russian satellite Sputnik sparked public attention and outrage, due to the perception that the USSR had surpassed the U.S. in the race for space. This event promoted a view that more "guidance counselors" were needed to identify and direct gifted students into the math and science fields. Federal monies were allocated to employ secondary school counselors to select outstanding students for these areas, so the United States could become more competitive (Herr, 2001). Teachers who were assuming guidance service positions were given training during the summer months and through year-long institutes (Gysbers, 2004; Herr, 2001) to learn how to guide students skilled in science and math.

In 1984, the Carl D. Perkins Vocational Education Act expanded career guidance and counseling programs so all students, regardless of gender, ethnicity, or handicapping conditions could develop skills in an identified occupation (Herr, 2001). This law was reauthorized in 1998 and again in 2006, with the intent of providing workers with skills that did not require an advanced degree. It was renamed the Carl D. Perkins Career and Technical Education Improvement Act of 2006.

The National Occupational Information Coordinating Committee (NOICC) of 1989 significantly impacted career guidance efforts in all schools (Herr, 2001). This federal interagency committee was designed to 1) facilitate communication between developers of occupational information; 2) help states meet the needs for vocational information; and 3) ease career decision making (Teacher's Guide to the U.S. Dept. of Education, 2000). The funding from this initiative assisted in the development of the career programs DISCOVER and SIGI Career Exploration.

In 1994, the School to Work Opportunities Act further addressed comprehensive guidance programs by passing legislation that assisted individuals in making and implementing occupational choices (Herr, 2001). This legislation provided students with the opportunity to seamlessly transition from secondary school to career, or to post secondary options. In addition, this legislation mandated that career awareness, exploration, and counseling were to begin as early as possible but no later than the seventh grade, with initial career selection to begin no later than the eleventh grade. Each of these enterprises served as forerunners to today's focus on the STEM careers, an acronym for Science, Technology, Engineering, and Math.

BOX 1.3 STEM SCHOOLS

Stem-focused schools were first developed to target students that excelled in the science and engineering occupations, so our youth would keep the United States as a leading nation in these areas. In 2009, the Program of International Student Assessment (PISA) reported that U.S. high school students ranked eighteenth in math and thirteenth in science compared to 34 other industrialized countries, with some of the higher ranked nations being much smaller with less wealth than the United States. Like the Sputnik incident, this report was a wake-up call, in that if our nation wanted to remain competitive, stronger educational efforts were needed in the areas of math, science, and technology. President Barack Obama stated, "The single most important determinant of how we do economically is going to be the skills of our workforce . . . . We used to be at the top of the heap when it came to math and science education; we are now 21st and 25th, respectively, in science and math" (Schram, 2013, B3). Identifying and enrolling gifted Hispanic and African American students who are underrepresented in these areas is a recent focus of this effort (Robeien, 2011).

Vocational concerns have obviously been the drive behind the school counseling profession, but even with this trend there were continued debates about the meaning of the term "guidance" and how it was to be delivered to students. In fact, it wasn't until 1931 that the term "counseling" was first used particularly with attention to the mental health concerns of students. This change of focus was partly due to mental health and progressive education that brought about a greater awareness of troubled youth (Gysbers, 2001) and the need for a new set of skills in the form of individual and group counseling.

Individual and Group Counseling

In the early 1900s, both Sigmund Freud and John Dewey generated an awareness of how mental health issues influenced the academic, personal, social, and moral growth of students. Guidance was seen as "problems of adjustment to health, religion, recreation, to family and friends, to school and to work" (Campbell, 1932, p. 4, as cited in Gysbers, 2001). Some argued that it was the vocational "guidance worker" who was responsible for the mental health of students, yet not everyone agreed guidance workers should assist with the emotional and moral concerns of youth (Gysbers, 2001).

E.G. Williamson (1900–1979) is one of the first individuals to emphasize the importance of a transition in the counseling profession from one that emphasized vocational development to one that focused on individual counseling. His theory, developed in the 1930s, largely borrowed from the work of Frank Parsons, outlined a six-step prescriptive model that included:

1. Analysis—gathering data about student

2. Synthesis—selecting information to better understand the student

3. Diagnosis—forming an initial hypothesis about the student's needs

4. Prognosis—problem-solving to determine an outcome

5. Treatment—identifying interventions to meet the outcome

6. Follow-up—evaluating how well the intervention worked

This directive approach, known as the Minnesota Model due to Williamson's work at the University of Minnesota (Neukrug, n.d.), was criticized due to its structured problem-solving approach, but was influential in that it created a framework for counselors to use when working with students and their individual concerns.

In contrast to Williamson's directive approach, Carl Rogers (1902–1987) influenced the counseling profession with his humanistic, indirect counseling theory. In his book *Counseling and Psychotherapy,* Rogers espoused a person-centered counseling which was contrary to the prevailing direct style of counseling. He believed that self-concept, or consistent beliefs and interpretation about oneself as a result of our life experiences, are facilitated when the core conditions of a counseling relationship exist.

Photo 1.2   E.G. Williamson in His Office at the University of Minnesota

Source: Image Courtesy of the University of Minnesota Archives, University of Minnesota—Twin Cities

Political and social upheaval in the 1960s brought renewed attention to personal/social issues, but because the guidance worker was laden with so many duties resembling those of an administrator, little counseling to address these concerns occurred (Gysbers, 2001). With the passage of Education for All Handicapped Children Act (PL 94–142) in 1975, the needs of students with special needs was highlighted, and with it the school counselor's role in assisting these students and their parents/guardians. With the school demographics continually changing, instruments with the capabilities to assess individual traits, abilities, and vocational interests appeared, and school counselors were given the additional task of testing and assessment.

Testing and Assessment

Due to the work of Albert Binet who developed the first intelligence test in 1905, educators began to see the benefits of tests as tools for assessing an individual's interests, abilities, and deficiencies. One of these tests, the Armed Services Vocational Aptitude Battery (ASVAB), formerly known as the Alpha and Beta Test, was developed during World War I to identify military jobs for which enlisted military would be best suited, and to determine candidates for leadership positions (ASVAB, n.d). As interest and aptitude tests expanded, the school counselor assumed a major role in administering and interpreting many of these tests. Counselor assessment and evaluation competencies are supported by ASCA and include knowledge and skills such as choosing assessment strategies and instruments, administering and interpreting test results, and using these results for decision making. Mandated testing and high-stakes testing are primary means for assessing student growth (Duffy, Giordano, Farrell, Paneque, & Crump, 2008).

Yet as indicated in the ASCA position statement on high stakes tests, "professional school counselors advocate for the use of multiple criteria when educational decisions are made about student performance and oppose the use of a single test to make important educational decisions affecting students and their schools" (ASCA, 2007, para. 1). Unfortunately, with the No Child Left Behind (NCLB) legislation of 2001 that requires assessments in reading/language arts, math, and science, many school counselors are assigned the role of "test coordinator." In fact, 80% of elementary school counselors reported that they were in charge of standardized testing in the district, and another 10% reported that they assisted with the testing procedures (Thorn & Mulvenon, 2002). This task requires an enormous amount of coordination and planning, takes time away from directly assisting students, and contributes to a tremendous amount of student, parent/guardian, and teacher stress. The poem in Box 1.4 was written by a counselor to express her views on the No Child Left Behind Law.

BOX 1.4 NO CHILD LEFT BEHIND?

No Child Left Behind, now in effect for 12 long years.
Trying, often failing, to equate students with their peers.
Teachers teaching to the test, ignoring other factors,
Counselors forced to jump on board, despite public detractors.
Academic reigns supreme as career falls to the side,
Personal/Social? No one cares, as long as scores are high.
You haven't eaten? No big deal. We expect you to perform.
You're being bullied? Get over it. For some kids, that's the norm.
Leave education to the teachers, or soon, we'll likely find,
Those students with no counselors will be the ones we left behind.

—Brittany Pollard

Throughout our history "guidance workers" were involved with numerous tasks and many continued to perform tasks that resembled those of a quasi-administrator. With a reduction in funding and difficult decisions regarding faculty and staff reductions, questions were raised as to how guidance activities could be evaluated to concretely demonstrate that outcomes were occurring as "guidance counselors" claimed (Gysbers, 2004).

Accountability

In partial response to the question as to how school counselors contributed to the academic mission as early as the 1930s, standards were created that measured the number of activities which were performed, the amount of time devoted to each activity, and the quality and consistency of the work (Myers, 1926, as cited in Gysbers, 2004). This emphasis continued in the 1940s with a focus on appropriate evaluative criteria that corresponded to the training and education of school counselors.

Throughout the next decades accountability efforts continued. During the 1960s a newsletter entitled *Guidance Counseling and Testing Program Evaluation* was prepared for the U.S. Office of Education that renewed the emphasis on outcome standards for students involved in a guidance and counseling program (Gysbers, 2004). During the 1970s the debate surrounding the efficacy of "guidance counselors" intensified, with pressure for these professionals to concretely document student outcomes using tangible methods (Gysbers, 2004). As insistence on providing documentation of service effectiveness continued, some individuals questioned whether or not school counselors could actually reveal how their interventions contributed to positive outcomes for students in preK–12 grades. Pressure to show program and performance effectiveness continued throughout the 1970s and 1980s, and despite the range of social problems such as child abuse, child-rearing problems, and divorce, decision-makers needed to reduce costs. School counseling was one area in which there were budget cuts, due to the lack of information regarding how these professionals contributed to student growth (Gysbers, 2004), and the numbers of students who were not receiving the urgently needed guidance assistance (Herr, 2001).

In 1994 Title I of the Elementary and Secondary Education Act was reauthorized and Goals 2000: Educate America Act (P.L. 103–227) was passed to support the development and implementation of standards-based educational reform at a national level (Superfine, 2005). By 1999 Goals 2000 was replaced by No Child Left Behind (NCLB), highlighting standards, assessment, and accountability systems in which "high-stakes" conditions were created. Furthermore, states were required to hold schools accountable for their performance on student assessments (Superfine, 2005). At the present time, there are many questions as to the practicality of this act, and there is some discussion that this legislation could be amended to give states more control.

Throughout these decades, the perception of the role of the "guidance worker" (now professional school counselor) differed depending on the person who was asked the question. Educational reform issues primarily have ignored guidance programs, partly due to guidance and counseling being considered as a separate entity from the academic mission. School "guidance counselors" were partially to blame for this omission because they had not advocated for themselves, did not partner with teachers, and tended to stay in their offices making themselves invisible to others (Aubrey, 1985). As an answer to these concerns, various guidance structures were proposed to standardize the role and position of the school counselor. In addition, credentialing and the formation of the ASCA contributed to school counselor identity by providing direction for state requirements and education.

Guidance Organizational Structure

A lack of an organized structure contributed to task differences among teachers who assumed the "guidance worker" position. Some believed that a centralized structure would help in standardizing duties, which would make the role of this professional more clearly understood. Therefore, throughout the 1930s the mental health movement dominated counselor practice with a clinical model of "guidance" that focused on the social and emotional needs of youth (Gysbers, 2001). In the 1930s and 1940s a pupil personnel format was proposed in which various educational practitioners such as attendance officers, school nurses, visiting teachers, school physicians, and "guidance workers" were organized into a structure of personnel who did not fit into any other organization. This solution was intended to maximize the services provided to students, but despite expectations for this organizational structure, guidance continued to be misunderstood and misinterpreted (Gysbers, 2001). To address this concern, a focus on student outcomes such as increased academic achievement, fewer disciplinary cases, fewer absences, better study habits, and so on were considered as necessary student outcomes (Gysbers, 2004) to achieve measurable results.

The pupil personnel services continued to be the organizational structure with "student services" as the more popular term (Gysbers, 2001), and "guidance counselors" took on a remedial connotation rather than one that was preventive and student-oriented. When the NDEA was passed in 1958, more and more full-time school counselors entered schools. School counselors continued with a service oriented structure known as the *nine dimensions of guidance,* with a focus on the areas in which school counselors were trained, ranging from orientation, student appraisal, counseling, information, placement, and follow-up services, regardless of the type of program that was in place. The need for better evaluation standards to assess how well guidance services are performed continued and persists today (Gysbers, 2004).

By the 1970s, there was debate as to whether the student services model was the best approach for confronting the numerous issues within educational arenas. Different program models were proposed and implemented. Myrick developed a competency-based guidance program in the 1970s and 1980s that identified student competencies associated with student success (Gysbers, 2001). Gysbers and Moore proposed a similar organizational structure with competencies, resources, and program components that included the guidance curriculum, individual planning, responsive services, and system support (Gysbers, 2001).

In 1997 the American School Counselor Association developed the ASCA National Standards (now known as the *ASCA Student Standards*), in which student competencies in the academic, career, and personal/social domains were identified. Although this was a positive step, more structure was needed. In response, the ASCA National Model® was created in 2003 and revised in 2012 as a prototype for counselors to use in developing a comprehensive, developmental school counseling (CDSC) program. This research-based model integrated the National Standards as outcome-based student competencies that are delivered through professional school counselor competencies.

The efficacy of CDSC programs is documented in the literature. For example, high school students who participated in a fully developed school counseling program had more positive attitudes toward school (Lapan, Gysbers, & Sun, 2007). School counselors in a CDSC program performed more activities that were compatible with their training and expressed more satisfaction with their jobs than did those who performed in a traditional school counseling program (Gysbers, Lapan, Blair, Starr, & Wilmes, 1999). With the ASCA model as a standardized program prototype, there is a greater understanding of how the school counselor plays an integral role in student achievement. Furthermore, the ASCA helped promote the profession by eliminating the outdated term "guidance counselor" and instead directed the term "***professional school counselor***" to be used as the preferred professional title.

Credentialing

CACREP

In the beginning stages of the guidance movement, there were no training programs for the teachers who assumed the guidance worker role. To alleviate this problem, Frank Parsons established vocational guidance in the Boston schools, and in 1908 the Boston YMCA offered a planned educational preparation program for teachers, known as the Boston School Vocational Counselors (Savickas, 2011). Anywhere from 16 to 25 people met on 16 Saturday evenings to obtain this training (Brewer, 1942, as cited in Savickas, 2011). Over the years, it was recognized that if "guidance counselors" were to be considered a profession, then in-service training was not enough (Bloomfield, 1914, as cited in Savickas, 2011), and to remedy this situation in 1911 Harvard University offered the first course on counseling for three weeks during the summer. Eventually, this course became a six-week course, and one-year later credit was applied toward an associate degree. During the 1940s, there was more emphasis on the type of training school counselors should receive (Gysbers, 2004), and in the 1960s, 38 states required minimal requirements for school counselor certification. Of these states, 34 required mandatory certification, and 20 required a master's degree (Wrenn, 1962).

In 1981 the Council for Accreditation of Counseling and Related Educational Programs (CACREP) was created to standardize training for all counseling professionals, including school counselors. This accrediting agency requires a minimum of 48 semester hours of coursework in core and specialty areas in an approved school counseling program. The ASCA "supports the credentialing and employment of those who hold a master's degree in counseling-related fields with training in all areas specified by the CACREP standards" (ASCA, 2003, para. 2). Today, there are approximately 228 CACREP accredited school counseling programs throughout the nation (CACREP, 2013).

Formation of the American School Counselor Association

The American Personnel and Guidance Association (APGA), now the American Counseling Association (ACA), was formed in 1952 from three like-minded groups. These groups were the National Vocational Guidance Association (NVGA), the National Association of Guidance and Counselor Trainers (NAGCT), now known as the Association for Counselor Education and Supervision (ACES), the Student Personnel Association for Teacher Education (SPATE), and the American College Personnel Association (ACPA). In 1983, the APGA changed its name to the American Association of Counseling and Development (AACD), and in 1992 it was again changed to the American Counseling Association. In 1953 the American School Counselor Association was initiated as a new division by the APGA senate (now known as the governing body).

With the various counseling specialty areas, it can be confusing as to how these specialties share skills and knowledge and how they differ. The ACA is considered as the parent organization for all counselors and includes 20 divisions organized according to interest and practice areas. For example, if you are interested in learning more about group work research and practice you might want to join the Association for Specialists in Group Work (ASGW). The ACA has an annual fee that is renewable yearly with an additional fee for membership in any of the divisions. The American School Counselor Association (ASCA) is the division that advocates for school counselors and has its own governing board and membership dues. The ACA divisions are found on the following table with a description of each specialty area.

Table 1.1 Summarization of ACA Divisions

Association for Assessment and Research in Counseling (AARC)

Originally the Association for Measurement and Evaluation in Guidance, and the Association for Assessment in Counseling and Education (AACE), AARC was chartered in 1965. The purpose of AARC is to promote the effective use of assessment in the counseling profession.

Association for Adult Development and Aging (AADA)

Chartered in 1986, AADA serves as a focal point for information sharing, professional development, and advocacy related to adult development and aging issues; addresses counseling concerns across the lifespan.

Association for Child and Adolescent Counseling (ACAC)

This newest association focuses on counselors who work with children and adolescents.

Association for Creativity in Counseling (ACC)

The Association for Creativity in Counseling (ACC) is a forum for counselors, counselor educators, creative arts therapists, and counselors in training to explore unique and diverse approaches to counseling. ACC's goal is to promote greater awareness, advocacy, and understanding of diverse and creative approaches to counseling.

American College Counseling Association (ACCA)

ACCA is one of the newest divisions of the American Counseling Association. Chartered in 1991, the focus of ACCA is to foster student development in colleges, universities, and community colleges.

Association for Counselors and Educators in Government (ACEG)

Originally the Military Educators and Counselors Association, ACEG was chartered in 1984. ACEG is dedicated to counseling clients and their families in local, state, and federal government or in military-related agencies.

Association for Counselor Education and Supervision (ACES)

Originally the National Association of Guidance and Counselor Trainers, ACES was a founding association of ACA in 1952. ACES emphasizes the need for quality education and supervision of counselors for all work settings.

The Association for Humanistic Counseling (AHC)

AHC, formerly C-AHEAD, a founding association of ACA in 1952, provides a forum for the exchange of information about humanistically-oriented counseling practices and promotes changes that reflect the growing body of knowledge about humanistic principles applied to human development and potential.

Association for Lesbian, Gay, Bisexual and Transgender Issues in Counseling (ALGBTIC)

Educates counselors to the unique needs of client identity development and a non-threatening counseling environment by aiding in the reduction of stereotypical thinking and homoprejudice.

Association for Multicultural Counseling and Development (AMCD)

Originally the Association of Non-White Concerns in Personnel and Guidance, AMCD was chartered in 1972. AMCD strives to improve cultural, ethnic, and racial empathy and understanding through programs to advance and sustain personal growth.

American Mental Health Counselors Association (AMHCA)

Chartered in 1978, AMHCA represents mental health counselors, advocating for client-access to quality services within the health care industry.

American Rehabilitation Counseling Association (ARCA)

ARCA is an organization of rehabilitation counseling practitioners, educators, and students who are concerned with enhancing the development of people with disabilities throughout their life span and in promoting excellence in the rehabilitation counseling profession's practice, research, consultation, and professional development.

(Continued)

Table 1.1 (Continued)

American School Counselor Association (ASCA)

Chartered in 1953, ASCA promotes school counseling professionals and interest in activities that affect the personal, educational, and career development of students. ASCA members also work with parents, educators, and community members to provide a positive learning environment.

Association for Spiritual, Ethical, and Religious Values in Counseling (ASERVIC)

Originally the National Catholic Guidance Conference, ASERVIC was chartered in 1974. ASERVIC is devoted to professionals who believe that spiritual, ethical, religious, and other human values are essential to the full development of the person and to the discipline of counseling.

Association for Specialists in Group Work (ASGW)

Chartered in 1973, ASGW provides professional leadership in the field of group work, establishes standards for professional training, and supports research and the dissemination of knowledge regarding groupwork.

Counselors for Social Justice (CSJ)

CSJ is a community of counselors, counselor educators, graduate students, and school and community leaders who seek equity and an end to oppression and injustice affecting clients, students, counselors, families, communities, schools, workplaces, governments, and other social and institutional systems.

International Association of Addictions and Offender Counselors (IAAOC)

Originally the Public Offender Counselor Association, IAAOC was chartered in 1972. Members of IAAOC advocate the development of effective counseling and rehabilitation programs for people with substance abuse problems, other addictions, and adult and/or juvenile public offenders.

International Association of Marriage and Family Counselors (IAMFC)

Chartered in 1989, IAMFC members help develop healthy family systems through prevention, education, and therapy.

National Career Development Association (NCDA)

Originally the National Vocational Guidance Association, NCDA was one of the founding associations of ACA in 1952. NCDA inspires and empowers the achievement of career and life goals by providing professional development, resources, standards, scientific research, and advocacy.

National Employment Counseling Association (NECA)

NECA was originally the National Employment Counselors Association and was chartered in 1966. The commitment of NECA is to offer professional leadership to people who counsel in employment and/or career development settings.

Source: Reprinted from www.counseling.org. The American Counseling Association. Reprinted with permission. No further reproduction authorized without written permission from the American Counseling Association.

The ASCA has its own governing body with one division charter per state, and holds an annual national conference that usually takes place in late June, and rotates among the four national regions. Student memberships are available and a few of the benefits of belonging include professional periodicals, professional development, liability insurance, and resources. In addition, the *ASCA Scene,* a networking site located on the ASCA website, is available to members with opportunities for school counselors to network through discussions, providing resources, and posing questions on problematic issues.

Most of the states have a chartered counseling association affiliated with ACA and a state school counseling division that is either an affiliate of the state counseling association or is an independent organization with its own governing body. Counseling divisions are found within each of the states for networking and professional development. To become a member of ASCA, go to the link http://www.schoolcounselor.org/ to join.

CONCEPTUAL APPLICATION ACTIVITY 1.2

Check the ASCA website to determine how to join your state division and region. Where is the closest chapter in your state? How can you join? What is the membership fee? What resources are available from ASCA that support school counselors?

As school counselors became more acknowledged at the national level, many at the state levels advocated for recognition and legislation within each state that would support the mission of school counseling. The following information summarizes state programs and models as well as a discussion of credentialing.

STATE PROGRAMS AND MODELS

As the ASCA became more vocal about the significance of comprehensive and developmental school counseling (CDSC) programs, more states began to legislate this type of programming. Today, 45 states have adopted a comprehensive developmental school counseling program model. Although the ASCA has recommended that school counselors have a minimum of a master's degree from a school counselor program, there are still several states that do not require this advanced degree in order to be employed as a professional school counselor. Each state determines its own requirements for entering and staying current in the profession, and the CACREP requirements serve as a benchmark even for those training institutions that are not accredited by this agency. However, be aware that some states require additional coursework such as human sexuality and/or substance abuse issues in addition to the curriculum that is mandated by the state board of education.

STATE CREDENTIALS AND REQUIREMENTS

Because teachers initially provided guidance services, teaching credentials were considered as a stepping-stone for entry into the school counseling profession. Therefore, many states believed it was essential for school counselors to have teaching credentials and experience as a teacher prior to entering the profession of school counseling. Since vocational guidance was the initial impetus leading the profession, many states mandated an additional requirement of documented work experience prior to entry into this career. Over the decades some believed that teaching experience was an unnecessary requirement and subsequently many states dropped both of these requirements. However, at the present time there are approximately six states that still require teaching experience in addition to a few states that still require proof of work experience prior to entering the profession.

When the teaching requirement was eliminated, some entering school counselors who did not have an education background were having difficulty understanding the educational environment and related tasks such as coordinating activities with teachers, conducting classroom guidance, and performing classroom management. In response to this dilemma, some state departments of education mandated extra fieldwork experiences in schools and/or classes in classroom management as a part of the school counselor training curriculum to supplement the practicum and internship experiences.

Tests such as the PRAXIS, communication and literacy tests, background and substance abuse screening, or being a U.S. citizen are some of the additional requirements some states mandate prior to entering the profession. Credentials also vary between states. Some states offer what is known as a "school counseling certificate" and others a "school counseling license."

BOX 1.5 PRAXIS

Some people wonder what the term PRAXIS stands for. It is not an acronym; it is the "exam required for teacher certification." The Educational Testing Service (ETS) administers the PRAXIS II School Counselor Exam. The exam content is based on counseling and guidance, professional issues, coordination, and consultation.

In some states the recipient is eligible to work in grades preK–12, and in others school counselors are only allowed to practice in specific grades, such as K–8 or 9–12, depending on the training received. Regardless of the type of credential, many school boards consider school counselors as 'teachers' and are placed on a teacher salary schedule with the same benefits, including sick leave, personal days, and so on. You may even need to consider whether or not to join an education association such as the National Education Association (NEA). Some educators choose to join this organization to access benefits such as liability insurance. Others join because the school district has agreed to a "closed shop" in which all teachers—and counselors—are required to pay union dues whether or not they concur with the philosophy of this organization.

CONCEPTUAL APPLICATION ACTIVITY 1.3

Check the requirements for the state or school district in which you would like to work as a professional school counselor. What are the requirements? Beginning level salary? Are school counselors placed on a teachers' salary schedule? Is teaching experience a requirement? If not, are there any special requirements that are needed to enter the school system? How do these requirements match your understanding of what is required of school counselors in the state in which you are interested in working?

There are other credentials school counselors may obtain that provide additional credibility. These include the National Board of Certified Counselors (NBCC) and the National Board for Professional Teaching Standards (NBPTS).

NATIONAL BOARD OF COUNSELOR CREDENTIALS (NBCC) AND NATIONAL BOARD FOR PROFESSIONAL TEACHING STANDARDS (NBPTS)

Recently, I was speaking with an elementary school counselor who had been working in the schools for 25 years. She revealed that when she graduated with her master's degree in counseling and received licensure as a school counselor, she decided a few years later to sit for the National Certified Counselor Exam (NCC). She was pleased when she successfully passed this examination, but she didn't realize the importance of this credential until a parent arrived at her school and demanded to know about her training and experience. Not only was this professional school counselor active in ASCA, she also maintained strong ties to her state and local professional counseling organizations. These professional relationships supported her personal and professional reliability, and the NCC designation provided further credibility to her professionalism.

The National Board of Certified Counselors (NBCC) provides certification in clinical mental health, addictions, and school counseling. The National Certified School Counselor (NCSC) is obtained upon successful completion of the National Certified School Counselor Examination (NCSCE). An annual recertification fee is required.

The National Board for Professional Teaching Standards (NBPTS) certifies teachers who have demonstrated high standards. Certification salary incentives are often available for educators (including school counselors) who have thoroughly met the 11 standards required by this organization (NBPTS School Counseling Standards, 2002). Requirements to become a candidate include the possession of a baccalaureate degree, three years of experience, and a valid license in the application area. At the present time, the fee for becoming Nationally Board Certified is $2,500.00, an application fee of $65.00, and a renewal fee of $1,250.00.

CONCEPTUAL APPLICATION ACTIVITY 1.4

Investigate and compare each of these credentials and the merits of receiving either of these credentials. Debate the pros and cons of each designation, and create a personal position statement on the merits of these credentials.

Regardless of whether or not you choose to receive an additional national credential, understanding counselor identity is a topic that has been debated throughout the ages and continues to be an issue today. As a member of the counseling profession you will need to answer the questions, "Am I a counselor with the abilities and skills to effectively work in any counseling specialty, or am I a school counselor trained to work only in the school counseling setting?"

COUNSELOR IDENTITY

As discussed previously, there are various counseling specialty areas and all of these specialty divisions embrace a wellness model of practice that supports prevention, social justice, and advocacy with a multicultural understanding of individuals. When the counseling organizations joined together in 1952, many hoped that this would provide a greater foundation of support without a loss of each organization's identity and autonomy. Despite the numerous similarities that exist among counseling specialties, there continues to be internal tension regarding the profession's vision and direction, particularly in regard to the distinctive role of each of the counseling divisions (Gazzola, Smith, King-Andrews, & Kearney, 2010).

In 2005, the ACA co-sponsored a collaborative initiative to unify the counseling profession, to define counseling, and to develop a strategy for reaching this goal by the year 2020. This enterprise became known as *20/20: A Vision for the Future of Counseling.* However, at this time the ASCA has chosen not to join this initiative due to the belief that there is more than one counseling profession (Kaplan & Gladding, 2011). Ironically, this is the same philosophy that was debated when the specialty counseling professions merged in 1952 to form the APGA.

CONCEPTUAL APPLICATION ACTIVITY 1.5

Investigate the 20/20 Vision for the Vision for the Future of Counseling. What are the various views regarding this initiative? What is your opinion about ASCA's decision to not support the enterprise?

Although the school counseling profession is relatively new in comparison with other occupations, some of the same issues that inundated the profession throughout the decades are still of concern today. Three decades ago, Aubrey (1983) asserted that counselors should pay greater attention to individual and family counseling in the schools, character development, stressors adversely impacting youth, accountability, prevention rather than remediation, leisure time activities for youth, and violence. School counselors continue to grapple with these issues and more. But before you get discouraged about the concerns impacting the school counseling profession, the ASCA and state affiliates have engaged in an active campaign of professional advocacy, education, and professional development that has been instrumental in advancing and enhancing a greater appreciation for the role of the school counselor. As you think about the various divisions within the counseling profession, think for a moment about the reason you decided to enter this profession. What are some of your attributes that you feel successful school counselors share? How do these characteristics match yours? Conceptual Application Activity 1.6 is designed to help you think about your characteristics that relate to the school counseling profession.

CONCEPTUAL APPLICATION ACTIVITY 1.6

Look at the list of adjectives found below and mark the traits you feel are characteristic of you.

Caring	Open	Flexible
Calm	Humble	Serious
Creative	Problem-solver	Tolerant
Curious	Sense of Humor	Trusting
Demanding	Understanding	Unique
Genuine	Listener	Consistent
Controlling	Friendly	Generous
Confident	Leader	Imaginative
Gregarious	Mature	Humorous
Sympathetic	Rigid	Naive
Empathic	Cooperative	Honest
Careful	Intelligent	Outgoing
Efficient	Opinionated	Proper
Fun-loving	Reliable	Loyal
Eager	Expert	Reflective
Compassionate	Risk-taker	Accepting
Forgiving	Perfectionist	Hard-worker
Hopeful	Quiet	Impulsive
Independent	Confident	Likeable
Judgmental	Self-conscious	Organized

Ask someone who knows you well to list the adjectives that he/she would use to describe you. Share and talk about the differences and similarities between the lists.

Which of these attributes do you feel are those that are essential to a successful school counselor?

The previous activity has given you an opportunity to reflect on your personal traits, and in the following section you have an opportunity to compare your list with the characteristics identified among successful practitioners.

CHARACTERISTICS OF SUCCESSFUL SCHOOL COUNSELORS

Counselor educators' attempts to determine the personality characteristics that encompass an effective counselor has been difficult due to the lack of adequate instruments, the indefinable nature of these qualities, and the complexity involved in researching these qualities. Although studies have investigated factors such as age, gender, religious beliefs, theoretical orientation, training, experience, and personality, the traits that make an effective counselor have not been conclusively verified (Reupert, 2006).

Traits such as empathy and rapport (Lazarus, 1985; Oke, 1994; as cited in Reupert, 2006), beliefs (Borcherdt, 1996, as cited in Reupert, 2006), genuineness and congruency, understanding, valuing counselee's ability to solve problems (Meador & Rogers, 1984, as cited in Reupert, 2006), and self-disclosure (Oke, 1994, as cited in Reupert, 2006) are considered essential to counseling outcome. Other characteristics include self-control, sympathy (Wicas & Mahan, 1966, as cited in Jennings & Skovholt, 1999), flexibility, sensitivity, and an ability to create a safe environment (Albert, 1997, as cited in Jennings & Skovholt, 1999). Jennings and Skovholt (1999) also investigated the personality characteristics of master counselors and found emotional well-being, humility, confidence, willingness to experience and process emotional and cognitive dissonance, nondefensiveness, willingness to seek feedback, and avid learning as aspects that create an inviting counseling relationship. Furthermore, in a separate study, counselors identified values as important to work satisfaction that include (Gazzola, et al., 2010):

- Helping others
- Using abilities and knowledge
- Growing and developing as a person
- Achievement
- Creativity and innovation
- Interaction with others
- Variety in work
- Comfort in working space
- Autonomous decision-making
- Financial security
- Career advancement
- Admiration
- Risk-taking
- Managing and directing others

Although there is no general agreement as to the most effective traits of successful counselors, there is agreement that it is the counselee him/herself who is the most essential component of the counseling relationship (Reupert, 2006).

As you have read this chapter, you have learned about the history of the profession and the trends that influenced its development. As you reflect on the past, think about the future and the movements that could have an influence on the future of the profession.

Table 1.2 Timeline of Significant Events That Shaped the School Counseling
Profession

Late 1800s—Early 1900s

- Industrial Revolution
- Child Labor Laws impacted education
- Compulsory Education Laws influenced the school environment
- First systematic guidance program was established by Jesse B. Davis in Grand Rapids, Michigan
- Eli Weaver and Anna Y. Reed infused guidance into the school curriculum
- Frank Parsons, also known as the "father of guidance" established vocational guidance in Boston
- Boston School Vocational Counselors established to provide guidance workers with information
- Sigmund Freud and John Dewey emphasized mental health issues of youth
- Albert Binet developed first intelligence test
- Alpha and Beta Tests developed (now known as the Armed Services Vocational Aptitude Battery [ASVAB])
- Harvard University established first course on counseling
- Emphasis on educational guidance rather than vocational guidance

1930s

- The Great Depression (begins in 1929)
- E.G. Williamson developed a directive counseling approach known as the Minnesota Model
- Carl Rogers developed a nondirective counseling approach also known as person-centered counseling
- "Guidance worker" standards created
- Pupil Personnel Model developed (also known as student services)
- Service Orientation Model organization developed (also known as the 9 Dimensions of Guidance)

1940s

- Vocational Education Act (George-Barden Act) passed into law
- Emphasis placed on training for school counselors

1950s

- National Defense Education Act (NDEA) legislated
- American Personnel and Guidance Association (APGA) formed (name changed to American Association of Counseling and Development (AACD) and now American Counseling Association (ACA))
- American School Counselor Association (ASCA) founded as APGA division

1960s

- Civil rights and women's movements emphasized personal/social student needs
- Guidance Counseling and Testing Program Evaluation developed
- 38 states established minimum requirements for school counseling certification

1970s

- Education for All Handicapped Children Act (PL 42–142)
- Developmental Counseling Model Developed

1980s

- Carl D. Perkins Vocational Education Act (renamed Carl D. Perkins Career and Technical Education Improvement Act of 2006)
- National Occupational Information Coordinating Committee (NOICC)
- The Council for Accreditation of Counseling and Related Educational Programs (CACREP) created

1990s

- School to Work Opportunities Act
- Elementary and Secondary Education Act reauthorized
- ASCA National Standards (now ASCA Student Standards) developed
- Goals 2000: Educate America Act (P.L. 103–227) legislated (now known as No Child Left Behind)

2000s

- No Child Left Behind Act (NCLB) (reauthorization of Elementary and Secondary Education Act)
- ASCA National Model® Developed
- 20/20: A Vision for the Future of Counseling initiative

Post 2010

- ASCA National Model Revised
- CACREP and the Council on Rehabilitation Education (CORE) released the Clinical Rehabilitation Counseling Standards
- The draft proposal of CACREP is proposing that beginning in July 2020, all accredited school counselor programs must be a minimum of 60 semester hours or 90 quarter hours

THE FUTURE OF THE SCHOOL COUNSELING PROFESSION

Although predictions for the future of school counseling and programs are obviously difficult to make, the history of the profession lends some insight into what we may expect in the future. Leaders in the counseling profession were asked about their views surrounding the future of the counseling profession (Shallcross, 2012) and their perceptions of the trends that could impact our profession. Predictions included the themes of violence and bullying, technology, globalization, health and wellness, poverty and marginalized students, accountability, students with special needs, family counseling, and the connection between neuroscience and counseling.

Violence and Bullying

School violence disrupts learning with the potential to impair emotional and cognitive growth. Targets of bullying, witnesses of aggressive behaviors, and perpetrators of bullying are all influenced by aggression. Although the media portrayals of violence in the schools (such as the shootings at Sandy Hook Elementary School in Newtown, Connecticut) make the public believe that these events are common everyday occurrences, statistics indicate that 1–2% of all homicides occur in schools, or in traveling to or from school (CDC, 2012).

Photo 1.3   Memorial Following Shooting at Sandy Hook Elementary School in Newtown, Connecticut

Source: © Lisa Wiltse/Corbis

Bullying is a type of school violence that reaches across all ages and grades and is associated with serious mental health issues such as suicide, homicide, and other acts of violence among victims. In addition, cyber bullies are at risk for continuing their deleterious behavior into the workforce, while targets of cyber bullying are at risk for experiencing poor psycho-social adjustment (Li, 2007).

Bullying often occurs on the playground, on the bus, or when supervision is lacking (Fredland, 2008), yet even when monitoring is increased, educators still do not recognize when bullying incidents occur. When students feel safe in schools there is a reduction in bullying, particularly when supplemented with individual counseling (Gottfredson, Gottfredson, & Skroban, 1998). School curricular intervention and prevention strategies that have been effective in reducing bullying include: 1) interpersonal skills such as assertiveness, problem solving, and character education; 2) conflict resolution and anger management; and 3) perspective taking and empathy. Individual and/or group counseling may assist targets of bullying in developing assertiveness skills and self-esteem, and aids bullies in acquiring empathy and perspective-taking skills.

Technology

The use and awareness of different types of technology is critical for supporting our role as a school counselor as it allows us to quickly and efficiently conduct our daily tasks. As our technology becomes obsolete, we often passively wait until the school system purchases new technology that may not always meet the needs of the school counselor. This is where we have an obligation to use our communication skills to reach out to the technology industry to request the hardware and software to make our program more effective (Forrester, 2011). Most software designers have never worked in schools and are unaware of the types of technology needed to perform various tasks or provide resources that could make the school counselor more productive.

Technology can assist school counselors with such things as tracking where time is spent, identifying youth at risk, assessing the effectiveness of our interventions, tracking communications with stakeholders, monitoring student progress, obtaining current information on specific issues, and developing websites to share events with stakeholders. With newer types of technology developed on a daily basis, the school counselor can receive training on technological innovations and skills. For instance, some school counselors are using new biofeedback software programs to help youth manage anxiety. There is even some discussion that an "artificial counselor" could assist students with issues that are commonly seen in the counselor's office today. This counselor avatar could provide advice and fill the need for closing the large student-counselor ratio, though this approach has not yet been studied sufficiently. However, there are also potential ethical issues to consider. Finally, technology also provides school counselors with an opportunity to raise global awareness by connecting with students in other countries, or to personally connect with school counselors in other parts of the world.

BOX 1.6 TWITTER AS A COUNSELING TOOL

You may be the only school counselor in a school or small school district, which creates a sense of isolation. School counselors in these situations have found the benefits of Twitter to immediately connect with others. Some of the advantages of Twitter are for information sharing, gaining ideas, or receiving immediate responses to a problem situation.

Globalization

Certain forms of counseling have a tradition in Western societies, and we are now recognizing that traditional counseling theories are not always applicable to individuals from other cultures. When counselors recognize how diverse worldviews and beliefs impact learning and peer relations both in the academic setting and at home (Ponterotto, Mendelowitz, & Collabolletta, 2008), they may be more receptive to engaging shaman, spiritual leaders, and other cultural healers as sources of support (Hohenshil, Amundson, & Nikes, 2013) and partnership. Due to internationalization and greater exposure to various attitudes and values, school counselors are combining traditional approaches with meditation, yoga, mind-body connection to teach students such skills as relaxation and stress reduction.

BOX 1.7 DID YOU KNOW? IMPROVING YOUR CULTURAL KNOWLEDGE

Learn about the culture of the students and the families with whom you work.

- When working with a student from Asia, remember that the term "counseling" is a taboo term. Instead, use the terms "learning" and "education" to introduce your role.
- In some countries the concept of counseling would more easily be understood as talking to a religious leader or "wise person."
- In India, mental health issues are now being introduced in schools, with the government beginning a 5-year plan of policy initiatives to address the needs of adolescents.

Health and Wellness

Our profession is founded on a philosophy of wellness, yet issues such as child obesity and a lack of leisure activities plague our youth. School counselors are instrumental in bringing about a greater awareness of techniques for healthful living through counseling. Furthermore, healthful living concepts can be integrated with academic areas. For example, school counselors could collaborate with science teachers to teach students gardening skills while they learn about healthy eating, where food comes from, and take responsibility for caring for the crops. In addition, the school counselor could work with the physical education teacher to engage students in physical activities to develop an interest in outside activities while keeping physically fit. Psychoeducational groups or small group counseling groups may also promote wellness while students learn about healthy lifestyles and develop a healthy body image.

BOX 1.8 COUNSELORS AND VICARIOUS TRAUMATIZATION

The term "burnout"—that is, compassion fatigue—was first used in the 1970s and is related to emotional exhaustion, emotionally distancing self from counselees, and feelings of ineffectiveness. These conditions lead to prolonged emotional stress vocationally and personally, and lowered self-esteem. In addition, counselors often suffer from vicarious traumatization when continually exposed to counselees in crisis. We have an ethical responsibility to be in touch with the needs of our students as well as our own needs and to find resources that will assist in stress alleviation.

Impoverished and Marginalized Students

Approximately 23% of 5- to 17-year-old youth live in poverty in the United States (Kids Count, 2012), which is associated with numerous personal, social, and academic challenges. For example, attendance and tardiness may be an issue for students who take responsibility for getting their younger siblings ready for school while their adult caregivers are working. Teens who need to work long hours to bring needed income into the home have little time to complete homework. Students can be living in temporary, transitional housing such as in shelters or with friends that could disrupt schooling.

Even when impoverished children and adolescents have permanent housing many cannot afford weather appropriate clothing or school supplies and may feel uncomfortable attending school for fear of embarrassment or being bullied. Many children come to school without breakfast or even miss this meal due to a late arrival. In other cases students may arrive for breakfast, often their only meal of the day, and leave after they are fed. All of these concerns could make it difficult to make friends or to sustain a consistent education. The school counselor is in a role to serve as an advocate to make these students and their families feel welcome by creating a positive culture and educating educators about the conditions impacting these students.

Accountability

As you have read in this chapter, accountability has been an issue throughout the history of the profession, yet school counselors have been reticent about revealing how their interactions make a difference in the lives of students. This omission has resulted in school counselors being among the first educational professionals to lose their jobs when funding is scarce. In a recent study (Studer, Diambra, Breckner, & Heidel, 2011), school counselor graduates trained in the ASCA National Model® were asked to indicate the extent to which they engaged in accountability practices within their school counseling program. The results revealed that school counselor participants across all school levels were collecting data about their programs at rates "slightly better than average." Although it is reassuring that efforts are made to collect data, it is difficult to understand why counselors are not engaged in collecting and analyzing data more frequently, particularly when school counselors are more likely to have a more comprehensive background in assessment and evaluation than do teachers and/or administrators (Ekstrom, Elmore, Schafer, Trotter, & Webster, 2004). Change from the status quo is difficult when school counselors do not demonstrate program effectiveness, and with today's educational climate school counselors are obligated to document activities, assess, analyze, and share program data.

Students with Special Needs

The numbers of students receiving special education services has increased over the decades with approximately 14% of students between the ages of 3 and 21 receiving these services (Education bug, n.d.). With the passage of the Individuals with Disabilities Education Improvement Act (IDEIA), growing numbers of students with special needs are placed in general education classrooms. Students with disabilities display characteristics such as depression, anxiety, few friends, lowered self-esteem, behavioral problems, and dropping out of school, with a greater risk for suicide (Romano & Herman, 2007). School counselors can serve an essential role by advocating for these students and their parents (Taub, 2006), as well as being aware of special education laws. In addition to working with special education teachers, the school counselor collaborates with general education teachers who need additional support, or access resources for the students with special needs who are placed in their classroom.

Family Counseling

As a practicing school counselor I realized the benefits of working with the child and his/her family, yet this goal was difficult to achieve as parents/guardians were often unable to leave work to attend a school conference. I suggested to my administrator that perhaps we could negotiate new working hours that would allow me to arrive at school later in the morning and stay later in the afternoons a few days of the week for the purpose of conducting parent consultations. My suggestion was met with the response, "We can't do that because teachers would not understand." Despite my repeated attempts to convince the administration that this plan could benefit the parent/school relationship, I was unsuccessful and the discussion ended. When we consider that the family and the school system are the two most essential support systems for the child, it makes sense that these two institutions work collaboratively for the benefit of the child.

BOX 1.9 BENEFITS OF PARENT/SCHOOL PARTNERSHIPS

Greater academic achievement is realized through school/family partnerships, and attendance increases when parents feel welcome and involved in the schools.

Providing mental health services in the school is particularly important when there are many families who do not have the means to access community mental health professionals (Nelson, 2006). Several factors serve as barriers to this partnership: 1) unlike other mental health professionals, school counselors are trained to focus on interventions that enhance academic growth (Nelson, 2006), and few school counseling training programs offer courses and supervision in family systems theory. Although the CACREP standards specify that training in family systems is necessary (Collaboration and Consultation; M.4 Knowledge), school counselors often receive cursory information about this approach; 2) school hours are often a negotiated agreement between the school board and teachers, and deviation from these hours may create difficulties in regard to available space; and 3) being alone in a school building after hours could create safety issues. Regardless of the reasons for not conducting family counseling, school counselors have an opportunity to work with families and are encouraged to take courses and receive training under supervision.

Neuroscience—The Mind and Body Connection

As technology and science advance, we are learning more about the roots of human behavior. We have historically looked at heredity, experiences, and environmental factors as the foundation of emotions and behavior, yet as the field of neuroscience develops there is evidence that the interrelated connections of memories, thoughts, and experiences leave a neural foundation. These structures are the source for creating new networks, as a basis and stimulus for change (Leanza, 2012).

Humans have the ability to grow new neuro-pathways, with brains changing and adapting as we engage in activities. Research has shown that counseling stimulates new brain networks (Leanza, 2012) that lead to neurological change. Engaging the student in creative techniques such as music, art, and dance have the potential to create a framework for new paths and change. Furthermore, activities such as smiling can stimulate mood and empathy, and staying intellectually active such as learning a new language enhances the synapses in the prefrontal cortex. When we consciously relax through mindfulness, breathing, or summoning images, the brain is affected, with evidence that yawning controls the brain temperature and assists with concentration. The school counselor could apply this research by prescribing yawning to students when concentration is needed, such as before an exam, or encouraging students to engage in aerobic exercise which protects the brain from stress, or dialoguing with others to strengthen emotions and behaviors (Blevins, 2012).

CONCLUSION

In this chapter, we have briefly discussed the history of the counseling profession, including the evolution from "guidance worker" to professional school counselor. Political, economic, and social events influenced the trends within the profession, and the American School Counselor Association has actively responded to these factors. The influences that shaped our profession include the Industrial Revolution as a stimulus for vocational guidance. With passage of child labor laws and recognition of mental wellness, individual and group counseling became a school counselor task, as did the testing movement and accountability. As school counselors proliferated in the school environment, organizational structures were proposed and with it, the recognition for credentialing and standardized training at the national and state levels.

As we respond to the needs of society and our school-age youth, we need to understand the "self" of the counselor and the personality traits that contribute to effective counseling. Finally, predictions about trends that may influence the future of school counseling are discussed.

REFERENCES

American School Counselor Association (n.d.). *The Role of the Professional School Counselor.* Alexandria, VA: Author.

American School Counselor Association (2003). *The professional school counselor and credentialing and licensure.* Alexandria VA: Author.

American School Counselor Association (2007). *The professional school counselor and high-stakes testing.* Alexandria VA: Author.

ASVAB. (n.d.). *History of Military Testing.* Retrieved from http://official-asvab.com/history_coun.htm

Aubrey, R. F. (1983). The odyssey of counseling and images of the future. *Personnel and Guidance Journal, 62,* 78–82.

Aubrey, R. F. (1985). A counseling perspective on the recent educational reform reports. *The School Counselor, 33,* 91–99.

Barrett, E. S. (1948). Vocational guidance and the george-barden act. *The High School Journal, XXXI* (1), 1–3.

Blevins, B. (2012, March). *Neuroscience and the impact on mental health.* Symposium conducted at the Smoky Mountain Counselor's Association, Jefferson City, TN.

Centers for Disease Control and Prevention (2012). School violence: Data & Statistics. Retrieved from http://www.cdc.gov/ViolencePrevention/youthviolence/schoolviolence/data_stats.html

Council for Accreditation of Counseling and Related Educational Programs (CACREP), 2013. *Directory.* Retrieved from http://www.cacrep.org/directory/directory.cfm?state=&degreeLevel=

Duffy, M., Giordano, V. A., Farrell, J. B., Paneque, O.M., & Crump, G. B. (2008). No child left behind: Values and research issues in high stakes assessments. *Counseling and Values, 53,* 53–66.

Education bug (n.d.). *Special education statistics.* Retrieved from http://www.educationbug.org/a/special-education-statistics.html

Ekstrom. R. B., Elmore, P. B., Schafer, W. D., Trotter, T. V., & Webster, B. (2004). A survey of assessment and evaluation activities of school counselors. *Professional School Counseling, 8,* 24–30.

Forrester, D. (2011). Take a risk. *School Counselor.* Alexandria, VA: American School Counselor Association.

Fredland, N. M. (2008). Sexual bullying: Addressing the gap between bullying and dating violence. *Advances in Nursing Science, 31,* 95–105.

Free Online Library (n.d.). *Meyer Bloomfield: Organizer of the vocational guidance movement (1907–1917).* Retrieved from http://www.thefreelibrary.com/Meyer+Bloomfield%3a+organizer+of+the+vocational+guidance+movement . . . -a0196723355

Gazzola, N., Smith, J. D., King-Andrews, H. L., & Kearney, M. K. (2010). Professional characteristics of Canadian counselors: Results of a national survey. *Canadian Journal of Counseling and Psychotherapy, 44,* 83–99.

Gottfredson, D. C., Gottfredson, G. D., & Skroban, S. (1998). Can prevention work where it is needed most? *Evaluation Review, 22,* 315–340. doi: 10.1177/0193841X9802200301

Gummere, R. M. (1988). The counselor as prophet: Frank Parsons, 1854–1908. *Journal of Counseling and Development, 66,* 402–405.

Gysbers, N. C. (2001). School guidance and counseling in the 21st century: Remember the past into the future. *Professional School Counseling, 5,* 96–105.

Gysbers, N. C. (2004). Comprehensive guidance and counseling programs: The evolution of accountability. *Professional School Counseling, 8,* 1–14.

Gysbers, N. C., Lapan R.T., Blair, M., Starr, M. F., & Wilmes, D. (1999). Closing in on the state-wide implementation of a comprehensive developmental guidance program model. *Professional School Counseling, 2,* 357–366.

Herr, E. L. (2001). The impact of national policies, economics, and school reform on comprehensive guidance programs. *Professional School Counseling, 4,* 236–245.

Hohenshil, T. H., Amundson, N. E., & Niles, S. G (2013). *Counseling around the world.* Alexandria, VA: ACA.

Jennings, L., & Skovholt, T. M. (1999). The cognitive, emotional, and relational characteristics of master therapists. *Journal of Counseling Psychology, 46,* 3–11.

Kaplan, D. M., & Gladding, S. T. (2011). A vision for the future of counseling: The 20/20 principles for unifying and strengthening the profession. *Journal of Counseling & Development, 89,* 367–372.

Katz, M. (1976). A history of compulsory education laws. *Phi Delta Kappa Educational Foundation. Retrieved from* ERIC database. (ED119389).

Kids Count (2012). Children in poverty. Retrieved from http://datacenter.kidscount.org/search/#q/united%20stats%20children%20in%20poverty

Lapan, R. T., Gysbers, N. C., & Sun, Y. (1997). The impact of more fully implemented guidance programs on the experiences of high school students. A statewide study. *Journal of Counseling & Development, 75,* 292–302.

Leanza, N. (2012, Oct.). Simple therapeutic interventions for rewiring the maladaptive brain. *Counseling Today.* Alexandria, VA: ACA.

Li, Q. (2007). New bottle but old wine: A research of cyberbullying in schools. *Science Digest, 23,* 1777–1791.

National Board for Professional Teaching Standards (2002). *NBPTS School Counseling Standards.* Author. Retrieved from http://www.nbpts.org/become_a_candidate/what_is_national_board_c

Nelson, J. A. (2006). For parents only: A strategic family therapy approach in school counseling. *The Family Journal: Counseling and Therapy for Couples and Families, 14,* 180–183. doi: 10.1177/1066480705285557

Neukrug, E. (n.d.). *Stories of the great therapists.* Retrieved from http://ww2.0du.edu/~eneukrug/therapists/williamson.html

Pontereotto, J. G., Mendelowitz, D. E., Collabolletta, E. A. (2008). Promoting multicultural personality development. A strengths-based, positive psychology worldview for school. *Professional School Counseling, 12,* 93–99.

Pope, K. (2009). Jesse Buttrick Davis (1871–1955): Pioneer of vocational guidance in the schools. *The Career Development Quarterly, 57,* 248–258.

Reupert, A. (2006). The counsellor's self in therapy: An inevitable presence. *International Journal for the Advancement of Counseling, 28,* 95–105.

Robeien, E. (2011, September 15). STEM-focused schools on the rise across nation. *Curriculum matters.* Retrieved from blogs.edweek.org

Romano, D. M., & Hermann, M. A. (2007, July). Advocates for all. *ASCA School Counselor.* Retrieved from http://www.ascaschoolcounselor.org/article_content.asp?article=936

Savickas, M. L. (2011). The centennial of counselor education: Origin and early development of a discipline. *Journal of Counseling & Development, 89,* 550–503.

Schram, M. (2013, January 13). Education must be new national security priority. *Knoxville Sentinel,* p. B3.

Shallcross, L. (March, 2012). What the future holds for the counseling profession. *Counseling Today.* Retrieved from http://ct.counseling.org/2012/03/what-the-future-holds-for-the-coun seling-profession/

Solomon-McCarthy, S. (2012). The history of child labor in the United States: *Hammer v. Dagenhart.* Retrieved from http://www.yale.edu/ynhti/curriculum/units/2004/1/04.01.08.x

Studer, J. R., Diambra, J. F., Breckner, J. A. & Heidel, R. E. (2011). Obstacles and successes in implementing the ASCA National Model® in schools. *Journal of School Counseling, 9* (2), Retrieved from http://www.jsc.montana.edu/pages/articles.html

Superfine, B. M. (2005). The politics of accountability: The rise and fall of goals 2000. *American Journal of Education, 112,* 10–43. Retrieved from http://www.jstor.org/stable/10.1086/444513.

Taub, D. (2006). Understanding the concerns of parents of students with disabilities: Challenges and roles for school counselors. *Professional School Counseling, 10,* 52–57.

Teachers' Guide to the U.S. Department of Education (Sept. 2000). *National Occupational Information Coordinating Committee (NOICC).* Retrieved from www2.ed.gov/pubs/teachers guide/noicc.html

Thorn, A. R., & Mulvenon, S. W. (2002). High-stakes testing: An examination of elementary counselors' views and their academic preparation to meet this challenge. *Measurement and Evaluation in Counseling & Development, 35,* 195–206.

Wrenn, C. G. (1962*). The counselor in a changing world.* Washington, D.C.: American Personnel and Guidance Association.

Zytowski, D. G. (2001). Frank Parsons and the progressive movement. *The Career Development Quarterly, 50,* 57–65

Chapter 2

THE SCHOOL COUNSELOR AND ETHICAL AND LEGAL ISSUES

 *CACREP STANDARDS

FOUNDATIONS

A. *Knowledge*

  2. Understands ethical and legal considerations specifically related to the practice of school counseling.

B. *Skills and Practices*

  1. Demonstrates the ability to apply and adhere to ethical and legal standards in school counseling.

  Laws and institutions must go hand in hand with the progress of the human mind

  -Sir Francis Bacon

Making ethical decisions is difficult enough, but is even more complicated when state and federal laws collide with our ethical standards. The American Counseling Association (ACA) developed ethical guidelines for counselors in all areas to use when confronted with difficult decisions. Likewise, the *ASCA Ethical Standards for School Counselors* (ASCA, 2010) were written to serve as a guide for the practice of school counseling, as a professional self-assessment, and expected professional responsibilities of school counselors (ASCA, 2010). Although the ethical guidelines of both ACA and ASCA are similar and essential resources to consult when problematic situations arise, this chapter will focus specifically on the ASCA Ethical Standards as a guide for school counselor decision making.

Ethics refer to the morals and choices an individual makes in his/her interactions with others (Remley & Herlihy, 2010) within a professional context. Ethical decision making is an organized, systematic process in which there are conscious efforts to logically weigh the pros and cons of determining a course of action (Wheeler & Bertram, 2012). In order to understand various terms, several important definitions are provided followed by the sections within the ASCA ethical code (See Appendix A).

DEFINITIONS OF TERMS

Legally, the counseling relationship is based on a duty, or a responsibility to act in the best interests of the client (in schools, the client would be the student) (Wheeler & Bertram, 2012). This duty is based on a *fiduciary* relationship, or one in which we act on what we consider to be the best interests of our counselee. This relationship is judged on a standard of care that is a benchmark upon which the knowledge, skills, and competence of practicing school counselors (Wheeler & Bertram, 2012) are judged.

In Loco Parentis, or the Latin term meaning *in the place of a parent,* refers to school personnel who act as a parent or guardian while school-age youth are under their care. With this care comes a responsibility to promote a cooperative atmosphere while looking out for the best interests of the students (Stone, 2005). In the case of *N.C. vs. Bedford Central School District,* the parents of a student who had been sexually abused by his cousin wanted to keep this abuse private, however the school social worker and school counselor ignored this request and provided the details to the school educators. Their intention in sharing this information was to help the educators have a better understanding of his behavior. The parents brought a lawsuit against the school due to this violation of confidentiality. However, in this case, the court found in favor of the school social worker and school counselor since it was believed that sharing this information did outweigh the student's and parents' request for confidentiality (Stone, 2006). Nonetheless, this disclosure probably irreparably damaged the relationship between the school counselor and the family.

Negligence is when the counselor has a responsibility to provide care and expertise with a counselee and fails with this obligation. For negligence to occur there must be a legal duty that exists in a specific relationship and the counselee suffers when this duty of care is violated (Wheeler & Bertram, 2012). *Malpractice* is based on negligence of professional responsibilities such as the counselor using unacceptable practices, lacking competence in a strategy, failing to use a more beneficial procedure, failing to warn or protect others, or failing to receive informed consent or explain consequences of a treatment (Wheeler & Bertram, 2012).

Numerous ethical decision-making models exist with steps to use in systematically determining a course of action in a difficult situation. In this chapter, the *Solutions to Ethical Problems in Schools* (STEPS) model developed by Carolyn Stone is outlined (Stone & Dahir, 2006; Williams, 2007). This model was developed specifically for school counselors due to the prevalence of rumors carried by many school-age youth, the significance of examining personal reactions, the unique situation of parental rights, and the chronological and the developmental considerations of youth (Stone & Dahir, 2006).

Figure 2.1 STEPS Decision-Making Model

1. Defining the problem emotionally and intellectually

2. Applying ASCA ethical code and the legal issues

3. Considering the student's chronological and developmental levels

4. Considering the setting

5. Identifying the moral principles

6. Determining a potential course of action and consequences

7. Evaluating the selection option

8. Consulting with peers

9. Implementing the selected course of action

Defining the Problem Emotionally and Intellectually

When we work with school-age youth we may have an immediate, strong reaction to the student and/or problem. All of us have values, beliefs, and biases yet being aware of how these influences affect the decision-making process is critical to the formulation of an ethical plan. Self-reflecting and asking yourself the question, "How might my personal values influence this process?" is an opportunity to step aside from the presenting dilemma to reconsider personal motivations. Some state legislators have passed laws that permit counselors to refer counselees whose values conflict with their own. However, what happens to the student when there is only one school counselor in the building? Does this mean valuable services would not be received? Is it possible to put aside personal biases while working with students whose beliefs/values differ from your own?

Assessing these reactions will help in guarding against any impulsive decisions that could inadvertently harm the student. For instance, if a counselor is working with an 18-year-old self-mutilator, it is easy to react at an emotional level and make premature decisions that have the potential for creating conflicts of interest.

Applying the ASCA Ethical Code and the Legal Issues

The ASCA ethical code offers guidance when faced with a troublesome situation; however, each situation is different and sometimes these codes are difficult when they conflict with state and federal laws. For instance, in 2012 the state of Tennessee passed a "Gateway Sexual Activity" bill that allows parents to sue teachers or others for promoting or condoning gateway sexual activity by students. The implications of this bill could mean that if a school counselor discusses sexual activity outside of "abstinence only" it could be construed that he/she is condoning sexual behavior (Ho, 2012). Opponents of this law point to activities such as handholding or hugging in hallways that could also be viewed as "gateway activities." Could educators who ignore these displays of affection be held liable? Does this mean counselors will need to report these behaviors if they are viewed in the school setting?

Considering the Student's Chronological and Developmental Levels

Our ethical principles guide us to promote autonomy and independence of our students, yet factors such as the student's developmental and chronological age intervene with the difficulty of this choice. A question to ask yourself is, "How will the age of this student impact the course of action I want to take?" For instance, a 12-year-old who has been taking care of her younger siblings by getting them up and dressed for school in the morning may be better able to make decisions for herself than a classmate of the same age who does not have this same responsibility.

Considering the Setting

School systems have policies in place that define how a counselor is to act in certain situations. For instance, some school principals require that the school counselor secure parent/guardian permission before individually counseling a student. Other principals believe that because counseling is considered as a part of the educational mission of the school, parental/guardian permission is not needed when counseling a student. Be aware of the institutional policies and procedures that impact your decisions.

Identifying the Moral Principles

An additional self-test to facilitate decision making includes looking at the issues of:

- Justice—or asking yourself if you would make this decision again for others in a similar situation
- Universality—if a counselor supervisor were to ask for advice, would you recommend this solution to him/her?
- Publicity—how would you feel after reading/seeing the outcome in the media?
- Moral traces—is there a slippery ethical slope—or possible conflicts of interest? (Gibbs & Lee, 2008).

Determining a Potential Course of Action and Consequences

Choices we make involve multiple people and factors. Significant individuals such as family members, friends, and teachers, in addition to extraneous variables such as culture, the counselee's age and maturity level, and environmental factors such as culture, race, and class, are influenced through the decision-making process.

In morally charged situations, take the time to gather as much information as possible, identify individuals who could provide needed information while respecting confidentiality, recognize obstacles that could endanger the outcome, and briefly state the problem with as many facts as are available. It is possible that there may be more than one decision that is needed. Taking the time to write down the options and pros and cons of each choice while researching the pertinent laws that are applicable to the situation provides a concrete method of determining an appropriate course of action.

Evaluating the Selected Option

Choose a course of action and be prepared to make alterations when other factors become clear. In forming a decision it is also a good idea to prepare for barriers that could jeopardize the final outcome. Documenting the action that was taken, including the individuals with whom you consulted helps you remember the steps that were taken in case a complaint is filed.

Consulting with Peers

Consulting with another professional provides a different perspective and an outside lens from which to view the dilemma. Although principals are available and serve as useful resources, their perspective on the situation is often different from that of the counselor. Selecting and maintaining positive professional relationships with individuals who are sensitive to the ASCA ethical code assists in reinforcing the values of ethical practice.

Implementing the Chosen Course of Action

Choose a course of action, prepare to alter the plan if other factors become clear, and identify barriers that could jeopardize the final outcome. Remember to document the chosen course of action.

As I indicated earlier, not only do the ACA ethical standards serve as a useful guide to difficult decision making, the *ASCA Ethical Standards for School Counselors* may be a more pertinent source when confronted with challenging situations. The remainder of this chapter focuses on specific sections with the ethical standards of the ASCA.

RESPONSIBILITIES TO STUDENTS

School counselors are concerned about the growth and development of all students, have respect for students' cultural background, an awareness of the multiple influences impacting the student's life, and are mindful of professional boundaries.

CONCEPTUAL APPLICATION ACTIVITY 2.1

Fifteen-year-old Tonya confides to you that her parents have forbidden her to see her boyfriend. She tells you that she has been sneaking out of her home at night to see her boyfriend, who lives in a neighboring town and attends a different high school. You are aware that the town in which her boyfriend lives is dangerous, as gang wars are often reported in the news. You are concerned about her safety when she sneaks out at night. Do you keep Tonya's confidence? Discuss this situation with your classmates.

Confidentiality

A second-grade girl came to her male elementary school counselor to talk about her friend who was being touched sexually by an older family friend. The school counselor brought the young girl into her office to talk with her about his responsibility to keep all students safe at school and at home. It became evident to the counselor that the young girl was embarrassed and really didn't want to talk with her male counselor, even though they had a good relationship. Together they decided that she would tell her female teacher what happened and then the teacher could relay the information to him. She disclosed that a sixth-grade boy who was enrolled in another school district had locked her in a closet with him in which he touched her in private places and forcefully made her do the same thing to him. Although they had discussed the limits of confidentiality in an age appropriate manner at all sessions, the young girl became outraged when the counselor explained that he was going to make a phone call to someone to assure her safety.

The young girl felt betrayed and stated that he had made a promise to her to not tell anyone, and had difficulty understanding he was trying to help her. The next day she came to his office and said, "Thanks a lot—I'm never going to get to see my friends again." The counselor again explained that he has to make decisions that students may not like or understand, but she could be certain that he would always do whatever he could to keep her safe, even though she may not like his decision. It took awhile for the relationship to get back to where it was at the beginning, but following through on ethical responsibilities was necessary even though the trusting relationship may be jeopardized.

Confidentiality is the foundation of the school counseling profession and a core condition of an effective counseling relationship. Without the assurance of confidentiality students will have difficulty self-disclosing or even seeking the help of a counseling professional. It is also possible that students will seek out information or support from an unreliable source or their peers. Confidentiality means that the information shared by your counselee will be kept private, with the exception of situations in which: 1) the student is a danger to self or others; 2) the student or parent requests that information be communicated to a third party; or 3) a court orders a counselor to disclose information. School counselors have a responsibility to inform students about the counseling process in a manner that is developmentally appropriate and discuss the limits of confidentiality, including the duty to warn when the student discloses information that is deemed to be of harm to self and/or others.

School counselors understand that their primary obligation is to the student, but are also aware that parents or guardians have rights to be the guiding voice in their children's lives, especially in value-laden issues (ASCA, 2010, A.2.d.). The dilemma resides in children having an ethical right to privacy and parents or guardians having a legal right to know about the information shared in a counseling session (Remley, 2007). These ethical and legal codes obviously conflict. To help resolve this impasse, a question to ask is, "Who is the counselee, the student or the parent/guardian?" When a parent is informed of confidences shared in counseling the law is not broken, but an ethical responsibility to the student is destroyed. When confidentiality is broken, the student may feel betrayed, which could be viewed as harm to a counselee.

The ASCA ethical codes also protect the information contained in student records. The Family Education Rights and Privacy Act (FERPA) and the Health Insurance Portability and Accountability Act (HIPAA) are two legislative acts that influence school counselors.

FERPA. This federal law, also known as the Buckley Amendment, applies to all schools that receive federal funding. This act protects the privacy of student educational records by providing parents/guardians certain rights in regard to academic documents. Parents/guardians have the right to see their child's record, and written consent is required before schools are able to release records. However, directory information such as names, date of birth, addresses, and so on, may be released as long as parent/guardian are informed about the release of these records and are provided with ample time to request that this information not be circulated.

In a recent survey, 65% of ASCA members indicated that they were not responsible for sending or receiving educational records (Stone, 2013). However, school counselors are often not aware of the latest FERPA revisions, such as the Uninterrupted Scholars Act (2012). This act permits school personnel to release education records to a state or local child welfare representative, or a tribal organization that is determined to address the student's education needs, or is authorized to receive these records without consent from the parent/guardian (Stone, 2013).

HIPAA. This is a federal law that came about as a result of privacy concerns regarding the transmission of health care information through the Internet or electronic means (Wheeler & Bertram, 2012). This law allows individuals to access their records and grant consent for the release of medical information. Although HIPAA regulations do not necessarily apply to school counselors, the law could apply particularly to the school nurse or school psychologist, both of whom have access to medical diagnoses.

Counseling Plans

School counselors work with all students in the academic, career, and personal/social domains integral to a comprehensive, developmental school counseling (CDSC) program. In addition, school counselors provide all students with an array of post-secondary options and advocate for resources to facilitate future plans.

CONCEPTUAL APPLICATION ACTIVITY 2.2

Maria is a Hispanic senior ranked in the top of her class. She has taken honors and Advanced Placement courses throughout high school and wants desperately to go to college to study biology, with the hopes of becoming a medical doctor. Maria's parents come into school outraged that you, as her counselor, would be encouraging their daughter to "dream about a future that will never happen." They are adamantly opposed to Maria attending college. How would you respond to Maria's parents? Discuss your response with your classmates.

School counselors acknowledge equitable opportunities for all students to graduate with skills that are necessary for career and college readiness (College Board, 2010). At the same time, school counselors respect the rights of parents and guardians. It is possible that Maria's parents, in the case above, are unaware of some of the resources that are available to facilitate college attendance. It is also possible that specific gender roles are part of the family's worldview. Family consultation, possibly with the inclusion of a leader from the Hispanic community, could make a difference in assisting Maria and her family make future plans.

Dual Relationships

School counselors play multiple roles that could create difficulty in maintaining professional boundaries. For instance, impaired relationships or objectivity could occur when working with neighbors' children, family friends, or even relatives. Social networking also has the potential to blur boundaries between students and school counselors. If situations arise in which there are concerns about multiple relationships, confidences, or boundaries, an ethical decision-making model aids in preventing harm to personal/professional relationships (Lonborg & Bowen, 2004).

CONCEPTUAL APPLICATION ACTIVITY 2.3

Lisa is a 13-year-old eighth-grader who lives with her divorced, custodial dad. You are a single school counselor and have worked in the school counseling profession for five years. Lisa has consistently received stellar grades, but when her younger brother died of lymphomatous cancer she lost interest in grades, school, and her activities. Her father came in to discuss Lisa's behavior with you, and after several parent meetings he has asked you out on a date. Are there any ethical implications if you agree to go out with him? Discuss your response with your classmates.

School counselors have a primary responsibility to their students. When roles are blurred there is a risk of mismanaged multiple roles, and these unintentional situations could create relationship complications. For instance, being the only counselor in the school in the school district in which you live creates concerns when working with a neighbor's child, or coaching a community soccer team to which one of the soccer players is also assigned to your caseload. As a member of the faculty, it is not unusual to have a teacher come to your office to seek counseling. As caring professionals it is acceptable to spend time with this individual to intervene in a crisis or to provide short-term assistance, yet a referral to a community mental health professional is warranted if long-term counseling is required (Wheeler & Bertram, 2012). In rural or small communities school counselors need to have an awareness of how their public behaviors may be perceived. For example, in these small communities your life may be scrutinized. A former student of mine was the recipient of hate messages and other unpleasant behaviors from parents who believed her classroom guidance lessons were defamatory and in conflict with their family values. These parents/guardians went so far as to question her religion and whether or not she attended church.

Appropriate Referrals

With a high caseload and teachers' reluctance to dismiss students from class, counselors are unable to provide long-term counseling, or counsel individuals on issues that are beyond the counselor's scope of training. In instances such as these, referrals are needed to ensure that the student receives the needed assistance and resources. When a referral is in the student's best interest, the counselor with whom he/she has developed a relationship may increase the student's feelings of abandonment during transition to another professional. A signed parent/guardian consent form allows all parties to communicate about the student's progress. In these cases, knowledge of terminology and diagnoses, collaborative plans for working with the student, and services to facilitate academic achievement aid in a smooth transition.

CONCEPTUAL APPLICATION ACTIVITY 2.4

Andrea, a 15-year-old sophomore, came to see her school counselor, Nat Brown, because she had been binging and purging for the past five months. Nat did not feel that he had the expertise to work with Andrea on this issue and referred her to a friend and community counselor, who specialized in eating disorders. Several weeks later Andrea's mother confronted Nat and accused him of trying to help out his friend rather than putting Andrea's needs first. Did Nat behave in an ethical manner? Discuss your answer with your classmates.

When a referral is needed, a network of resources is desirable. Providing at least three experts in a particular area allows parents/guardians to make their own decision about the professional they feel is best equipped to work with their child. If a problem does occur, then the responsibility for the decision belongs to the family. This guideline was particularly evident to me when I was a practicing school counselor and I provided a referral for a teenage female who was having difficulties with substance use and abuse. Several weeks after I provided the name of a local resource, the mother of the teen called me and communicated that her daughter had a horrible incident with this counselor. She reported that during one session her daughter tearfully ran out of the counselor's office and was so disturbed that she wasn't able to discuss what occurred and refused to return for follow-up sessions.

The example above and other agency referrals could unintentionally lead to negative consequences. For example, a third-grade boy was having difficulty with work completion and exhibited odd behaviors such as licking and hiding under his desk. His teacher referred him to the school counselor, who found him to be very non-communicative. The counselor wasn't making much progress until he got the idea of asking the student to draw images on the chalkboard and write answers to questions posed by the school counselor. Using this creative approach the counselor learned that the young boy had been exposed to pornographic and violent media, lived in an unstable family in which the father left home, and his teenage brother had been in trouble with the law. Furthermore, this young student had nightmares in which he was chased and killed. The school counselor called the Department of Children's Services (DCS) and when the young student's mother learned that a call to DCS had been made, she assumed it was from the school counselor, and immediately called the school and requested that her son not see the school counselor anymore. Not only was this request detrimental to the individual counseling services the student had been receiving, this demand also prevented the student from participating in classroom guidance lessons where he could have learned and practiced essential life skills.

It is also possible that the school system may have a policy regarding referrals. In some school districts personnel are not allowed to make any referrals to outside sources, due to the fear that the district could be held monetarily liable for any expenses that could be accrued as a result of a professional recommendation. This policy severely limits professionals' ability to best meet the student's needs.

Group Work

Both the Association for Specialists in Group Work and ASCA outline ethical guidelines for school counselors conducting work in groups. According to the

ASCA position statement, providing group counseling is an "efficient and effective way to meet students' developmental and situational needs" (ASCA, 2008, para. 2). Knowledge and skill in group facilitation, including the establishment of group rules, pre-screening, and emphasizing confidentiality are necessary components for preventing physical and/or psychological harm. Post-group meetings with members and documentation of the group activities are also considered best practices.

CONCEPTUAL APPLICATION ACTIVITY 2.5

You are a school counselor at a middle school and you decide to start a group to educate sixth-grade students about bullying and methods for handling incidents of bullying. You have selected 8 students to participate in the group, and during one of the sessions Tabitha tearfully reveals that she sent a picture of herself naked to her boyfriend. After the group, one of the group members asked Tabitha's boyfriend to show her the picture. How should the counselor handle this situation? Discuss your response with your classmates.

Although the importance of confidentiality is to be stressed at every session, privacy cannot be guaranteed. Consequently, thoughtful group planning within an educational setting that includes screening group members, discussing participant's responsibilities to other group members, and considering constraints within a school building can serve as potential safeguards from member harm. Furthermore, leader qualifications, attention to group process, unanticipated situations, and appropriateness of interactions while attending to individual issues (Wheeler & Bertram, 2012) also contribute to group effectiveness. Although group counseling is a respected function of the counselor's role in a school setting, soliciting parent/guardian written permission indicating consent for their child to participate in a group is considered good clinical preparation.

Danger to Self or Others

Reminding students about the limits to confidentiality at the beginning of each counseling session provides transparency about the counseling process. In addition, this disclosure may prevent a sense of betrayal when appropriate individuals are notified if the student indicates a danger to self and others.

CONCEPTUAL APPLICATION ACTIVITY 2.6

Ella Fitzhugh is a fifth-grader with a history of depression. Recently, she came to see you because her grandmother died and her mother is having difficulty coping with the death. Ella's grades have dropped and she is giving away some of the gifts that she received on her birthday. She also made the statement that, "she would like to visit her grandmother." What are the counselor's ethical/legal responsibilities in this case? Discuss your response with those of your classmates.

A suicide assessment is required when working with any individual who indicates that he/she is contemplating suicide. In the case of 13-year-old Nicole Eisel, several students told their school counselor that Nicole, who attended a different school, was involved in Satanism and mentioned that Nicole was talking about killing herself. The school counselor informed Nicole's counselor and Nicole was questioned about these statements, which she denied. Later, Nicole and a friend killed themselves, which resulted in Nicole's parents bringing a lawsuit against the school and the counselors. In this case the court ruled that school counselors have a "duty to use reasonable means to attempt to prevent a suicide" (Stone, 2003, para. 9). If you believe that there is a possibility of suicide with a student, but your assessment indicates a low risk, be sure to consult with colleagues and document these procedures and information in your case notes.

When you assess a student to be at a low risk for suicide, parents/guardians can be informed about your concern in two ways: 1) personally call parents and guardians regarding your concern and document the conversation; 2) tell the student that you are concerned about his/her well-being, and if the child is capable, ask him/her to tell parents/guardians with the stipulation that they are to contact you immediately after being told. If you do not receive a call from the responsible adult in a designated time, then it is your responsibility to call home to speak directly to the parent/guardian.

If a student is at serious risk for committing suicide, immediate action is required (Remley, 2007). After consulting and documenting your concern, explain to the student you have a responsibility to notify parents/guardians so that he/she can receive the necessary help. Describe what will happen in a developmentally appropriate manner and make certain that the child is not left alone until a responsible adult arrives. In the case that a dependable person cannot be located, keep the student in a safe place until someone does arrive. In some cases, this may mean that you will be with this student for an extended period of time, and if after a reasonable amount time there is still no responsible adult to transport the student, an ambulance will be needed for transport to a hospital that has psychiatric services. It may even be necessary to ride with the student to the hospital. Once you have contacted the parent/guardian, it is helpful to have a consent form signed so that you can speak openly with the treating professional about the student. Furthermore, be sure you document the details of the conversation, including the time and date, for legal protection.

The Tarasoff case provided the legal basis for warning others when there is evidence of clear danger to others. In 1969, a client told his counselor that he intended to kill an identified woman, and after receiving this information the counselor notified the campus police who picked up the client, but later released him and he followed through on his threat. The parents of the deceased woman sued the therapist for not warning them or their daughter about the threat. This case served as the catalyst for most states establishing the legal requirement that mental health professionals have a duty to warn.

Student Records

School counselors maintain and protect student records. Personal records are created for memory assistance, and because they belong solely to the originator they are kept separately from educational records. School counselors often wonder how much documentation is necessary, particularly since excessive documentation takes away valuable professional time that could be used to work with students. In certain circumstances, however, a more detailed summary is necessary in the event that they become the basis of a legal issue. It is helpful to separate personal notes into two separate columns labeled objective and subjective. Under the objective section, write specifically what the counselee said and did, including exact dates and times with personal, objective observations. In the subjective column record notes for future reference, personal impressions, speculations as to the student's problems, and plans for future sessions. Even though these case notes are considered as your own personal property, they may become educational records in the event that they are subpoenaed (if your state doesn't recognize privileged communication), shared with others, or other information is included other than your observations or professional opinion.

Throughout the years, files of notes accumulate and take up much needed space, leading school counselors to wonder when it is appropriate to destroy personal records. Although there are no general guidelines regarding the length of time records should be kept, six years is the recommended number of years for legal purposes (Remley, 2007). Best practices suggest that documents are to be shredded on a scheduled time line, or if certain school records are destroyed on a regular schedule, the school counselor files can be destroyed at this same time.

However, if you believe that a court of law may need this record at a future date, it would be wise to save these records for future reference.

CONCEPTUAL APPLICATION ACTIVITY 2.7

The principal is aware that you have been seeing Lila on a regular basis and that you keep personal notes on the sessions you have with each student. Lila's mother comes to school and the principal mentioned that Lila had been seeing you regularly, and that you have records of your sessions with her. The mother and principal come to your office to talk about your meetings with Lila. How would you handle this? Discuss your responses with your classmates.

Case notes help you become a more effective counselor, and although there is no legal requirement for maintaining these notes, it is considered as a best practice. Keep notes in a locked file drawer to which only you have access, or if you decide to keep notes on a computer, it is important that these records are not accessible to anyone, and that appropriate software is installed for security purposes.

Finally, school counselors have a duty to provide accurate information to stakeholders. When students are relying on you to provide factual information and you fail in this role, this is considered professional negligence (Stone, 2005). In the case of *Sain v. Cedar Rapids Community School District,* Bruce Sain attended high school in Cedar Rapids during his eleventh- and twelfth-grade years. Sain was an outstanding basketball player and received a scholarship to play basketball at an NCAA Division 1 University following high school graduation. During Sain's senior year, his school counselor granted him permission to drop a core NCAA English course and enrolled him in a different course to meet his English requirements. However, since the new English class was not included on the list of classes meeting NCAA approval, he lost his scholarship to Northern Illinois University, and as a result Sain and his parents filed a lawsuit against the high school and school counselor. This case highlighted the importance of school counselors using reasonable care, demonstrating they can be held liable for providing inaccurate advice.

Evaluation, Assessment, and Interpretation

Testing and assessment has been a component of the school counselor's role almost since the inception of the profession, and continues to be a major task today. School counselors are trained in areas such as test selection, norming, orientation, administration, and interpretation. They are also aware of the multiple factors used to make decisions in regard to students' placement in programs and educational plans, rather than relying on a single score.

CONCEPTUAL APPLICATION ACTIVITY 2.8

Katherine Towns has a huge caseload that exceeds the ASCA recommendation of 250 students to 1 counselor ratio. The ACT results arrived, and since she has difficulty getting into classes to schedule a group interpretation session, she decides that she will conduct an online webinar to explain the results to students and their families. She decided that she will also meet with any student individually if results need to be explained in more detail. What do you think of Katherine's decision? Discuss your response with your classmates.

Understanding the purpose of various tests and receiving the training that is necessary to administer and interpret tests is critical to counselor competence. Tests range in complexity from intelligence tests that require intense training to vocational assessments that are easily administered and interpreted. I am aware of some school counselors who were assigned the task of administering an intelligence test when the school psychologist was not available, which created inaccurate results and frustrated parents when the school counselor was not able to answer questions they had regarding the assessment. School counselors do not usually have the training that is required to administer and interpret these tests, and it is unethical to do so without proper training. Counselors have a responsibility to inform the student and/or parent/guardian of the test purpose, what the test is designed to measure, how the test will be used (Wheeler & Bertram, 2012), and the test results.

Technology

As technology proliferates, school counselors need to be savvy consumers of technological applications that are developmentally appropriate, understand privacy laws to prevent inappropriate information from being released, and develop proactive intervention strategies to prevent cyber bullying. It is also a good idea to educate school secretaries about keeping records private and to teach them about FERPA laws.

CONCEPTUAL APPLICATION ACTIVITY 2.9

Jon Devlin carefully selected students to serve as "guidance helpers" during their study halls. He trained the peers to assist students with computer generated career searches and showed them how to access career interest inventories for students who were uncertain as to the career they wished to pursue. Was this a good decision? Discuss your response with your classmates.

Students without technological resources are at a disadvantage when teachers require assignments to be completed and submitted electronically, or technological means are used to communicate with parents/guardians. School counselors have an opportunity to advocate on behalf of these individuals and make arrangements for alternative means of conveying information. Furthermore, when personal notes and records are stored on computers, savvy individuals are able to find ways to break security codes and access records. At one point in my career, a talented student was able to figure out the computer passwords that provided access to grades and other student information. This breech of security took months to resolve, not to mention the enraged reactions of parent and student.

No school bullying policy will be effective without attention to cyber bully issues, defined as using technology to harass, exclude, or degrade another through such means as instant messaging, e-mail, chat rooms, and videos through cell phones, social networking sites, and so on (Espelage, 2004). Cyber bullying influences the school climate and student well-being. With the increasing number cyber bullying incidents schools are legally mandated to develop bullying policies with attention to this type of harassment. Unfortunately, many school personnel are reluctant to address this type of aggression, particularly when it occurs outside of school hours. However, school personnel have a legal obligation to intervene with cyber bullying that occurs off campus, particularly when evidence suggests that the incident disrupted the school environment (Hinduja & Patchin, 2008).

Student Peer Support Programs

Peer support programs are based on the premise that students are more likely to talk with and receive information and support from their peers than an adult. These programs include models such as peer tutoring, peer mentors, or peer mediation. Peer program models include: 1) a separate course limited to students who enroll in the class; 2) as a part of the curriculum in which all the students learn skills in a scheduled class; or 3) as a student club in which students are selected and meet at a designated time under the guidance of a school faculty member.

CONCEPTUAL APPLICATION ACTIVITY 2.10

Mr. Rodriquez, a middle school counselor, has read about the benefits of peer facilitation groups. He decides to start a peer mediation group with eighth-grade students who display leadership skills and have good grades. He meets with the selected students once for training, and on the PA system announces to the student body that trained mediators are available if anyone would like to resolve a conflict with another student.

He arranges a room and times for the students to conduct their mediation, and tells the peer mediators that if they run into a problem to come and see him. What are your reactions to this type of arrangement? Discuss your reaction with your classmates.

Peer facilitation is an opportunity for students to participate in their own learning and apply what they learn. Through peer-led activities, students are able to work with their peers one-on-one in multiple ways. As in any school program the endorsement from the building administrator and support of all educational personnel is necessary for program success. Sharing goals, rationales, strategies, and evaluation are crucial aspects for gaining program support. Training, coordination, evaluation of effectiveness, identifying the students to participate, selecting topics, and finding a location where the peers will meet are additional aspects of peer programming. Peer programs are likely to be ineffectual without continual commitment and monitoring.

RESPONSIBILITIES TO PARENTS/GUARDIANS

Parent Rights and Responsibilities

School counselors have a primary responsibility to promote students' well-being, an obligation that becomes complicated due to school counselors also having a responsibility to the students' parents and guardians. These multiple commitments are often difficult to balance.

CONCEPTUAL APPLICATION ACTIVITY 2.11

Maxton's parents have been divorced for several years and he lives with his custodial mom. One morning Maxton's noncustodial father comes to school to get copies of Maxton's grades and progress reports. You realize the importance of involving parents in the student's education, but are uncertain whether or not to provide Maxton's father with this information. Should this information be released? Discuss your answer with your classmates.

In most states non-custodial parents are granted the same rights as custodial parents; however, in some states the rights of non-custodial parents are limited. Providing parents/guardians with information about the school counseling program at the beginning of each school year and providing information to parents who are transferring to your school can prevent miscommunication. A professional disclosure form assists in informing others of who you are through information such as your credentials, training, theoretical approach, the benefits of a CDSC program, and ethical statutes including the limits of confidentiality. Program brochures, and "tips of the week" placed on the school website also show the relevancy of the school counseling program and facilitate an understanding of how the program is connected with the school goals. A school counselor website and business cards that include contact information such as your e-mail, phone number, and program web address provide a professional impression. Business cards can be made inexpensively from http://www.vistaprint.com.

Parents/Guardians and Confidentiality

It is sometimes difficult to know how much information to communicate to parents/guardians. Some counselors feel that they should not reveal any information given by a student, whereas others believe that parents/guardians are more likely to work harmoniously with the counselor when general information is shared. This information could include strategies to engage the child at home rather than providing detailed information. For instance, making a statement such as "Jackson is having difficulty concentrating and I would like to share some techniques that you can use at home to help him" shows respect to both the child and parent.

CONCEPTUAL APPLICATION ACTIVITY 2.12

Bo is an 8-year-old, third-grader whose parents are divorced but have joint custody. Bo's father is recently remarried and his wife, Bo's stepmother, comes to school to request Bo's progress reports and grades. Do you give her these reports? Discuss your answer with your classmates.

The developmental maturity of the child is a factor in deciding how much information to share. In general, greater loyalty is to be given to the parent/guardian of the younger the child. Moyer, Sullivan, and Growcock (2012) revealed that school counselors believed that breaking the confidentiality of younger students was more ethical than revealing the confidences of older students, particularly in regard to behaviors such as sexual activity and tobacco use.

According to FERPA, a stepparent is entitled to review the child's records and is considered as a "parent" if the stepparent lives with a custodial parent on a day-to-day basis (U.S. Department of Education, 2004). Both parents are eligible to receive educational records unless school officials have been notified otherwise (Stone, 2005). In the *Page v. Rotterdam-Mohonasen Central School District* case, the school district refused to provide a noncustodial father with his son's school records. Although the parents were separated and the mother was the custodial parent, the school district was charged with a neglect of duty by not acting in the best interests of the child when educational information was not released to both parents. Unless there is a court order stating otherwise, both parents have a right to their child's educational records.

Other guidelines for communicating with parents/guardians include:

- Asking the child if he/she is willing to disclose the information that was discussed in counseling
- Discussing the importance of confidentiality and the nature of a counseling relationship while assuring the parent/guardian that contact will be made if there is any indication of harm to self or others
- Arranging for a collaborative session with the parent/guardian and child and allow the student to share as much information as is comfortable
- If the suggestions above are not options, inform the child ahead of time that you are going to share the information that was revealed in the counseling sessions (Remley, 2007).

RESPONSIBILITIES TO COLLEAGUES AND PROFESSIONAL ASSOCIATES

Professional Relationships

Collaborative relationships in which positive, respectful working relationships with colleagues are established improve the academic, career, and personal/social growth of students. There are some teachers who are easier to work with than others, and knowing these colleagues is an initial step for school counselors to develop programs/activities or other curricular offerings that benefit all students.

CONCEPTUAL APPLICATION ACTIVITY 2.13

Mrs. Adams teaches English at the high school in which you are employed. Every year she complains about the number of students that are placed in her honors English class. You are aware that the class is large but it is the only twelfth-grade honors class that is offered. A new senior enters your school and as luck would have it, this student was enrolled in a twelfth-grade honors English class at the previous high school. Reluctantly, you place this student in Mrs. Adams' class and that afternoon an irate Mrs. Adams arrives at your office, demanding to have this new student removed from her class. What do you do? Discuss your response with your classmates.

School counselors are often in the middle of situations such as that described above, and rather than arguing your position it is sometimes better to allow time for the teacher to vent while you use active listening skills and ask him/her to provide you with suggestions as to how the situation could be better addressed. Building an alliance with the teacher, creating a collegial atmosphere, and understanding personal views facilitates collaborative problem-solving.

Sharing Information with Other Professionals

When individuals and agencies work together the student is often the beneficiary, yet most school professionals do not have a code of conduct in which confidentiality is required and part of their ethical, professional responsibilities. Therefore, it is difficult for individuals to understand the reason counselors do not share information that could be viewed as essential to teaching and learning.

CONCEPTUAL APPLICATION ACTIVITY 2.14

You are an elementary counselor and you have been working with 8-year-old Mia, who has been sad and lethargic. Mia's mom comes into your office and mentions that Mia is now seeing a community mental health counselor for her depression. Can you talk with this professional about Mia? Discuss your response with your classmates.

When information needs to be shared, school counselors are not able to communicate with outside mental health professionals without a signed release from the parent or guardian. Once this release is signed both professionals are able to work together to support the student's counseling goals. Colleagues in the school environment have a personal interest in the well-being of the student and often want to know the reasons a student is performing poorly. You may be aware that a student's dad has recently been incarcerated or that a student's mother has recently remarried and step-siblings are in the home, which has created personal turmoil for the student. Although this information may give teachers an awareness of the student's situation, you are bound to the confidential trust of the student. Two questions you could ask yourself in these situations are: "Does the teacher need to know this information?" and, "How will revealing this information help the student?"

COLLABORATING AND EDUCATING AROUND THE ROLE OF THE SCHOOL COUNSELOR

It is evident that stakeholders have varied perceptions of the school counselor's role and how well they believe you perform your job. These views are often based on experiences they have had with school counselors as students, classes they have taken, or professional interactions with school counseling professionals.

CONCEPTUAL APPLICATION ACTIVITY 2.15

Mrs. McCarthy's son, Ryan, is a starting quarterback on the high school football team. She was just informed that Ryan is ineligible to play for the next two games due to his failing grades. She was irate that you, Ryan's counselor, didn't inform her about his poor grades. She was so upset with what she perceived to be your negligence that she sent a blog to the community members in which you were the target of her anger. What do you do? Discuss your response with your classmates.

School counselors support the academic growth of their students, and although many school counselors continually address student grades that could put them in jeopardy for academic success, awareness of athletic eligibility is generally not part of a school counselor's role. It is obvious in the conceptual application activity that the parent believed that this was a school counselor task. If we don't take the opportunity to educate others about our job responsibilities, then perceptions rather than reality will guide how others evaluate us. Brochures, websites, letters, and so on, in addition to discussing our role at PTA meetings, at the beginning of the year at faculty meetings, and at the new teacher orientation are all methods of communicating what we do. Visiting classrooms at the beginning of the year to introduce yourself, or reminding returning students of your role provides information as to who you are, how they can make appointments, and where your office is located. This gives students an opportunity to see you as an ally and someone with whom they can confide.

RESPONSIBILITIES TO SCHOOL, COMMUNITIES, AND FAMILIES

Today's school counseling program is an integral part of the educational mission; it is designed to meet the needs of all students as opposed to being a traditional, ancillary school program. A CDSC program creates a healthy, productive school climate in which all students are able to reach their fullest potential. The ASCA mandates that school counselors inform administrators of activities that could jeopardize, create damage, or destroy property, a difficult directive when student confidentiality is jeopardized (Moyer, et al., 2012). For example, in the case of *Davis v. Monroe County Board of Education*, the mother of a fifth-grade student alleged that the school authorities did not prevent the sexual harassment of her daughter and placed her daughter in a toxic educational environment. The courts ruled against the school board, citing that the harassment complaints were ignored.

CONCEPTUAL APPLICATION ACTIVITY 2.16

Judy Sommers was in a quandary. She finally landed a job at her dream high school and was excited about counseling with the students in her caseload. The principal approached her and stated that because he was responsible for the welfare of the students, he wanted to know the names of students who were pregnant. Judy felt uncomfortable about this request and pointed out that she felt this was a violation of her ethical code of conduct. The principal replied that he was the building administrator and that she needed to comply with his request. How should Judy handle this? Discuss your response with your classmates.

It is difficult to work in a school setting when administrators make requests that you feel jeopardize the student/counselor relationship. In my first year as a high school counselor, the principal asked me to take urine samples of girls who were suspected they might be pregnant to the local health department (this was before home pregnancy kits) and to notify him if any of the test results were positive. I told him I did not feel comfortable with this task, but he felt that it was important for the girls to know as early as possible that they were pregnant and that this knowledge would protect their safety when they were in activities that required strenuous physical activity, such as physical education. I left this position after one year when I realized that my beliefs did not correspond with his.

Potential conflicts such as this could be avoided when you interview for a job. Ask about expectations, ask to see a job description, ask about their vision for school counseling, and if their vision is different from yours perhaps this isn't the position for you. Since the acceptance of employment implies agreement with the general policies and procedures of the school, try to reach an agreement with employers concerning acceptable standards of conduct and procedures for optimal student growth. Furthermore, read school policies and procedures and request an interpretation of ambiguous phrases or words. Administrator requests should be followed unless you are asked to do something that is illegal, unethical, or against school procedures. If you feel your request is unreasonable you could protest, but in the end, you will need to follow the request. It is possible to appeal to your administrator's supervisor regarding tasks that you feel are unacceptable, but you may also be dismissed for insubordination (Remley, 2007).

Responsibility to the Community

We do not work in isolation. Students and their families are beneficiaries when resources and experts work together to seek referral sources and consult on personal/professional issues.

CONCEPTUAL APPLICATION ACTIVITY 2.17

You live in a very small community that has few resources. You are a licensed school counselor and also have a license to work independently as a mental health counselor. Seven-year-old Zaida has numerous family, school, and peer relationship issues and you do not have the time to work with her in a school setting. You mention to her guardian that you have a private practice and would be willing to serve as her counselor outside of school. Is this ethical? Discuss your answer with your classmates.

School counselors in rural settings are at a disadvantage when there are limited available resources. Every effort needs to be made to ensure that you do not use your role as a school counselor to promote any private practice you may have outside of the school.

RESPONSIBILITIES TO SELF

Professional Competence

Wellness, a tenet of our counseling profession, refers to the promotion of health within our counselees as well as ourselves. Too often we get caught up in the devastating stories of our students and ignore the vicarious stress that impacts us as we offer assistance to our troubled youth.

CONCEPTUAL APPLICATION ACTIVITY 2.18

Sue Lange works as a school counselor for youth who have been placed in an alternative school setting due to their behavioral issues. She likes to be with her friends on the weekends to relax and separate herself from the toxic situations her students discuss with her. She parties long and hard on the weekends, and several times the neighbors have called the police due to the loud noise that emanates from her apartment. Are there any ethical principles that Sue is violating? Discuss your responses with your classmates.

As school counselors, we are role models. Our behaviors reflect who we are and serve as guidelines for the students with whom we work. Engaging in questionable behavior outside of school gives the perception that we are not holding ourselves to the highest standards of conduct.

Multicultural and Social Justice Advocacy and Leadership

Woodcock v. Orange Ulster B.O.C.E.S., 2006/2008 illustrates a situation in which a practicing school counselor did not feel she was given administrative support. The school counselor had years of experience and favorable evaluations up until she was assigned to a school counselor position in a school for students with special needs. Her administrator at this new site was an intern completing his master's degree who was supervised by a principal in a neighboring school. At this school a student with special needs engaged in disruptive and extremely troubling behaviors including smearing feces on walls, endangering others, and attempting suicide. The counselor expressed her concerns to her administrator and his supervisor but did not receive any assistance or action from either administrator. The school counselor documented these attempts, but because she did not follow protocol to express her complaints, she was forced to resign her position (Stone & Zirkel, 2010). In this case, although her advocacy efforts fell on deaf ears, not following appropriate procedures for expressing concern was critical. Competent school counselors are aware of the environmental, academic, family, and community factors that support student growth across ages and abilities. Systemic change occurs when we advocate for our students and their parents, and at times sensitivity and political savvy are skills that facilitate this advocacy.

CONCEPTUAL APPLICATION ACTIVITY 2.19

Aliyah came to your school from Jordan. She is a practicing Muslim and according to her religious tenets, is required to wear a hijab (scarf) to cover her hair. She is scheduled for English class with Mr. Van Ness, who makes the comment, "I don't know why people who come to this country can't learn to dress like we do." Aliyah has come to you because he has made reference to her religion on several occasions and she isn't sure if it is because he is prejudiced against her culture/religion or if she doesn't understand Western customs. What would you do in this situation? Discuss your response with your classmates.

School counselors are aware of the impact of school climate on learning and growth, and are committed to making the school environment as positive as possible. Continually self-assessing personal beliefs and values and how these personal values influence counseling relationships are critical for an ethically responsive school counselor (Lambie, Davis, & Miller, 2008). Addressing multicultural issues that impact student learning in faculty meetings, or discussing cultural norms and working as student advocates for those who feel oppressed are all part of working for social justice for our students and their families.

Advocacy and awareness was particularly evident in the *Nabozny v. Podlesny* case in which Jamie Nabozny was awarded a monetary sum due to suffering injuries at Ashland Middle and High Schools, located in Ashland, Wisconsin. Jamie was assaulted, sexually harassed, urinated and spitted upon, and had objects thrown at him by his peers due to his sexual orientation. The school officials were found guilty for not protecting Jamie, despite having knowledge of these incidents. The school counselor can be proactive in preventing incidents such as this by addressing the absence of policies that are designed to protect students, or assist in revising policies that create unfair treatment of students.

RESPONSIBILITIES TO THE PROFESSION

Professionalism

School counselors have a responsibility to conduct themselves professionally and stay informed of the trends within the counseling profession, including the importance of assessing student growth and professional interventions. Research protocol and professionalism includes following school district protocol in conducting research with minors, seeking parent/guardian consent before collecting data, maintaining anonymity of student information, and securing data in a locked file.

CONCEPTUAL APPLICATION ACTIVITY 2.20

Darold Malone is a staunch supporter of a person who is running for state senator. He has a campaign sign hung on his office door in support of this individual. Is Mr. Malone within his ethical rights to voice this opinion? Discuss your opinion with your classmates.

When such things as policies, finances, or opinions negatively impact school-age students, it is difficult to not express personal opinions on how you believe things could be better; however, stakeholders could view public statements or expressions of personal views as questionable professional behaviors. When expressing personal opinions, be sure to differentiate between personal actions/statements and those made as a member of the school and counseling program. For instance, at one point a school counselor felt quite strongly in her views about reproductive choice and participated in a march in favor of funding for the local family planning clinic, for which there was a proposed reduction in funding. Several parents and community members decided that if this was her belief, they did not want her working with their children because they thought her values would harm their children.

Contribution to the Profession

School counselors are busy individuals. Not only are their days filled with work-related tasks, they often go home to children who are involved in after-school activities, not to mention the other personal or professional activities that take time. It is a difficult balance between work, family, self, and other personal/family responsibilities. Participating in professional organizations is often given a lower priority when there are other activities pressing for attention. However, if you do not keep up on the current movements in the counseling profession it is difficult to be viewed as a competent professional.

CONCEPTUAL APPLICATION ACTIVITY 2.21

Blanche has been a school counselor for 15 years. She attended several conferences over the years and returns to her school inspired about new ideas, connections she made, and knowledge she gained from the sessions. Her principal has notified the faculty that money will no longer be available to support attendance at conferences, and that personnel will no longer be allowed to attend professional events during the school day. What can Blanche do to stay actively involved in her professional organizations? Discuss your response with your classmates.

When monies are tight and financial support is unavailable to attend professional conferences, it is difficult to network with other colleagues who serve as sources of support and information; however, other opportunities are available for developing these needed networks. For instance, the ASCA SCENE is a networking site sponsored by the ASCA, available for members at https://schoolcounselor.groupsite.com/main/summary.

This resource serves as a professional meeting place where you can post questions, join discussions, search files, and learn about professional opportunities. Furthermore, the ASCA National conference is traditionally held in late June, at a time most school counselors have completed their school year. As a member of the ASCA, you are able to access numerous professional resources for members that range from position statements to webinars and other professional resources. In addition, your state counseling organization provides state and local professional conferences, workshops, and seminars. Consider submitting a proposal for a conference presentation to share ideas, programs, or events from your school program. Sometimes presenters are given a fee reduction in exchange for sharing their expertise.

Supervision of School Counselor Candidates

Providing supervision for students entering the school counseling profession is an opportunity to serve as a mentor, supervisor, and eventually a colleague for those entering school counseling. The CACREP standards indicate that supervisors are to have a minimum of two years of school counseling experience with training in supervision. Unfortunately, receiving training in supervision can be difficult since this is generally not a course that is taught in master's level programs. However, this training can be accessed through additional coursework or through professional conferences.

CONCEPTUAL APPLICATION ACTIVITY 2.22

Andrea Keller is desperately seeking help and decides that hosting a school counseling internship student at her school would be the ideal solution. Ms. Keller has gone to several workshops on supervision and believes she is ready to take on this responsibility. She agrees to be the supervisor for Mikade, who is in his final semester of his school counseling program. She has him helping with many of the activities that she finds to be time consuming such as testing and monitoring cafeteria and bus duty, and on occasion has him work with students scheduling their classes. What are your thoughts about her supervision? Discuss your responses with your classmates.

According to the CACREP requirements, the clinical experiences include the practicum, entailing a minimum of 100 clock hours, of which a minimum of 40 direct hours are to be spent in direct counseling service with students. The internship is a minimum of 600 hours, of which a minimum of 240 hours are spent in direct contact with counseling students. The site supervisor of the practicum or internship is to provide at least one hour of supervision each week and is required to evaluate the progress of the supervisee. Although not all school counseling programs are CACREP accredited, these requirements serve as a guide for non-CACREP programs.

The school counseling program is aligned with a data-driven developmental, comprehensive program including beliefs, mission and vision statements, and program goals, including methods for evaluating the program and school counselors. The practicing school counselor and program faculty member supervise students in their school counseling clinical experiences and evaluate the student's ability to perform tasks aligned with the ASCA National Model.

Collaboration and Education About School Counselors and School Counseling Programs with Other Professionals

The school counselor does not work in isolation but rather meets students' needs through interactions with other professionals. School counselors are one of the few school-based professionals who have an ethical code with confidentiality standards. Providing a copy of the ASCA ethical code to interested individuals while explaining how confidentiality is the cornerstone of a counseling relationship could alleviate misperceptions surrounding our role.

CONCEPTUAL APPLICATION ACTIVITY 2.23

Rose Alvarez has not been herself lately. You have seen her change from a gregarious, happy seventh-grader to one who seems sad and lonely. You decide to talk with the school nurse to see whether or not Rose has complained of health issues. The nurse informs you that Rose has been to her office with complaints of headaches and stomach problems. Who would be some of the other professionals who could provide additional information about Rose? Discuss your responses with your classmates.

School counselors are not the only major provider of mental health services for youth. Collaboration and holistic interventions with the school psychologist, school social worker, or nurse complement the work of school counselors. When collaboration occurs stakeholders have a better understanding of our work, and those who are skeptical of our role may turn out to be our greatest advocates when given an opportunity to discuss concerns and learn about the program.

Maintenance of Standards

Maintain ethical standards and behaviors at all times. In situations where individuals behave in ways that may be construed as unethical, there are several steps that can be taken to resolve any suspicious behaviors.

CONCEPTUAL APPLICATION ACTIVITY 2.24

You are concerned about reports from students talking about their friend, Molly, who was a senior at a neighboring school. They were upset because Molly stopped "hanging out" with them, and whenever they called her to do something over the weekend she was consistently busy. A few weeks ago they saw her at a restaurant with an "older man" and when they went to her table to speak with her, they felt as if they were intruding on something between the two of them. One of your students mentioned that Molly had been talking about a boyfriend named John King, and believed that this was the man she was with at the restaurant. As the girls talk with you, you realize that this man is the counselor at the neighboring school. What do you do? Discuss your response with your classmates.

Whenever you have a dilemma—consult, consult, consult! If you are concerned about the behavior of a counseling professional, discuss your apprehensions with a colleague. If this person believes the situation is an ethical violation, the best recourse is to talk, if possible, with the professional about whom you are concerned. If a resolution is not reached, then the established school or district networks and procedures need to be explored. If the issue is still not resolved then a referral to the state ethics committee is necessary, and if a resolution still isn't reached, then the ASCA ethics committee will need to be contacted.

CONCLUSION

The ASCA Ethical Standards for School Counselors serve as the basis for school counselor responsibilities in providing ethical practices, self-appraisal, and informing stakeholders of expected school counseling practices. At times decision making is difficult when ethical and legal issues are not congruent. The Solutions to Ethical Problems in Schools (STEPS) ethical decision-making model assists in understanding the issues and the people who will be impacted when a particular resolution is determined. Consideration of justice, universality, publicity, and moral traces facilitates the ethical decision resolution, in addition to asking the question, "What would a reasonably similarly trained school counselor practicing in this school have done in this situation at this time?" (Remley, 2007).

The American Counseling Association and the American School Counselor Association have ethical codes to consult, yet in this chapter the ASCA Ethical Standards for School Counselors serve as the foundation for the discussion in this chapter. Although these ethical guidelines do provide a reference, counselors are advised to be knowledgeable about local, state, and federal laws and policies prescribed by their school board. Consulting with colleagues before taking action, documenting the steps that were taken, and maintaining liability insurance provides protection in the event your professionalism is questioned.

REFERENCES

American School Counselor Association (2008). *The Professional School Counselor and Group Counseling.* Retrieved from http://www.schoolcounselor.org/

American School Counselor Association (2010). *Ethical Standards for School Counselors.* Retrieved from http://www.schoolcounselor.org/

College Board (2010). School Counselor Strategic planning tool. Retrieved from NOSCA Strategic planning tool-1.pdf

Espelage, D. L., (2004). An ecological perspective to school-based bullying prevention. *The Prevention Researcher, 11,* 3–6.

Gibbs, K. & Lee, R. (2008, Feb.). *Legal and ethical issues for professional school counselors.* Paper presented at the School Counselor Institute Aim for Success: Assess Implement Measure. Murfreesboro, TN.

Hinduja, S., & Patchi, J. W. (2008). Cyberbullying: An exploratory analysis of factors related to offending and victimization. *Deviant Behavior, 29,* 129–156.

Ho, E. (2012, April 30). Tennessee passes abstinence-based "gateway sexual activity" bill. *Time NewsFeed.* Retrieved from http://newsfeed.time.com/2012/04/30/tennessee-passes-abstinence-based-gateway-sexual-activity-bill/

Lambie, G. W., Davis, K. M., & Miller, G. (2008). Spirituality: Implications for professional school counselors; Ethical Practice. *Counseling and Values, 52,* 211–223.

Lonborg, S. D., & Bowen, N. (2004). Counselors, communities, and spirituality: Ethical and multicultural considerations. *Professional School Counseling, 7,* 318–325.

Moyer, M. S., Sullivan, J. R., & Growcock, D. (2012). When is it ethical to inform administrators about student risk-taking behaviors? Perceptions of School Counselors. *Professional School Counseling, 15,* 98–109.

Remley, T. (2007, November*). Legal and ethical issues: Counseling children in schools and community agencies.* Pre-conference session presented at the Tennessee Association for Counselor Education and Supervision, Franklin, Tennessee.

Remley, T. & Herlihy, B. (2010). *Ethical, legal, and professional issues in counseling* (3rd ed.). Upper Saddle River, NJ: Pearson.

Stone, C. (2003). Suicide: A duty owed. *The ASCA School Counselor.* Retrieved from http://www.ascaschoolcounselor.org/article_content.asp?edition=91&section=140&article=780

Stone, C. (2005). *Ethics and law for school counselors.* Alexandria, VA: American School Counseling Association.

Stone, C. (2006, Sept-Oct). *In Loco Parentis,* substantial interest and qualified privilege. ASCA *School Counselor.* Alexandria, VA: ASCA.

Stone, C. (2013, July-Aug.). FERPA: The ever-changing federal statute. *ASCA Counselor, 50,* 6–9.

Stone, C. B., & Dahir, C.A. (2006). *The transformed school counselor.* Boston: Lahaska Press.

Stone, C. B., & Zirkel, P.A. (2010). School counselor advocacy: When law and ethics may collide. *Professional School Counseling, 13,* 244–247.

U.S. Department of Education (2004, Sept*). Letter to parent re: Disclosure of education records to stepparents.* Retrieved from http://www2.ed.gov/policy/gen/guid/fpco/ferpa/library/hastings082004.html

Wheeler, A. M., & Bertram, B. (2012). *The counselor and the law: A guide to legal and ethical practice* (6th ed.). Alexandria, VA: American Counseling Association.

Williams, R. (2007, November). Solutions to ethical problems in schools. *ASCA School Counselor.* Alexandria, VA: ASCA.

APPENDIX A

ETHICAL STANDARDS FOR SCHOOL COUNSELORS

(American School Counselor Association, 2010; Adopted 1984; revised 1992, 1998, 2004 and 2010)

Preamble

The American School Counselor Association (ASCA) is a professional organization whose members are school counselors certified/licensed in school counseling with unique qualifications and skills to address all students' academic, personal/social and career development needs. Members are also school counseling program directors/supervisors and counselor educators. These ethical standards are the ethical responsibility of school counselors. School counseling program directors/supervisors should know them and provide support for practitioners to uphold them. School counselor educators should know them, teach them to their students and provide support for school counseling candidates to uphold them.

Professional school counselors are advocates, leaders, collaborators and consultants who create opportunities for equity in access and success in educational opportunities by connecting their programs to the mission of schools and subscribing to the following tenets of professional responsibility:

- Each person has the right to be respected, be treated with dignity and have access to a comprehensive school counseling program that advocates for and affirms all students from diverse populations including: ethnic/racial identity, age, economic status, abilities/disabilities, language, immigration status, sexual orientation, gender, gender identity/expression, family type, religious/spiritual identity and appearance.
- Each person has the right to receive the information and support needed to move toward self-direction and self-development and affirmation within one's group identities, with special care being given to students who have historically not received adequate educational services, e.g., students of color, students living at a low socio-economic status, students with disabilities and students from non-dominant language backgrounds.
- Each person has the right to understand the full magnitude and meaning of his/her educational choices and how those choices will affect future opportunities.
- Each person has the right to privacy and thereby the right to expect the school-counselor/student relationship to comply with all laws, policies and ethical standards pertaining to confidentiality in the school setting.
- Each person has the right to feel safe in school environments that school counselors help create, free from abuse, bullying, neglect, harassment or other forms of violence.
- In this document, ASCA specifies the principles of ethical behavior necessary to maintain the high standards of integrity, leadership and professionalism among its members. The Ethical Standards for School Counselors were developed to clarify the nature of ethical responsibilities held in common by school counselors, supervisors/directors of school counseling programs and school counselor educators. The purposes of this document are to:
- Serve as a guide for the ethical practices of all professional school counselors, supervisors/directors of school counseling programs and school counselor educators regardless of level, area, population served or membership in this professional association;
- Provide self-appraisal and peer evaluations regarding school counselors' responsibilities to students, parents/guardians, colleagues and professional associates, schools, communities and the counseling profession; and
- Inform all stakeholders, including students, parents and guardians, teachers, administrators, community members and courts of justice, of best ethical practices, values and expected behaviors of the school counseling professional.

A.1. Responsibilities to Students

Professional school counselors:

a. Have a primary obligation to the students, who are to be treated with dignity and respect as unique individuals.

b. Are concerned with the educational, academic, career, personal and social needs and encourage the maximum development of every student.

c. Respect students' values, beliefs and cultural background and do not impose the school counselor's personal values on students or their families.

d. Are knowledgeable of laws, regulations and policies relating to students and strive to protect and inform students regarding their rights.

e. Promote the welfare of individual students and collaborate with them to develop an action plan for success.

f. Consider the involvement of support networks valued by the individual students.

g. Understand that professional distance with students is appropriate, and any sexual or romantic relationship with students whether illegal in the state of practice is considered a grievous breach of ethics and is prohibited regardless of a student's age.

h. Consider the potential for harm before entering into a relationship with former students or one of their family members.

A.2. Confidentiality

Professional school counselors:

a. Inform individual students of the purposes, goals, techniques and rules of procedure under which they may receive counseling. Disclosure includes the limits of confidentiality in a developmentally appropriate manner. Informed consent requires competence on the part of students to understand the limits of confidentiality and therefore, can be difficult to obtain from students of a certain developmental level. Professionals are aware that even though every attempt is made to obtain informed consent it is not always possible and when needed will make counseling decisions on students' behalf.

b. Explain the limits of confidentiality in appropriate ways such as classroom guidance lessons, the student handbook, school counseling brochures, school Web site, verbal notice or other methods of student, school and community communication in addition to oral notification to individual students.

c. Recognize the complicated nature of confidentiality in schools and consider each case in context. Keep information confidential unless legal requirements demand that confidential information be revealed or a breach is required to prevent serious and foreseeable harm to the student. Serious and foreseeable harm is different for each minor in schools and is defined by students' developmental and chronological age, the setting, parental rights and the nature of the harm. School counselors consult with appropriate professionals when in doubt as to the validity of an exception.

d. Recognize their primary obligation for confidentiality is to the students but balance that obligation with an understanding of parents'/guardians' legal and inherent rights to be the guiding voice in their children's lives, especially in value-laden issues. Understand the need to balance students' ethical rights to make choices, their capacity to give consent or assent and parental or familial legal rights and responsibilities to protect these students and make decisions on their behalf.

e. Promote the autonomy and independence of students to the extent possible and use the most appropriate and least intrusive method of breach. The developmental age and the circumstances requiring the breach are considered and as appropriate students are engaged in a discussion about the method and timing of the breach.

f. In absence of state legislation expressly forbidding disclosure, consider the ethical responsibility to provide information to an identified third party who, by his/her relationship with the student, is at a high risk of contracting a disease that is commonly known to be communicable and fatal. Disclosure requires satisfaction of all of the following conditions:

- Student identifies partner or the partner is highly identifiable
- School counselor recommends the student notify partner and refrain from further high-risk behavior
- Student refuses
- School counselor informs the student of the intent to notify the partner
- School counselor seeks legal consultation from the school district's legal representative in writing as to the legalities of informing the partner

g. Request of the court that disclosure not be required when the release of confidential information may potentially harm a student or the counseling relationship.

h. Protect the confidentiality of students' records and release personal data in accordance with prescribed federal and state laws and school policies including the laws within the Family Education Rights and Privacy Act (FERPA). Student information stored and transmitted electronically is treated with the same care as traditional student records. Recognize the vulnerability of confidentiality in electronic communications and only transmit sensitive information electronically in a way that is untraceable to students' identity. Critical information such as a student who has a history of suicidal ideation must be conveyed to the receiving school in a personal contact such as a phone call.

A.3. Academic, Career/College/Post-Secondary Access and Personal/Social Counseling Plans

Professional school counselors:

a. Provide students with a comprehensive school counseling program that parallels the ASCA National Model with emphasis on working jointly with all students to develop personal/social, academic and career goals.

b. Ensure equitable academic, career, post-secondary access and personal/social opportunities for all students through the use of data to help close achievement gaps and opportunity gaps.

c. Provide and advocate for individual students' career awareness, exploration and post-secondary plans supporting the students' right to choose from the wide array of options when they leave secondary education.

A.4. Dual Relationships

Professional school counselors:

a. Avoid dual relationships that might impair their objectivity and increase the risk of harm to students (e.g., counseling one's family members or the children of close friends or associates). If a dual relationship is unavoidable, the school counselor is responsible for taking action to eliminate or reduce the potential for harm to the student through use of safeguards, which might include informed consent, consultation, supervision and documentation.

b. Maintain appropriate professional distance with students at all times.

c. Avoid dual relationships with students through communication mediums such as social networking sites.

d. Avoid dual relationships with school personnel that might infringe on the integrity of the school counselor/student relationship.

A.5. Appropriate Referrals

Professional school counselors:

a. Make referrals when necessary or appropriate to outside resources for student and/or family support. Appropriate referrals may necessitate informing both parents/guardians and students of applicable resources and making proper plans for transitions with minimal interruption of services. Students retain the right to discontinue the counseling relationship at any time.

b. Help educate about and prevent personal and social concerns for all students within the school counselor's scope of education and competence and make necessary referrals when the counseling needs are beyond the individual school counselor's education and training. Every attempt is made to find appropriate specialized resources for clinical therapeutic topics that are difficult or inappropriate to address in a school setting such as eating disorders, sexual trauma, chemical dependency and other addictions needing sustained clinical duration or assistance.

c. Request a release of information signed by the student and/or parents/guardians when attempting to develop a collaborative relationship with other service providers assigned to the student.

d. Develop a reasonable method of termination of counseling when it becomes apparent that counseling assistance is no longer needed or a referral is necessary to better meet the student's needs.

A.6. Group Work

Professional school counselors:

a. Screen prospective group members and maintain an awareness of participants' needs, appropriate fit and personal goals in relation to the group's intention and focus. The school counselor takes reasonable precautions to protect members from physical and psychological harm resulting from interaction within the group.

b. Recognize that best practice is to notify the parents/guardians of children participating in small groups.

c. Establish clear expectations in the group setting, and clearly state that confidentiality in group counseling cannot be guaranteed. Given the developmental and chronological ages of minors in schools, recognize the tenuous nature of confidentiality for minors renders some topics inappropriate for group work in a school setting.

d. Provide necessary follow-up with group members, and document proceedings as appropriate.

e. Develop professional competencies, and maintain appropriate education, training and supervision in group facilitation and any topics specific to the group.

f. Facilitate group work that is brief and solution-focused, working with a variety of academic, career, college and personal/social issues.

A.7. Danger to Self or Others

Professional school counselors:

a. Inform parents/guardians and/or appropriate authorities when a student poses a danger to self or others. This is to be done after careful deliberation and consultation with other counseling professionals.

b. Report risk assessments to parents when they underscore the need to act on behalf of a child at risk; never negate a risk of harm as students sometimes deceive in order to avoid further scrutiny and/or parental notification.

c. Understand the legal and ethical liability for releasing a student who is in danger to self or others without proper and necessary support for that student.

A.8. Student Records

Professional school counselors:

a. Maintain and secure records necessary for rendering professional services to the student as required by laws, regulations, institutional procedures and confidentiality guidelines.

b. Keep sole-possession records or individual student case notes separate from students' educational records in keeping with state laws.

c. Recognize the limits of sole-possession records and understand these records are a memory aid for the creator and in absence of privileged communication may be subpoenaed and may become educational records when they are shared or are accessible to others in either verbal or written form or when they include information other than professional opinion or personal observations.

d. Establish a reasonable timeline for purging sole-possession records or case notes. Suggested guidelines include shredding sole possession records when the student transitions to the next level, transfers to another school or graduates. Apply careful discretion and deliberation before destroying sole-possession records that may be needed by a court of law such as notes on child abuse, suicide, sexual harassment or violence.

e. Understand and abide by the Family Education Rights and Privacy Act (FERPA, 1974), which safeguards student's records and allows parents to have a voice in what and how information is shared with others regarding their child's educational records.

A.9. Evaluation, Assessment, and Interpretation

Professional school counselors:

a. Adhere to all professional standards regarding selecting, administering and interpreting assessment measures and only utilize assessment measures that are within the scope of practice for school counselors and for which they are trained and competent.

b. Consider confidentiality issues when utilizing evaluative or assessment instruments and electronically based programs.

c. Consider the developmental age, language skills and level of competence of the student taking the assessments before assessments are given.

d. Provide interpretation of the nature, purposes, results and potential impact of assessment/evaluation measures in language the students can understand.

e. Monitor the use of assessment results and interpretations, and take reasonable steps to prevent others from misusing the information.

f. Use caution when utilizing assessment techniques, making evaluations and interpreting the performance of populations not represented in the norm group on which an instrument is standardized.

g. Assess the effectiveness of their program in having an impact on students' academic, career and personal/social development through accountability measures especially examining efforts to close achievement, opportunity and attainment gaps.

A.10. Technology

Professional school counselors:

a. Promote the benefits of and clarify the limitations of various appropriate technological applications. Professional school counselors promote technological applications (1) that are appropriate for students' individual needs,

(2) that students understand how to use and (3) for which follow-up counseling assistance is provided.

b. Advocate for equal access to technology for all students, especially those historically underserved.

c. Take appropriate and reasonable measures for maintaining confidentiality of student information and educational records stored or transmitted through the use of computers, facsimile machines, telephones, voicemail, answering machines and other electronic or computer technology.

d. Understand the intent of FERPA and its impact on sharing electronic student records.

e. Consider the extent to which cyberbullying is interfering with students' educational process and base guidance curriculum and intervention programming for this pervasive and potentially dangerous problem on research-based and best practices.

A.11. Student Peer Support Program

Professional school counselors:

a. Have unique responsibilities when working with peer-helper or student-assistance programs and safeguard the welfare of students participating in peer-to-peer programs under their direction.

b. Are ultimately responsible for appropriate training and supervision for students serving as peer-support individuals in their school counseling programs.

B. Responsibilities to Parents/Guardians

B.1. Parent Rights and Responsibilities

Professional school counselors:

a. Respect the rights and responsibilities of parents/guardians for their children and endeavor to establish, as appropriate, a collaborative relationship with parents/guardians to facilitate students' maximum development.

b. Adhere to laws, local guidelines and ethical standards of practice when assisting parents/guardians experiencing family difficulties interfering with the student's effectiveness and welfare.

    c. Are sensitive to diversity among families and recognize that all parents/ guardians, custodial and noncustodial, are vested with certain rights and responsibilities for their children's welfare by virtue of their role and according to law.

    d. Inform parents of the nature of counseling services provided in the school setting.

    e. Adhere to the FERPA act regarding disclosure of student information.

    f. Work to establish, as appropriate, collaborative relationships with parents/ guardians to best serve student.

B.2. Parents/Guardians and Confidentiality

Professional school counselors:

    a. Inform parents/guardians of the school counselor's role to include the confidential nature of the counseling relationship between the counselor and student.

    b. Recognize that working with minors in a school setting requires school counselors to collaborate with students' parents/guardians to the extent possible.

    c. Respect the confidentiality of parents/guardians to the extent that is reasonable to protect the best interest of the student being counseled.

    d. Provide parents/guardians with accurate, comprehensive and relevant information in an objective and caring manner, as is appropriate and consistent with ethical responsibilities to the student.

    e. Make reasonable efforts to honor the wishes of parents/guardians concerning information regarding the student unless a court order expressly forbids the involvement of a parent(s). In cases of divorce or separation, school counselors exercise a good-faith effort to keep both parents informed, maintaining focus on the student and avoiding supporting one parent over another in divorce proceedings.

C. Responsibilities to Colleagues and Professional Associates

C.1. Professional Relationships

Professional school counselors, the school counseling program director/site supervisor and the school counselor educator:

    a. Establish and maintain professional relationships with faculty, staff and administration to facilitate an optimum counseling program.

b. Treat colleagues with professional respect, courtesy and fairness.

c. Recognize that teachers, staff and administrators who are high-functioning in the personal and social development skills can be powerful allies in supporting student success. School counselors work to develop relationships with all faculty and staff in order to advantage students.

d. Are aware of and utilize related professionals, organizations and other resources to whom the student may be referred.

C.2. Sharing Information with Other Professionals

Professional school counselors:

a. Promote awareness and adherence to appropriate guidelines regarding confidentiality, the distinction between public and private information and staff consultation.

b. Provide professional personnel with accurate, objective, concise and meaningful data necessary to adequately evaluate, counsel and assist the student.

c. Secure parental consent and develop clear agreements with other mental health professionals when a student is receiving services from another counselor or other mental health professional in order to avoid confusion and conflict for the student and parents/guardians.

d. Understand about the "release of information" process and parental rights in sharing information and attempt to establish a cooperative and collaborative relationship with other professionals to benefit students.

e. Recognize the powerful role of ally that faculty and administration who function high in personal/social development skills can play in supporting students in stress, and carefully filter confidential information to give these allies what they "need to know" in order to advantage the student. Consultation with other members of the school counseling profession is helpful in determining need-to-know information. The primary focus and obligation is always on the student when it comes to sharing confidential information.

f. Keep appropriate records regarding individual students, and develop a plan for transferring those records to another professional school counselor should the need occur. This documentation transfer will protect the confidentiality and benefit the needs of the student for whom the records are written.

C.3. Collaborating and Educating Around the Role of the School Counselor

The school counselor, school counseling program supervisor/director and school counselor educator:

a. Share the role of the school counseling program in ensuring data-driven academic, career/college and personal/social success competencies for every student, resulting in specific outcomes/indicators with all stakeholders.

b. Broker services internal and external to the schools to help ensure every student receives the benefits of a school counseling program and specific academic, career/college and personal/social competencies.

D. Responsibilities to School, Communities, and Families

D.1. Responsibilities to the School

Professional school counselors:

a. Support and protect students' best interest against any infringement of their educational program.

b. Inform appropriate officials, in accordance with school policy, of conditions that may be potentially disruptive or damaging to the school's mission, personnel and property while honoring the confidentiality between the student and the school counselor.

c. Are knowledgeable and supportive of their school's mission, and connect their program to the school's mission.

d. Delineate and promote the school counselor's role, and function as a student advocate in meeting the needs of those served. School counselors will notify appropriate officials of systemic conditions that may limit or curtail their effectiveness in providing programs and services.

e. Accept employment only for positions for which they are qualified by education, training, supervised experience, state and national professional credentials and appropriate professional experience.

f. Advocate that administrators hire only qualified, appropriately trained and competent individuals for professional school counseling positions.

g. Assist in developing: (1) curricular and environmental conditions appropriate for the school and community; (2) educational procedures and programs to meet students' developmental needs; (3) a systematic evaluation process for comprehensive, developmental, standards-based school counseling programs, services and personnel; and (4) a data-driven evaluation process guiding the comprehensive, developmental school counseling program and service delivery.

D.2. Responsibility to the Community

Professional school counselors:

a. Collaborate with community agencies, organizations and individuals in students' best interest and without regard to personal reward or remuneration.

b. Extend their influence and opportunity to deliver a comprehensive school counseling program to all students by collaborating with community resources for student success.

c. Promote equity for all students through community resources.

d. Are careful not to use their professional role as a school counselor to benefit any type of private therapeutic or consultative practice in which they might be involved outside of the school setting.

E. Responsibilities to Self

E.1. Professional Competence

Professional school counselors:

a. Function within the boundaries of individual professional competence and accept responsibility for the consequences of their actions.

b. Monitor emotional and physical health and practice wellness to ensure optimal effectiveness. Seek physical or mental health referrals when needed to ensure competence at all times.

c. Monitor personal responsibility and recognize the high standard of care a professional in this critical position of trust must maintain on and off the job and are cognizant of and refrain from activity that may lead to inadequate professional services or diminish their effectiveness with school community members Professional and personal growth are ongoing throughout the counselor's career.

d. Strive through personal initiative to stay abreast of current research and to maintain professional competence in advocacy, teaming and collaboration, culturally competent counseling and school counseling program coordination, knowledge and use of technology, leadership, and equity assessment using data.

e. Ensure a variety of regular opportunities for participating in and facilitating professional development for self and other educators and school counselors through continuing education opportunities annually including: attendance at professional school counseling conferences; reading *Professional School Counseling* journal articles; facilitating workshops for education staff on issues school counselors are uniquely positioned to provide.

f. Enhance personal self-awareness, professional effectiveness and ethical practice by regularly attending presentations on ethical decision-making. Effective school counselors will seek supervision when ethical or professional questions arise in their practice.

g. Maintain current membership in professional associations to ensure ethical and best practices.

E.2. Multicultural and Social Justice Advocacy and Leadership

Professional school counselors:

a. Monitor and expand personal multicultural and social justice advocacy awareness, knowledge and skills. School counselors strive for exemplary cultural competence by ensuring personal beliefs or values are not imposed on students or other stakeholders.

b. Develop competencies in how prejudice, power and various forms of oppression, such as ableism, ageism, classism, familyism, genderism, heterosexism, immigrationism, linguicism, racism, religionism and sexism, affect self, students and all stakeholders.

c. Acquire educational, consultation and training experiences to improve awareness, knowledge, skills and effectiveness in working with diverse populations: ethnic/racial status, age, economic status, special needs, ESL or ELL, immigration status, sexual orientation, gender, gender identity/expression, family type, religious/spiritual identity and appearance.

d. Affirm the multiple cultural and linguistic identities of every student and all stakeholders. Advocate for equitable school and school counseling program policies and practices for every student and all stakeholders including use of translators and bilingual/multilingual school counseling program materials that represent all languages used by families in the school community, and advocate for appropriate accommodations and accessibility for students with disabilities.

e. Use inclusive and culturally responsible language in all forms of communication.

f. Provide regular workshops and written/digital information to families to increase understanding, collaborative two-way communication and a welcoming school climate between families and the school to promote increased student achievement.

g. Work as advocates and leaders in the school to create equity-based school counseling programs that help close any achievement, opportunity and attainment gaps that deny all students the chance to pursue their educational goals.

F. Responsibilities to the Profession

F.1. Professionalism

Professional school counselors:

a. Accept the policies and procedures for handling ethical violations as a result of maintaining membership in the American School Counselor Association.

b. Conduct themselves in such a manner as to advance individual ethical practice and the profession.

c. Conduct appropriate research, and report findings in a manner consistent with acceptable educational and psychological research practices. School counselors advocate for the protection of individual students' identities when using data for research or program planning.

d. Seek institutional and parent/guardian consent before administering any research, and maintain security of research records.

e. Adhere to ethical standards of the profession, other official policy statements, such as ASCA's position statements, role statement and the ASCA National Model and relevant statutes established by federal, state and local governments, and when these are in conflict work responsibly for change.

f. Clearly distinguish between statements and actions made as a private individual and those made as a representative of the school counseling profession.

g. Do not use their professional position to recruit or gain clients, consultees for their private practice or to seek and receive unjustified personal gains, unfair advantage, inappropriate relationships or unearned goods or services.

F.2. Contribution to the Profession

Professional school counselors:

a. Actively participate in professional associations and share results and best practices in assessing, implementing and annually evaluating the outcomes of data-driven school counseling programs with measurable academic, career/college and personal/social competencies for every student.

b. Provide support, consultation and mentoring to novice professionals.

c. Have a responsibility to read and abide by the ASCA Ethical Standards and adhere to the applicable laws and regulations.

F.3. Supervision of School Counselor Candidates Pursuing Practicum and Internship Experiences:

Professional school counselors:

a. Provide support for appropriate experiences in academic, career, college access and personal/social counseling for school counseling interns.

b. Ensure school counselor candidates have experience in developing, implementing and evaluating a data-driven school counseling program model, such as the ASCA National Model.

c. Ensure the school counseling practicum and internship have specific, measurable service delivery, foundation, management and accountability systems.

d. Ensure school counselor candidates maintain appropriate liability insurance for the duration of the school counseling practicum and internship experiences.

e. Ensure a site visit is completed by a school counselor education faculty member for each practicum or internship student, preferably when both the school counselor trainee and site supervisor are present.

F.4. Collaboration and Education About School Counselors and School Counseling Programs with Other Professionals

School counselors and school counseling program directors/supervisors collaborate with special educators, school nurses, school social workers, school psychologists, college counselors/admissions officers, physical therapists, occupational therapists and speech pathologists to advocate for optimal services for students and all other stakeholders.

G. Maintenance of Standards

Professional school counselors are expected to maintain ethical behavior at all times.

G.1. When there exists serious doubt as to the ethical behavior of a colleague(s), the following procedure may serve as a guide:

1. The school counselor should consult confidentially with a professional colleague to discuss the nature of a complaint to see if the professional colleague views the situation as an ethical violation.

2. When feasible, the school counselor should directly approach the colleague whose behavior is in question to discuss the complaint and seek resolution.

3. The school counselor should keep documentation of all the steps taken.

4. If resolution is not forthcoming at the personal level, the school counselor shall utilize the channels established within the school, school district, the state school counseling association and ASCA's Ethics Committee.

5. If the matter still remains unresolved, referral for review and appropriate action should be made to the Ethics Committees in the following sequence:

   - State school counselor association
   - American School Counselor Association
   - The ASCA Ethics Committee is responsible for:
   - Educating and consulting with the membership regarding ethical standards
   - Periodically reviewing and recommending changes in code
   - Receiving and processing questions to clarify the application of such standards. Questions must be submitted in writing to the ASCA Ethics Committee chair.
   - Handling complaints of alleged violations of the ASCA Ethical Standards for School Counselors. At the national level, complaints should be submitted in writing to the ASCA Ethics Committee, c/o the Executive Director, American School Counselor Association, 1101 King St., Suite 625, Alexandria, VA 22314.

G.2. When school counselors are forced to work in situations or abide by policies that do not reflect the ethics of the profession, the school counselor works responsibly through the correct channels to try and remedy the condition.

G.3. When faced with any ethical dilemma, school counselors, school counseling program directors/supervisors, and school counselor educators use an ethical decision-making model such as Solutions to Ethical Problems in Schools (STEPS) (Stone, 2001):

1. Define the problem emotionally and intellectually

2. Apply the ASCA Ethical Standards and the law

3. Consider the students' chronological and developmental levels

4. Consider the setting, parental rights and minors' rights

5. Apply the moral principles

6. Determine your potential courses of action and their consequences

7. Evaluate the selected action

8. Consult

9. Implement the course of action

Chapter 3

COMPREHENSIVE AND DEVELOPMENTAL SCHOOL COUNSELING PROGRAMS

MICHAEL BUNDY

*CACREP STANDARD

FOUNDATIONS

A. *Knowledge*

> 5. Understands current models of school counseling programs (e.g., American School Counselor Association [ASCA] National Model) and their integral relationship to the total educational program.

COUNSELING, PREVENTION, AND INTERVENTION

C. *Knowledge*

> 2. Knows how to design, implement, manage, and evaluate programs to enhance the academic, career, and personal/social development of students.

ASSESSMENT

G. *Knowledge*

> 3. Identifies various forms of needs assessments for academic, career, and personal/social development.

ACADEMIC DEVELOPMENT

K. *Knowledge*

1. Understands the relationship of the school counseling program to the academic mission of the school.

2. Understands the concepts, principles, strategies, programs, and practices designed to close the achievement gap, promote student academic success, and prevent students from dropping out of school.

LEADERSHIP

O. *Knowledge*

3. Knows how to design, implement, manage, and evaluate a comprehensive school counseling program.

P. *Skills and Practices*

1. Participates in the design, implementation, management, and evaluation of a comprehensive developmental school counseling program.

I may be extreme, but I believe counselors must realize their role in the school building is as important as any other professional. Counselors are not in the building to "serve" others; they are in the school to implement a program and apply the distinct skills and knowledge that only they possess. (Anderson, 2002)

Professional school counselors use a comprehensive developmental school counseling (CDSC) model to deliver programs and services to all students (Baker, 2001; Gysbers & Henderson, 2001; Herr, 2001). A CDSC program is an integral part of the overall school curriculum that delivers data-driven services to and for students that promote student development through large group curriculum, small group counseling, individual counseling, collaboration, and consultation (ASCA, 2012a).

CACREP

School counselors are able to contribute to academic, career, and personal/social development of all students when leading a CDSC program (Campbell & Dahir, 1997). This organized approach evolved from the position-based model and later the service-oriented approach that school counselors previously used to address vocational planning and mental health needs of students (Baker, 2001; Gysbers & Henderson, 2001; Herr, 2001). The strength of this new model lies in its systematic structure, its connection to the overall educational environment for students (Baker, 2001; Herr, 2001), and its intent to close achievement gaps among underserved student populations (Bemak & Chung, 2005; Ratts, DeKruyf, & Chen-Hayes,

2007). The CDSC model uses data to ensure students are engaged in standards-based programs and interventions that use evidenced-based practices with outcome-based accountability (Carey, Dimmitt, Hatch, Lapan, & Whiston, 2008).

However, providing leadership to establish a CDSC model can be overwhelming for new counselors, and it can even provide challenges to experienced counselors who need to set their priorities annually (Baker, 2001). While there are several models for designing CDSC programs, this chapter is written to complement the *ASCA National Model®-Third Edition* (ASCA, 2012a) as a framework for building CDSC counseling programs. The ASCA National Model is shown in Figure 3.1.

Figure 3.1 The ASCA National Model

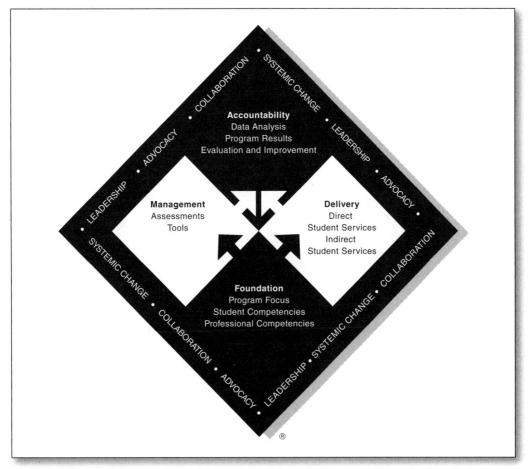

Source: Reprinted with permission, American School Counselor Association, www.ASCANation alModel.org. The ASCA National Model diamond graphic is a registered trademark of the American School Counselor Association and may not be reprinted or modified without permission.

COMPREHENSIVE SCHOOL COUNSELING PROGRAMS AS AN INTEGRAL PART OF THE EDUCATIONAL PROGRAM

The *ASCA National Model* provides a framework for building comprehensive school counseling programs that are connected to the school mission and are integral to the total educational program. The model provides a structure for designing standards-based programs that use evidence-based best practices and have outcome-based accountability methods.

Standards-Based School Counseling Programs

Standards- and outcomes-based education has been the goal of educational reformers since the early 1980s, but this movement gained momentum with the passage of two pieces of legislation: *Goals 2000: Educate America Act* (Goals, 1994) and the *No Child Left Behind Act of 2001* (NCLB, 2002). Fortunately for professional school counselors, ASCA leaders and school counseling scholars had already established standards for school counseling with the publication of the *ASCA National Standards for School Counseling Programs* (Campbell & Dahir, 1997) that was later renamed the *ASCA National Standards for Students* (ASCA, 2012). The *ASCA National Standards for Students* (ASCA, 2012) identify three standards for each of the three core developmental domains of school counseling: Academic, Career, and Personal/Social (See Figure 1.), with specific competencies and indicators for preK–12 students contained within these student standards. These competencies and indicators enable counselors to set more specific objectives for counseling programs based upon what students learn and do as a result of participating in school counseling programs. How these national standards can be used to guide school counselors in establishing standards-based programs will be presented later in this chapter. The three domains and nine specific standards are in Table 3.1.

By using the *ASCA National Standards for Students,* counselors have a uniform system to design CDSC programs that connect to the overall educational mission of their schools, and a method to show how their programs enhance the academic performance of their students. For example, seventh-graders who are distracted from their schoolwork because of the difficulties they experience with their peers could benefit from counselor-conducted social-skills training. As a result of standards-based group counseling, the seventh-graders are able to make friends, grow in confidence, and improve their grades. The counselor can then show how the counseling programs helped produce the academic gains among the seventh-graders.

Table 3.1 ASCA National Standards for Students

Developmental Domain		Student Standard
Academic	A	Students will acquire the attitudes, knowledge, and skills contributing to effective learning in school and across the lifespan.
	B	Students will complete school with the academic preparation essential to choose from a wide range of substantial post-secondary options, including college.
	C	Students will understand the relationship of academics to the world of work and to life at home and in the community.
Career	A	Students will acquire the skills to investigate the world of work in relation to knowledge of self and to make informed career decisions.
	B	Students will employ strategies to achieve future career goals with success and satisfaction.
	C	Students will understand the relationship between personal qualities, education, training and the world of work.
Personal/Social	A	Students will acquire the knowledge, attitudes and interpersonal skills to help them understand and respect self and others.
	B	Students will make decisions, set goals and take necessary action to achieve goals.
	C	Students will understand safety and survival skills.

Evidence- and Outcome-Based School Counseling Programs

Selecting which program or intervention strategy to use with an identified student population can be challenging to professional school counselors, and to assist in this process Carey, et al. (2008) established a model to help counselors evaluate counseling programs and strategies. These researchers propose criteria that include: measurement instruments, comparison of treatment groups to control groups, rigor of statistical analysis, fidelity of program delivery, replication of studies, implementation in public schools with diverse populations, and the persistent effect of the program. To illustrate their model, Carey et al. (2008) examined research on two counseling programs (*Student Success Skills* and *Second Step Violence Prevention Curriculum*) and found evidence that these two programs "cause positive changes in student outcomes" (p. 203).

To support school counselors in selecting evidence-based school counseling programs, the Center for School Counseling Outcome Research & Evaluation (www.umass.edu/schoocounseling/index.php) established a clearinghouse of effective programs: this service identifies school counseling programs that work best with students under specific circumstances. The Center also distributes periodic bulletins that describe the current best practices in school counseling programs and illustrate interventions that work.

Outcome-based evaluation methods enable counselors to show how their efforts make a difference with the population they serve (Whiston, Tai, Rahardja, & Eder, 2011), provide evidence that school counseling programs support the school mission (Lapan, 2001), and are linked to the overall goals of the school (Stone & Dahir, 2010).

The meta-analysis findings of Whitson et al. (2011) provide evidence that core curriculum activities and group responsive services by school counselors can be effective in producing cognitive, behavioral, and affective changes among students. School counseling programs that focus on outcomes can answer such general questions as: "What do school counseling programs do to contribute to the education of students?" and, "What do students gain as a result of participating in comprehensive school counseling programs?"

With robust accountability data in hand, school counselors are better able to promote their programs and to develop collaborative relationships among administrators, teachers, parents, and others. It is, therefore, strongly recommended that

Photo 3.1   School Counselor Reading Book to Students in Classroom

counselors infuse robust evaluation methods in the design of comprehensive school counseling programs. How to design school counseling programs based upon specific outcomes and how to measure the effectiveness of counseling programs against identified outcomes will be discussed in more detail later in this chapter.

ADDRESSING SOCIAL JUSTICE THROUGH COMPREHENSIVE, DEVELOPMENTAL SCHOOL COUNSELING PROGRAMS

The themes of the ASCA National Model (2012) give professional school counselors a path to address social justice issues within schools. The achievement and opportunity gaps in the educational experience of many young people are a concern of many educators (Ratts, et al., 2007). As our society becomes more diverse, the faces of our students will increasingly mirror the many cultures and groups that comprise our country. This demographic trend requires a change in which curricula are presented, how instruction is delivered, and who is allowed the opportunity to engage in educational programs. All students require rigorous academic experiences, and researchers have found that students of color and low-income youths must be held to standards of excellence that are just as high, if not moreso, than students in the majority (Bemak, & Chung, 2005).

Recognizing the influence of school counselors on student achievement, the Education Trust established the National Center for Transforming School Counseling (NCTSC) in 2003 (Thompson, 2012). The aim of this center is to change the role of school counselors from one that is ancillary and service-oriented to one that includes taking the role of advocate for students who face tremendous barriers to their academic success. This expanded role is intended to encourage school counselors to be more active in social justice and systemic change issues on behalf of those who possess fewer resources, fewer support systems, and are least able to take advantage of educational opportunities.

To accomplish this mission, the NCTSC focused on training school counselors in the use of data and technology to identify achievement and opportunity gaps (Dollarhide & Saginak, 2008). The NCTSC involved ASCA members, counselor educators, and other leaders in school counseling in retooling counselors with a new vision and agenda. The ASCA accepted this challenge by developing a new school counseling model that emphasized the use of data and the themes of Leadership, Advocacy, Collaboration, and Systemic Change (ASCA, 2003, 2005, & 2012).

Leadership

The theme of *Leadership,* though seemingly straightforward, involves more than developing and implementing a vision for comprehensive school counseling programs and persuading others to participate in these programs. While promoting the importance of school counseling programs is essential, counselors must also provide leadership in identifying and removing barriers that prevent students from accessing opportunities and achieving academic success (Campbell & Dahir, 1997; Dollarhide, 2003).

For example, professional school counselors can influence administrators to change school policies so that more students are allowed access to educational opportunities, and they can also encourage teachers to keep their expectations high for all students. School counselors need not try to take on more than they can change by themselves; rather, counselors should work with others to make changes in their schools for the benefit of all students.

Counselors can make other educators aware of achievement gaps by using data that breaks down student performance into subgroups. Using these data changes in school policies and expectations can effectively occur with a vision for equal access to a rigorous educational program.

Advocacy

Advocacy promotes school success for all students. School counselors are not gatekeepers of a status quo that denies some students educational opportunities; rather, counselors serve as advocates who support and facilitate equality and access for all students. School counselors advocate in a variety of forms, such as empowering students to take constructive action on their own behalf, intervening in support of students, organizing community backing to address a concern, and initiating school-wide or district-wide changes (ASCA, 2012).

The *ACA Advocacy Competencies* that are discussed in more detail in chapter 11 provide school counselors with guidelines on how to enhance their abilities as advocates and how they can transform their practice for students (Ratts et al., 2007). It is through leadership and advocacy that school counselors can remove educational and social barriers, and in so doing, allow more students to experience academic and career success.

Collaboration

Collaboration is an essential skill for counselors to master in order to effectively implement every aspect of comprehensive school counseling programs (ASCA, 2012). The more success counselors have in building working partnerships with administrators, teachers, parents, students, and others both in and outside of the school setting, the more impact they will have in promoting student achievement (Balfanz & Byrnes, 2012) and addressing critical issues that impede academic success (Epstein & Van Voorhis, 2010; Steen & Noguera, 2010).

On one level, counselors may team with others to design, manage, deliver, and evaluate school counseling programs (Dimmitt, 2003; Sink, 2005), but a higher objective for counselors is to use their collaboration and team-building skills for systemic changes and advocacy for underserved students (Barona & Barona, 2006). Within the role and function of school counselors, collaboration is inextricably linked with leadership, advocacy, and systematic change because counselors must garner the support of others to build developmentally appropriate school counseling programs and to enhance "equity, access, and academic success for every student" (ASCA, 2012, p. 6).

Systemic Change

Systemic Change represents the significant efforts of school counselors at the school-wide and district-wide level to address gaps in educational access, opportunity, and aspiration from a systems perspective (ASCA, 2012). Counselors generally focus on helping students to deal with their issues, either individually or in groups, but student problems may be the result of systems functioning inappropriately or insensitively toward subgroups of students. For example, low-income students may not be as college- or career-ready as are students who possess the economic means to access rigorous academic programs.

Counselors must be prepared to address other systemic changes that impede student performance such as social oppression, intolerance, and bullying. School counselors can confront educational disparity and inequality by collaborating with others to remove systemic barriers, promote programs, raise expectations, expand services, change curriculum guidelines, or improve instructional strategies, which will create opportunities for all groups of students to achieve academic success (Singh, Urbano, Haston, & McMahon, 2010).

CONCEPTUAL APPLICATION ACTIVITY 3.1

ASCA Model Themes

 1. Discuss with a classmate how leadership as a school counselor can be used to advocate for underserved students.

(Continued)

(Continued)

2. Explain how data empowers counselors to promote systemic changes in schools.

3. Reflect on your abilities to be a leader who advocates for systemic change as a school counselor. What knowledge do you need to acquire? What skills do you need to develop? What attitude do you need to develop? Share your responses with a classmate.

DESIGNING, IMPLEMENTING, MANAGING, AND EVALUATING A CDSC PROGRAM

As the demand for accountability increases and as economic constraints continue to restrict school budgets, counselors will increasingly be expected to show how they affect student achievement and academic success. Consequently, it is essential that counselors acquire the skills to systematically build school counseling programs that are developmental in nature, comprehensive in scope, accountable in design, collaborative in implementation, and supportive of the total educational school program. The question becomes: "How does one do all this?"

For over a decade, ASCA has supported professional school counselors by providing a vision and framework to design, implement, and evaluate CDSC programs. The *ASCA National Standards for Students* (ASCA, 2012) offers counselors a vision of *what* students should learn regarding their academic, career, and personal/social development. The *ASCA National Third Edition,* officially released at the ASCA Annual Conference in Minneapolis in June 2012, provides a structure on *how* counselors can facilitate student development. The revisions offer greater flexibility for counselors to adapt their counseling programs to local school issues than was provided by previous editions (ASCA, 2003; ASCA, 2005; ASCA 2012). The four components of *ASCA National Model-Third Edition* (2012) are Foundation, Management, Delivery, and Accountability.

CACREP

The remainder of this chapter presents a basic approach to designing, implementing, and evaluating a CDSC program using the ASCA National Model as the framework. In addition to the information provided in the ASCA National Model and this chapter, the American Student Achievement Institute has developed an online program called Redesigning School Counseling for counselors-in-training and experienced counselors seeking to transform their programs. This Internet resource guides counselors in the use of data to build CDSC programs one component at a time within the ASCA Model framework. For more details, see http://cgi.asainstitute.org/cgi-bin/rsc/intro.

The four components of ASCA National Model (ASCA, 2012) address key parts of planning and implementation and focus on purpose, design, and outcomes of comprehensive school counseling programs. The *Foundation* component answers the question: What knowledge, attitudes, and skills will students learn from participation in school counseling programs? The *Management* component addresses the questions: Why do students benefit from school counseling programs? Who determines the program focus? When will program activities occur? The *Delivery* component answers the question: What activities and strategies will be used to address student needs? The *Accountability* component answers the question: How have students changed as a result of the counseling programs?

THE FOUNDATION COMPONENT

Program Focus, Student Competencies, and Professional Competencies are three subsections within the Foundation component. The *Program Focus* component ensures that the school counseling program is built upon a well-defined and understood set of beliefs that is aligned with the school's mission and guided by well-defined program goals. The *Student Competencies* section reminds counselors to use the *ASCA National Standards for Students* and to incorporate individual state standards when writing outcome objectives for counseling programs and strategies. The *Professional Competencies* section encourages counselors to seek professional development by providing a self-assessment instrument that is based upon the *School Counselor Professional Competencies* (ASCA, 2007) and the *ASCA Ethical Standards for School Counselors* (ASCA, 2010).

Program Focus

The program focus integrates the counselor's personal philosophy with the school's mission to generate distinct program goals. The vision for the school counseling program is sweeping in scope with a long-term view of what the program should look like in the future, and aligns with the mission statement of your school district. Based upon your beliefs and program vision, your mission statement becomes a bold declaration that communicates your intent to design a school counseling program to address the academic, career, and personal/social development of all students. See Table 3.2 as an example of a mission statement of a school counseling program that is fully aligned with its school district.

The final task within the *Program Focus* segment is to develop school counseling goals that operationally define what you will do to fulfill your vision and mission in clear, measurable terms. These goals reflect work previously done on your beliefs, vision, philosophy, and mission statement. To assist counselors in

Table 3.2 School Counseling Program Mission Statement

School District Mission Statement	*All students graduate from Ottumwa High School prepared for a successful post-secondary transition.*
School Counseling Program Mission Statement	*As professional school counselors at Ottumwa Community Schools, we are dedicated to empowering every student to achieve academic success, through personal and social growth, wellness and career exploration.*

Source: Retrieved from http://www.ottumwaschools.com/

establishing effective program goals, the *SMART* acronym is used to identify *s*pecific issues to be addressed, determine how to *m*easure outcomes, establish outcomes to *a*ttain, write goals that use *r*esults-oriented data, and ensure goals can be achieved within a specified *t*ime.

Before you write school counseling goals you will need to review school data and discuss school goals with your principal. Data on student success will enhance your program planning by aligning it with the overall educational system in your school, as well as identifying areas where student performance needs to be improved and where your counseling program can contribute to this improvement. Although the information in Table 3.3 provides basic demographic information of

Table 3.3 Example of Foundations High School

School Profile Grades Served: 9–12 School Enrollment: 1,168		
	Number	*Percent*
African American	240	21.5
Asian/Pacific Islander	24	2.1
Hispanic/Latino	98	8.4
Native American	6	0.5
White	656	56.2
Female	553	47.3
Male	615	52.7
Economically Disadvantaged	499	42.7
Students with Disabilities	44	3.8
Limited English Proficiency	25	2.1

a fictitious school, it does not provide us with specific data we need to set program goals. We would need to gather additional school data to better guide our planning and goal setting.

A thorough analysis of school data involves more than merely reviewing the demographics of the student population or glancing at a summary of test results. You will need to drill deeper into your school data to discover the specific areas in which students are thriving and those areas in which your support is needed to achieve success. Critical data on student achievement and behavior can be found in your school's report cards, NCLB reports, school improvement plans, and student data management systems. To gain a thorough profile of your students' data, you should examine school reports on the following:

- Achievement test scores
- Attendance/absenteeism rates
- Number of promotions
- Discipline reports
- Post-secondary enrollment rates
- Number of drop-outs/graduations
- Enrollment demographics in advanced courses

Table 3.4 presents an overview of the attendance and graduation data from our example school. It appears that some improvements have been made in its graduation rates during the past three years; however, almost one out of five (or 20%) of students still do not graduate. We would need more data to determine where the school counseling program can best address the issue of the graduation rate.

Table 3.4   Example of Foundations High School Attendance and Graduation Rates

	2009	2010	2011
Attendance Rate (%)	90	90	91
Graduation Rate (%)	71	80	81

The most effective way to identify gaps in student achievement and opportunity is by disaggregating your school data. Breaking down student information by subgroups such as race/ethnicity, gender, economic status, special needs status, grade level, and program enrollment will inform you as to the student subgroups that are not as successful in school as others. For example, a counselor who looks more closely at the data from the school report cards might find that Latino male students have scored below proficiency level in math at a higher proportion than other ethnic groups in the school. This could certainly be a significant area of concern for the school that may affect graduation rates and, by extension, the school counselor.

Additionally, disaggregated data can inform principals, the school counseling advisory council, and other school stakeholders of those critical student issues that should be addressed through CDSC programs. Table 3.5 presents graduation rates by student subgroups at our example school. We can see that some subgroups of students are more challenged to complete high school than other subgroups. This information directs our attention to the student populations that need more support.

Table 3.5   Example of Foundations High School Graduation Rates by Subgroup

Subgroup	2009	2010	2011
African American (%)	51	69	84
Asian/Pacific Islander (%)	100	100	100
Hispanic (%)	69	75	67
Native American (%)	50	75	75
White (%)	85	87	90
Female (%)	73	87	91
Male (%)	69	79	81
Economically Disadvantaged (%)	69	72	77
Students with Disabilities (%)	62	66	72
Limited English Proficiency (%)	58	62	78

Complete Conceptual Application Activity 3.2 below and discuss your answers with a classmate

CONCEPTUAL APPLICATION ACTIVITY 3.2

Foundation-program focus

1. Describe the vision for your school counseling program based upon your beliefs. What do you want your program to look like in three years? In five years?

2. Present your beliefs and vision in a bold mission statement that aligns with the mission of a given school.

Student Competencies

To ensure that CDSC programs are standards-based activities, the ASCA National Standards for Students (ASCA, 2012) are identifed. These standards provide school counselors with direction in what attitudes, knowledge, and skills students should acquire as a result of their participation in CDSC programs. The nine national standards not only guide school counseling programs, but they also explain how the CDSC program supports the overall educational program by linking student competencies with student success.

School counselors should use the competencies and the indicators associated with the standards in writing specific objectives (learner outcomes) for all counseling programs to address student developmental needs; however, many of the competency indicators require adaptation in order to create objectives that can be measured (Brown & Trusty, 2005). See Table 3.6 for examples of how to translate competencies and indicators from the *ASCA National Standards for Students* (ASCA, 2012) into learner outcome statements for your school counseling programs.

Table 3.6 Converting *ASCA National Standards for Students* to Outcome Statements

ASCA National Standards for Students	*Outcome statements*
A:A1.4 Accept mistakes as essential to the learning process	Student will demonstrate acceptance of mistakes by applying feedback from teachers to improve final products.
C:A1.6 Learn how to set goals	Student will demonstrate goal-setting by writing one goal as part of a planning process.
PS:A2.6 Use effective communication skills	Student will demonstrate effective communication skills by using one I-message to express hurt feelings.

In addition to the national student standards, most counselors have state and local standards that they must incorporate into their school counseling programs. While these expectations are often generated from regional public concerns and political pressures, you will frequently find that these state and local standards are consistent with the goals of a CDSC program. For example, character education curriculum teaches such principles as fairness, responsibility, and respect, which are attitudes that are also found in the personal/social development standards of the *ASCA National Standards for Students* (ASCA, 2012). Other programs that school counselors must consider include college and career readiness, Twenty-First Century Standards, and health education curricula.

As the number of standards generated by state and local educational agencies continues to grow, it would be prudent to complete a curriculum and standards crosswalk (ASCA, 2012). The crosswalk process should be a collaborative venture among school counselors and key school stakeholders to map out how all relevant standards are being addressed in your school. The crosswalk will provide a scope and sequence guide for your school counseling program, and it is possible that local, state, and national standards can be addressed within a single program activity. See Table 3.7 for an example of a standards crosswalk of three programs that many school counselors are required to implement.

Table 3.7 Standards and Curriculum Crosswalk

ASCA National Standards for Students	Core Counseling Curriculum	Character Counts	21st Century	Health Education Curriculum
A:A3.1 Take responsibility for their actions	Y	Y	Y	Y
C:A1.4 Learn how to interact and work cooperatively in teams	Y	Y	Y	Y
PS:C1.2 Learn about the relationship between rules, laws, safety and the protection of rights of the individual	Y	Y	Y	Y

Y = Yes—Standard is met in designated curriculum

CONCEPTUAL APPLICATION ACTIVITY 3.3

Identify state standards required for students.

1. Design a curriculum crosswalk aligning state and national standards for a school counseling program.

2. Reflect on how you could use this approach in planning your counseling program. Discuss your responses with a classmate.

Professional Competencies

As you develop your CDSC program, a self-assessment of your own professional competencies is necessary in order to perform the range of tasks to assist students. The ASCA National Model (2012) emphasizes the *ASCA School Counselor Competencies* by placing them foremost in the *Foundation* component, and again in the *Management* component as a self-assessment tool. With this dual emphasis, you are encouraged to focus on the full range of knowledge, attitudes, and skills needed to effectively assist students.

In addition to the competencies, the *ASCA Ethical Standards for School Counselors* (2010) and other professional codes of conduct guide the behavior of professional school counselors. As a counselor in a school setting, you are presented with unique challenges to your practice that other mental health counselors may not have. You are expected to act within the boundaries required by your school board, school administration, and state laws; at the same time, you must adhere to laws and guidelines that protect the rights of parents in addition to the rights of the students.

CONCEPTUAL APPLICATION ACTIVITY 3.4

Foundation-Professional Competencies

1. Complete the ASCA School Counselor Competencies Assessment.

2. Devise a professional development plan to address your competency needs using professional association resources, or under the supervision of a practicing school counselor.

3. Reflect what you learned about yourself as a school counselor. Share your plan for improvement with a classmate.

MANAGEMENT COMPONENT

The *Management* component provides program implementation guidelines for setting up an advisory council, using data, developing action plans, and establishing an annual program calendar. Furthermore, an advisory council affords counselors the support and resources essential for creating a successful school counseling program. Effective planning involves using data for informed decision making, composing detailed plans for implementing programs, and recording important events on calendars. The management component outlines some strategic planning steps to ensure counselors launch their programs in an organized fashion.

Management Component: Annual Agreements

Once you have analyzed your school data, determined your student needs, and formulated a few ideas on what you might do to address these needs, you will be ready to meet with your school administrator, the one person in your school who has the potential to have the most influence on your role and function as a counselor (Dollarhide, Smith, & Lemberger, 2007).

In your ongoing conversations and interactions with principals, you should have four goals: 1) to develop a collaborative relationship with your school administration; 2) to share your analysis of school data and student needs; 3) to actively listen to the goals that are identified by your administrator; and 4) to explain what comprehensive school counseling programs can do to support student success and the school mission. Sharing school counseling program planning, monitoring, and accomplishments with your principal can ultimately expand how you deliver services to students. Complete Conceptual Application Activity 3.5.

CONCEPTUAL APPLICATION ACTIVITY 3.5

Management: Annual Agreement

1. With a classmate, use the Foundations High School data to write one school counseling program goal.

2. Role play with your classmate to practice the conversation you would have with your principal to present your school counseling program goal.

3. Write a reflection of your role play activity. What did you do that you believe was effective? What did you learn about yourself as a counselor? What would you do differently?

4. How is your view of what is an important goal different from that of your principal?

Advisory Council

An advisory council can serve as a collaborative resource and a support system for your CDSC program. Your advisory group assists by identifying key issues to address, offering program guidance, generating additional resources, and providing system and community support.

A school counseling advisory council should be composed of representatives of key stakeholders chosen in collaboration with administration and appointed by the school board. Members include teachers, parents, administration, and community groups. Given the specific needs of each school within a given district, each counseling department should establish its own School Counseling Advisory Council to focus problem-solving efforts on the unique needs of individual schools. Depending upon the size of the school and the scope of issues to be addressed, the composition of a school-based advisory counseling group should range between 4 to 8 members, each of whom represents various school stakeholders.

A meeting with the advisory council should occur within the first three weeks of the school year, after you and your principal have reviewed school data and have developed a purpose or mission for the advisory council. This group assists in making plans for the academic year. Subsequent advisory council meetings should occur as needed to monitor school counseling programs, but certainly meeting near the end of the school year to review collected data to evaluate results and to develop a campaign to promote the effectiveness of your school's counseling programs is desirable.

CONCEPTUAL APPLICATION ACTIVITY 3.6

Management: Advisory Council

1. With a classmate, generate a list of potential members of a school-based School Counseling Advisory Council. What groups are represented?

2. How would you extend an invitation to serve on the advisory council? What is the purpose? What is the member's role?

3. Develop an agenda for the first meeting of the Advisory Council. What data would be presented? What action plans would be proposed?

4. Reflect on challenges you will have in setting up an advisory council. What can you do to address those challenges? Share with a classmate.

Needs Assessment Data

When you, your principal, and your advisory council conduct a review of disaggregated school data, it may reveal that further data should be collected, especially perception type data which is the stakeholder's view of student attitudes, behaviors, or skills acquired due to participation in a school counselor program. One of the first questions to ask in developing a needs assessment is: "What do you want to know?" Methods for measuring needs should be determined according to your available resources—for example, money, time, materials, and labor. Some assessments of needs require a lot of time to administer and collect, while other survey approaches can be organized and tabulated with less effort and fewer resources. Additional information on needs assessment is provided in chapter 4.

Program Results Data

Data are used extensively in addressing, planning, and evaluating CDSC programs, and clarifying student issues within the three domains. As you design your program, it is important that you systematically collect evaluation data in order to monitor progress.

Three types of evaluation data include process, perception, and outcome. *Process* data answers the questions: What activity was done, when, and with whom? To collect *process* data, you will record the number of times you engaged in a program activity, when you did it, and who participated in your program. For example, a group of counselors logged each time they conducted a classroom lesson, facilitated a small counseling-intervention group, and held an individual student planning session.

A *process* evaluation should also include demographic data regarding the program participants, such as grade, race, gender, special needs, or whether they are on the free/reduced lunch program, and so on. Collecting *process* data over time can reflect any milestones that may occur, such as increased stakeholder participation. Summary reports of *process* data present a profile of counseling program activities that show how you spend your time and the range of stakeholders you reached through your counseling program activities.

The *EZAnalyze Time Tracker* is a free piece of software that can facilitate this method of data collection and can generate impressive reports that you can share with your principal and advisory council. (For more information, see: http://www .ezanalyze.com/.) Figure 3.2 presents a sample of an EZAnalyze report that shows time allocation by an elementary school counselor. This counselor began inputting her contact data into EZAnalyze throughout the school year from August to May. Other reports were generated by EZAnalyze from this counselor's data, such as tables of individual counseling sessions, group counseling sessions, classroom activities, and overall time allocation. Presenting reports such as these will impress administrators and advisory councils and inform them of your workload and the range of services you provide. Pictures of data tell more than words can express.

Figure 3.2 An EZAnalyze Time Tracker Report

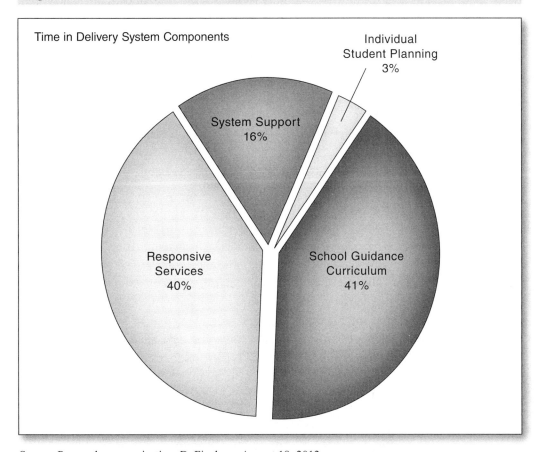

Time in Delivery System Components

Individual Student Planning 3%

System Support 16%

Responsive Services 40%

School Guidance Curriculum 41%

Source: Personal communication, D. Finchum, August 18, 2012

Perception data answers the question: What did students think, know, or demonstrate as a result of a school counseling program? To answer this, counselors need to design evaluation methods that measure student gains in their knowledge, skills, and attitudes toward standards and competencies. Common assessment methods include post-surveys, pre- and post-assessments, role-play activities, presentations, class participation, and checklists. In addition to student assessments, surveying the perceptions of teachers, parents, and other stakeholders can be evidence of student proficiency and can indicate deficit areas that need to be addressed. For example, survey questions to students, parents, and teachers could identify any of the following: What percentage of eighth-graders report that they know how many credits are required for graduation? What percentage of third-graders report knowing how to deal with bullying and feel safe at school as a result of school counseling programs? What percentage of eleventh-graders has examined the result of their college/career interest inventory and made plans accordingly?

Outcome data answer the question: So what? In other words, what changes in academic performance, career/college decisions, and personal/social development took place among the students who participated in your CDSC programs? Did attendance, promotion, or graduation rates improve as indicated in school reports? Did student behavior improve as measured by office referrals, suspensions, and expulsion rates? Did more underserved students register for advanced placement courses?

Outcome results include short-term data that assess change within a few weeks or months, intermediate data that measure program effectiveness for an academic-long timeframe, and long-term data that analyze changes year-over-year for multiple years. Attendance reports, discipline referrals, progress reports, and unit/semester exams provide short-term data that you can use to monitor the impact of school counseling intervention programs on student behaviors. Annual achievement/ performance tests, promotion/retention reports, and course registration records provide intermediate outcome data for school counseling accountability.

Outcome evaluations compare pre-program data with post-program data as presented in school report cards, student data management systems, and other measures of student performance. Those outcome data analyzed in your school counseling accountability methods can be used to focus your programs on the critical concerns of your school. Because outcome data are linked to the school's improvement goals, evidence is shown that your school counseling program supports academic success and the school's mission.

CONCEPTUAL APPLICATION ACTIVITY 3.7

Management: Use of Data

1. Discuss with a classmate how you would incorporate evaluation data in your plans for your school counseling program. What stakeholders would you assess? When? How?

2. Give an example of process data, perception data, and outcome data.

3. Reflect on what you understand as a result of this activity. Share with a classmate.

Action Plans

Mastering the discipline of recording a vision for your school counseling program can be an intimidating process; nonetheless, writing action plans is an important element of program management and planning that many school administrators require today. The action plan includes what is to be accomplished in the program, how it is to be done, who will be involved, and how the program will be evaluated. Utilizing a team approach in writing action plans builds support and investment from key stakeholders in your school counseling program which will enhance the program's effectiveness and potential for success.

The ASCA National Model (2012) provides an action plan template that requires good planning information: 1) the goals to be addressed; 2) the domains, standards, and competencies that align with school and program goals; 3) a description of your school counseling activities; 4) the curriculum or activity title; 5) a timeline; 6) the name of person responsible; 7) the evaluation methods, including the type of data to be used; and 8) your expected results for students. When you use this planning aid you are able to deliver programs more efficiently and effectively because you have a clear roadmap on what you are to do, who will assist you, and when you will implement your plan; in other words, this planning process provides you with a greater chance at success. Table 3.8 illustrates an Action Plan for the school counseling core curriculum topic about the way to give ninth-graders information on how they can earn course credits toward graduation.

Table 3.8 School Counseling Core Curriculum Action Plan Ninth-Grade Lesson on Graduation Requirements

Grade	Lesson Topic	Presented in Class/ Subject	ASCA Standard	Curriculum and Materials	Start/End Dates	Process Data	Perception Data	Outcome Data
9th	What does it take to graduate from high school?	Career Success classes	A:A3.1 A:B2.6 A:C1.6	White board, markers, handouts	9/15 to 10/15	EZAnalyze results of class sessions, number of students, time in class	Pre- and post-survey results	Promotion data in School Report Card

The ASCA National Model contains action plan templates for three counseling program activities: core curriculum lessons, small-group sessions, and closing-the-gap endeavors. The core curriculum lessons provide a systematic means to promote student development in the academic, career, and personal/ social domains. Some of the counseling core curriculum programs include college and career readiness, personal safety skills, academic motivation, and school success. When you collaborate with stakeholders to review the disaggregated data, achievement and performance gaps among subgroups of students will emerge that need to be addressed. The ASCA action plan templates for closing-the-gap activities provide a guide for developing CDSC program strategies.

CONCEPTUAL APPLICATION ACTIVITY 3.8

Management: Action Plans

1. With a partner, choose a group from those listed in Table 3.5. Looking at the data provided, what gap can you see that needs to be addressed?

2. Complete a Closing-the-Gap Action Plan to address the gap you identified above.

3. Write a brief reflection of this activity. What did you learn? What would you do differently?

Calendars

Effectively managed CDSC programs are visually organized around calendars. Weekly calendars offer more specific details like the date, time, and location of each activity and also give the name and contact information of the persons responsible for events. For best results, consider the best visibility for calendars, including hallway bulletin boards and in high-traffic areas, as well as your program website. With centralized locations, your calendars can create greater awareness for special theme weeks, school-wide programs, special events, and significant school activities that require a lot of community support for success. Table 3.9 illustrates one month of activities for our sample high school counseling program.

CONCEPTUAL APPLICATION ACTIVITY 3.9

Management: Calendar Activity

1. Working with a classmate, select a school level and generate a list of school counseling programs for a school year, including parent events, curriculum themes, promotional weeks, and so on.

2. Write a brief reflection on the benefits of calendars in your school counseling program. Share your reflections with your classmate.

Table 3.9 Example of Foundations High School Counseling Department Calendar: September

September					
					1
					2
3 Advisory Council	4 9th Classes Earning Credits	5 ACT PLAN Review	6 New Student Meetings	7 9th Classes Earning Credits	8
					9
10 Jr. Class Presentation	11 9th Classes Graduation Requirements	12 PSAT Info to 10th Grade	13 11th & 12th Parent Meetings	14 9th Classes Graduation Requirements	15 ACT test
					16
17 Applying to College Presentation	18 A&D group Counseling	19 Peer Facilitator Training	20 D-group Counseling	21 GLSEN Club	22
					23
24 Financial Aid Talk	25 AS Group	26 Faculty Presentation: School Report Card	27 AS Group	28 Dept. Meeting	29 College Fair
					30

THE DELIVERY COMPONENT

The *Delivery* component categorizes various functions counselors perform as either Direct Services or Indirect Services. Direct Services are defined as those face-to-face meetings and interactions school counselors have with students in individual and small group counseling and classroom curriculum sessions. Indirect Services are those contacts counselors have with teachers, parents, and others on behalf of students. The *Delivery* component of your CDSC program describes *how* activities and services will be implemented.

A wide range of school counseling programs and interventions include compo nents such as core curriculum (e.g., classroom instruction and group activities), individual student planning (e.g., appraisal and advisement), responsive services (e.g., counseling and crisis response), referrals, consultation, and collaboration. How you allocate and distribute your time in order to deliver program activities depends upon your overall school goals, counseling program objectives, and those priorities you set in conjunction with your administrators and advisory council. The ASCA National Model (2012) offers some guidance on how best to allot your time for delivering developmentally appropriate programs and intervention services.

Eighty percent of the time, counselors should be engaged in a combination of Direct Services *to* students and Indirect Services *on behalf of* students. This combined approach provides flexibility to determine how time is best distributed to address the identified student needs in your school. School counselors spend 20% or less of their time on planning and evaluating in the foundation, management, and accountability domains.

Direct Student Services

In providing direct services, school counselors work with students individually or in groups to enhance their academic, career, and personal/social developmental needs. The implementation of direct services to students takes the forms of *school counseling core curriculum, individual student planning,* and *responsive services.*

The *school counseling core curriculum* is a structured set of developmentally appropriate standards-based lessons that align with the school's overall curriculum. These counseling curriculum activities are considered to be preventive, planned with a scope and sequence that connects with the school's mission, and designed to support student success. These lessons are usually presented to students through classroom instruction, but they can be delivered in other large group formats, such as grade-level meetings and in special group meetings.

Individual student planning activities are counseling sessions to provide students with information that will empower them to make good decisions regarding their own goals. Counselors can meet with students individually or in small groups to share appraisal results of their achievement, aptitude, careers, interests, and skills. In these sessions, school counselors also advise students on their academic, career, college, and other post-secondary options, and/or help them develop short- or long-term plans to achieve their desired goals.

Responsive services focus on individual and small-group counseling sessions designed to help students address their immediate concerns and episodic issues. Students often require short-term support and intervention from school counselors in order to face many challenges and crises such as family disruptions, peer pressure, abuse, loss, bullying, relocation, and other personal/social concerns. Students with more significant mental health issues requiring more than six or seven weeks of counseling should be referred to outside therapy for treatment.

CONCEPTUAL APPLICATION ACTIVITY 3.10

Delivery: Direct Student Service

1. With a partner, identify a student need from the data provided in Table 3-6.

2. What direct student intervention would you provide to address that need? Describe how you would deliver that intervention.

3. What would be an expected student outcome after delivering this direct student service?

4. Reflect on how using data would guide what you do as a school counselor. Share with a classmate.

Indirect Student Services

Indirect student services are those school counselor activities performed on behalf of the students, but in which students are not engaged directly. These services include *referrals, consultation,* and *collaboration.* When students have needs and issues beyond the expertise, resources, and skill of school counselors, the counselor may make a *referral,* which directs the student to other resources within the school or outside the school setting. For example, students who struggle with math proficiency may need to be referred to a math tutor, or students displaying significant mental health issues may need to see a therapist in the community for long-term treatment.

Consultation is a problem-solving process in which a person seeks the advice of a consultant to provide better service to a third party (Dougherty, 2009). The school counselor in the role of the consultant is able to assist a parent or teacher who is seeking help to work with a child or student (i.e., third party). It also could be that the school counselor needs assistance from a consultant on how to best support a student. For example, you might consult with your principal on a student bullying issue or you might consult with a local psychologist on how to counsel children of divorce.

Collaboration is another problem-solving process in which the counselor (or the collaborator) and a significant stakeholder (or the collaboratee) work together in order to achieve positive outcomes for a student (or the client) (Dougherty, 2009). Both the collaborator and the collaboratee have a vested interest in the process outcome and share responsibilities regarding the implementation of interventions, services, and programs. For counselors, teaming up with others can be a powerful indirect strategy to promote student success and achievement. For example, you may collaborate with teachers on strategies to help students perform better in class or you may work with others to create a systemic change in a school culture to encourage and enhance academic achievement and positive student behaviors.

CONCEPTUAL APPLICATION ACTIVITY 3.11

Delivery: Indirect Student Services

1. With a partner, identify and describe a student need in which you would respond by providing indirect student intervention. Describe this need and the resulting service.

2. What would be the expected student outcome from delivering the indirect student intervention you identified above?

3. Reflect on what you take away from this activity as school counselor. Share with a classmate.

ACCOUNTABILITY COMPONENT

The *Accountability* component describes how to track data over time, how to generate program reports, and how to use information for program improvement. It is critical for school counselors to produce reports that indicate how school counseling programs impact student performance and success. Tracking student data over time provides important information, but does not provide information on the effectiveness of your interventions. To close the accountability loop, it is important that counselors provide key stakeholders with concrete reports on programs and interventions. Using these elements of accountability generates respect for school counselors and support for school counseling programs.

Now more than ever in the history of our profession, professional school counselors are expected to demonstrate the effectiveness of their CDSC programs (Dimwit, 2003; Gysbers & Henderson, 2006). The essential question to answer in the *Accountability* component is: How do students benefit from school counseling programs?

Throughout the design and implementation of school counseling programs, competent school counselors use data to monitor the efficacy of their programs and interventions. They 1) review data to establish program goals, 2) incorporate data collection into the program implementation and delivery phase; and, 3) analyze data during the implementation of their programs and after the end of the program.

Data Analysis

Counselors use various data to measure student behavioral changes and academic gains. The school profile, school report card, and school improvement plan that were initially reviewed to establish counseling program priorities should now be re-examined to identify where student performance improved over the course of the program.

When counselors compare data, questions can be answered about the impact of school counseling programs on student success. For example, what changes can be found in the disaggregated data on student achievement, promotion rates, graduation rates, discipline, attendance, course participation, and other measures of pupil performance? What does the evidence indicate regarding systematic changes in closing gaps in student achievement, opportunity, and/or attainment?

Further analysis of disaggregated data will answer more than evaluative questions; it will identify the areas in which counseling programs could focus next. For example, does the disaggregated data reveal additional access and equity issues in the school? What other programs or services should counselors deliver in order to remove barriers to learning for certain student populations? In addressing these questions, counselors can look to the data to provide important evidence that reveals the degree to which they were effective in meeting the overall school goals.

Use-of-time analysis should be done at the end of each semester to ensure that counselor time is aligned with their annual agreement and with the designed delivery of their programs. Counselors can analyze their calendars to determine how much time was spent in program delivery tasks such as small group counseling, curriculum, individual planning, and direct-responsive services to students.

CONCEPTUAL APPLICATION ACTIVITY 3.12

Accountability: Data Analysis

1. With a classmate, determine two sources of accountability data which you will use to evaluate your school counseling program.

2. Describe how you will analyze your data in order to determine the impact your counseling program had in the areas of student success and development.

3. Write a brief reflection on how and what you learned. How would you manage your time to collect and analyze data? Why is it important to use data in evaluating your program?

Program Results

Program results enable counselors and stakeholders to review data on efficacy of such school counseling programs as the core curriculum, small-group interventions, and closing the gap initiatives. Process, perception, and outcome data are incorporated in the program results to offer a complete report of accountability (Poynton & Carey, 2006). As part of program or intervention design, formative assessment data are collected during implementation of lessons and summative assessment data are collected after each lesson is delivered (Poynton & Carey, 2006). An example of a formative assessment is to ask students a few short-answer questions related to a counseling goal such as, "Name one strategy you have used to make better grades" or "What should you do when someone is bullying you?"

Summative assessments are designed to gauge how well students have acquired the skills, knowledge, or affective goals relative to the program standards. An example of a summative assessment is to conduct a pre- and post-test that measures the knowledge of good homework habits that students acquired from the core curriculum lesson. Figure 3.3 is a pre- and post-assessment to determine knowledge of bullying prevention.

Figure 3.3   Pre- and Post-Test Example

Third-Grade Core Curriculum: Bully Prevention		
Not in My School!		
I feel safe in school.	Yes	No
I have seen bullying in school.	Yes	No
I know how to stop bullying of my friends.	Yes	No
I know three things to do when I am being bullied.	Yes	No
I know three adults who will listen when I report bullying.	Yes	No
It is my responsibility to report bullying when I see it.	Yes	No
I should tell someone being bullied that I support them.	Yes	No

In order to produce complete accountability reports, counselors are expected to show results of their closing-the-gap initiatives. School counseling programs aligned with school improvement plans that address social justice issues demonstrate the impact they had upon educational gaps among underserved student populations. Closing-the-gap reports require counselors to compare data on student performance, access, and participation. For example, closing-the-gap reports can answer such questions as: Has the graduation rate among African American male students increased? Has the college enrollment rate among Hispanic male students increased? Are more female students enrolling in advanced math and science courses? Program results that reflect positive changes in closing-the-gap issues increase the image of school counselors as leaders, advocates, and change agents in schools.

When presenting program results to stakeholders, highlight your accomplishments and indicate where changes will be made to improve program effectiveness. Some of the questions that program results could address include: Did the school counseling program accomplish its intended purpose? Was student performance impacted in the way that was envisioned? Did student behaviors change in the expected way? How can programs be modified to improve effectiveness or to increase positive results? Can resources and time be allocated differently to improve program outcomes?

Sometimes comprehensive school counseling programs produce small gains, especially when program goals include raising graduation rates, improving student attendance, increasing minority participation in advanced placement courses, or decreasing disruptive student behaviors. In such cases, you can compare program data over time to display the cumulative effect of your counseling program. For example, graphing the data of small program improvements over three years or more can give your results a more dramatic presentation that will make a lasting impression on principals, teachers, parents, and other stakeholders.

CONCEPTUAL APPLICATION ACTIVITY 3.13

Accountability: Program Results

1. Based upon the data you collected in your previous activity, what reports would you generate to show accountability?

2. With a classmate, describe how you would share your reports to key stakeholders.

3. Write a brief reflection on the development of accountability reports for your school counseling program. In what areas do you think you could improve? Where can you obtain the knowledge, skills, or disposition you need to grow in your ability to produce accountability reports?

Evaluation and Improvement

School counselors have an opportunity to reflect upon the overall quality of their school counseling program as well as their performance after analyzing evaluation data, generating accountability reports, and sharing the results of their comprehensive school counseling programs with key stakeholders. Due to the fact that many principals do not fully understand the role and function of school counselors (Kirchner & Setchfield, 2005), and also because your local school district will likely require an evaluation of your work as an employee, the ASCA offers a *School Counselor Performance Appraisal* tool as a guide to local administrators and school districts in evaluating your work as a professional school counselor. Administrators who use this instrument are likely to be more cognizant of how the school counselor's role is integral to student growth.

CONCEPTUAL APPLICATION ACTIVITY 3.14

Accountability: Evaluation and Improvement

1. With a classmate, discuss how you envision using the School Counselor Competencies Assessment, the School Counseling Program Assessment, and the School Counselor Performance Appraisal in your career.

2. Role-play a conversation you might have with your principal about the School Counselor Performance Appraisal.

3. Write your reflections on the role-playing activity and discuss them with your classmate. What do you think you did well in the activity? How can you improve?

CONCLUSION

The ASCA National Model® advances the role and function of professional school counselors through a foundational framework for building and managing programs, delivering services to students and parents, and providing a process for evaluating CDSC programs. In addition, student development in the academic, career/college, and personal/social domains are found in the *ASCA National Standards for Students.* Both documents enable counselors to systematically build programs that are based on student developmental needs and allow them to align their programs with the overall educational program of their schools.

The ASCA National Model identifies the four central themes of leadership, collaboration, advocacy, and systemic change to guide professional school counselors in fulfilling their mission to enhance the success and development of all students. As the role of school counseling evolves, the profession will need practitioners who embrace a vision that promotes school success for all students, who are passionate about designing a CDSC program to enhance student development, and who equip themselves to be leaders and advocates for those students most in need of support.

REFERENCES

American School Counselor Association (2003). *The ASCA National Model: A framework for school counseling programs.* Alexandria, VA: Author.

American School Counselor Association (2005). *The ASCA National Model: A framework for school counseling orograms* (2nd ed.). Alexandria, VA: Author.

American School Counselor Association (2012). *The ASCA National Model: A framework for school counseling programs* (3rd ed.). Alexandria, VA: Author.

American School Counselor Association (2012a). ASCA National Model 3.0: When it's time to change. *ASCA School Counselor, 49* (6), 10–13.

American School Counselor Association (2007). *School counseling standards: School counselor competencies.* Alexandria, VA: Author. Retrieved July 15, 2012 from www.*schoolcounselor*.org/files/SC*Competencies*.pdf

American School Counselor Association (2010). *Ethical standards for school counselors.* Alexandria, VA: Author. Retrieved July 15, 2012 from www.*schoolcounselor*.org/files/*Ethi calStandards*2010.pdf

Anderson, K. (2002). A response to common themes in school counseling. *Professional School Counseling, 5,* 315–321.

Baker, S. B. (2001). *Reflections on forty years in the school counseling profession: Is the glass half full or half empty?* Retrieved from http://www.thefreelibrary.com/Reflections+on+forty+years+in+the+school+counseling+profession%3a+is . . . -a084152027

Balfanz, R. & Byrnes, V. (2012). *Chronic absenteeism: Summarizing what we know from nationally available data.* Baltimore: Johns Hopkins University Center for Social Organization of Schools.

Barona, A. & Barona, M. S. (2006). School counselors and school psychologists: Collaborating to ensure minority students receive appropriate consideration for special education programs. *Professional School Counseling, 10,* 3–13.

Bemak, R. & Chung, R. C. (2005). Advocacy as a critical role for urban school counselors: Working toward equity and social justice. *Professional School Counselor, 8,* 196–202.

Brown, D. & Trusty, J. (2005). *Designing and leading comprehensive school counseling programs: Promoting student competence and meeting student needs.* Belmont, CA: Thomson Brooks/Cole.

Campbell, C. A. & Dahir, C. A. (1997). *The National Standards for School Counseling Programs.* Alexandria, VA: American School Counselor Association.

Carey, J. C., Dimmitt, C., Hatch, T. A., Lapan, R. T., & Whiston, S. C. (2008). Report of the National Panel for Evidence-Based School Counseling: Outcome Research Coding Protocol and Evaluation of Student Success Skills and Second Step. *Professional School Counseling,* 11, 197–201.

Dimwit, C. (2003). Transforming school counseling practice through collaboration and the use of data: A study of academic failure high school. *Professional School Counseling, 6,* 340-349.

Dollarhide, C. T. (2003). School counselors as program leaders: Applying leadership contexts to school counseling. *Professional School Counseling, 6,* 304-308.

Dollarhide, C. T. & Saginak, K. A. (2008). *Comprehensive School Counseling Programs: K-12 delivery systems in action.* Boston, MA: Pearson Education, Inc.

Dollarhide, C. T., Smith, A. T., & Lemberger, M. E. (2007). Critical incidents in the development of supportive principals: Facilitating school counselor-principal relationships. *Professional School Counseling, 10,* 360–369.

Dougherty, A. M. (2009). *Psychological consultation and collaboration in school and community settings* (5th ed.). Belmont, CA: Brooks/Cole.

Epstein, J. L. & Van Voorhis, F. L. (2010). School counselors' roles in developing partnerships with families and communities for student success. *Professional School Counseling, 14,* 1–14.

Goals 2000: Educate America Act. P.L. No. 103–227, Sec. 318, § 108, Stat.186 (1994).

Gysbers, N.C. & Henderson, P. (2001). Comprehensive Guidance and Counseling Programs: A rich history and a bright future. *Professional School Counseling, 4,* 246–256.

Gysbers, N. C. & Henderson, P. (2006). *Developing and Managing Your School Guidance Program* (4th ed.). Alexandria, VA: American Counseling Association.

Herr, E. L. (2001). The impact of national policies, economics, and school reform on comprehensive guidance programs. *Professional School Counseling, 4,* 236–245.

Kirchner, G. L. & Setchfield, M. S. (2005). School counselors' and school principals' perceptions of the school counselor's role. *Education, 126,* 10–17.

Lapan, R. T. (2001). Results-based comprehensive guidance and counseling programs: A framework for planning and evaluation. *Professional School Counseling, 4,* 289–299.

No Child Left Behind (NCLB) Act of 2001. P.L. No. 107–110, § 115, Stat. 1425 (2002).

Poynton, T. A. & Carey, J. C. (2006). An integrative model of data-based decision making for school counseling. *Professional School Counseling, 10,* 121–130.

Ratts, M. J., DeKruyf, L., & Chen-Hayes, S. C. (2007). The ACA Advocacy Competencies: A social justice advocacy framework for professional school counselors. *Professional School Counseling, 11,* 90–97.

Schwallie-Giddis, P., Maat, M., & Pak, M. (2003). Initiating leadership by introducing and implementing the ASCA National Model. *Professional School Counseling, 3,* 170–173.

Singh, A. A., Urbano, A., Haston, M., & McMahon, E. (2010). School counselors' strategies for social justice change: A grounded theory of what works in the real world. *Professional School Counseling, 13,* 135–145.

Sink, C. A. (2005). Fostering academic development and learning: Implications and recommendations for middle school counselors. *Professional School Counseling, 9,* 128-135.

Steen, S. & Noguera, P. A. (2010). A broader and bolder approach to school reform: Expanded partnership roles for school counselors. *Professional School Counseling, 14,* 42–52.

Stone, C. B. & Dahir, C. A. (2010). *School counselor accountability: A MEASURE of student success* (3rd ed.). Upper Saddle River, NJ: Prentice Hall.

Thompson, R. A. (2012). *Professional school counseling: Best practices for working in the schools* (3rd ed.). New York: Routledge/Taylor & Francis.

Whiston, S. C., Tai, W. L. Rahardja, D. & Eder, K. (2011). School counseling outcome: A meta-analytic examination of interventions. *Journal of Counseling & Development, 89,* 37–55.

Chapter 4

THE SCHOOL COUNSELOR'S ROLE IN ASSESSMENT AND RESEARCH

*CACREP STANDARDS

ASSESSMENT

G. *Knowledge*

   3. Identifies various forms of needs assessments for academic, career, and personal/social development

H. *Skills and Practices*

   2. Selects appropriate assessment strategies that can be used to evaluate a student's academic, career, and personal/social development.

   3. Analyzes assessment information in a manner that produces valid inferences when evaluating the needs of individual students and assessing the effectiveness of educational programs.

RESEARCH AND EVALUATION

I. *Knowledge*

   1. Understands how to critically evaluate research relevant to the practice of school counseling.

   2. Knows models of program evaluation for school counseling programs.

   3. Knows basic strategies for evaluating counseling outcomes in school counseling (e.g., behavioral observation, program evaluation).

   4. Knows current methods of using data to inform decision making and accountability (e.g., school improvement plan, school report card).

CACREP

5. Understands the outcome research data and best practices identified in the school counseling research literature.

J. *Skills and Practices*

1. Applies relevant research findings to inform the practice of school counseling.

2. Develops measurable outcomes for school counseling programs, activities, interventions, and experiences.

3. Analyzes and uses data to enhance school counseling programs.

> *I didn't go into the school counseling profession to do research and collect data—I went into the profession to counsel students.*

> *When I collect data and show my principal how students have achieved as a result of my work with them, he is more willing to sit down and talk with me about my training.*

The two above statements made by school counselors are at opposite ends of the continuum in regard to accountability. Although most school counselors grasp the idea that data collection and evaluation are key components for demonstrating that school counseling programs enhance student growth, there is still reticence about engaging in this significant process.

The focus on accountability in schools has ushered in an era of evidence-based programs and educational interventions to demonstrate the growth of school aged youth. When school counselors repeatedly fail to reveal the positive influences of counselor interventions on student growth, the perception is that school counseling programs are peripheral to academics. Although many educators claim that the passage of No Child Left Behind (NCLB) is responsible for evidence-based results, the fact is that the need for school counselor accountability practices has been communicated for decades (Aubry, 1985; Baker, 2012).

A HISTORY OF SCHOOL COUNSELOR ACCOUNTABILITY

In the early 1920s, Payne (1924, as cited in Gysbers, 2004) cautioned school counselors that without active involvement in verifying and documenting how student involvement with the school counseling program promotes achievement, others would define and evaluate what we do. In partial response, a checklist of guidance and counseling activities was created in the 1930s that stipulated a number or percentage of specific school counselor tasks (Gysbers, 2004) to be performed throughout the academic year. Although these types of data are useful in showing where time is spent, these data do not provide evidence as to the quality or importance of these tasks and how they were performed.

In the 1960s the Elementary and Secondary Education Act (ESEA) was passed and federal dollars were allocated to improve educational opportunities for disadvantaged youth (Duffy, Giordano, Farrell, Paneque, & Crump, 2008). With standards-based reform such as *The Goals 2000: Educate America Act,* school counselors continued to practice "as usual" with the rationale that it was difficult to objectively study counseling relationships or how school counseling contributed to student growth. Instead, they relied on the favorable comments expressed by students or encouraging communications from teachers or parents. When No Child Left Behind mandated substantial reform in the areas of testing, accountability, and teacher quality, counselors were assigned new responsibilities such as testing coordinator, assessor, and test technician (Duffy, et al., 2008), tasks that only peripherally relate to direct student contact.

BOX 4.1 BENEFITS OF DATA COLLECTION AND ANALYSIS

Implementing strategies for collecting and assessing data leads to increased student academic growth and is a catalyst to facilitate school counselor contributions.

Leaders in the school counseling profession (Cobia & Henderson, 2006; Gysbers & Henderson, 2006, as cited in Sink, 2009) acknowledge: 1) the use of objective data to reveal established outcomes in Comprehensive Developmental School Counseling (CDSC) programs; 2) systematic assessment of program personnel; and 3) needs assessments to ascertain stakeholder views. School counselors can no longer hope that enumerative data or a checklist of activities will be sufficient. Evidence of how the school counseling program impacts students is essential if we want our skills and knowledge to be valued and acknowledged. School counselors take classes in research and statistics as a part of their professional program, yet apprehension is expressed when applying this training to their work within the schools.

ACTION-BASED RESEARCH

Action research, also known as systematic inquiry (Dahir & Stone, 2009), is a method of gathering information to gain a better understanding of intervention effectiveness to improve practice (Mills, 2000). This strategic plan is conducted in a real-life setting for the purpose of demonstrating and evaluating students' mastery of competencies and goals, and is key for demonstrating efficacy (Borders & Drury, 1992). The steps to be taken when conducting action research include identifying a problem, planning a strategy, collecting and organizing data, interpreting data, and evaluating its effectiveness.

- *Identifying a problem.* This step requires discovering an area of interest that is engaging and meaningful to you. Once you have chosen an area to investigate, look at the existing literature on this topic to better understand the problem. Researching the topic offers an opportunity to reflect on the problem from a different viewpoint and the strategies that were implemented to better understand the issue.
- *Planning a Strategy.* Once you have had the opportunity to define the issue and interventions for addressing it, you are able to create and implement a plan. There are myriad ways a particular problem can be addressed. Is a group approach the best intervention to address the issue? An individual counseling approach? Or, an in-service workshop?
- *Data collection.* Now that a plan is created for addressing the problem, data are collected using the population and intervention you have chosen. Data gathering can take different forms, including the use of scales or questionnaires, making observations, examining records such as attendance and discipline, and analyzing graduation rates. More specific details on these strategies are found later in the chapter.
- *Interpreting Data.* Action research is dependent upon formative and summative data that include stopping and reflecting on the process at different intervals to make certain necessary data are captured, and again at the end to identify program intervention results (Mills, 2000). Complicated statistical analyses are not necessary when reporting data. Results do not need to be complicated. The use of descriptive data, or summarizing a sample through such means as mean, median, or mode, provide clear data in an easily understood format. These data are often preferred to more complex inferential data in which inferences are made between groups.
- *Evaluating the Intervention.* At this point you are conveying what the study revealed about your program or intervention. An action chart visually outlines the scope of the research project such as outlined in Table 4.1.

IDEAS! (Lapan, 2005, as cited in Gysbers & Henderson, 2012), SOARING (Gilchrist, 2006, as cited in Holcomb-McCoy, 2007), and M.E.A.S.U.R.E (Dahir & Stone, 2009) are acronyms that may be applied for conducting action research.

Table 4.1 Outline of Action Research Project

Purpose	Persons Involved	Assessment	Location	Evaluation
Why is this research being conducted? Why is it important?	Who will be responsible for the intervention? School counselor? Teacher?	What will be assessed? Knowledge? Behavior? Skills? Attitude?	Where will the intervention occur? In the guidance suite? Classroom?	What are the indicators that this intervention was effective?

IDEAS!

IDEAS! is a guide for school counselors to methodically identify a problem, design an intervention to address the issue, examine and analyze the data, and share the results with decision makers (Lapan, 2005, as cited in Gysbers & Henderson, 2012).

(I) identify the problem

(D) describe the situation

(E) existing school data are used to analyze the problem

(A) analysis of data to examine the impact of the intervention

(S) summarize the results and share with stakeholders

SOARING

SOARING is an acronym that describes another type of system that guides school counselors to assess and evaluate workshops, lessons, and other types of interventions (Gilchrist, 2006, as cited in Holcomb-McCoy, 2007).

S = Standards	O = Objectives
In using this acronym as a guide, school counselors use S to determine what *standard* the counseling activity is to tackle. Is it in the domain of Academic? Career? Personal/Social? It is also possible that the standard is addressed in more than one domain.	The O is used to determine the *objective* that is to be mastered. For example, at the end of a lesson on friendship, "students will be able to demonstrate two ways to address a friend." The objective addresses critical needs and is measurable.

(Continued)

(Continued)

A = Assessment	R = Results
The A is used to identify the type of data that are needed to *assess* the objective. Are grades needed? Standardized tests? Skill demonstration? Or, are subjective responses from students regarding perceived knowledge of an activity enough?	The R part of the abbreviation refers to how *results* are to be gathered and analyzed. Descriptive data (percentages) are easy to understand, particularly when illustrated on graphs.
I = Impact	N = Network
The I, or *impact* describes how the strategy affected students' knowledge, attitudes, or skills. For instance, "as a result of participating in a friendship activity, 90% of the students were able to effectively demonstrate how to meet new friends, an increase of 50%."	The N relates to *network*, or communicating program results to stakeholders. For instance, are program results to be publicized through presentations? Newsletters? Website?
G = Guide	
The G stands for *Guidance* or the measures that need to be taken to alter this activity for the future	

M.E.A.S.U.R.E.

The M.E.A.S.U.R.E process developed by Stone and Dahir (2003) is an acronym for "systematically collecting, analyzing, and using critical data elements to understand the current achievement story for students, and to begin to strategize, impact, and document how the school counseling program contributes toward supporting student success" (Dahir & Stone, 2003, p. 216). Mission, analyze, stakeholders, unite, reanalyze, and educate are the key terms that comprise the acronym.

Mission—Connect to the Mission of the School	A mission statement defines the reason the school counseling program exists. Without an effective mission school counselors are unsure of how to plan and prepare for what they want to accomplish. This mission includes school counselors' philosophy, goals, and values that are consistent with the educational mission of the school. The foremost school counselor responsibility is to support the academic achievement of all students as articulated through the three Ps (purpose, practice, and principles) that guide the development of the mission by answering the questions:
	What are the opportunities or needs of students? (purpose)
	What are we doing to address those needs? (best practices)
	What beliefs guide our work (principles we hold)

Elements—Identify Critical Data Elements	Available data assist in identifying elements that could impair the educational growth of some students. By examining data that are available on the school report card, or accessing records such as discipline referrals, attendance, tardiness, report cards, or attrition, critical conditions are identified and studied.
Analyze—Critical Data Elements	Careful analysis of identified data and disaggregating the information by looking at such elements as ethnicity, gender, grade level, or subject assists in gaining a more accurate understanding of the issue. Asking the question, "What are some of the factors that could be contributing to this problem?" facilitates an examination of the barriers that are impacting student success. For instance, you may be concerned with the large number of ninth-grade females who are failing English. Through further analysis you might realize that 45% of these girls had a certain eighth-grade English teacher, and recognize that these students did not master certain competencies that were to be addressed in this class. As a result, it may be necessary to assist the eighth-grade English teacher in teaching skills that were not attained, and/or to design a strategy to help struggling students master necessary skills.
	Once the critical factors are identified, a benchmark for achievement is established, in addition to identifying a strategy to meet this goal. For example, you may decide that you will hold a study skills group for these girls to attain the skills that they missed in their English class the previous year. Your benchmark could be identified as English scores being 10% higher the grading period following the intervention. After the intervention, the group strategy can be evaluated by gauging whether or not this benchmark was reached.
Stakeholders Unite	Once an intervention is decided upon, the next step is to identify individuals who are able to address the problem. For instance, the ninth-grade English teachers who have the failing female students in class will need to indicate the skills that need to be retaught. If a group approach is used to improve these skills the principal will need to support and approve this strategy. In this case, teachers may need to release these students from class to attend the group, and parents and/or guardians will need to be informed and provide permission for their daughters to attend the group sessions. An action plan that outlines the skills to be taught, the days and times the group will meet, and the individuals responsible for group implementation are developed. In addition, documentation of the action plan, and responsible stakeholder roles and tasks are indicated on the timeline.
Reanalyze, Reflect, and Revise	Formative and summative data determine what parts of the plan were effective and those that did not work as expected. Formative data are collected while a specific strategy is being conducted, and the intervention may be adjusted based on this feedback. This information provides timely, critical data to determine student progress with space to adapt the plan to meet student needs. Summative data are collected after the plan is finished

(Continued)

(Continued)

	to assess plan effectiveness for future considerations. At this point you may wish to examine the benchmark that was established and compare it with the final results (in the example, the benchmark was set at increasing English grades 10% from the previous grading period). If this benchmark was not met, rather than being discouraged, determine what steps need to be altered or eliminated. Or, it may be more realistic to lower the benchmark to a more reasonable goal.
Educate	Documenting and reporting the results of the systematic process reveal how school counselors contribute to school goals. *The School Counseling Program Accountability Report Card* (SPARC) is one method of sharing the results of an identified intervention (Stone & Dahir, 2003). This accountability report succinctly categorizes the process in a one to two page document with information such as: School demographics and key individuals Comment from principal The goal or school issue including critical data Stakeholders involved Results that are graphed Systemic changes that occurred Anecdotal reports

Photo 4.1   School Counselor Talking With Student

As an example of how school counselor training concepts can be implemented in a real-life setting, a school counseling intern conducted an action research project in which she taught various study skills to struggling students. She used a pre/post-test to evaluate student perceptions of ability to use various skills before the group intervention, and again at the end of the intervention. An example of a graph that was used to illustrate a middle school student's progress is in Figure 4.1.

Figure 4.1   Example Student Progress Graph

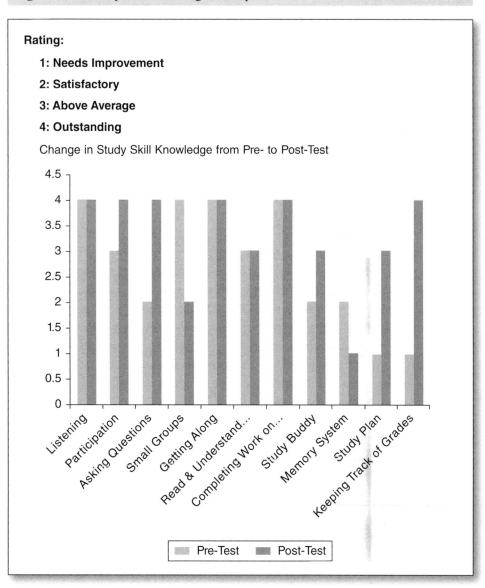

As revealed in the graph, the student perceived an improved ability to utilize the various study skills that were taught in the group.

CONCEPTUAL APPLICATION ACTIVITY 4.1

Choose a school and analyze the report card for this chosen school. Use the data from the report card and with the steps in the IDEAS! SOARING, or M.E.A.S.U.R.E models, identify a critical issue that needs to be addressed and develop an action plan to address the problem.

IDEAS!, SOARING, and M.E.A.S.U.R.E all require knowledge of action research and assessment, "an umbrella term for the evaluation methods counselors use to better understand people, places, or things" (Hays, 2012, p. 4). Experimental designs, single-subject designs, and retrospective assessments are additional methods of revealing counseling effectiveness among groups.

COMPARATIVE STUDIES

Experimental Designs

This methodology could be applied if you are interested in studying the effects of a program (*variable*) on a group of students. For instance, suppose you were interested in creating a group intervention to reduce discipline referrals. Using an experimental design you could *randomly assign* identified students to a group that is designed to teach students self-management skills (*experimental group*), or to a *control group,* in which they receive no group intervention. At the end of the experiment you would statistically compare the discipline referrals for each group to verify whether or not the intervention made a significant difference in discipline referrals. Although this approach appears straightforward, it is difficult to conclude if the group was the only *variable* influencing the outcome. Furthermore, if you use this method, keep in mind that ethically you would need to offer the same group intervention for those students who were originally placed in the control group.

Single-Subject Design

In this design you would compare the results of an intervention with a single, identified subject. *Baseline* data to determine the frequency of an identified behavior or degree of knowledge would be collected prior to beginning the strategy. For instance, suppose you decided to use narrative counseling with an elementary-age student who was having difficulty with aggressive behaviors. In this design the individual is the focus, and there is no comparison or control group. In this case, suppose you decided to use the *Beliefs About Hitting Scale* that the student completes prior to receiving the narrative counseling intervention. After the counseling has ended the student would complete the inventory again to determine whether or not the counseling was effective in reducing aggressiveness. As in the experimental design, it is difficult to determine whether the counseling was responsible for the outcome or whether it was the result of other *intervening variables.*

Retrospective Assessment

A retrospective assessment recreates past events through the recollection of memories or events. Suppose a student expresses anxiety about transitioning to a new grade. This student could be asked to think back to the previous school year when he/she matriculated to the present grade and the feelings he/she experienced. The counselor could design a Likert scale and the student would be asked to think about each scale item and to put an "0" on the scale based on his/her feelings at the end of the previous year. After the student has completed this scale, the student is asked to look at the same items and to put an "X" next to the number that best represents how he/she feels at the present time. If there is a positive change, the counselor could discuss skills that helped in making the situation better and then ask the student to use these same skills as he/she adjusts to the new grade. Table 4.2 is an example of a retrospective assessment scale.

Table 4.2   Example of a Retrospective Assessment

Directions to student: I want you to think about the feelings you had last year when you were moving to a new grade. Put an "0" on the number that best represents your feelings at that time.

Feelings at End of Last Year about Moving to a New Grade

	1	*2*	*3*	*4*	*5*
Stressed		0			
Nervous			0		
Angry				0	
Frustrated				0	
Content	0				

(Continued)

Table 4.2 (Continued)

Key: 1 = rarely had this feeling 5 = almost always had this feeling

My Feelings about School Right Now

	1	*2*	*3*	*4*	*5*	*Change*
Stressed		X				—
Nervous	X					+
Angry	X					+
Frustrated		X				+
Content				X		+

Key : 1 = Rarely have this feeling 5 = I almost always have this feeling

—No change + = indicates positive change

In comparing these data there was no change in perceived level of stress; however, there were perceived improvements in nervousness, anger, frustration, and contentment.

These designs are examples of methodologies the school counselor is able to employ to disclose effectiveness and contributions to student development. Test results as well as other sources of information are necessary for decision making and outcome dissemination (Whiston, 2000). However, no decision is to be made solely on the basis of one test.

ASSESSMENT INSTRUMENTS

Instruments to collect data with validated psychometric properties assist with evidence-based practices. An appropriate assessment instrument is identified and selected based on the purpose of the intervention, the needs of the student, or the objectives of the program. Several online sites provide instruments school counselors can access for program or intervention assessment.

The U.S. National Library of Medicine (http://wwwcf.nlm.nih.gov/hsrr_search/index.cfm) provides resources, databases, and a list of instruments to select for the purpose of investigating issues. In addition, the Center for Disease Control (CDC) offers a compendium of comprehensive instruments to investigate numerous topics such as aggression, emotional competence, beliefs, and conflict resolution

strategies for youth from the ages of 5 to 24. This guide is available at http://www
.cdc.gov/ncipc/pub-res/pdf/YV/YV_Compendium.pdf

Although it is preferable to use an instrument that is validated with acceptable
psychometric properties, there are times when an instrument is not available for a
specific purpose. In these instances, you will need to create an instrument using
the following steps.

- Research the area you are investigating to better understand the problem and
  the factors surrounding the issue
- Operationally define the criteria that needs to be evaluated based on the
  objectives of the intervention or program
- Determine the type of question format that will provide the most information. Assign point values to allow for scale comparison
- Determine the validity of the tool by looking at the relevance of the measurable criteria
- Design the instrument and pilot-test it with participants from the same norm
  group as those for whom the instrument is designed. Use the lowest possible
  reading level to catch participants with varying reading abilities
- Decide how the assessment tool will be given and scored

Assessments are designed in the form of checklists, scales, questionnaires,
observations, interviews, counseling goals, and portfolios.

Checklists

Checklists are used to establish whether a behavior, skill, piece of knowledge,
or value is present. The score is generally expressed as the total number of items
or percentages. An example is found in Figure 4.2.

Figure 4.2   Example of a Checklist

Check if you have observed (*Name of Student*) exhibiting any of the following
behaviors in the last month.

_____ aggressive behaviors (starting fights)	_____ inattentive in class
_____ cheating on tests	_____ difficulty completing work
_____ tardiness to class	_____ disrespectful to others
_____ difficulty with peers	_____ blames others when things go wrong

In the example above the counselor will choose the individuals who are best able to complete the checklist (e.g., teachers, parents, administrators), and responses are tallied to verify if there are commonalities or a pattern across people or situations.

Scales

Attitudes, values, and interests are common self-report rating scales used in schools (McMillan, 1996) to ascertain either the frequency and/or quality of behaviors or views. Likert-like scales, commonly used in schools due to their ease in development and data collection, contain either odd or even numbers. The use of odd-numbered scales provides a neutral or undecided middle value (e.g., 1–5), whereas even numbered scales create a forced choice in which the participant indicates a preference toward one end of the scale or the other (e.g., 1–4). A weight is assigned to each point on the scale and scores for each individual are averaged (Salkind, 2000). Examples of a Likert scale are in Figure 4.3.

Figure 4.3   Examples of a Likert-Type Scale

1. Statements can be used to express an opinion or attitude.

   Circle the statement that best expresses your viewpoint: The primary role of school counselors is to:

   support the academic improvement of school-age youth

   work directly with students

   work collaboratively with teachers

   advocate for disenfranchised students

2. A scale is given to express the degree of agreement. For instance:

   The confidentiality of students in counseling is to be protected at all costs:

   SA   Strongly agree

   A   Agree

   U   Undecided

   D   Disagree

   SD   Strongly Disagree

Questionnaires

Questionnaires collect descriptive data from individuals using a set of structured, focused questions (Ebel, 1965) that are generally self-administered and easy to score. When developing a questionnaire, it is a good idea to pilot-test the instrument with a group of individuals who are similar to the identified participants, and to revise the questionnaire from the suggestions provided by this pilot group. Questionnaires are designed with time, age of participants, and ease of scoring considerations. An example of a questionnaire is in Figure 4.4.

Figure 4.4   Example of a Questionnaire

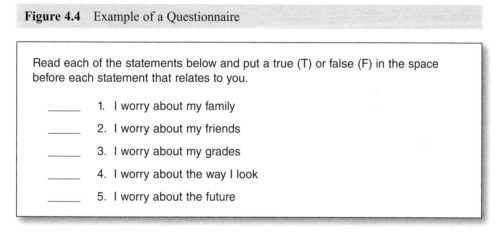

Read each of the statements below and put a true (T) or false (F) in the space before each statement that relates to you.

_____   1. I worry about my family

_____   2. I worry about my friends

_____   3. I worry about my grades

_____   4. I worry about the way I look

_____   5. I worry about the future

Observations

Observational techniques are used when you wish to document behavioral patterns without interfering with the behavior being observed (Salkind, 2000). This type of assessment requires identifying the specific behaviors to be observed, creating a system for coding and documenting, and making decisions regarding the observed behavior (McMillan, 1996). For instance, if a teacher is concerned about a student who frequently wanders around the classroom and does not sit in his/her seat, a school counselor observer may be asked to come into the classroom to watch this behavior using one of several observational approaches. Using *duration recording,* the length of time an identified behavior occurs is recorded. In the case above, the amount of time that passed while the student is out of his/her seat would be recorded. *Frequency recording* is used to document the number of times the identified behavior occurs in a period of time. For instance, if the class period is 50 minutes, the observer would keep track of the number of times the student is out of his/her seat during the class session. *Interval recording* is another observational strategy in which the observer would designate a time frame and record the number of times the behavior occurred within this time. For example, the observer might choose five minutes as the observation interval, and record each time the student is out of his/her seat during this five-minute interval. Finally, using *continuous recording,* the observer notes behaviors seen within a classroom period. For instance, in the example above, the observer would record every noticeable action of the target student (Salkind, 2000), such as talking to peers, not raising hand to answer a question, or sleeping at his/her desk, not just the times he/she is out of the classroom seat. An example of an observation checklist is in Figure 4.5.

Figure 4.5 Sample Observational Checklist

Location _____   Name _____   Date _____

Defined Behavior for Observation _____

Time   Tally/Description of Behaviors

_____   _____

_____   _____

_____   _____

_____   _____

Summary

Signature of Observer

Interviews

Data are also collected through interviews. Through the use of a structured format all participants are asked the same questions in a setting in which verbal as well as nonverbal responses and behaviors are observed and recorded. Similar to the questionnaire, it is wise to pilot-test the questions and revise the questions based on feedback. A combination of both "open-ended" questions that elicit deeper information and "closed" questions which are usually answered with a single "yes" or "no," or a phrase are used to obtain different types of information. Interviews provide information that may not ordinarily be available through other methodologies. When interviews are combined with other techniques such as observations or analysis of records (Salkind, 2000), a better understanding of an area of concern unfolds. An example of interview questions to assist transfer students is below.

Figure 4.6   Examples of Interview Questions

1. What are some of your questions about this school?

2. What are your greatest concerns about entering as a new student?

3. What are some of the things that would make this a good experience for you?

4. What goals would you like to set and reach this year?

5. Tell me what your plans are for the future?

6. What do you need to do to reach these goals?

Counseling Goals

Identifying counseling goals to serve as a guide for counseling effectiveness is frequently the most difficult part of the counseling process. It is not unusual for a student to talk about multiple concerns that are influencing his/her life, making it difficult for the counselor to pinpoint the direction to take in counseling. The Target Complaints (TC) procedure helps in identifying and rating the extent to which problems are influencing effective functioning. Using TC, students are asked to identify a maximum of 3 complaints, or problems they wish to address in counseling, and to rate the severity of these complaints on a scale of 1 (no problem) to 5 (severe problem) (Battle, et al., 1966, as cited in Hays, 2012). For instance, the student may state that grades are a concern with a severity rating of 4, friendships as another issue with a severity rating of 5, and parents' fighting with an assigned number of 3. The student can then choose one of these problems to address in counseling. Once a target area is identified the S.M.A.R.T acronym discussed in chapter 3 can be used to specifically elaborate a goal for evaluative purposes. Once a goal is defined and a plan of action is determined, progress toward the goal is assessed at each session (formative) and again at the termination of counseling (summative). Subjective measures to track progress are in Figure 4.7 (p. 138).

Keeping track of the student's progress using a visual representation provides concrete data for the counselor and a pictorial reminder of progress for the student. Verbal subjective responses can also be used to evaluate the student's perceptions of counseling. An example is in Figure 4.8 (p. 138).

Figure 4.7   Example of Evaluating Counseling Goals

At the beginning of each individual session, ask the student to choose a number on the ruler (1 = not making progress, and 5 = making great progress) that best illustrates how much progress toward the goal he/she believes is occurring.

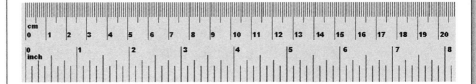

At the end of the session, once again ask the student to choose a number that best represents how well the counseling session helped toward reaching the goal.

Figure 4.8   Evaluating Goals Through Subjective Responses

Please provide feedback on your perceptions of the counseling process.

In what ways has counseling helped you achieve your goals?

What were the most helpful parts of counseling?

What suggestions do you have for your counselor?

Portfolios

Portfolios are becoming an increasingly popular assessment method. Portfolio analysis evaluates progress over a period of time with the progression of student work from the first assignment until the last. The portfolio may consist of reflection papers, a response assignment, or write-ups that are organized and accompanied with a final reflective paper. A career portfolio may contain such artifacts as the results of interest inventories, career papers, or a list of academic subjects that relate to a specific career.

Other assessment techniques that can be used following group guidance or other formats to assess knowledge are below.

Assessment	Purpose
Minute Paper	At the end of the lesson the participants are given an index card to answer the questions: "What was the most important thing you learned during this class?" "What else do you want to know?"
Muddiest Point	This strategy can be used after a lesson, reading assignment, discussion, or video. Students complete the following question: "What was the muddiest point in today's lesson?"
One-sentence Summary	Participants summarize the information they learned by answering the questions, "Who did what to whom, when, where, how, and why?"
Pros and Cons	Participants create a list of pros and cons to a situation presented by the school counselor. For example, "After reading the situation, write three pros and three cons about making the choice Louisa made."

Each of these strategies is used to document and analyze interventions to answer the question, "How are students different as a result of the school counseling program?" The objectives of the intervention and the needs of the student dictate the type of assessment to be used.

Practitioners are now more actively involved in data collection to concretely demonstrate how students have grown academically, vocationally, and personally/socially, yet school counselors lament the difficulty of demonstrating how their contributions impact student achievement (Barna & Brott, 2011). Not only is the link of school counseling programs to academic achievement limited, but when school counselors use a combination of strategies, it is difficult to verify which intervention is directly connected to academic growth.

CONCEPTUAL APPLICATION ACTIVITY 4.2

From the issue you identified in conceptual activity 4.1, find, or design, an assessment instrument that you could use to gather data to address this issue. Think in terms of project objectives, developmental level of potential participants, and how you will gather the information.

EVIDENCE-BASED SCHOOL COUNSELOR INTERVENTIONS

CACREP

Counselors at all levels engage in strategies that document their contributions to the educational mission within the academic, vocational, and personal/social domains. Numerous school counselor interventions are found in the literature, and several examples of school counselor influences are described below.

Academic Interventions

Four high schools in the Rockwood Missouri School District implemented a results-based project to increase graduation rates. The target population consisted of identifying high school juniors who were identified as not on track to graduate with their class. A letter was sent to the identified students' parents/guardians that documented the student's credits along with suggestions for credit recovery. Throughout the year the counselors met individually with the struggling students to review credits, progress toward credit recovery, and regularly contacted parents/guardians with updates on their child's progress. As a result of this intervention the graduation rate increased from 90 percent to 95 percent (Sevier, 2010), which concretely revealed school counselors' ability to collaborate with others to address and positively influence an identified outcome.

In another study school counseling portfolios were developed for elementary school students to demonstrate proficiency in competencies addressed through classroom guidance lessons (Curry & Lambie, 2007). The PTA provided folders in which each student placed materials with various activities that addressed student standards. Materials placed in the folder included personal academic goals and student identified steps to reach those goals. Drawings and written summaries about a career of interest, and activities from other group guidance lessons were additional artifacts placed in the folder. The end result of this project concretely demonstrated student growth in reaching identified standards (Curry & Lambie, 2007).

Kayler and Sherman (2009) discussed the results of a psychoeducational study skills group provided to ninth-grade students at risk for academic success. The purposes of this group were to improve academic skills, and to form long-lasting relationships with these students and their families. Although the results of this program revealed no difference in students' GPA as a result of the intervention, students did report using more study skills by the end of the program, and an improved relationship between the school counselor, parents, and students. Although a desired outcome of a higher GPA did not occur in this intervention, the counselors were able to analyze the program and procedures, and made revisions to the interventions to address and increase students' GPA the following year.

Career Interventions

In a study aimed at improving the occupational self-efficacy of female adolescents, school counselors implemented and evaluated the influence of a nontraditional career fair in determining career choices. Students completed the *Career Attitudes Scale* prior to the career fair and then again at the end of the fair. The results of this study revealed that occupational self-efficacy among female adolescents significantly increased (Kolodinsky et al., 2006).

In another study, career self-efficacy was measured based on high school students' current career choice and responses on portions of the *Self-Directed Search,* a career interest inventory by Holland. This study demonstrated that when school counselors provide practical learning experiences, self-efficacy in career selection increased (Tang, Pan, & Newmeyer, 2008).

Personal/Social Interventions

Barna and Brott (2011) investigated elementary school counselors' perceptions of the extent to which their personal/social development interventions supported academic growth. In their study, the participants implemented personal/social standards at a "slightly higher" rate than academic standards. This led to the conclusion that elementary school counselors perceived no difference in targeting academic or personal/social standards to support academic achievement. Other outcome data support this conclusion.

A group counseling format was used to examine the impact of a group intervention on social development, academic growth, and learning (Steen, 2011). Fifth-grade students recommended by their teachers were placed in either a group intervention or were waitlisted to participate in the group at a later date. In this study the students' GPAs were calculated in language arts and math, and the Learning Behaviors Scale and Students' Social Skills Scale were given to both teachers and participating students as pre- and post-tests. The results of this group intervention revealed a significantly higher GPA for the group participants compared with the wait-listed students. However, there were no significant differences between the two groups in math GPA, learning behavior, or social skills. Although these results are mixed and the anticipated results were not attained, this information contributes to the counseling field in that it provides valuable information to strengthen and revise plans for future groups (Steen, 2011).

As you are becoming more aware of dilemmas that the school counselor encounters, it is hoped that you are beginning to think in terms of some focus areas that you would like to tackle. With a classmate, complete conceptual application 4.3.

CACREP

CONCEPTUAL APPLICATION ACTIVITY 4.3

With a partner, review the school counselor literature to select a problem that is prevalent in schools today. Select an area you would like to address and analyze assessment strategies that are appropriate to address this issue. Develop measurable objectives and design an intervention to tackle this issue. Be sure to identify assessment instruments and measurable outcomes. Discuss your project with those of your classmates.

RESEARCH AND ASSESSMENT RESOURCES

Each of the examples described above provides evidence as to how school counselor interventions and data analysis contribute to the academic mission and program/strategy effectiveness. Additional resources available to support evidence-based counseling are listed below.

School Counseling Analysis and Leadership and Evaluation (SCALE)	The SCALE research center is available through the American School Counselor Association. SCALE disseminates research conducted by school counselors that demonstrates improved school counseling practice. ASCA members are able to access this site at: http://scale.schoolcounselor.org/content. asp?pl=657&contentid=657
School Counseling Outcome Research and Evaluation Center (CSCORE)	CSCORE at the University of Massachusetts at Amherst (http://www .umass.edu/schoolcounseling/our-services.php) assists school counselors in such areas as professional development, research opportunities, and program evaluation.
The Education Trust National Center for Transforming School Counseling	The Education Trust is a network of individuals and institutions committed to helping school counselors promote success for all students, particularly those who have been historically underserved. This resource is available at http://www.edtrust.org/dc/tsc
The What Works Clearinghouse	This resource is established by the Department of Education (http:// ies.ed.gov/ncee/wwc/default.aspx) in which evidence-based studies such as reducing drop-out rates, improving social/emotional behaviors, and peer assisted learning strategies are found.
The Substance Abuse and Mental Health Services Administration (SAMHSA)	This government-funded clearinghouse provides publications, data, and resources surrounding prevention, treatment, and behavioral health. This resource is available at http://www.samhsa.gov/index .aspx

CONCEPTUAL APPLICATION ACTIVITY 4.4

Check out the resources listed above and choose a research area to investigate. Discuss what you have learned with your classmates.

Demonstrating how well tasks are performed is the foremost consideration whenever engaging in a project, intervention, or program. Although this may seem to be an intimidating responsibility, it will become a consistent part of your day when these tasks are conducted on a regular basis. It is not enough to continually engage in program assessment and repeated self-assessment. Awareness of professional competencies keeps you informed about current trends and areas in which additional training is necessary. An annual evaluation by an administrator or a designated individual occurs using a variety of procedures. Some of these evaluations are based on sound strategies that correlate with a mutually determined job description; however, some counselors lament that their assessment is based on an instrument that is more reflective of a teacher's role than that of the school counselor. In these cases, the school counselor has a responsibility to collaborate with decision-makers to create an assessment instrument based on a mutually agreed-upon job description. Examples of evaluations based on job descriptions are below.

PROFESSIONAL SCHOOL COUNSELOR COMPETENCIES AND EVALUATION

The school counselor is involved in numerous tasks that form a basis for supervisor evaluations, self-evaluation, and feedback from stakeholders. A comprehensive, inclusive evaluation based upon mutually agreed-upon tasks and goals takes into account the multiple facets of the school counselor's job. Without this statement of responsibilities, stakeholders will be disappointed when expected tasks are not undertaken or completed, and professional evaluations will be a product of stakeholder assumptions of what the school counselor should be doing. The *ASCA School Counselor Competencies* specifies the necessary knowledge, abilities, skills, and attitudes school counselors at all grade levels need to address what are integral to the themes, foundations, accountability, management, and delivery system of the ASCA National Model. These competencies can be used as an evaluation and/or self-assessment. Members can access these competencies at: http://www.schoolcounselor.org/content.asp?pl=325&sl=133&contentid=133

A template of an evaluation instrument is in Table 4.3.

Table 4.3   School Counselor Evaluation Template Adapted From the ASCA School Counselor Competencies

LEADERSHIP	Needs Improvement	Satisfactory	Exceeds Expectations
Supports academic achievement and student development			
Advances effective delivery of CDSC program			
Promotes professional identity			
Overcomes challenges of role inconsistency			
ADVOCACY			
Student Empowerment. Acts with students to facilitate the identification of external barriers and development of self-advocacy skills, strategies, and resources in response to those barriers			
Student Advocacy. Acts on behalf of students to assess the need for direct intervention within the system on behalf of the student, identifying allies and carrying out a plan of action			
School/community Collaboration. Acts on behalf of students in which the school counselor and community collaborate to address a problem and devise an advocacy plan.			
Systems Advocacy. Acts on behalf of students by identifying systemic problem, gaining information and insight from those who are most affected and implementing advocacy at systems level.			
Public Information. Acts on behalf of students in collaboration between the school counselor and community in efforts to alert the public to macro-level issues regarding human dignity.			
Social/Political Advocacy. Acts on behalf of students in recognizing when student problems must be addressed at a policy or legislative level and advocating for change within those areas.			
COLLABORATION			
Interprofessional. Collaborates with other helping professionals			

LEADERSHIP	Needs Improvement	Satisfactory	Exceeds Expectations
Youth-centered collaboration. Views youth as experts who share responsibility and accountability for results			
Parent-centered collaboration. Views parents/guardians as experts whose engagement and well-being influence and determine their child's well-being			
Family-centered collaboration. Views family systems as partners whose engagement influences and determines the well-being of children, parents, and grandparents, as well as the future of the family			
Intra-organizational collaboration. Collaborates with people in the same school such as secretaries, custodians, cafeteria workers, bus drivers, and so on			
Inter-organizational collaboration. Works with community organizations such as social service agencies, faith-based institutions, and so on			
Community collaboration. Works with legitimate stakeholders within the school community.			
SYSTEMIC CHANGE			
Identifies systemic barriers to student achievement			
Proactive efforts with students, parents, teachers, administrators, and the community to remove systemic barriers and to promote systemic change			
FOUNDATION			
Develop and reassess belief statements			
Develop and reassess a vision statement			
Develop and reassess a mission statement			
Develop and reassess program goals			
Identification of student competencies based on ASCA, state, and school district competencies			
Maintenance of ethical standards and adherence to legal standards			

(Continued)

Table 4.3 (Continued)

LEADERSHIP	Needs Improvement	Satisfactory	Exceeds Expectations
MANAGEMENT			
Self-assessment of school counselor competencies			
Self-assessment of school counseling program			
Assessment of direct student services			
Assessment of indirect student services			
Development of Annual Agreements			
Development of an advisory council			
Review of the school's data			
Use of data to monitor student progress			
Collect and analyze process data			
Collect and analyze perception data			
Collect and analyze outcome data			
Development of Action Plans			
Development of Lesson Plans that include identified competencies			
Creation of Annual Calendar			
Creation of Weekly Calendar			
DELIVERY SYSTEM			
Delivers the school counseling curriculum			
Provides Individual Student Planning			
Provides individual counseling			
Conducts small group counseling			
Provide support and assistance to students in crisis			
Engages in referrals			
Provides consultation			
Collaborates with others			
ACCOUNTABILITY			
Analysis of data to make decisions about student needs and school/community trends			
Analysis of school data profile to assess program progress and impact			

LEADERSHIP	Needs Improvement	Satisfactory	Exceeds Expectations
Analysis of use-of-time to determine where time is spent			
Analysis of curriculum results			
Analysis of small-group results			
Analysis of closing-the-gap results			
Presentation of results to stakeholders			
Self-analysis of knowledge, abilities, skills, and attitudes			
Assessment of school counseling program			
Review of program goals			

Source: Adapted from: American School Counselor Association (2012). *ASCA National Model: A framework for school counseling programs* (3rd ed.). Alexandria, VA: Author.

Supplementary School Counselor Evaluations

Several school districts and states have actively created an evaluation model to serve as an inclusive assessment of school counselor performance. As a part of the federal Race to the Top funds that are available to states for the purpose of improving education and learning, the state of Tennessee developed several assessment procedures from which school districts can choose. The TEAM Model School Services Personnel Rubric is one of the more widely used tools to evaluate school counselors in Delivery of Services, Environment, and Planning of Services domains. Identified indicators are specified in each domain.

Delivery of Service	Planning of Services
Standards and Objectives	Scope of Work
Motivating Students	Analysis of Work Products
Delivery of Professional Services	Evaluation of Services or Programs
Service Structure and Pacing	
Activities and Materials	**Environment**
Communication	Expectations
Consultation	Managing Student Behavior
Developing Educational Plans for Students	Environment
Professional Content Knowledge	Respectful Culture
Knowledge of Students	
Organization of Services	
Problem Solving	

The Delivery of Services indicators include program objectives and standards, communication, consultation, and professional knowledge. The Environment indicators include managing student behavior, establishing a respectful culture, and meeting community expectations. The Planning of Services indicators are analysis of work products and an evaluation of services and/or programs. The TEAM rubric guidelines specify that the school counselor is to receive multiple observations and engage in conversations with the evaluator in which the counseling role is discussed and evidence in the form of a portfolio or artifacts is presented. Artifacts used to demonstrate work effectiveness include such items as the school counseling website, with program brochures, interest inventories, documentation of individual and group counseling, planning calendars, consultation logs, newsletter, evaluations, programs conducted, intervention plans, licenses and certificates, participation in professional development, and/or self-assessment.

The TEAM evaluation is a positive shift away from the use of a teacher's evaluation to one in which the school counseling professional is evaluated from a rubric based on accepted practices. When this form is used as intended, one of the benefits is that the evaluator and school counselor are able to have an honest discussion of the activities that the school counselor performs. During these conversations, the school counselor has an opportunity to educate the administrator about his/her training, education, and the benefits of a CDSC program.

The School Counseling Program Component Scale (SCPCS) is another instrument that was designed concurrently with the ASCA National Model to evaluate school counselor perceptions of the Model components most essential to their training (Hatch & Chen-Hayes, 2008). The content of the instrument was derived from an extensive review of the literature regarding the roles and subsequent functions of professional school counselors in CDSC school counseling programs, and information gathered from focus groups and discussions with professional leadership at state and national levels. The scale contains 18 items where respondents use a 5-point Likert scale to rate their subjective beliefs about the importance of various ASCA National Model elements.

The *School Counselor Activity Rating Scale* (SCARS) was developed for the purpose of processing data on activities of school counselor (Scarborough, 2005). The SCARS contains a 50-item verbal frequency scale to measure school counselors' activities in two dimensions: the frequency with which school counselors actually perform activities, and the frequency with which they would prefer to perform activities in five areas: counseling, consulting, curriculum, coordination, and other activities (Scarborough, 2005). Some items on this scale reflect school counselor activities that are congruent with those of the ASCA National Model, whereas other activities are those that school counselors commonly perform but are more reflective of a traditional school counseling program.

An annual review of the school counseling program and personnel supports strategies and duties that are effective and those that are not as successful. Furthermore, as stated by Cobia and Henderson (2006), a needs assessment is an additional instrument that functions as an aid for program improvement and professional direction.

NEEDS ASSESSMENTS

Needs assessments reflect a picture of the discrepancies between what is currently available in the school and what is desirable (Gysbers & Henderson, 2012), or the gap between what currently exists and what ideally should exist. Needs assessments do not have to be costly and do not have to be complex. Data may be collected from numerous stakeholders such as students, parents/guardians, administrators, teachers, community members, and other educational personnel. Each of these groups has different needs and all are important for smooth program functioning. From the results of the needs assessment the school counselor is able to plan program content and the best method for delivering content.

The needs assessment serves three purposes (Palacios, 2003):

- Determining the purpose of the inventory
- Identifying the scope of the assessment
- Deciding what to assess

The scope of the assessment requires looking at issues such as the target population, individuals to administer the instrument, complexity, and timelines (Palacios, 2003). Ethnicity, reading level, and language difficulties play a role in instrument design.

Additional questions to consider in implementing needs assessments include, "Who will have access to the data?" "Who will assess the data?" and "Should the assessments be given individually or in groups?" Finally, the format the assessment is to take will contribute to the types of information that is gathered.

The needs assessment can take the form of quantitative data gathered from the school report card or test scores, multiple choice questions, sentence completion, or choosing the top five needs out of a list of items. Additional methods for designing the needs assessment include program competency items, or item selection based on observation or feedback from others. Reporting results in an organized method assists stakeholders in understanding and supporting the establishment of a solid program (Palacios, 2003). Figure 4.9 is an example of a needs assessment.

Figure 4.9 Example of a Student Needs Assessment

Instructions: Circle your grade: 9   10   11   12

Circle your gender: Female   Male

Check all items below that concern you.

CONCERNS	CHECK
Getting along with friends or others	
Fear of making mistakes	
Receiving one or more failing grades	
Coping with change/new situations	
Difficulty controlling anger	
Having a problem with alcohol or drugs	
Dealing with divorce or separation of parents	
Struggling with loss of a loved one	
Dealing with bullying/harassment	
Teenage pregnancy	
Coping with stress	
Hurting/cutting oneself	
Thinking/talking about suicide	
Feeling sad or depressed most of the time	
Dropping out of school	
Coping with eating disorders	
Controlling test anxiety	
Not getting along with teachers	
Coping with family issues	
Feeling unsafe at school	

List other concerns you have:

_____

_____

CONCEPTUAL APPLICATION ACTIVITY 4.5

1. Collaborate with a classmate to design a needs assessment. What area of concern will you investigate and at what grade level?

2. Determine the resources you have to support your method of study. How much time do you have? Who can help collect and compile results? What method will you use to deliver the survey?

3. Reflect on how you designed a needs assessment. What more do you need to learn about designing and implementing surveys? How can you use them effectively in school counseling?

Technology has increased counselors' ability to design needs assessments and to collect, analyze, and share data much more easily than counselors were able to do before the proliferation of technology and associated computer programs. Computers also allow students to complete testing with instantaneous feedback.

THE USE OF TECHNOLOGY IN ASSESSMENT

Software has enabled school counselors to be more organized by allowing for scheduling, keeping records, tracking students' progress, and eliminating the need to store paper files. However, despite the benefits of technology there are also negative consequences. For instance, with this media there are concerns surrounding confidentiality, online assessments with questionable psychometric properties, limited Internet access due to remote locations or lack of financial resources, and dehumanizing the testing process (Sampson, 2000).

With the availability of test instruments available on the Internet, school counselors have a responsibility to be aware of test descriptions and psychometric properties. Test information is available through test publisher links. For instance, the Buros Center for Testing provides reviews on tests. This link may be accessed at http://buros.org/. From here, you can click on the "test reviews & information" located on the menu bar and enter either the name of a particular test, or the category of a topic such as "achievement," from which a listing of various tests that assess this topic are provided.

CONCEPTUAL APPLICATION ACTIVITY 4.6

Go to the Buros website and locate a testing instrument that could be used in a school setting. Read the reviews and summarize your findings to your peers.

Technologies also provide counselors with the opportunity to conduct research and easily compute statistics without having to rely on the complex formulas taught in statistics classes. For instance, Survey Monkey at http://www.survey monkey.com/ and Counseling Surveys www.counselingsurveys.org are free online survey software and questionnaire tools that are used to design a survey from templates that are provided, gather information, and analyze the survey.

An excellent website that is devoted specifically to counselor literacy and use is available at http://schoolcounselor.com/newsletter/newsletter140.htm. This website assists in learning more about technology problems, particularly as they relate to school counselors.

Counselors often complain about the difficulty of tracking the myriad tasks they perform each day. The *Time Elapsed Analysis & Reporting System* (T.E.A.R.S.) is a program that calculates activities, time spent in these tasks, and offers a summary to share with stakeholders. This system can be accessed at http://www.schoolcoun selor.com/tears/

Finally, using graphs to communicate results to stakeholders is an essential step to demonstrate intervention or program effectiveness. For those who have difficulty creating these graphs, the National Center for Education Statistics (http://nces.ed.gov/) has a Kids' zone link that is located under the Data & Tools menu. Users are able to create simple graphs in various formats.

CONCLUSION

School counselors are no longer able to rest on their laurels without analyzing, documenting, and sharing how the school counseling program supports the educational mission. Accountability in school counseling is not a new issue; demands for data-driven results have been expressed for many decades. Action research models are designed for school counselors to better understand school counseling interventions. Comparative research designs such as experimental, single-subject, and retrospective procedures are additional methods for school counselors to consider in showing how the school counselor contributes to the school mission.

In addition to assessing program interventions, an evaluation of school counselor performance as leaders of a comprehensive, developmental school counseling program is essential. The *ASCA School Counselor Competencies* is one evaluative assessment that could be used in evaluating school counselors, or state designed instruments that match the focus of the school counseling trends within that state may be helpful tools. Needs assessments are another resource for determining program content and delivery. Finally, technology has facilitated assessment and has made the task easier, but school counselors are responsible for being aware of some of the negative consequences of using electronic devices.

REFERENCES

Aubrey, R. F. (1985). A counseling perspective on the recent educational reform reports. *The School Counselor,33,* 91–99

Baker, S. B. (2012, December). A new view of evidence-based practice. *Counseling Today.* Alexandria, VA: American Counselor Association

Barna, J. S., & Brott, P. E. (2011). How important is personal/social development to academic achievement? The elementary school counselor's perspective. *Professional School Counseling, 14,* 242–249.

Borders, L. D., & Drury, S. M. (1992). Comprehensive school counseling programs: A review for policymakers and practitioners. *Journal of Counseling & Development, 70,* 487–498.

Cobia, D. C., & Henderson, D. A. (2006). *Developing an effective and accountable school counseling program.* Upper Saddle River, NJ: Prentice-Hall.

Curry, J., & Lambie, G. W. (2007). Enhancing school counselor accountability: The large group guidance portfolio. *Professional School Counseling, 11,* 145–148.

Dahir, C. A., & Stone, C. B. (2003). Accountability: A M.E.A.S.U.R.E. of the impact school counselors have on student achievement. *Professional School Counseling, 6,* 214–221.

Dahir, C. A., & Stone, C. B. (2009). School counselor accountability: The path to social justice and systemic change. *Journal of Counseling & Development, 87,* 12–20.

Duffy, M., Giordano, V. A., Farrell, J. B., Paneque, O. M., & Crump, G. B. (2008). No Child Left Behind: Values and research issues in high-stakes assessment. *Counseling and Values, 53,* 53–66.

Ebel, R. L. (1965). *Measuring educational achievement.* Oxford, England: Prentice-Hall.

Gysbers, N. C. (2004). Comprehensive guidance and counseling programs: The evolution of accountability. *Professional School Counseling, 8,* 1–14.

Gysbers, N. C., & Henderson, P. (2012). *Developing & managing your school guidance & counseling program* (5th ed.). Alexandria, VA: ACA.

Hatch, T., & Chen-Hayes, S. F. (2008). School counselor beliefs about ASCA national model school counseling program components using the SCPCS. *Professional School Counseling, 12,* 34–42.

Hays, D. (2012). *Assessment in counseling* (5th ed.). Alexandria, VA: ACA.

Holcomb-McCoy, C. (2007). *School counseling to close the achievement gap: A social-justice framework for success.* Thousand Oaks, CA: Corwin.

Kayler, H., & Sherman, J. (2009). At-risk ninth-grade students: A psychoeducational group approach to increase study skills and grade point averages. *Professional School Counseling, 12,* 434–439.

Kolodinsky, P., Schroder, V., Montopoli,G., McLean, S., Mangan, PA., & Pederson, W. (2006). The career fair as a vehicle for enhancing occupational self-efficacy. *Professional School Counseling, 10,* 161–167.

McMillan, J. H. (1996). *Educational research: Fundamentals for the consumer* (2nd ed.). New York, NY: Harper Collins.

Mills, G. E. (2000*). Action research: A guide for the teacher researcher.* Columbus, OH: Prentice Hall.

Palacios, K. N. (2003). *Developing a comprehensive needs assessment model for implementation in continuing education.* (Master's thesis, Southwest Texas State University.) Retrieved from digital.library.txstate.edu/handle/10877/3743

Salkind, N. J. (2000). *Exploring research* (4th ed.). Upper Saddle River, NJ: Prentice Hall.

Sampson, J. P. (2000). Using the internet to enhance testing in counseling. *Journal of Counseling & Development, 78,* 348–356.

Scarborough, J. L. (2005). The school counselor activity rating scale: An instrument for gathering process data. *Professional School Counseling, 8*(3), 274–283.

Sevier, S. F. (2010, Nov./Dec.). The ultimate transformers. *ASCA School Counselor,* pp. 38–41. Alexandria, VA: ASCA.

Sink, C. A. (2009). School counselors as accountability leaders: Another call for action. *Professional School Counseling, 13,* 68–74.

Steen, S. (2011). Academic and personal development through group work: An exploratory study. *The Journal for Specialists in Group Work, 36,* 129–143. doi: 10.1080/01933922.2011.562747

Stone, C. & Dahir, C. (2003). *School counselor accountability: A MEASURE of student success.* Upper Saddle River, NJ: Pearson.

Tang, M., Pan, W., & Newmeyer, M. D. (2008). Factors influencing high school students' career aspirations. *Professional School Counseling, 11,* 285–295.

Webb, L. D., & Brigman, G. A. (2006). Student success skills: Tools and strategies for improved academic and social outcomes. *Professional School Counseling, 10,* 112–120.

Whiston, S. C. (2000). *Principles and applications of assessment in counseling.* Belmont, CA: Wadsworth.

SECTION II

COUNSELING, INTERVENTION, AND PREVENTION

Chapter 5

THE SCHOOL COUNSELOR AS A GROUP LEADER AND FACILITATOR

TARA JUNGERSEN & CAROLYN BERGER

 CACREP Outline

COUNSELING, PREVENTION, AND INTERVENTION

C. *Knowledge*

    5. Understands group dynamics—including counseling, psycho-educational, task, and peer helping groups—and the facilitation of teams to enable students to overcome barriers and impediments to learning.

COLLABORATION AND CONSULTATION

M. *Knowledge*

    2. Knows strategies to promote, develop, and enhance effective teamwork within the school and the larger community.

    3. Knows how to build effective working teams of school staff, parents, and community members to promote the academic, career, and personal/social development of students.

> *Group counseling is an efficient and effective way to meet students' developmental and situational needs. Group counseling makes it possible for students to achieve healthier academic and personal adjustment in a rapidly changing culture. Groups are an integral part of a comprehensive school counseling program and should be included and supported by every educational institution. ASCA Position Statement (2008, para. 4).*

In this chapter we discuss group counseling principles and techniques that are particularly useful for school counselors. Although you probably are taking a designated course within your school counselor training program that focuses exclusively on group dynamics, this chapter is specifically devoted to an overview of groups in schools and the types of groups commonly found in the school environment. Next, we review leadership strategies for school counselors who facilitate groups at the elementary, middle, and high school levels. Finally, we consider legal, ethical, and multicultural issues in relation to groups in schools, and discuss the roles school counselors occupy in developing teamwork and consultations among school personnel.

Like many specialized work environments, schools have a unique culture in which a variety of formal and informal groups operate for a myriad of purposes. Groups can form inside or outside the classroom. They can include students, teachers, staff, administration, parents, and outside stakeholders. Groups can be fairly homogenous in nature, but more often within the school system they involve a heterogeneous mixture of people, personalities, and purposes.

DEFINITIONS OF GROUP

Many definitions of 'group' and 'group work' exist to promote a deeper understanding of the dynamics and processes involved. The Association for Specialists in Group Work (ASGW, 2000) defines group work as:

A broad professional practice involving the application of knowledge and skill in group facilitation to assist an interdependent collection of people to reach their mutual goals, which may be intrapersonal, interpersonal, or work related. The goals of the group may include the accomplishment of tasks related to work, education, personal development, personal and interpersonal problem solving, or remediation of mental and emotional disorders (pp. 329–330).

Gladding (2012) defines a group as "a collection of two or more individuals who meet face-to-face or virtually in an interactive, interdependent way, with the awareness that each belongs to the group and for the purpose of achieving mutually agreed-on goals" (p. 3). Erford's (2010) definition uses components that are specific to the school environment. These components include:

- Family, Educational Rights and Privacy Act (FERPA) compliant ethical and legal group leader interactions

- The scope and purpose of the group work promote the academic and career goals of the students
- The promotion of learning through intentional group-based interactions

Regardless of the setting in which a group occurs, groups help people learn about themselves (Kottler, 1994).

CONCEPTUAL APPLICATION ACTIVITY 5.1

Think about a group in which you were a member. What were some of your feelings about being part of this group? What were some of the dynamics that occurred in the group that made this a positive or negative experience?

HISTORY OF GROUPS IN SCHOOLS

The history of counseling group development within the school system parallels the development of the counseling profession as a whole. Counseling groups in schools can be traced back to the early 1900s, where guidance classes were conducted to assist with career planning and social adjustment (Paisley & Borders, 1995). The founder of the American Group Psychotherapy Association (AGPA), S. R. Slavson, utilized activity groups for children and adolescents, which facilitated this modality in schools (Erford, 2010).

School counselors utilize groups to meet the increasing needs of vocational aptitude and intelligence assessment (Dahir & Stone, 2012; Paisley & Borders, 1995). Currently, the American School Counseling Association (ASCA) in the *ASCA National Model* (2012) promotes the use of groups in its mission to foster equitable access delivered in a systematic fashion of a comprehensive school counseling program. Outside the school setting, the practice of group counseling has undergone several adaptations in response to outside demands (e.g., rapid and least costly treatments) (Yalom & Leszcz, 2005). Similarly, group work in the school must continue to adapt to meet the needs of students and schools alike.

CONCEPTUAL APPLICATION ACTIVITY 5.2

Interview a school counselor and discuss some of the obstacles and successes he/she has had in leading groups in schools. What were some of the strategies that were used for students to be released from classes to attend group?

GROUPWORK AND THE SCHOOL COUNSELOR

Group counseling is a required core counseling competency in every school counseling program accredited by the Council for the Accreditation of Counseling and Related Education Programs (CACREP, 2009). While 80% of a school counselor's time should be spent in direct student services, this time is divided between both individual and group modalities (ASCA, 2012). Group work provides both an effective and efficient method for reaching the most students within this prescribed time (Gladding, 2012; Pérusse, Goodnough, & Lee, 2009). Large groups are typically conducted with a whole classroom in which curriculum is provided to all students. Small groups are for students who need more in-depth counseling than is provided in the large group setting. Small groups are a good alternative to individual counseling because counselors can reach more students at once; however, there are, of course, times when individual counseling is necessary. This concept is referred to in the counseling literature as the *law of parsimony* (Dahir & Stone, 2012). All groups must support the academic mission of the school and must ultimately meet the needs of all students, not just a few (ASCA, 2012; Dahir & Stone, 2012).

Leadership Strategies

School counselors have a remarkable opportunity to be "change agents" in students' lives (Kulic, Horne, & Dagley, 2004, p. 149). It may come as no surprise that the more experienced and well trained a group leader is, the more effective the group will be (Kulic et al., 2004). However, as counselor training programs continue to focus on group leadership skills, the disparity between seasoned and novice group leaders will continue to shrink (Kulic et al., 2004).

School counselors need to understand both the populations with whom they are working as well as group dynamics. Understanding the population means that group topics and materials are developmentally appropriate for the particular group members. Materials that are either too advanced, uninteresting, or unchallenging may result in disengaged students. For example, a group discussion on test anxiety might yield less than interested students, whereas having the students design and act out a skit in which they are given a pop quiz or have to take a standardized test, so the students would enact behaviors and responses to test anxiety and perform behavioral and cognitive strategies to combat this stress. This action-based activity keeps the lesson interesting, as well as grounded in actual experiences. Additionally, counselor awareness of both the spoken and unspoken communications within the group can impact the success or failure of the group process.

PURPOSES OF GROUPS IN SCHOOLS

Groups in schools serve many growth-enhancing processes (Dahir & Stone, 2012) in the academic, career, and personal/social development of students (CACREP, 2009). Whether targeted or general, formal or informal, groups provide members opportunities to hone tolerance skills, build trust, and to grow both interpersonally and psychologically. School counselors must assist in the preparation of children and adolescents for the rapidly changing occupational workforce which they will enter (Gysbers & Henderson, 2012). School counselors also utilize their group facilitation skills with adults, such as families and school personnel.

Groups can serve the purpose of being proactive/developmental or reactive in nature, though these may overlap in actual practice (Dahir & Stone, 2012). Proactive or prevention groups focus on developmentally relevant issues that include age, gender, and maturity level. Reactive groups are more targeted at a specific issue or concern, and involve interventions that remediate behaviors, crises, and interpersonal problems (Erford, 2010; Gladding, 2012). All of these groups target students with identified concerns and needs (ASCA, 2012).

Prevention and Growth

School counselors utilize prevention groups to address common developmental issues affecting students, with the goal of maintaining or learning coping skills and preventing the development of problems (Gladding, 2012). These proactive groups are growth-oriented and address developmental milestones and social interactions that are expected in the course of a student's educational experience. Examples of prevention groups include bullying prevention, how to give and receive feedback, team-building, and controlling alcohol and drug use.

Intervention

Intervention groups are sometimes referred to as remediation groups, as they assist students who have impairments that affect their learning and development (Perusse et al., 2009). The purpose of intervention groups is to develop students' coping skills and to "empower students to regain control over their lives and engage (or reengage) in the learning process" (Perusse et al., 2009, p. 226). Examples of intervention group topics include coping with divorce, grief, anger management, military deployments, and natural disasters.

BOX 5.1 A NOTE ABOUT SCHOOL GROUPS AND TERMINOLOGY

The "Counseling Group" is a common type of group conducted in schools (Whiston & Quinby, 2009); however, before we explore these concepts, a word about terminology must be included.

Many school counselors are faced with concerns over use of the words "counseling" and "guidance" in their group work. Many school counselors have moved away from the use of the terms "guidance counseling" or "guidance group" which may represent simply the conveyance of information (Waldo, Kerne, & Kerne, 2007). Instead, the terms "counseling" or "counseling group" convey a more accurate picture of the professional standards, training, and practice of school counselors. However, school counselors may encounter resistance from parents or school personnel when a group is described as a "counseling group," due to the erroneous impression that these counseling groups somehow meet the criteria of a "psychotherapy group" (which is neither accurate nor appropriate in a school setting).

To navigate this terminology issue, we suggest that school counselors first become aware of the school climate and culture. Counselors must review school/district policies and consult with administration and other school counselors to discern the more commonly used terms and develop strategies to accurately describe the purpose of counseling groups. Additionally, school counselors may avoid use of these terms altogether, instead focusing on group topics and content for the most accurate description of the type of group being conducted.

For the purposes of this section, we will utilize the term "counseling group" to describe small group activities and reserve the term "classroom guidance' to describe formal classroom guidance.

TYPES OF GROUPS IN SCHOOLS

The school setting offers countless opportunities for successful group outcomes. Counseling groups, psychoeducational groups, task groups, and others that are led in the school are discussed in the following sections.

Counseling Groups

Counseling groups focus on a situational issue, with the goal of changing or resolving each person's behavior, development, or cognition (Gladding, 2012). Counseling groups are therapeutic by nature, as group members vicariously learn from their peers. Within these groups, students discover what they have in common and what distinguishes them from their peers (Perusse et al., 2009; Yalom & Leszcz, 2005). As students apply this information to themselves, they begin to process the experience, which leads to self-disclosure and eventual growth and development (Perusse et al., 2009). While counseling groups are therapeutic in nature, the ultimate goal of these groups is to help students overcome emotional barriers to achievement. Sample topics of counseling groups include anxiety, stress, and anger management.

The crisis group is one specialized type of counseling group. While a specific protocol for conducting crisis groups related to disasters, school crises, and other trauma-causing events is beyond the scope of this chapter, school counselors are trained to facilitate groups that allow for mutual healing and the development of resilience during school crises (Echterling, Presbury, & McKee, 2005).

An anger management group is one example of a counseling group. This group focuses on helpful and unhelpful ways of dealing with anger. One possible group activity is called "Don't Pop Your Balloon." Students begin by talking about a recent event that made them angry, but where they were able to control their anger. Each student is then given a balloon and asked to blow up the balloon (without tying it closed) to the size that represented his or her highest level of anger during that event. Students' balloons will be of different sizes (e.g., lemon, grapefruit, cantaloupe-sized) depending on the event.

The school counselor then asks students to think about what they did during and/or after the event that helped them keep their anger under control. As the students describe these anger reduction techniques, they are asked to let some of the air out of their balloons to represent the effect of these coping mechanisms. Next, rather than have the students burst their balloons, the school counselor can facilitate a discussion about what would have happened if they had allowed their anger to take control instead. Students then discuss what would happen to their balloon as a consequence of uncontrolled anger.

Psychoeducational Groups

Psychoeducational groups provide didactic interactions to disseminate information (Perusse et al., 2009). Therefore, the purpose of these groups is to provide information on a particular topic (e.g., managing test anxiety, how to talk to your child about sex). Regardless of a particular group's type, purpose, or makeup, most groups contain this psychoeducational component.

Due to its primary objective of disseminating information, these groups may be comprised of a large number of members, thus requiring the school counselor to be aware of any group members who may not receive adequate time to speak or raise issues (Gladding, 2012). Typically, a psychoeducational group involves the dissemination of written materials. The school counselor should ensure that resources and his/her contact information are included in these materials to provide appropriate follow-up.

A social skills group is an example of a psychoeducational group. The "Put Your Listening Ears On" activity teaches students basic listening concepts through modeling instruction of key skills. In this group, the school counselor shows a video where a student is being a good versus a bad listener, and processes what the students in the group notice about each example. Then, the counselor can identify the skill concepts of being a good listener. For example: 1. Look at the person who is speaking, 2. Use non-verbals to show you are listening, 3. Think about what the person is saying, 4. Answer questions the speaker asks you, and 5. Ask questions if you need more information (Weltmann-Begun, 1996).

CONCEPTUAL APPLICATION ACTIVITY 5.3

Look at the ASCA Student Competencies in the academic, career, and personal/social domains. Select those competencies that could be cross-walked with the competencies that are identified within the curriculum that could be addressed through team-teaching in a psychoeducational group.

Task Groups

Task groups focus on the accomplishment of a preset task or work product, and involve all group members toward the accomplishment of this goal (ASGW, 2012; Gladding, 2012). Within schools, task groups may take the form of committee work (e.g., the students finishing their career/college portfolio or training peer mediators) or may be larger in scope (e.g., building a new "peace garden" for the school in which students and adults plant flowers and outdoor foliage to create a tranquil environment). Task groups may require the school counselor to take on an organizational, management, or consultative role (ASGW, 2012).

Other Groups

The list of the myriad ways in which groups form both formally and informally within the school environment is limitless. School counselors find themselves interacting with types of groups that may not fit precisely in one of the above categories. There may be groups that are a combination of counseling groups and psychoeducational groups. In addition to groups directed primarily at students, school counselors engage parents, guardians, families, and school personnel in their work, which often includes collaboration of a group nature. Groups occur during the course of administrative and consultative functions such as during parent-teacher conferences, or Individualized Education Program Plan (IEP) meetings. School counselors may not be in charge of a specific group such as an IEP meeting; however, counselors do play a key role in advocating for student needs.

School counselors often facilitate teams, which may require clear accountability of each member and result in strong emotional connectivity between members (Gladding, 2012). These teams may be comprised of students, school staff, parents, and/or community members as they work toward a common goal (e.g., Response to Intervention, Positive Behavior Support teams). Other groups include different forms of committee work (e.g., curriculum committee), or groups involving stakeholders (e.g., a law enforcement agency providing a drug prevention program within the school).

Groups go through a progression of phases with the type of group dictating the length and breadth of each stage. For instance, task group members may be focusing more on the product than forming lasting relationships and developing self-awareness. A review of these group stages is below.

STAGES OF GROUP WORK

Regardless of their purposes and goals, groups proceed through common stages. Tuckman and Jensen (1977) describe these group stages as Forming, Storming, Norming, Performing, and Adjourning. The effective school group facilitator recognizes how the particular group stage corresponds with expected group dynamics and manages the group accordingly.

Forming

During the forming stage, the establishment of group norms is the primary task that the group must accomplish. Group norms are the spoken and unspoken rules by which members abide. During this stage, it is critical that the school group facilitator model the behaviors that are expected throughout the group. For example, beginning and ending on time, facilitating who talks when and for how long, encouraging positive interchange among group members (Gladding, 2012), and advising students that they are not to abuse the rules of the school (e.g., on-time attendance) or they will be excused from participation in the group (Perusse et al., 2009). See Student Activity 5.1 for an example of a strategy that can be used in the forming group stage.

STUDENT ACTIVITY 5.1. THINGS THAT ARE IMPORTANT TO ME

Objective: To identify valued items/people

Directions: Students are asked to select an object that represents something of value to them.

This introductory activity encourages discussion and promotes relationship building by asking group members to select one object from their wallet, purse, or backpack that has particular meaning. Each member is to share the importance of that item with the group. For instance, when this activity was introduced in a group, a sixth-grade student showed a picture of her dog that recently died. After she shared information about her dog and her special bond with her pet, another group member was able to disclose that her pet cat died a few weeks earlier. This activity served as a catalyst for forming a friendship that may not have occurred if the girls had not had been group members.

Storming

The storming stage occurs when conflict or disagreement arises during the group process, and offers an opportunity for transition. Negativism, rivalry, and high emotion may occur during this stage (Tuckman & Jensen, 1977).

During the storming stage, the school group facilitator carefully navigates any spoken or unspoken conflict in order to keep all members psychologically safe. The facilitator must expect and welcome the storm, and see it as a necessary step in an effective group process. Key facilitator skills in this area include a tolerance for discord, patience, and solid conflict resolution skills. The group leader intervenes when it becomes clear that the group members cannot handle the conflict themselves, but is careful not to intrude to the point where members do not have the opportunity to use their own conflict resolution skills.

The facilitator should allow a tolerable level of discord as members try out new behaviors and problem-solving skills because growth occurs as a result of dissonance (Yalom & Leszcz, 2005). For example, if a fifth-grade group member calls another fifth-grade group member "stupid" during the group, the school group facilitator should allow either the target of this remark or the group to respond to this negative outburst. When the counselor doesn't jump in to "rescue" the targeted student, this individual will have the opportunity to practice assertive communication and to reflect to the speaker the hurtful nature of his/her words. The facilitator has a responsibility to intervene if the exchanges become excessive or abusive, as vulnerable members need protection from harmful members. See Student Activity 5.2 as an example of a group activity that is appropriate in the storming stage for children whose parents are divorcing.

STUDENT ACTIVITY 5.2. FEELINGS COLLAGE

Objective: To identify feelings about parents' divorce

Materials: Magazines, large sheets of paper, scissors, and paste/glue

Directions: Students are asked to select and cut out pictures from magazines that best express their feelings about their parents' divorce. The pictures are arranged and glued onto the paper to make a collage and then are asked to write descriptive statements that describe the pictures. Group members discuss their collages.

Norming

Group norms are rules that govern how the group operates and are constructed by the group in order to ensure its predictability (Gladding, 2012). The norming stage of a group allows members to experience cohesiveness, as well as further differentiate their roles in the group.

During the norming stage, school counselors encourage empathy, support, and self-disclosure through the use of basic counseling skills. Additionally, the norming process allows the exploration of group members' values; therefore, the school counselor must be sensitive to cultural diversity issues during this stage. For example, if a sixth-grade group member's cultural norms are such that self-disclosure is discouraged, the school counselor may facilitate understanding that not every group member is required to speak, while helping the sixth-grader to explore how her lack of self-disclosure affects her relationships with peers and teachers. Student Activity 5.3 is an example of an activity that is appropriate at this group stage.

STUDENT ACTIVITY 5.3. MY ANIMAL, MYSELF

Objective: To identify one's own personality traits

Materials: Whiteboard or large paper, writing utensils, crayons, and drawing paper

Directions: Students are asked to think of animals that are either family pets, at the zoo, or animals they have read about. The group leader writes the names of animals identified by students on the board or paper. After students have finished naming animals, each member draws an animal he/she perceives to best represent him/her. Students are instructed to not disclose this picture to the group members. Next, group members guess the animal that he/she believes each member drew and reasons for this choice. Each member describes his/her personality traits that are representative of the animal and him/herself.

Performing

The performing stage is also called the working stage, as group members take action to achieve tasks and goals (Gladding, 2012). A successful group at this stage demonstrates trust among members, and members who feel included are more apt to take risks.

The most challenging interventions at this stage occur as a result of high cohesion and fluid communication. For example, if the school counselor plans a learning activity related to body-image and obesity that requires group members to draw a picture of their perceived and ideal body, the performing stage would allow group members to safely share and process the strong emotions this activity could evoke. Student Activity 5.4 can be used at this group stage.

STUDENT ACTIVITY 5.4. STRAW HOUSES

Objectives: To discuss the importance of planning projects and tasks

Materials: Straws, tape, scissors, paper clips, hole punches, stopwatch

Directions: Group members are asked to build a straw house that must be at least a foot tall using straws, tape, scissors, paper clips, and hole punches. Students are given 3 minutes to plan the house and 15 minutes to build the house. After houses are built, 3 other group members try to blow each house down within 20 seconds but are not allowed to touch the house or the surface it is on. The group leader leads a discussion asking the following questions:

Who had the best plan and implementation for the project?

Would you rather plan a project or jump right in with both feet?

Do you remember a time when you did not plan but should have?

Photo 5.1 Straw Tower Designed by Group Members

Adjourning

Tuckman and Jensen's (1977) final stage is adjourning or termination. During this stage, group members prepare to transition out of the group and undergo an assessment of goals that were achieved, as well as discussing the process of ending (Gladding, 2012).

The school counselor prepares group members for termination by setting clear boundaries about the duration and purpose of the group from the beginning, and throughout the duration of the group. Termination allows for processing of feelings about the experience and typically involves a formal ritual or activity that signifies that the group has come to an end (e.g., a certificate of completion or a booklet of collected written exercises completed during the group). See Student Activity 5.5 as an example of a termination activity.

STUDENT ACTIVITY 5.5. THREE COMPLIMENTS AND A WISH

Objective: To reinforce personal goals

Directions: The group leader asks each student to give group members 3 compliments and a wish. This activity is designed for members to acknowledge strengths each person has and a sense of direction for future life decisions. For example: "Jose, during the time we have spent in group together I have noticed that 1) you are thoughtful in our discussions; 2) you have an ability to relate to others; and 3) you are willing to take risks in sharing your thoughts. My wish for you is to be able to use these skills whenever you feel your parents misunderstand you."

Throughout these stages the school counselor builds consensus to foster collaboration and cooperation (ASCA, 2012). Part of this consensus building requires the group facilitator to effectively manage the exchange of verbal and non-verbal information between him/herself and the group, and between group members themselves. For example, when the facilitator notices that a group member is being ignored, he/she can prompt the other members to make eye contact with the student who is speaking and comment about how important it is when what we say matters to others around us.

The unique characteristics of each individual group member are considerations in monitoring the health and tone of the group. Certain issues can arise when differences of age, grade level, and developmental level are too dichotomous to allow for the group stages to progress. Erford (2010) describes a variety of roles that students may adopt throughout various stages of the group process. As students struggle for control, they may display hostility towards the leader or other group members, or they may withdraw as they resist the intimacy required in a small group setting. The facilitator's task throughout this process is to cultivate self-awareness of each group member, while avoiding being 'sucked in' to the conflict or to a group member's desire to remain invisible.

School counselors are also required to complete administrative and accountability tasks related to termination. Any process and measurable outcome evaluation data (i.e., pre-test/post-test) are to be collected, analyzed, and disseminated appropriately according to the school's requirements to enhance school counseling programs. Documentation should include a Small-Group Results Report, which contains data on the process, perceptions, and outcomes of the group (see *The ASCA National Model* for more information; ASCA, 2012) without revealing individual data.

STARTING A GROUP IN THE SCHOOL

There are several practical considerations involved in conducting groups in the schools. Prior to beginning the group, school counselors consider the following suggestions to provide a smooth group experience that will function optimally within the school's curriculum.

Preplanning and Organization of Groups

Effective school-based groups require planning and consideration of many practical issues. Initially, school counselors should devise an action plan template to help focus and organize the group intervention, and to provide documentation of the group content and intervention outcomes (ASCA, 2012). This action plan will detail the topics, target population, number of students (i.e., a large or small group), rationale, goals, and assessment plan for the course of the group (Geroski & Kraus, 2010). Effective groups have clear objectives and planned activities. Additionally, school counselors are aware of any program evaluation measures that schools require in order to collect and track data (e.g., number of students served, aggregate outcome results of group interventions).

School counselors are required to implement evidence and research-based practices (ASCA, 2012; CACREP, 2009). By targeting a problem and coupling it with a directed technique that has been shown to be effective, the school counselor can support his/her intervention plans within the larger school counseling curriculum.

CONCEPTUAL APPLICATION ACTIVITY 5.4

Find a research-based article about groups in schools. Read the article and discuss how this group was formed, the purposes of the group, the materials used, and how it was evaluated. Share your article with your classmates.

Additionally, school counselors apply counseling theory to group work. The *ASCA National Model* (2012) describes the following theories school counselors understand in order achieve a basic level of competency: rational emotional behavior therapy, reality therapy, behavioral therapy, Adlerian, solution-focused brief counseling, person-centered counseling, and family systems. Regardless of the theoretical orientation, solution-focused group techniques are time-limited in scope as recommended by the ASCA *Ethical Standards for School Counselors* (2010).

The facilitator weighs practical considerations when planning a group, including chairs, desks, and floor space, if needed. Group space must be private, with few to no interruptions allowed. With regard to group session duration, a typical group for adolescents could range from 1–2 hours, whereas groups for children and pre-adolescents may last 20–45 minutes (Gladding, 2012). One of the more challenging aspects of conducting groups in schools is finding a time that will interfere the least with the overriding educational priorities. Perusse et al. (2009), note that some school counselors meet with resistance from administrators and teachers when a group occurs during a class meeting time. However, they also note that many students are excused from class for other educational adjuncts (i.e., student athletes excused from class in order to travel to an away volleyball game). A well-developed group plan (with clear rationale and goals) can emphasize the equally important benefits of school counseling interventions on the social/personal, career, and academic success of the students involved.

Oftentimes, administration limit when and how the school counselor pulls students from classes to attend group. This is a challenging hurdle to overcome and it often takes time to demonstrate to the administration that the group counseling intervention is just as crucial, if not more so, than having the student in the classroom. If teachers are aware of how acquiring skills in group may facilitate academic success, they will be more willing to dismiss students. When presented with this obstacle, creativity is necessary. Lunchtime is a viable alternative, but students do not like to miss socializing with their friends. Providing students with free pizza may eliminate this problem, but the question then becomes financing this "free" lunch. Furthermore, lunch periods are often fairly short, and running a group in 25 minutes or less may be acceptable for elementary-age students but is challenging for adolescent-age students. A few suggestions here would be to request if the students can leave class a little early to get to the lunch group and then be released a little late to return to class. Funding options for lunches can be found by advocating for this need at a Parent Teacher Association meeting (sometimes these parent groups have a small fund from which you can request monies), requesting local businesses to donate, or requesting that the funds be pulled from the school counseling budget (if you are fortunate enough to have one).

Administrators may also allow students to be pulled from electives (e.g., physical education, art, music, etc.). Again, students may not like this option because these classes are often those to which the student most relates, so the school counselor may risk losing student participants. Another option could be for the group to rotate the meeting time so students do not miss more than 45 minutes of any one subject. Regardless of the time chosen for the group, it is imperative that the school counselor collect data on the students' success in the group so in the future the administration and teachers will see the value of leading the group, and how the group relates to academic success even if class time is interrupted.

When the group's time is set according to the administration's requirements, the school counselor communicates with the teachers whose classes will be missed by the students in the group. Sometimes the student cannot miss a particular class period—for example, if the student has to take a test or do a group presentation. At this point, excusing the student from the group is the most respectful thing to do in order to accommodate the teacher's class schedule, or arrangements can be made with the teacher and the student to reschedule the test. It is courteous to inform teachers in advance so they have an opportunity to prepare for the student's absence; this prevents many problems from arising in the future.

It is also imperative that school counselors communicate with the group members about their class absences as a result of the group meetings. Students need to understand that it is their responsibility to make up any work missed in a timely manner. While the group is an excuse for missing a portion of class, it is not an excuse for the student to hand in the homework late. Teachers need to know that school counselors are not allowing the student to use the group to get out of classwork.

Photo 5.2 Students in a Counseling Group

Source: © Comstock Images/ThinkStock.com

Promotion of the Group

After the group plan is determined, school counselors utilize various methods to appropriately communicate and promote group activities that clearly describe the purpose and target of the group. If the school counselor decides to send an e-mail to teachers to solicit students for a Study Skills Group for high school freshmen, he/she may consider wording the e-mail such that the teacher can quickly and easily forward it on as written (targeted to ninth-graders) to his/her student e-mail list. Such gestures save the teacher valuable time, yet include him/her in the process.

Additionally, electronic solicitation of group members can occur through social media, but only when appropriate security and confidentiality measures are put in place. For example, on the school counselor's school-supported Facebook page, he/she may place an announcement regarding an upcoming Divorce Support Group, along with instructions on how to contact him/her for more information. However, the Facebook page settings must prevent anyone from publicly commenting on the announcement so students cannot publicly reply, for privacy reasons.

Screening of Group Members

Prior to conducting group interventions, school counselors are responsible for screening potential group participants (ASGW, 2000). The facilitator will want enough *homogeneity* to allow commonalities and bonding among members, while allowing for the personal growth required of members in *heterogeneous* groups—those which contain members with dissimilar backgrounds (Gladding, 2012).

Teachers may refer students to the group; however, the school counselor will still perform some form of screening to ensure that the student can benefit from the group and all group members feel safe. Typically, the school counselor will want to avoid the inclusion of highly disruptive students in the group. Once these organizational and planning aspects are in place, the school counselor can proceed to group interventions.

GROUP TOPICS AND GROUP LABELS

There is a wide range of group topics that school counselors can implement at the various grade levels. This section will cover some of the commonly used groups within the three ASCA model domains: academic, personal/social, and career (ASCA, 2012). Small group topics should be chosen based on the students' needs that can be determined by analyzing school data (e.g., test scores, discipline, attendance data, etc.) and by conducting a needs assessment (Dimmitt, Carey, & Hatch, 2007). Consulting with stakeholders either informally or formally is essential when selecting group topics (Stockton & Toth, 2000). Developmental levels are considerations when selecting group topics and activities. For instance, students in the lower elementary school grades (i.e., preK–2) may not be able to verbally explain the circumstances leading up to their parents' divorce, but they may be able to process the feelings associated with it through creative strategies such as art.

Certain topics are not appropriate for small groups in the school setting. Consultation with other school counselors and administration will help the school counselor determine whether or not a small group counseling topic is appropriate for his/her specific population. For example, psychotherapy groups that focus on a mental health disorder are not an appropriate intervention choice in the school setting (e.g., a group for students who struggle with Obsessive-Compulsive Disorder) (Sink, Edwards, & Eppler, 2012). Students struggling with mental health disorders need to be referred out to mental health providers. However, the school counselor should continue to work with students having mental health concerns by advocating for the student, collaborating with community agencies, and working with the student on overcoming academic barriers he/she may face (Brown, Dahlbeck, & Sparkman-Barnes, 2006; Walley, Grothaus, & Craigen, 2009). Group counseling interventions may be appropriate for students with mental health concerns; however, the primary focus should be on academics rather than the mental health disorder.

Group topics can fit within all three of the domains outlined in the American School Counselor Association's *National Model* (ASCA, 2012). Sample group topics within the academic domain include study skills, time management, organizational skills, goal setting, positive classroom behaviors (e.g., paying attention, participating, listening, etc.), test taking skills, and test anxiety. Sample group topics within the personal/social domain include friendship/social skills, conflict mediation, grief, changing families, anger management, bullying prevention, peer pressure, appreciating diversity, transition groups (i.e., new student groups), self-esteem, assertiveness, body image, and groups for specific at-risk populations (e.g., drug/alcohol abuse, drug/alcohol abuse within student's family (ALATEEN), teens with babies/pregnant teens, etc.). In the career domain, many counseling interventions will be held at the whole school or large group level; however, the school counselor may recognize a smaller group of students that needs more intensive assistance with career development and/or college preparation. Sample group topics within the career domain include career exploration/concerns, college exploration/concerns, financial aid, scholarships, career shadowing/mentoring, transitioning to college, choosing a major, career preparation (e.g., resume building, interviewing), and exploring personal assets (Sink et al., 2012; Wittmer & Thompson, 2000). Some of these topics are more appropriate for elementary-level students, while others better fit the needs of middle or high school students. See Table 5.1 for a sample list of topics by school level.

Table 5.1   Sample Group Topics by Grade Level

Elementary School	Middle School	High School
Study skills/Test taking skills	Study skills/Test taking skills	Study skills/Test taking skills
Test anxiety	Test anxiety	Test anxiety
Positive classroom behaviors	Organizational skills, time management	Organizational skills, time management
Friendship/social skills	Goal setting	Goal setting
Conflict mediation	Relationship issues	Relationship issues
Changing families	Conflict mediation	Conflict mediation
Grief/loss	Familial issues and transition	Familial issues and transition
Bullying prevention	Grief/loss	Grief/loss
Appreciating diversity	Anger management	Anger management
Early career exploration	Bullying prevention	Peer pressure
	Peer pressure	Financial aid/scholarships
	Appreciating diversity	Career Shadowing/mentoring
	Transition group (to middle school and to high school)	Choosing a major
	Self-esteem/assertiveness training	Career preparation
	Body image	Exploring personal assets
	Career exploration/concerns	
	Career shadowing	
	Exploring personal assets	

The HOPS program is a group intervention that incorporates Homework, Organization, and Planning Skills to address the academic domain for middle school students (Langberg, Epstein, Becker, Girio-Herrera, & Vaughn, 2012). In this program, 16 group sessions lasting 20 minutes are offered over 11 weeks, with topics such as school materials organization, homework recording and management, and planning/time management. In this program, the school counselor provides psychoeducational groups addressing the different topics and implements tracking checklists, bookbag checks, and two parent meetings. The parent meetings, along with the checklists, provide key pre-post test data, which is useful for outcome measures and accountability for the school counselor.

There are some group topics that require more sensitivity; for instance, students struggling with their sexual identity could certainly benefit from a support group, but due to the polarized opinion on openly discussing sexual identity in a school environment, this type of group may prove challenging to hold in schools. When groups such as these have been introduced in schools, some parents/guardians have the false impression that the group encourages their children to "convert" and administration may not be comfortable with an LGBTQ group in the school. However, the school counselor is responsible for advocating for the needs of LGBTQ students by promoting a positive school climate (Byrd & Hays, 2012). If a group for LGBTQ students is not permitted by the administration, the counselor could encourage LGBTQ youth, in addition to their supportive friends, to attend a general group on self-esteem improvement or assertiveness, without overtly labeling the group as one for the LGBTQ population.

Similarly, groups that are designed for students who are victims of abuse, children of alcoholics/addicts, or other such sensitive topics must be implemented with caution (if at all) in schools. While students struggling with these types of sensitive topics could certainly benefit from a group, due to the nature of the school environment, groups focusing on these topics may do more harm than good. The students' confidentiality will be at risk as teachers, staff, and students may find out the student is in a group that addresses a sensitive subject. The group leader cannot guarantee in-group confidentiality; therefore, the group members' privacy could be at risk. If school counselors decide to hold groups that have topics of a sensitive nature, it is imperative that the counselors inform the students that privacy of what is shared within the group (Corey, Corey, & Corey, 2014) cannot be guaranteed.

Labeling groups is an important consideration for any group, regardless of the topic. Problems may arise out of group labeling because others in the school will know the issues of students in the group. Students may also feel the negative impact of labeling; it may lead to a reduction in self-esteem and cause students to internalize the problem. A positive group label that does not clearly identify the personal issues of students in the group is important. For example, instead of calling a group "Communication Skills Group," a better title would be, "Let's Be Friends" (elementary) or "Let's Talk It Out" (middle, high school). One school counselor formed a group for children of divorced parents and decided to call the group "The Loss Group." At the beginning of the first meeting the group members arrived in the front office and reported that they were the "Lost Group" and someone needed to find them. Although this is a humorous anecdote, the title of the group is a serious consideration in planning.

ETHICAL AND LEGAL CONSIDERATIONS

As mentioned in the previous section, implementation of groups requires sensitivity and attention to the needs of students. This section will briefly address the ethical and legal issues essential to conducting small groups. This overview is not comprehensive because ethical considerations are vast and complex; in all likelihood you will take a more in-depth graduate-level training on the codes of ethics of the profession. The *Ethical Standards for School Counselors* are the codes of ethics most specific to school counselors and therefore is the focus of this section (ASCA, 2010). In addition, the American Counseling Association and the Association of Specialists in Group Work also have codes of ethics by which school counselors also abide (ACA, 2005; ASGW, 2000).

School counselors are encouraged to stay current on the ethical standards for running groups. Journal articles or professional conferences that address ethical issues pertaining to group counseling are professional resources to gain necessary information (Hermann, Remley, & Huey, 2010). Member screening, protecting students from harm, establishing guidelines and rules, documentation, confidentiality, parent/guardian consent, school policies and procedures, and consultation are ethical items to which the group leader abides when facilitating groups.

Member Screening

Section A.6. of the ASCA ethical standards is devoted specifically to group work (2010). As previously mentioned, according to ASCA (2010), school counselors must properly screen students for the group to ensure that the group is a good fit for each member. The question needs to be asked, "Will each member's needs be met by the group activities?" Many students will be referred to participate in the group, and some students may not feel comfortable in a group setting. For example, a mother of a seventh-grader referred her son to a grief group due to the loss of his father two months ago. The student adamantly protested about participating in the group and did not feel comfortable talking about the death of his father in front of other students. This group member would most likely not benefit from the group, at least not at the current time. He may need more time to grieve privately and should not be forced to participate. The school counselor and the student together may determine whether or not a group is appropriate for the student at a specific time, and whether or not the student is able to comfortably share and work within a group setting (Gladding, 2012).

Protecting Students From Harm

"Reasonable precautions" must be made to protect students from harm while participating in the group (ASCA, 2010, p. 3). Therefore, school counselors carefully consider anything related to group participation that might cause the student any kind of harm, including emotional harm or damage to the student's reputation for participating in the group. In addition, some students may not be appropriate for group counseling due to their history of physical violence or verbal abuse towards other students. While these students need counseling services, it is best to refer them out to community agencies and/or work with the student individually so other group members are not put at risk (Sink et al., 2012).

CONCEPTUAL APPLICATION ACTIVITY 5.5

You are a high school counselor working with a female senior about the guilt she is experiencing because she received an abortion several months ago. You are aware of two other girls in the school who were also struggling with the pregnancies that they terminated. You decide that bringing these girls together for weekly group counseling sessions would be the most appropriate way to work with these girls. Read the ASCA Ethical Standards and discuss whether or not this was a good decision. Discuss your responses with your classmates.

Guidelines and Rules

It is important that school counselors have a method for introducing group guidelines to students (Corey et al., 2014). Some school counselors have group members develop guidelines and rules in the first session so that they are more invested in the process. It is also helpful to have these rules and guidelines clearly posted for students in the group to view during each session. ASCA also stresses the importance of follow-up with group members. When the group concludes, "booster sessions" or individual student follow-up meetings to ensure that the students are progressing (Brigman & Goodman, 2008) are recommended. ASCA specifies that the groups should be brief and solution-focused because long-term groups are not appropriate for the school setting. School counselors establish clear short-term goals and objectives for the group to direct the content of the group sessions and to evaluate the effectiveness of each session and the entire group outcome.

Documentation

The ASCA ethical codes also mandate that school counselors document group sessions (ASCA, 2010). While the codes do not specifically state what needs to be documented, at a minimum school counselors should document the topics of the group, dates of the group, and a list of group members present at each group meeting. School counselors may also find it helpful to clearly record the specific activities, worksheets, and discussion questions used during the group sessions. Clear documentation with results that are easy to interpret will assist in replicating the group in the future, and reveals how the school counselor contributes to the mission of the school. Finally, documentation needs to be filed in a safe, locked cabinet in the school counselor's office.

Confidentiality

It is imperative that when leading groups that the school counselor explains in a clear, age-appropriate manner, that he/she cannot guarantee confidentiality (ASCA, 2010). For example, an elementary school counselor might say to fourth-graders, "As a school counselor, I can promise that what you share with me will be kept private, unless you tell me that you or someone you know is being hurt or is in danger. Do you know what I mean by keeping information private? (Make sure students can explain privacy and give examples of things you will have to share with others.) I have asked you each to keep what is said in this group private. However, I can't promise that the other students in this group will follow this rule and respect your privacy. So, please keep that in mind when deciding what to share with the group." Although school counselors strongly encourage confidentiality within the group, students also need to know that there is no way for the school counselor to ensure this confidentiality (Corey et al., 2014).

CONCEPTUAL APPLICATION ACTIVITY 5.6

Judy Sommers is a middle school counselor leading a relationship group of 8 sixth-graders. She pre-screened potential members, discussed the group purpose and objectives, obtained consent forms, and discussed the limits of confidentiality. After three weeks of meeting with the group she learned that a member broke the confidentiality rule. How should she approach this?

Parent/Guardian Consent

Parent consent is addressed in ethical code A.6.b: "Recognize that best practice is to notify the parents/guardians of children participating in small groups" (ASCA, 2010, pg. 3). Therefore, parents/guardians are to be notified that their child is participating in a group at school. Sink et al. (2012) recommends that written consent of both the group members and their legal guardians is necessary. It is important to consider whether or not the consent form needs to be translated for non-English-speaking parents, and a call home to obtain consent would be important for parents with visual or literacy challenges. Figure 5.1 contains a Sample Student Assent Form and Figure 5.2 (p. 180) is an example of a Parent/Guardian Consent Form.

Figure 5.1 Sample Student Assent Statement

Student Name: _____

I, _____, will be participating in a "Get Along Group" at XXXX School on Tuesdays from 12:00–1:00 pm.
   When I am in group, I will abide by the group rules*:

   1. I will keep my hands to myself

   2. I will be respectful of everyone in the group

   3. I will be on time for group and leave on time to return to class

   4. I will talk about what my other group members say only during group time

   5. I will try my best to have fun!

   I understand that if I do not like participating in the group, I can talk to my school counselor about it.

Student Signature _____

School Counselor Signature _____

Note: This section can be modified as appropriate. Some counselors choose to create the rules with all the group members so that it is a collaborative process.

School Policies and Procedures

In addition to obtaining proper training on ASCA's ethical codes for conducting groups, school counselors must be well-versed in their school and school district policies that pertain to small group counseling. Some schools may not allow small groups at all, and if this is the case, the school counselor should adhere to this policy but also advocate for the need for small groups. Some schools may not

Figure 5.2 Sample Parent/Guardian Consent Statement**

Student Name: _____

I, _____, give permission for my child _____ to participate in the Get Along Group at XXXX School with the school counselor.
   The school counselor explained to me:

- Who will be leading the group
- When the group will meet/what class time will be missed
- How my child can make up any work missed (if necessary)
- The purpose of the group
- The group is voluntary and I can request for my child to be removed at any time and without any penalty

Parent Signature _____   Date: _____

School Counselor Signature _____   Date: _____

**Note:* It is always best practice to explain the group to the parent verbally, but sometimes logistics do not permit this discussion to take place. The school counselor can choose to explain these elements in detail on the form or can speak to the parent/guardian to go over these details.

approve of groups that focus on certain topics—for example, a group of high school teens who are parents. The school administration may feel this group encourages students to have babies even though that is neither the intent nor the purpose of the group. When starting a new group, the principal of the school is to be consulted for permission to conduct a group on a particular topic. When proposing a new counseling group to the school principal, consider how the group will fit with the principal's mission and strategic plan for the school. Violence prevention, academic excellence, and attendance are examples of topics that could be explored through targeted group interventions. As mentioned earlier, it is also important that the school counselor consider the label given to the group. Some may view a "Tai Chi" group for students as inappropriate, but a "Relaxation Skills Group" as more acceptable.

Consultation

In addition to consulting administrators when running groups, it is important to have experienced, knowledgeable, and ethical school counselors with whom to consult to prevent ethical and legal problems from arising (ASCA, 2010). There are many gray areas when running groups and getting a second professional opinion is always a best practice. Other school professionals, including teachers, exceptional student education specialists, and English Language Learner specialists can also be consulted when issues or ethical questions arise. However, always remember to observe the limits of confidentiality when consulting.

MULTICULTURAL CONSIDERATIONS

Just as when working with students individually and in the classroom, multicultural awareness is crucial for effective small groups in a school setting. School counselors have a responsibility to monitor their own cultural biases to prevent these biases from negatively impacting their students (Delgado-Romero, Barfield, Fairley, & Martinez, 2005). When leading a group, school counselors may find that there is a clear cultural difference between him/herself and the members of the group. For example, the school counselor leading a career exploration group in a rural, low socioeconomic status (SES) community must be aware of the diverse expectations regarding post-secondary career options, and provide support and information for first generation college students who choose to continue their formal education. It is always important for counselors to become familiar with students' backgrounds by educating themselves about students' cultures. Understanding students' cultural backgrounds takes time and to gain cultural knowledge you could: 1) go into the community and attend cultural events; 2) consult with teachers or other school professionals; or 3) seek out community cultural leaders regarding their knowledge about the students' cultural backgrounds.

We do not want to place our value system on our students and this can happen, albeit unintentionally, if we are not aware of the value differences. For example, some cultures place higher reliance on family members. School counselors who come from a background with more "Western" cultures typically value independence over dependence on others. If leading a college exploration group with students, the school counselor may be inclined to encourage students to be independent and move away from their families to seek out their dreams. This encouragement may be well-intentioned; however, if the group members come from families that value inter-family reliance over independence, the school counselor could be doing more harm than good. The students could go home and share this group session topic with their families and the end result could be the administration's decision to end the group.

DEVELOPING TEAMWORK, COLLABORATION, AND CONSULTATION AMONG SCHOOL PERSONNEL

School counselors must take a strong teamwork approach when implementing small group counseling. First of all, it is crucial that the counselor link the small groups to the goals of the school. Due to federal education initiatives such as No Child Left Behind and Race to the Top, states often require public schools to present annual goals for progress. School counselors need to be aware of their school's goals and link direct services, including small group counseling, to these goals. The counselor should present this linkage between the goals and the small group intervention to school stakeholders, including the administration and teachers (Dahir & Stone, 2012). For example, if a school goal focuses on ninth-grade students in the bottom 25% of reading ability, the school counselor could develop a small group dedicated to teaching relaxation and imagery strategies to assist students in this population in improving reading scores. The outcomes of this group relate directly to the school improvement plan (i.e., annual goals). To gain support for small groups in schools, the school counselor could go a step further and find research studies that demonstrate improved test scores as a result of a specific counseling intervention (Dimmitt, et al., 2007). Linking the small group counseling intervention with the school goals and demonstrating the effectiveness of the group counseling intervention will strengthen the counselor's advocacy efforts. Through these accounts, administration and teachers will be more likely to see the benefits of the small group and more cooperative and collaborative in supporting group work in the school.

Ideally, a school counselor should research the needs of the students at the very beginning of the school year to develop a plan for small group counseling interventions. The plan first needs to be presented to the administration, and once the administration is committed, the plan needs to be presented to all faculty, possibly at a faculty meeting. This presentation could include the plan for group counseling throughout the school year, the linkage between the school's annual goals and the group, and any available research in the group counseling topic area that demonstrates the effectiveness of group counseling. For example, if the school counselor is trying to get administration and faculty support for a group counseling intervention for ninth-graders whose academic performance is below average, a peer reviewed study that shows improvement can be found and presented for intervention support. For instance, Kayler and Sherman (2009) conducted a group intervention that focused on improving the grade point average and study skills of ninth-grade students. Their study demonstrated support for this intervention, with students in the group strengthening their study behaviors as a result of group participation.

Another example is a mentoring group with the goal of improving overall self-efficacy and classroom behaviors for culturally diverse students. Phillips, Hagan,

Bodfield, Woodthorpe, and Grimsley (2008) conducted a study utilizing mentoring and group work with culturally diverse students and revealed that mentoring had a positive impact on students' self-esteem, behavior, and well-being.

Research such as this shows the importance of school counselor collaboration and consultation with staff to increase success of counseling interventions (Paisley & Milsom, 2007). Presenting information on group interventions such as this educates stakeholders, and the school counselor is better able to request support for the group counseling effort from the teachers. Teacher support is essential for two main reasons: 1) teachers are often the source of referrals for students into the group, and 2) sometimes the student will miss the teacher's class in order to attend the group. If teachers do not see the importance of the group, they will be less likely to refer students and they could even hold the student back from attending the group.

Finally, once the group is concluded, data are gathered and revealed to demonstrate the success of the group. When the results of the group are shared with stakeholders, the school counselor can build support for future groups to be held in the school. For example, after a school counselor leads a small group that focuses on lowering test anxiety, the counselor should plan to share the results of this group in a faculty meeting. The counselor can put together handouts and/or a PowerPoint presentation that includes bar charts showing the difference in student anxiety reports and test scores before and after the group.

CONSULTATION AND COLLABORATION WITH COMMUNITY MENTAL HEALTH PROVIDERS

Unfortunately, not all school counselors will be able to find time to conduct small groups at their schools (Steen, Bauman, & Smith, 2007). School counselors in this position should not rule out the possibility of groups due to high work demands. One way to overcome this obstacle is by consulting with community mental health agencies or counseling centers to see if they are willing to come into schools to conduct counseling groups, such as a program for attention-deficit hyperactivity disorder or for coping with parental drug use.

As always, the administration needs to be consulted prior to bringing in a community agency worker/counselor. Oftentimes, the school/school district has a security clearance protocol to follow before an outside agency counselor is able to work with children at the school. In addition, best practices suggest that a professional disclosure form that provides parents/guardians with a statement of credentials as well as signed informed consent forms are essential before this community leader can lead groups with students.

One challenge to using community stakeholders to conduct groups is finding qualified mental health providers who are willing and able to come into schools. School counselors should seek out these connections by calling community agencies to ask if a trained group facilitator is available to lead a group in a school setting. When a group facilitator is identified, inquire about his/her credentials to confirm that this group leader is appropriately trained to work with children and adolescents in a group setting. Stress the importance of communication while consulting with the person from outside of the school prior to the beginning of the group. If the group leader has concerns about a specific student in the group but does not share these concerns with the school counselor, no one at the school will be aware that this student needs additional attention.

CONCLUSION

In this chapter we have outlined some key components that specifically relate to groups in schools. ASCA's national standards emphasize reaching students through academic, career, and personal/social domains, with group work as an efficient method for engaging more students than is possible through individual counseling strategies. A brief history of group work in schools is discussed in addition to a definition of groups, purposes of groups in the schools, and types of groups that are commonly created in schools. Furthermore, the school counselor as a group leader is aware of methods for releasing students from classes, including the importance of obtaining administrator's approval for conducting groups during the school day. In addition, time limitations for conducting groups during students' scheduled day, collecting data to reveal the effectiveness of group work, advertising, indentifying students for the group, and appropriately labeling the group without misleading students as to the purpose of the group are significant factors when designing and implementing this type of student intervention.

Group leaders also consider the diversity of students and make efforts to become educated regarding the composition of group members, their values, beliefs, and personal culture. The ASCA Ethical Standards and the ethical code of the Association of Specialists in Group Work guide school counselors as they develop groups in an academic setting. Presenting data that concretely reveal how these groups benefit teachers and the academic growth of students are critical tasks to garner support for group work in schools.

School counselors are able to develop partnerships with families and community members to expand services to students that a single counselor is unable to do alone. Collaborating with various individuals and agencies helps in obtaining these valuable services for the benefit of school-age youth.

REFERENCES

American Counseling Association (2005). *ACA code of ethics.* Alexandria, VA: Author.

American School Counseling Association (2008). *The professional school counselor and group counseling position statement.* Alexandria, VA: Author.

American School Counseling Association. (2012). *The ASCA National Model: A framework for school counseling programs* (3rd ed.). Alexandria, VA: Author.

American School Counselor Association (2010). *Ethical standards for school counselors.* Retrieved from http://schoolcounselor.org/files/EthicalStandards2010.pdf

Association for Specialists in Group Work. (2000). Professional standards for the training of group workers. *Journal for Specialists in Group Work, 25,* 327–342. doi:10.1080/01933920008411677

Brigman, G. & Goodman, B. E. (2008). *Group counseling for school counselors.* Portland, ME: J. Weston Walch.

Brown, C., Dahlbeck, D. T., & Sparkman-Barnes, L. (2006). Collaborative relationships: School counselors and non-school mental health professionals working together to improve the mental health needs of students. *Professional School Counseling, 9*(4), 332–335.

Byrd, R., & Hays, D. G. (2012). School counselor competency and lesbian, gay, bisexual, transgender, and questioning (LGBTQ) youth. *Journal of School Counseling, 10*(3). Retrieved from http://www.jsc.montana.edu/articles/v10n3.pdf

Corey, M. S., Corey, G., & Corey, C. (2014). *Groups: Process and practice* (9th ed.). Belmont, CA: Brooks/Cole.

Council for the Accreditation of Counseling and Related Education Programs. (2009). *CACREP standards.* Retrieved from http://www.cacrep.org/doc/2009%20Standards%20with%20cover.pdf

Dahir, C. A., & Stone, C. B. (2012). *The transformed school counselor* (2nd ed.). Belmont, CA: Brooks/Cole.

Delgado-Romero, E. A., Barfield, J., Fairley, B., & Martinez, R. (2005). Using the multicultural guidelines in individual and group counseling situations. In M. G. Constantine & D. W. Sue (eds.), *Strategies for building multicultural competence in mental health and educational settings* (pp. 29–55). Hoboken, NJ: John Wiley.

Dimmit, C., Carey, J. C. & Hatch, T. (2007). *Evidence-based school counseling.* Thousand Oaks, CA: Corwin Press.

Echterling, L. G., Presbury, J. H. & McKee, J. E. (2005). *Crisis intervention: Promoting resilience and resolution in troubled times.* Upper Saddle River, NJ: Pearson.

Erford, B. T. (Ed.). (2010). *Group work in the schools.* New York, NY: Pearson.

Geroski, A. M. & Kraus, K. L. (2010). *Groups in schools: Preparing, leading, and responding.* New York, NY: Pearson.

Gladding, S. T. (2012). *Groups: A counseling specialty* (6th ed.). New York, NY: Pearson.

Gysbers, N. C., & Henderson, P. (2012). *Developing and managing your school guidance program* (5th ed.). Alexandria, VA: American Counseling Association.

Hermann, M. A., Remley, T. P., & Huey, W. C. (Eds.). (2010). *Ethical and legal issues in school counseling* (3rd ed.). Alexandria, VA: American School Counselor Association.

Kayler, H. & Sherman, J. (2009). At-risk ninth-grade students: A psychoeducational group approach to increase study skills and grade point averages. *Professional School Counseling, 12*(6). 434–439. doi: 10.5330/PSC.n.2010–12.434

Kottler, J. A. (1994). *Advanced group leadership.* Pacific Grove, CA: Brooks/Cole.

Kulic, K. R., Horne, A. M., & Dagley, J. C. (2004). A comprehensive review of prevention groups for children and adolescents. *Group Dynamics, Theory, Research, and Practice, 8*(2). 139–151. doi:10:1037/1089–2699.8.2.139

Langberg, J. M., Epstein, J. N., Becker, S. P., Girio-Herrera, E. & Vaughn, A. J. (2012). Evaluation of the Homework, Organization, and Planning Skills (HOPS) intervention for middle school students with Attention Deficit Hyperactivity Disorder as implemented by school mental health providers. *School Psychology Review, 41*(3), 342–364.

Paisley, P. O., & Borders, L. D. (1995). School counseling: An evolving specialty. *Journal of Counseling and Development, 74*(2), 150–153. doi:10.1002/j.1556–6676.1995.tb01840.x

Paisley, P. O.. & Milsom, A. (2007). Group work as an essential contribution to transforming school counseling. *Journal for Specialists in Group Work, 32,* 9–17.

Perusse, R., Goodnough, G. E., & Lee, V. V. (2009). Group counseling in the schools. *Psychology in the Schools, 46*(3), 225–231. doi:10.1002/pits.20369

Phillips, D., Hagan, T., Bodfield, E., Woodthorpe, K., & Grimsley, M. (2008). Exploring the impact of group work and mentoring for multiple heritage children's self-esteem, well-being and behaviour. *Health and Social Care in the Community, 16*(3), 310–321. doi: 10.1111/j.1365–2524.2008.00761.x

Sink, C. A., Edwards, C. N., & Eppler, C. (2012). *School based group counseling.* Belmont, CA: Brooks/Cole.

Steen, S., Bauman, S. & Smith, J. (2007). Professional school counselors and the practice of group work. *Professional School Counselors, 11,* 72–80.

Stockton, R., & Toth, P. (2000). Small group counseling in school settings. In J. Wittmer (Ed.), *Managing your school counseling program: K-12 developmental strategies* (pp. 111–122). Minneapolis, MN: Educational Media Corporation.

Tuckman, B. W., & Jensen, M. A. C. (1977). Stages of small group development revisited. *Group and Organizational Studies, 2.* 419–427. doi:10.1177/105960117700200404

Waldo, M., Kerne, P. A., IV, & Kerne, V. V. H. (2007). Therapeutic factors in guidance versus counseling sessions of domestic violence groups. *Journal for Specialists in Group Work, 32*(4), 346–361. doi:10.1080/01933920701476672

Walley, C. T., Grothaus, T. & Craigen, L. M. (2009). Confusion, crisis, and opportunity: Professional school counselors' role in responding to student mental health issues. *Journal of School Counseling, 7*(36). Retrieved from http:///jsc.montana.edu/articles/v7n36.pdf

Weltmann Begun, R. (1996). *Social skills lessons and activities for grades 7–12.* San Francisco, CA: Jossey-Bass.

Whiston, S. C., & Quinby, R. F. (2009). Review of school counseling outcome research. *Psychology in the Schools, 46*(3). 267–272. doi:10.1002/pits.20372

Wittmer, J., & Thompson, D. W. (2000). *Large group guidance activities* (2nd ed.). Minneapolis, MN: Educational Media Corporation.

Yalom, I. D., & Leszcz, M. (2005). *The theory and practice of group psychotherapy* (5th ed.). New York, NY: Basic Books.

Chapter 6

INDIVIDUAL COUNSELING IN THE SCHOOL ENVIRONMENT

CACREP OUTCOME

COUNSELING, PREVENTION, AND INTERVENTION

C. *Knowledge*

   1. Knows the theories and processes of effective counseling and wellness programs for individual students and groups of students.

   3. Knows strategies for helping students identify strengths and cope with environmental and developmental problems.

D. *Skills and Practices*

   2. Provides individual and group counseling and classroom guidance to promote the academic, career, and personal/social development of students.

   3. Designs and implements prevention and intervention plans related to the effects of (a) atypical growth and development, (b) health and wellness, (c) language, (d) ability level, (e) multicultural issues, and (f) factors of resiliency on student learning and development.

   Susan Roberts is a school counselor at Sharpton Middle School and has been working with 10-year-old Charlea one hour a week for the entire school year. Is this type of work considered as counseling or therapy?

When the draft copy of the revised ASCA National Model® was released, appropriate and inappropriate school counseling activities were outlined with "working with one student at a time in a therapeutic, clinical mode" (p. 21) listed as an inappropriate task. When the draft became available for public comment, school counseling professionals debated this position. Some professionals supported this position statement due to the multiple school counselor responsibilities that preclude devoting sufficient time to work intensely with individual students (Saginak, 2012). Others expressed that the terms "counseling" and "therapy" refer to the same process in that a theoretical framework is employed to bring about desired change (Canfield, 2012). School counselors are as skilled in counseling as those in the mental health counseling specialty field, and have the same knowledge and skills to bring about effective change in the students with whom they work, yet they do not have the time to work intensively with individual students at the expense of the majority of the student body. For example, the ASCA recommends a 250:1 student/counselor ratio, yet the national average is 459:1 (U.S. Department of Education, 2010-2011). In addition, administrators sometimes prohibit the use of the word "therapy" to describe a school counselor activity due to parent/guardians' negative perceptions of their child receiving therapy. In this chapter the word "counseling" as the therapeutic task school counselors perform, and the term "student" or "counselee" will be used in reference to the term "client."

Approximately 1 out 5 school-age youth has a diagnosed mental disorder (NIH, 2013) with statistics that indicate that during the 2005–2006 academic year, approximately 12% of youth received mental health assistance in a school setting (SAMHSA, 2008). Conceptual Application Activity 6.1 is designed for you to start thinking about the differences between these terms and the school counselor's role in this process. As you think about this process, keep in mind that the school counselor is often the only mental health professional in the educational setting and when personal or social issues are not addressed, students may experience significant barriers to personal growth and development.

CONCEPTUAL APPLICATION ACTIVITY 6.1

What are your own definitions of the words "therapy" and "counseling"? Look up the definitions as described by the American Counseling Association and the American School Counselor Association. Discuss your description of these terms with your peers. Based on this discussion, do you believe school counselors provide counseling or therapy? What do you believe is the difference?

Regardless of how you define this task, school counselors do work with students through a relationship that is intended to help the student resolve areas of personal concern. When working with students remember that for the most part children do not voluntarily choose to come to counseling. They are usually referred or brought in by another adult, and as in any new situation they will have many questions regarding the counseling process such as:

- Who are you?
- Why am I here?
- Will it hurt?
- Am I in trouble?
- What do I have to do in here?
- Are you going to tell my parents/guardians?

At times the school counselor is the only trustworthy adult in a child's life and instrumental in providing support and succor to navigate life's challenges. As an example, a public school counselor enrolled a ninth-grade female who had spent all her school years in a private, Christian school. The mother of this shy girl was deaf but was able to communicate that she wanted her daughter to participate in softball. Unfortunately, due to state law she needed to wait to receive permission for athletic eligibility. The girl made frequent visits to the counselor to talk about her lack of friends and her wish to drop out of high school. Eventually, she made a friend with the help of her counselor, but at the end of the year the friend moved to a new school. When eligibility to participate in sports was finally granted the counselor suggested that the lonely student join the girls' swim team due to her interest in competitive swimming, and the hope that she would make friends with her team members. By the student's senior year of high school this once shy female was actively involved in several activities, no longer complained of being friendless, decided to stay in school, and eventually graduated. Several years later she stopped by the counselor's office to thank her for the time she spent with her.

Forming a relationship with students, understanding their needs, answering questions students may have about counseling, as well as discussing limits of confidentiality and other concerns will facilitate productive counseling sessions. Motivational Interviewing (MI) is a helpful "front-loaded" intervention (precedes a standard counseling approach) that works as a respectful approach in tandem with the theoretical counseling theory you choose (Frey, et al., 2011).

MOTIVATIONAL INTERVIEWING (MI)

Motivational interviewing (MI) supports an empathic counseling style (Enea & Dafinoiu, 2009; Frey et al., 2011; Miller & Rose, 2009). The MI counselor listens to the student's verbalizations, attends to language that emphasizes readiness to change (Miller, 2010), and listens for *motivational ambivalence.* Motivational ambivalence refers to the struggle between the counselee's wish to change a behavior while simultaneously not wanting to change problematic conduct.

The counselor considers two interrelated phases of MI (Frey et al., 2011). During phase 1, or the pre-commitment phase, the counselor uses basic skills such as the use of open-ended questions, reflective listening, affirmation, and summarization (Miller & Rose, 2009) while listening for "change talk." Counselor encouragement and reminders of past successes reinforce the willingness to change and is facilitated through the question, "How will changing this behavior make life better for you?" Through change talk the counselee is better able to recognize the advantages of altering behaviors and attitudes (Frey et al., 2011). Phase 1 serves as a catalyst for phase two, in which the counselor and student collaborate in formulating goals, brainstorm options for reaching these goals, determine a plan for change, and commit to a plan.

During phase 2, a self-efficacy scale is used to ascertain the student's confidence in completing the goal. A 1–10 scale is used, with the number "1" representing "little confidence to be able to achieve the goal" and "10" indicating "high probability in achieving the goal." The counselor promotes a discussion of goal attainment by asking a question such as, "Using the scale, how confident are you that you are able to accomplish this goal?" From here a conversation of barriers to goal attainment assists in planning for potential difficulties that could arise. Student Activity 6.1 *To Change or Not to Change* is a concrete, visual activity for counselors to use with students to identify goals, motivation to change, and potential barriers that could frustrate success.

STUDENT ACTIVITY 6.1. TO CHANGE OR NOT TO CHANGE

Take a piece of paper, fold it into nine sections, and label each section with a number from 1–9. Open the paper and either draw a picture or write words to answer the following questions.

1 What behavior do you want to change?	2 What are some of your strengths (or competencies)?	3 Can these strengths be used to help you change?
4 What are your reasons for not changing this behavior?	5 What are your reasons for continuing this behavior?	6 What goal do you want to reach?

7	8	9
What are some of the strategies you can implement to reach your goal?	On a scale from 1–10, how confident are you that you can accomplish your goal?	When will this goal happen? How will you know when you have reached this goal?

After the student has completed this chart, the counselor and student are able to discuss the answers and identify tasks that can be accomplished during the following week to reach the goal.

Regardless of the initial method you choose to establish a relationship with students, selecting a counseling theory that is best suited to your personality and values gives direction to plan the counseling sessions. Research has not consistently identified the variables that most prominently contribute to a positive counseling outcome. However, Hubble, Duncan, and Miller (1999, as cited in Selekman & Gil, 2010) identified four contributing factors that assist in counseling effectiveness including: a) counselee characteristics such as strengths, expectations, and coping strategies; b) the counselor's ability to express empathy and warmth; c) the counselor's ability to convey hope in the counselee's ability to change; and d) the counseling theory and techniques. Of these, the counselee's characteristics are those that contribute most to a successful outcome. Surprisingly, counseling theories do not have empirical evidence to support their effectiveness (Archer & McCarthy, 2007) in generating change. In fact, the chosen theoretical approach only accounts for 15% of counseling effectiveness (Hubble et al., 1999, as cited in Selekman & Gil, 2010). Nevertheless, intentional principles such as those in MI provide a foundation for the counseling relationship to facilitate the change process.

You may have already taken a class or have yet to take a class specifically devoted to counseling theories in your school counseling program curriculum. The information in this chapter is not intended to replace this course, but to supplement theoretical models used in school settings. A personal awareness of beliefs, values, personal interests, and biases is an essential foundation for understanding others' worldviews. Self-awareness assists in evaluating cultural practices and how these practices impact counseling relationships. In choosing a theoretical counseling model and/or creative approach to use with students, an understanding of differences within cultural groups, in addition to unique individual differences (Locke & Bailey, 2014) are critical considerations. As you read the following section, keep in mind the cultural influences that could influence the growth and development of each individual student with whom you work.

Person-centered, Adlerian Counseling, Reality Therapy, Rational-Emotive Behavior Therapy, Solution-focused, and Narrative theories are discussed below. A brief summary of the theory, techniques, multicultural considerations, and applications in a school setting are also summarized.

PERSON-CENTERED COUNSELING

Dr. Carl Rogers is credited with a phenomenological, non-directive counseling theory based on a humanistic philosophy. Rogers believed that each individual has an innate desire to meet basic needs while moving toward self-actualization (Archer & McCarthy, 2007) or, as stated in the popular Army slogan, "Be all you can be."

Techniques

Rogers believed specific techniques interfere with the counseling process. Instead, the counselor tries to understand the world from the counselee's perspective. According to Rogers, personal problems arise when there is a discrepancy between the perceived self and the ideal self, or the self-concept that is desired but not yet attained (Archer & McCarthy, 2007). Core conditions need to be created for effective counseling to occur which include congruence, unconditional positive regard, and empathy. Through the counselor's use of active listening, reflection, paraphrasing, clarification, and summarizing, the counselee is able to accept and respect self, the foundation for solving personal problems.

Congruence. When the counselor is genuine and authentic and able to openly express thoughts, feelings, and attitudes, openness is modeled, and the student begins to feel comfortable and accepted (Corey, 2009).

Unconditional Positive Regard. This core condition relates to the counselor's ability to see the student as worthy of acceptance without judgment. Through the stance of caring and accepting, the student develops unconditional positive self-regard, or a sense of self-worth (Corey, 2009).

Accurate Empathy. As the counselor enters the student's world of feelings and thoughts, a sense of understanding emerges. Accurate understanding is the foundation to person-centered counseling and is a key to promoting change (Corey, 2009).

Multicultural Considerations

All cultures accept the tenets of person-centered counseling due to the emphasis on value and dignity and the opportunities for personal growth (Ivey, D'Andrea, & Ivey, 2012). However, because an understanding of the essence of the counselee's experiences serves as the foundation of person-centered theory, it could be difficult for the counselor to completely enter and understand a worldview of a counselee from a diverse culture (Archer & McCarthy, 2007). Person-centered counseling has shown success in Asian cultures through the ideologies of empathy, harmony, and relationships that parallel those found in Confucianism and Zen Buddhism, yet the nondirective approach may be difficult for those from cultures who prefer a hierarchical, directive approach (Lee & Yang, 2013).

Applications in Schools

As a school counselor, you both respond to and model the basic skills you learn in your program. Through these skills you are responsible for creating an inviting environment that facilitates self-growth and autonomy (Thompson, Rudolph, & Henderson, 2004). Person-centered counseling facilitates self-esteem development, with success and achievement used as stepping-stones to develop a greater sense of self-worth. Student Activity 6.2 *ME!* assists students in identifying personal strengths.

STUDENT ACTIVITY 6.2. ME!

Bring in different types of magazines that represent different aspects of life (e.g., sports, school, fashion, family, etc.). Students are asked to make a collage that represents their successes and achievements by cutting out pictures in the magazines. Students will share their accomplishments with their classmates or group members.

ADLERIAN COUNSELING

Alfred Adler was the founder of Adlerian Counseling, also known as Individual Psychology. Initially, as an admirer of Sigmund Freud, he joined the Vienna Psychoanalytic Society but later resigned, due to disagreements with Freudian theory. Adler believed that each person constructs his/her own reality based on experiences and biological factors, which form a unique lifestyle as he/she strives to overcome inferiority, a normal condition of everyone regardless of culture, gender, or ethnicity (Archer & McCarthy, 2007). In addition, an individual forms opinions about life and how to meet life challenges based on perceptions of events that they encounter. These perceptions form the foundation for their lifestyle and the mistaken goals that lead to problems, which are largely created due to a fear of not belonging. Counselors view their counselee from a social, holistic perspective in the areas of work/school, love, and friendships.

Techniques

The counselor is an active participant in the counseling relationship, and works hard to understand the counselee's "private logic" while teaching the counselee about his/her mistaken beliefs, where they have originated, and strategies for change. Adler's approach is one that incorporates listening, instruction, demonstrations, and practicing (Thompson et al., 2004). Socratic questioning such as "What would happen if? . . ."; "How would your life be different and what would you do if you didn't have this problem?"; or "Can this be seen differently?" help the student develop insight. Although Adler himself did not view his approach as one that used techniques, Adlerian counselors use numerous strategies including encouragement, the family constellation and early recollections, and acting "as if."

Encouragement. Discouraged individuals behave inappropriately, and encouragement is the key to changing impaired beliefs and behaviors. Adlerian counselors attempt to make their counselees feel heard and accepted and work cooperatively with their counselee to create goals. Encouragement is given before a task is undertaken with the intention of: 1) helping the counselee gain a sense of confidence, and, 2) to break self-defeating beliefs and behaviors when goals are accomplished. Encouragement serves as a foundation for the creation of hope with an expectation that self-confidence will emerge (Thompson et al., 2004).

Family Constellation and Early Recollections. Adlerian counselors make efforts to get a picture of the student's social world and lifestyle by understanding his/her view of the family dynamics. A questionnaire is used to understand this structure in which the student describes his/her parent and sibling personalities, relationships to one another, talents, interests, and so forth. To better understand how the student views his/her world, the counselor considers that the psychological position of the family members as more important rather than the chronological position.

Furthermore, the use of early recollections serve as additional metaphors for understanding the counselee's present world view. To retrieve these memories the counselor says, "Think back to a time when you were young and tell me one of your earliest childhood memories." A minimum of three memories is used to assess personal beliefs, strengths, assets, and mistaken beliefs, and although these recollections may not be accurate, what is important is the child's perception of these events. Box 6.1 is an example of some of the questions that can be asked to determine lifestyle and mistaken goals. A nonverbal student may do better in drawing pictures to answer the questions.

BOX 6.1 LIFESTYLE QUESTIONNAIRE

1. Write the names of your parents and their ages.

   a. Father _____ age _____

List 3 of his personality characteristics

Describe his education/occupation

   b. Mother _____ age _____

List 3 of her personality characteristics

Describe her education/occupation

2. If you have siblings, write the names, ages, and 3 personality characteristics of each

   c. Sibling(s) _____ age _____

   _____

   Move to next section if you do not have siblings.

3. Which sibling is most and least like you, your dad, your mom? _____

   _____

4. If you have more than one sibling, which sibling is most and least athletic, studious, friendly, popular, serious, funny?_____

Early Childhood Memories

Think of three of your earliest childhood memories and describe these recollections in detail below. Think in terms of your age, who you are with, where you are, what can you see, smell, hear, touch, taste?

(Continued)

(Continued)

Memory 1 _____

_____

Memory 2 _____

_____

Memory 3 _____

_____

From here, the counselor looks at themes to determine the student's mistaken beliefs, and makes tentative guesses about the student's lifestyle that are shared with the student.

Acting "As If." Collaborative goal-setting is essential to an effective counseling session. A counselee may have a picture of how he/she would like to be in the future, but may believe reaching this goal is impossible. With counselor encouragement and an instruction for the student to act "as if" he or she would like to be in the future, a glimpse of their goal emerges. The counselor uses the following steps while working with a student:

1. Visualize what you would be doing, saying, thinking, and doing when your goal is reached. Who is with you? Where are you? Hold onto this picture.

2. Now that you have this picture in your mind, act "as if" you have already achieved this goal.

3. When you leave my office I want you to behave and think as you just described to me. Pay attention to your feelings and thoughts when you are acting as you envision.

Multicultural Considerations

Adlerian counseling works well with individuals from any culture due to the counselor's basic respect for others' beliefs and values, the egalitarian relationship, and the importance of family influences on culture. Recently, Adlerian counselors added the concept of spirituality as a supplementary life task and critical component for understanding individuals from a holistic viewpoint, which is consistent with an emphasis some cultures place on sacrosanctity (Ivey et al.,

2012). Furthermore, the preventive focus inherent to this theory that emphasizes fostering mental wellness and psychological well-being before problems occur facilitates skill development, as marginalized individuals (Ivey et al., 2012) confront prejudice and other discriminatory behaviors and attitudes. Finally, Adlerian counseling is a good alternative for those in cultures who have difficulty with the idea of receiving counseling about social/personal issues, but value the concept of exploring educational concepts (Strasser, 2013).

Applications in Schools

Students who are having life difficulties often have problems that are evident in multiple areas of life. If a student is having conflict at home, this stress will be viewed in the school setting and in peer relationships. People who are anxious are difficult to be around, and as problems continue friends and family often distance themselves from this student. This social withdrawal leaves the student without the critical support system that is needed to buffer painful events. When a student finally seeks counseling or is referred, the student often has difficulty identifying a certain area in which to focus the counseling session. When this occurs, the school counselor can use Student Activity 6.3 *Good News/Bad News* to identify a counseling goal.

STUDENT ACTIVITY 6.3. GOOD NEWS/BAD NEWS

The counselor asks the following questions and records the student's response. "I'm going to ask you to think about school, family, and friends and I would like you to tell me the 'good news' or 'bad news' in each of these areas."

1. Good News School _____

2. Bad News School _____

3. Good News Family _____

4. Bad News Family _____

5. Good News Friends _____

6. Bad News Friends _____

This activity serves as a guide for addressing problems the child perceives as presenting the most difficulty and provides a focus for the counseling session.

REALITY THERAPY

William Glasser is the founder of Reality Therapy, also known as Choice Therapy. This approach emphasizes that all individuals are motivated to fulfill the five basic needs of survival, love and belonging, power or achievement, freedom or autonomy, and fun (Glasser, 2001). Each of us has the ability to choose how we want to meet our unmet needs. In our minds we store "picture albums" that contain images of what we think we need for our "quality world." When these images are different from the way we presently view life, we choose something we believe will be more satisfying. The acronym W-D-E-P is useful in helping our students evaluate goals and present behaviors to reach these ideals (Wubbolding, 2000).

W = Wants-   What do you want?

D = Doing-   What are you doing to get what you want?

E = Evaluate-   Is what you are doing working?

P = Planning-   What can you do to get what you want?

Techniques

Goal-Setting. The counselor uses skillful questioning such as, "What do you want?" to help the counselee identify what he/she wants to meet their needs and identified goal. Goal setting is facilitated through the SAMIC acronym: S = simple; A = attainable; M = Measureable; I = Immediate; C = Commit (Wubbolding, 2000). By providing more direction for the counselee at the beginning of counseling sessions and helping the student accomplish small steps toward goal attainment, the student is eventually able to evaluate wants and plans without the help of the counselor (Corey, 2009).

Multicultural Considerations

Many counselees from diverse backgrounds respond better to a thinking and behaving focus rather than one that concentrates on feelings (Corey, 2009). Therefore, the counselor needs to adapt questions to fit the needs of the student. For example, some cultures tend to be more direct and assertive, where others may be resistant to candid questioning. Furthermore, because people from different cultures hold different perspectives and values that comprise their "quality world," the counselor has a responsibility to examine and understand the values, traditions, and worldviews of each student.

Applications in Schools

When needs are not satisfied, destructive behavior, poor achievement, and unsupportive social relationships could result. Many students are not aware of the relationship between need satisfaction and destructive behaviors (Loyd, 2005). When students are able to make decisions that are mentally and physically healthy, they are able to become more autonomous and in control of their lives. Active techniques such as role-playing, humor, confrontation, and goal-setting teaches students concepts integral to reality therapy. Student Activity 6.4 *Recipe for Meeting Needs* could be implemented to determine personal needs and a plan for reaching them.

STUDENT ACTIVITY 6.4. RECIPE FOR MEETING NEEDS

Directions: Write out "ingredients" that are needed to make a "recipe for success." Identify people, values, events, and so on that can be used to meet each of the needs identified in each of the cells. When finished, answer the questions below.

To make a recipe for freedom, the following ingredients are needed: FREEDOM	To make a recipe for love and belonging, the following ingredients are needed: LOVE & BELONGING
To make a recipe for survival, the following ingredients are needed: SURVIVAL	To make a recipe for fun, the following ingredients are needed: FUN

What are you *doing* to meet each of these needs?

Evaluate how well your behaviors are working

Write out a goal (S-A-M-I-C) for each of the needs above, and make a *plan* to meet or fulfill your needs.

RATIONAL-EMOTIVE BEHAVIOR THERAPY (REBT)

Albert Ellis is credited with developing Rational-Emotive Behavior Therapy (REBT). REBT practitioners adhere to the belief that everyone is capable of irrational, or what is often referred to as "stinking thinking" (Archer & McCarthy, 2007), as well as rational thought (Corey, 2009). According to this theory, it is not an event that creates emotional and behavioral consequences but rather the belief or thought about the event that creates anxiety and/or distress. This is known as the A-B-C-D-E-F steps of REBT. For example, Rachel sees her boyfriend, Carl, talking with Susan, the homecoming queen.

A = activating event (seeing Carl talking with Susan)

B = Belief ("I MUST not be popular enough for Carl")

C = Emotional and/or behavioral consequences (Rachel gets angry)

D = Disputing belief ("I am a worthwhile person, too")

E = Effect of new belief ("Just because Susan is the homecoming queen doesn't mean Carl doesn't care for me")

F = New feeling (Relief)

Techniques

REBT is an educational model in which individuals are taught how to manage irrational emotions and thoughts through cognitive restructuring and behavioral strategies (Banks & Zionts, 2009). School counselors may wish to consider a different theoretical approach with children under the age of seven due to their developmental level and their difficulty in disputing irrational beliefs (Bernard, Ellis, & Terjesen, 2006; Vernon, 2011).

Disputing Irrational Thoughts. Counselees who are able to think more abstractly are able to challenge their irrational thoughts by recognizing and replacing absolute language such as "must," "ought," or "should" with rational, self-affirming language. Homework, imagery, role-playing, and humor are additional techniques associated with REBT.

Multicultural Considerations

Ellis has long been considered as having a respect for human differences; however, he has also been criticized for his ethnocentric approach to mental health (D'Andrea, 2000, as cited in Ivey et al., 2012). REBT works well with individuals from cultures in which a directive, active approach is preferred (Thompson et al., 2004). Therefore, the counselor needs to adapt the types of questions to ask counselees (Thompson et al., 2004), in order not to appear confrontational and offensive to those who prefer a more indirect approach (Ivey et al., 2012). When the individual's culture is not explored, it is difficult for the counselor to understand the context in which the irrational thoughts are occurring (Archer & McCarthy, 2007). REBT has been successful with counselees from some cultures in the

Middle East when counselees are taught to alter their beliefs such as that behaviors originate from the devil or "evil eye" (Mikhemar, 2013). A counselor may confront an analogous belief among those from the U.S. and other cultures who have been taught to believe that their actions are prompted by the devil and that an evil spirit may be within them.

Applications in Schools

Practical, comprehensive interventions with a wide range of activities and strategies have been successful with individuals and groups; even children around the age of 7 are able to accept responsibility for their emotions through REBT programs. A red light/green light construct can be implemented in which the student and counselor identify and dispute the "red light" thoughts that disrupt communication and produce conflict. "Green light" thoughts are identified to dispute the conflict-producing thoughts and behaviors. Student Activity 6.5 *Helpful Thinking* can be used as a homework assignment with a student to assist him/her in refuting irrational thoughts associated with an event.

STUDENT ACTIVITY 6.5. HELPFUL THINKING

Complete the worksheet after an upsetting event has occurred.

A. What event occurred? (Activating Event can be something that happened in the past, present, or future)

B. What was your irrational thought about the event (A)?

To identify this thought look for:

- Dogmatic thoughts include "shoulds," "oughts," or "musts"
- "Awfulizing" thoughts include "it's awful," "terrible," "the worst"

C. Identify your unhealthy behavioral or negative emotions to the event? (These may include anxiety, hurt, shame, rage)

D. What are some of your disputing beliefs from B?

To identify these thoughts, ask yourself the following questions:

- Is this belief helping or hurting me?
- What are the facts to support this belief?
- Does this belief seem logical?

(Continued)

(Continued)

E. What is your new effective belief in response to D?

To answer this question consider:

- Identifying beliefs that are not absolutes
- Evaluating the extent of the belief

F. What are the feelings/behaviors that are healthy?

Identify the new productive feelings and behaviors

- New healthy emotions and behaviors

Adapted from Ellis (2001, as cited in Rosenthal, 2001)

SOLUTION-FOCUSED BRIEF COUNSELING (SFBC)

Steve de Shazer and Insoo Kim Berg are credited as the founders of Solution Focused Brief Counseling (SFBC; Archer & McCarthy, 2007), also known as Brief Counseling. Counselors using this approach believe that people are able to work through their own problems when there is a focus on what is wanted rather than what is not desired. Too often people focus on the problem that brought them to counseling, which hinders their ability to focus on a more favorable outcome. The theory is strength-based as the focus is on the successes that have been achieved so far in life, and on the idea that small changes lead to greater outcomes (Thompson, et al., 2004). Change is seen as inevitable (Archer & McCarthy, 2007), and solution-focused counselors concentrate on goal-setting to allow students to think about what they want. Asking the question, "What would you like to see happen in your time with me?" gives the student an opportunity to provide a direction for counseling or goal setting. The SAMIC acronym described in the reality therapy description also applies to SFBC in establishing goals.

Once a goal is identified, the counselor will want to establish the times that the goal is happening, or the *exceptional times* that that the problem is not happening. The student is encouraged to discuss events in which the goal was present, the people involved in these exceptional times, when these events occurred, how the goal transpired, and to recall feelings, behaviors, and thoughts. Once these times are identified the student is given a homework assignment to make more of these exceptional times occur.

At times students are unable to recall exceptional times. When this occurs the *miracle question* is asked to help the student visualize possibilities and what life would be like when the problem no longer exists. For instance, "Suppose you went to bed at night and when you woke up in the morning all of your problems were gone. What would you be doing, thinking, feeling that would make you realize that the miracle occurred?" For younger students the question could be, "Suppose I waved a magic wand that wiped away all your problems. How would you know that the magic worked?" The counselor then has a responsibility to keep the student focused on what he/she would be do when the miracle happened, and to assign this visualization as homework to complete prior to the next counseling session.

Techniques

Scaling Questions. Scaling questions help students evaluate their willingness to achieve goals and their commitment to change. To gauge commitment, the counselor asks the question, "On a scale of 1–10 with '10' meaning the problem is completely gone, and '1' meaning the problem is the worst it has ever been, how would you rate where you are today?" Suppose the student responds with "3." The counselor would then ask, "What do you need to do from the time you leave my office until the next time I see you to move to a '4'?" The school counselor uses this information to assign homework to help the student experience a move up the scale.

Coping Questions. When the student is able to identify unique times without the problem, the counselor reinforces personal skills and talents that may not have been previously recognized through questions such as, "How were you able to manage to do so well given the things that have happened to you?"

Flagging the Minefield. The counselor and student collaboratively create a plan to identify possible people or events that might stand in the way of goal attainment. Advance planning teaches skills that may be activated if a barrier stands in the path of a personal objective.

Multicultural Considerations

SFBC requires that the counselor understand the counselee's perception of the problem for the purpose of generating solutions to the dilemma (Archer & McCarthy, 2007), and it is possible that the counselor may have difficulty grasping the problem without an understanding of the student's values and culture. In addition, a necessary ingredient to SFBC is an equalitarian relationship that may be difficult for those from cultures in which a hierarchical relationship is expected. Finally, SFBC may not work with individuals who prefer a direct, cognitive focused method of dealing with problems; in these cases, a consultant role may be the preferable strategy (Thompson et al., 2004).

Applications in Schools

SFBC has been used successfully with numerous issues youth bring to counseling. For instance, greater completion and accuracy in math assignments resulted when SFBT was used with students who had difficulty completing math homework (Fearrington, McCallum, & Skinner, 2011). In addition, SFBC has also been effectively used in Response to Intervention, classroom management, counseling, and social skills groups (Jones et al., 2009). SFBC was also effective with both bullies and targets of bullying when students were encouraged to view exceptions to the bullying, identify strengths, visualize life without the problem, and develop strategies for the potential of future bullying incidents (Paterson, 2011). Student Activity 6.6 *I Am Capable* could be implemented as an SFBC strategy to assist students in identifying goals and exceptional times.

STUDENT ACTIVITY 6.6. I AM CAPABLE

Directions: Complete the following worksheet

1. Describe in detail the problem you would like to resolve.

2. The circle below represents 100% of the time. In the circle, shade in the percentage of time you are currently having this problem.

3. Now look at the unshaded area that indicates times the problem isn't occurring (exceptional times) and describe in detail what is happening during these times.

4. What do you need to do make the percentage of time that the problem doesn't occur larger? Describe in detail.

5. Use the S-A-M-I-C acronym to establish a goal.

6. What can you do between now and next week to make the "unshaded "times occur?

NARRATIVE COUNSELING

Michael White is credited as the founder of Narrative Counseling, a theoretical approach that focuses on the stories we choose to tell in counseling. These selected narratives are based on perceptions of interactions with others, social factors, and experiences. The problems that bring the student to counseling, or *dominant plots,* are uncovered as the counselor carefully listens and assists the student in authoring new possibilities for living (Archer & McCarthy, 2007). Through the counselor/student relationship and the counselor's use of wisely couched questions, attention is given to *alternative discourses* or other interpretations of the problem (Carey, Walther, & Russell, 2009). This collaborative approach deconstructs or "re-examines" the problem with the intent of developing alternative stories or plots for problem resolution (Archer & McCarthy, 2007).

Techniques

Narrative counseling consists of defining the problem, mapping the influence of the problem, evaluating the effects of the problem, identifying unique outcomes, and restorying (White & Epston, 1990). Movement through these stages is facilitated through skillful questions, metaphors, strength identification, and unique outcomes.

Questions. Questions are used to gain a clearer understanding of how the student views the problem. *Relative influence questions* are used to separate the student from the problem and to "map" the influence of the problem on the student's life. The counselor and student collaboratively determine how the problem influences school, peers, and family, and so on. For example, the counselor could ask, "How has the issue gained control over your life?" or, "When would your mom say you have control over the situation?"

Use of Metaphors. Figurative language offers the student an opportunity to objectify the problem by giving the problem a name. This externalization of the problem aids the counselee in re-authoring the stories by recognizing that "the person is not the problem, the problem is the problem" (Schofield, 2013). In addition, externalization symbolizes the problem as peripheral to the student, gives the student an opportunity to "view" the problem from a distance (Carey et al., 2009; Lambie & Milsom, 2010), and facilitates a more comfortable counseling environment to tell a story (Lambie & Milsom, 2010). For example, the counselor could say, "You have been telling me about your experiences in school and the difficult time you are having. Could you come up with a name for the trouble?" I once worked with a high school student who had test anxiety. In working with her from a narrative perspective, she named the text anxiety as "Fred," and from here on our counseling consisted of talking about Fred and the frequency Fred would visit, the duration of his visit, and the intensity of his influence in different aspects of life. Or, as in the questions above, "How has Fred gained control over you?" or, "When would your teacher say you have control over Fred?"

Strengths and Unique Outcomes. As the counselor listens to the student's story, attention is given to individual strengths as resources to generate positive change. These *unique outcomes* or *sparkling moments* are then used to re-author a new story that is facilitated by: a) emphasizing the unique outcomes; b) focusing on the new problem-free story; c) asking about strategies to make the new narrative happen; and d) questioning how unique outcomes can continue outside counseling sessions (Lambie & Milsom, 2010). These skills invite inquiries about intention and purposes. For instance, "What were you hoping would happen when you decided to do that?" or, "How did this action reflect what is important to you?" (Carey et al., 2009).

Multicultural Considerations

Through narrative counseling, counselors are able to listen to students' stories and explore their cultural views (Semmler & Williams, 2000). Although there is a paucity of literature surrounding narrative therapy and diverse populations, it is a powerful counseling approach in which to explore the influence of culture on counselee's lives (Semmler & Williams, 2000). Narrative counseling is also a respectful method for telling narratives among some indigenous communities in Africa and Australia (Mpofu et al., 2013; Schofield, 2013).

Applications in Schools

Clearly, this theoretical orientation provides students with an opportunity to tell their story, yet not all youth are able to verbalize events in their lives. In these cases the counselor could consider combining a narrative approach with creative arts. For example, drawing a self-portrait is an alternative, creative strategy for students to "tell" their story (Carlson, 1997), or the counselor could ask the student to draw a picture of a person with the same problem he/she is currently experiencing. These activities give the counselor an opportunity to ask about the influences of the problem on the student's life while he/she is able to distance him/her self from the problem. From here, the student could visualize the illustrated person having control over the problem and draw a picture of that person controlling the problem. Through a combination of art and narrative counseling the counselor is able to get a better understanding of the dominant story, and the student is able to externalize the situation and recognize new behaviors that lead to a new, revised life story. In addition to art, visualization and the use of puppets in counseling are also effective techniques to externalize the problem (Butler, Guterman, & Rudes, 2009). Student Activity 6.7 *Powerful Me* is an example of bridging narrative counseling with creative methods.

STUDENT ACTIVITY 6.7. "POWERFUL ME"

Write out or draw your answers to the following questions in as much detail as possible.

1. Name the problem. Describe this issue in as much detail as possible.

2. How is this a problem for you? (Is it evident in relationships, behaviors, feelings, or in other ways?)

3. How is it influencing your life? (Evaluate how it is influencing school, friends, work, activities, family, etc.)

4. When do you have control over the problem?

5. When is the problem easier to handle?

6. What strengths or skills do you have that can be used to solve the problem?

7. Describe how you can use these skills to conquer the problem.

Traditional counseling theories such as those summarized above can be supplemented with expressive, creative approaches to better meet the developmental needs of individual students. Expressive arts is the " . . . use of techniques, such as drawing, painting, collage and sculpting, to help a person express and visualize emotions" (Bauer, 2011, para. 2). Not only are expressive strategies conceptualized as a mode of working with children, individuals of all ages are able to engage in these methodologies (Murphy, 2010). Advantages for using creative arts in counseling include the following: 1) students are able to express themselves in ways that cannot be conveyed through "talk"; 2) a chance to give voice to people marginalized due to race, gender, diversity, or any other reason (Ledger & Edwards, 2011); 3) a "hook" for engaging youth in ways that other techniques are unable to do (Olson-McBride & Page, 2012); and 4) an opportunity for collaboration and group connectedness. Creative interventions take a number of forms, such as walking with a student around the playground or track, making collages, or bringing in photographs. Spontaneity and flexibility and selecting the types of media that would best meet the needs of the counselee are essential in determining when to use a creative intervention. Play in counseling, art media, literature, music, and movement in counseling are discussed below.

EXPRESSIVE ARTS IN COUNSELING

Play in Counseling

Play is a child's natural activity and is therefore a useful developmental approach for working with children who have not yet mastered their verbal skills or abstract reasoning (Hall, Kaduson, & Schaefer, 2002). Through play, children are able to indirectly view and express a problem from a different perspective while learning about themselves and others (Shallcross, 2010).

Careful consideration of the types of materials to include in counseling facilitates the communication process. Media to consider include: 1) playdoh; 2) puppets that fit into the categories of real-life toys (doll houses, dolls, household items, telephones, fruit and vegetables, etc.); 3) acting-out and aggressive toys (handcuffs, suction darts, hammer, toy soldiers and military equipment, masks, etc.); or 4) creative media (chalk, markers, colored paper, tape, paste, pipe cleaners, etc.). Toys that represent violence such as toy guns and plastic knives are useful in play counseling rooms, yet because of "zero-tolerance" policies many school administrators do not allow any semblance to weapons in the schools. (See Box 6. 2 for toy selection ideas). However, if you believe these toys are essential to the goals of counseling, discuss the importance of these toys with your principal for permission for their inclusion into your array of counseling materials. Student Activity 6.8 *The Feeling Game* is a creative approach for students to recognize the link between feelings and physiological responses.

STUDENT ACTIVITY 6.8. THE FEELING GAME

Everyday toys such as blocks or even the Jenga game can be used to assist students in recognizing feelings and understanding issues influencing the student. The counselor evenly divides the Jenga blocks between him/herself and the student. A block is placed on the table and each person selects a block and places it on top of the already placed blocks to make a tower. As each block is placed, a specific event is discussed along with a feeling statement and physiological response. For instance, "When my girlfriend ignores me I feel sad." "I know I am sad because my stomach hurts and I cry." If the child is having difficulty identifying an incident, feeling, and response, the counselor can write down open-ended statements on index cards. For example, "I am happy when . . . ," and "I know I am happy because. . . . ." The child reads the statement on the card and places a block on top of the previous block. The game continues until the tower tumbles over.

BOX 6.2 TOYS FOR PLAY IN COUNSELING

Counselors select toys that represent all facets of life. A list of toys that facilitate expression is below.

Nurturing Toys	Expressive Toys	Cultural Considerations	Nature	Aggressive Toys
Dolls	Pipe Cleaners	Dolls with various skin tones	Shells	Representations of "scary" animals (e.g., sharks)
Families	Crayons	Variety of jewelry or utensils from other countries	Stones and rocks of various sizes	Toy soldiers
Furniture	Newsprint	Cultural toys	Sand	Handcuffs
Nursing bottle	Blunt scissors	Doll clothes representing culture	Leaves	Rubber knife
Play dishes & Utensils	Popsicle sticks	Pictures	Twigs	Aggressive hand puppets

Adapted from Landreth, Ray, & Bratton (2009)

Considerations in Play. The benefits of play in counseling are documented (VanVelsor, 2013); however, teachers and parents may not fully understand how play can actually be a useful counseling approach for helping children and youth. They naturally want to know the purpose of play in counseling, particularly if instructional time will be missed (Landreth, Ray, & Bratton, 2009). If you wish to garner support for dismissing students from class who may be struggling academically, conduct an in-service workshop at the beginning of the year to discuss the benefits of play in counseling (Landreth et al., 2009) and to solicit parent/guardian and teacher cooperation. Ideally, a fully equipped room designed specifically for play is recommended, yet few school counselors have the luxury of having a room dedicated specifically for counseling. Many school counselors have to share an office with another person such as the speech therapist, or travel from building to building. In these instances a tote bag filled with items that can be transported from place to place is helpful. In your school counseling program you will learn about theoretical models, child development, and basic responding skills. If the use of play in counseling is an approach that you would like to incorporate into your school counseling program, identify an experienced school counselor to receive appropriate training under supervision to develop personal insight, skill, and practice in the use of toys in counseling.

Visual Arts in Counseling

The use of art in counseling involves creating or viewing art, and emotionally processing the final product. It is also a useful method for fostering cultural awareness, personal growth, and mental wellness (Gladding, 2005) in a nonthreatening manner. Several visual arts methods include using already existing artwork such

Photo 6.1   Students Expressing Themselves Through Chalk Drawings

as that which appears in magazines, or postcards, posters, art prints, in addition to photos taken by the counselee, of the counselee, self-portraits, or any photograph that creates emotional responses. Although these types of methods speak to individuals from all ethnicities and cultures, the counselor has a responsibility to be aware of the counselee's cultural heritage to more thoroughly understand the meaning of the imagery and metaphor (Gladding, 2005). Student Activity 6.9 *My Future Timeline* is an example of a creative art activity to identify long-term goals.

STUDENT ACTIVITY 6.9. MY FUTURE TIMELINE

The student with whom you are working is given a piece of paper on which a horizontal line is drawn. On the far left side of the line, the student draws or locates a picture from a magazine or other source to represent his/her birth date. On the far right side, the student selects or draws a picture to represent an appropriate long-term, future goal. The student then draws a short vertical segment on the horizontal line between the two points to represent his/her age at the present time. Next, the student is asked to write words, draw a picture, or paste pictures on line segments that represent significant life events that have occurred. For instance, birthdays, holidays, preschool, or traumatic incidents can be indicated. As the events are recalled, the student is encouraged to discuss these events in as much detail as possible, while the counselor asks questions such as, "How did you feel when this happened?" or "How do you feel now?" or "Is there anything that you could do to make this situation better today?" Then, the student can identify future events he/she hopes will occur to reach the specified goal indicated by the year on the far right. The counselor is able to prompt the student through questions such as, "How can you make this event happen?" The use of pictures provides a concrete reminder of the steps needed to reach the designated goal and to envision future possibilities.

2/14/2006   2008 Sister Born   2010 Parents Divorced   Age Today   2020

The Use of Literature in Counseling

Bibliocounseling, poetry, storybooks, fairytales, and nursery rhymes are all forms of literature that aid in personal growth and self-understanding. Children's literature teaches lessons about handling personal issues, inspires courage, aids in overcoming fears, teaches interpersonal communication skills, and interconnects fictitious characters whose feelings and challenges parallel the student's issues. Identification, catharsis, insight, and universality are four interrelated stages when literature is used in counseling. During the

Photo 6.2   Art Is a Nonthreatening Vehicle for Communicating and Expressing Oneself

identification stage, characters, situations, and settings are recognized with the intention of creating emotional involvement and reactions. Identification with the story characters including recognition of characteristics, motivations, thoughts, behaviors, and feelings brings about insight. Universality is an outcome when the counselor processes these factors with the student, having the intention of gaining self-awareness with newly experienced thoughts, feelings, and behaviors (Gladding, 2005).

Mutual storytelling is another bibliocounseling technique in which the counselor and student tell a story together. The counselor starts the story with the words "Once upon a time . . ." and narrates a tale that is similar to the student's current issue. At a certain point the counselor invites the student to add to the story and only gives assistance when the student is stuck. This creative approach facilitates insight as the student subconsciously reveals aspects of him/herself while indirectly resolving life events.

Adolescents can also bring in literature that is personally meaningful, write stories, or create poetry. Bibliocounseling can also be used to meet academic standards as school counselors collaborate with teachers to integrate reading and writing competencies while learning about self and others. Or, teachers of language arts and history can collaborate with the school counselor through discussing narratives that teach culturally specific information. For example, in a history class a poem written from a certain sociocultural perspective may facilitate the reader's ability to move beyond his/her culture and empathize with the affect behind the poetry. Literature also has the potential to increase an appreciation for one's own culture and ethnicity (Pehrsson & McMillen, 2003). The school counselor, in partnership with a social studies teacher, could work with students to write a poem or song lyrics that depict a character from a different country, a dissimilar ethnicity from the student, or from a different period of time. Or, the school counselor could share a poem that has personal meaning for him/her, discuss the key concepts, special connection with the characters, and offer a particular empathic reflection of the characters (Ingram, 2003).

The needs and the developmental level of the student are points to consider when using literature in counseling because there is always a danger that the student does not identify with the story protagonists, may refuse to discuss topics that create discomfort, or may not follow through on the application of appropriate solutions to personal problems (Eppler, Olsen, & Hidano, 2009). Student Activity 6.10 *A Personal Diamante* is an example of a literary counseling strategy that could address the student competencies identified in the counseling program and in language arts classes.

STUDENT ACTIVITY 6.10. A PERSONAL DIAMANTE

A diamante is a poem that forms a diamond when finished. The first and last line consist of one word that starts and ends with an antonym, a synonym, or the same word. The second line of the poem consists of two adjectives about the first word. The third line contains three "ing" words about the beginning topic. The fourth line includes four nouns or a short phrase linking the topic. The fifth line contains three "ing" words that relate to the ending topic. The sixth line contains two adjectives about the final word.

Dark

Ebony   Eternal

Prohibiting   Tossing   Thinking

Shadows   Demons   Voices   Visitors

Flickering   Guiding   Beckoning

Hopeful   Visible

Light

After reading the poetry, respond to the following questions.

1. What are you feeling about the poem or story?

2. If you were the writer of the poem or story, how would you feel? Behave?

Music and Dance

Regardless of culture or ethnicity, music produces a range of mental, emotional, physical, and/or spiritual responses (Gladding, 2005). Children are naturally energetic, and although movement is a natural means for expressing self (Gladding, 2005), unfortunately outside of physical education or recess, the educational environment does not always welcome this form of expression as a learning strategy. Music connects people, and youth are much more likely to participate in group activities when they are allowed to listen, and share feelings and thoughts about music that "speaks to them" (Olson-McBride & Page, 2012). Music in counseling can take the form of writing lyrics, listening, playing an instrument, or singing.

Photo 6.3 The Use of Literature in Counseling Is a Creative Approach for Helping Students Develop Personal Insight While Reinforcing Academic Skills

Songs help individuals relax, learn, or develop self-understanding. The counselor could ask the student to select a song that has special meaning to better understand the student's attitudes and values, or students may wish to write a song with lyrics that express their feelings, thoughts, or behaviors. Olson-McBride and Page (2012) conducted intervention groups with at-risk adolescents in which the use of poetry and music provided the means for self-disclosure. In these sessions students selected songs that contained themes of special personal significance, and as the group progressed members shared song lyrics that were meaningful to them. This process of moving from "song-to-self" facilitated movement from a discussion of lyrics to personal thoughts, feelings, and experiences, while a community of trust was created in which students felt comfortable in sharing horrific acts of sexual abuse, mental illness and substance abuse. These disclosures resulted in members having the courage to form meaningful relationships with group members from whom they were previously distanced. Student Activity 6.11 *Rapping Science Vocabulary* is an example of a strategy for using music that meets counseling standards as well as standards in academic classes such as science.

STUDENT ACTIVITY 6.11. RAPPING SCIENCE VOCABULARY

Students can create a rap song using the concepts they learned in science class. Have the students talk about ways songs can help them learn and remember academic terms.

Movement in Counseling

Dance and movement facilitate a mind-body connection in which actions are integrated with emotion. Counselors often combine dance/movement with activities such as martial arts, yoga, breath-work, and relaxation. Although some movement strategies such as yoga are not part of traditional forms of counseling, its use significantly enhances psychological growth through its emphasis on feelings and senses, while reducing a focus on performance. Koshland, Wittaker, and Wilson (2004) conducted a 12-week dance/movement program with elementary-age children that focused on socialization and self-regulation. As a result of participating in this program, children showed a significant decrease in the frequency of aggressive behaviors and negative classroom behaviors.

Khalsa, Hickey-Schultz, Cohen, Steiner, and Cope (2011) also revealed the benefits of movement. Adolescents were randomly assigned to either a regular physical education class or to a yoga class over an academic semester. The study results revealed that the students in the yoga group reported improvements in stress compared to those who participated in the regular physical education class.

Regardless of the type of approach that is chosen, school counselors talk about the difficulty of counseling with school-age youth while respecting the rights of parents/guardians and teachers who work with students on a daily basis. Whether or not to tell parents that their child is receiving counseling services, and how to safeguard confidentiality are two of the most difficult concerns expressed by school counselors (Williams, 2007, 2009). The next section provides information on best practices for communicating the school counselor's role with respect to the various school stakeholders.

CONFIDENTIALITY AND WORKING WITH STAKEHOLDERS

Some school districts consider counseling as a part of the educational services provided by the district, whereas other school districts require parent/guardian permission before any child can be seen for counseling (Williams, 2009). The rights of students to seek counseling while being assured of a confidential relationship that complies with laws, policies, and ethical standards is of paramount importance to school-age youth. In a 1995 study by Collins and Knowles, as cited by Williams (2007), over 53% of surveyed adolescents stated that confidentiality with their school counselor was essential to an effective relationship, with another 46% who responded that confidentiality was important. Regardless of the approach that is taken by your school board, educating others about your program is a prerequisite to a healthy, supportive relationship among all stakeholders. A professional disclosure statement that outlines your professional education, experience, and training that is offered to interested parties is considered a best practice. Box 6.3 is an example of a professional disclosure statement and can be used as a template to develop your own disclosure statement.

BOX 6.3 PROFESSIONAL DISCLOSURE STATEMENT

Melissa Martin

Licensed Professional School Counselor

Hartley Middle School

This Disclosure Statement is designed to inform you of my professional credentials, types of services I provide and therapeutic orientation and style.

Education

M.S. in School Counseling, Technology College, 2007

B.S. in Psychology, University of Excellence, 2004

Work Experience

Hartley Middle School 2007–present

Case Manager, 2004–2007

Professional Organizations

American Counseling Association (ACA)

American School Counselor Association (ASCA)

Counseling Philosophy

My role in the school is to support the academic, career, and personal/social growth of all the students enrolled in the school. I provide consultation, advocacy for students, and individual and group counseling. Within these roles I recognize that my primary responsibility is confidentiality to your child, but I also recognize parental rights as primary voices in the lives of their children. In order to work most effectively with your child, I collaborate with individuals who have a primary role in your child's life, and in doing so I respect the child's right to privacy. However, I will disclose information your child shares if he/she indicates harm to self or others.

Counseling Approach

I feel every child is unique and a complex being; therefore, the approach I take with your child will be based on his/her development and needs. I use a variety of counseling approaches including person-centered, cognitive-behavioral, reality, rational-emotive counseling, narrative, and solution-focused brief counseling. In addition, I use creative approaches to help your child gain a better understanding of the issues that brought him/her to counseling. Most sessions will focus on self-awareness, choice, problem-solving, and setting goals for the present and future to support academic growth. There are times I will assign homework such as journal writing, reading, or art.

You are encouraged to discuss any questions or concerns you have about my role as a school counselor or the counseling process. Thank you for the opportunity to work with your child.

Although ASCA ethics discuss the importance of confidentiality, we must also follow school policy and procedures, and there are some school districts that require parental/guardian permission for counseling, or specify a specific number of counseling meetings before parent/guardian permission is needed. With policies such as these in place, students who desperately need the counseling services will miss an opportunity for receiving the support they need. If this is the established requirement there are several steps you can take. Clarifying the counseling relationship with both parents and children through informed consent at the beginning of each school year is an opportunity to begin the year with clear boundaries. In addition, the importance of confidentiality should be included in the student handbook, on the school counseling website, or in brochures. Through straightforward communication from the beginning problems can be avoided.

Finally, how do school counselors convince teachers to release students from classes when there is so much pressure for students to spend as much time in the classroom to master identified concepts? Some school counselors work with students when they are in related classes such as music, art, or physical education, yet these are often the classes that students who are struggling enjoy more than the more academic-based classes. Furthermore, the teachers of these classes tend to feel that this practice devalues the content of these subjects. Perhaps the most essential approach to gain the support of teachers to release students from their classes is to demonstrate how counseling can aid in supporting academic progress. Figure 6.1 depicts the progress of students who worked with a school counselor on academic goals, and when the counselor shared this information with teachers they had a greater appreciation for counselor interventions and the usefulness of counseling to their subject content.

Figure 6.1　Results of Students' Improved GPA After Receiving Counseling

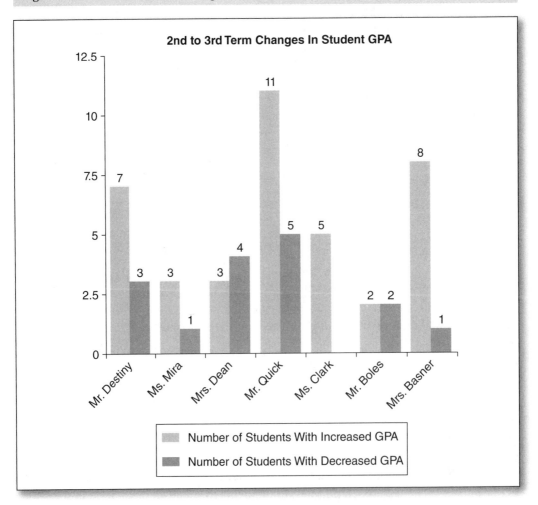

CONCLUSION

School counselors provide individual counseling for students who are struggling academically, vocationally, and personally. The practice of motivational interviewing is a useful strategy to use in conjunction with any counseling theoretical approach. Person-centered Counseling, Adlerian counseling, Reality Counseling, Rational-Emotive Behavior Therapy, Solution-Focused Brief Counseling, and Narrative Counseling are commonly used theoretical approaches adopted by school counselors. When students are unable or uncomfortable talking through personal issues, creative techniques can complement these methods. Play, visual arts, literature, music, and movement in counseling are expressive arts methodologies that are successful in facilitating change. In selecting an expressive art for a particular student, the school counselor considers the child's developmental needs and interests to best facilitate change.

Although many school districts consider individual counseling as an essential component of the academic mission, other school districts have been reluctant for counseling to occur without full knowledge and consent of the parent or guardian. School counselors are often placed in a precarious position when they have an ethical obligation to maintain the confidences of the child while maintaining their obligations to parents/guardians. A professional disclosure form that emphasizes the school counselor's experiences, education, and training provided to all stakeholders from the beginning assists in role clarification and educating others about the counseling relationship.

REFERENCES

Archer, J., & McCarthy, C. J. (2007). *Theories of counseling and psychotherapy: Contemporary applications.* Upper Saddle River, NJ: Pearson.

ASCA (2010). Ethical standards for school counselors. Retrieved from www.schoolcounselors .org/files/EthicalStandards 2010.pdf.

ASCA (n.d.). Careers/Roles. Retrieved from http://www.schoolcounselor.org/

Banks, T., & Zionts, P. (2009). REBT used with children and adolescents who have emotional and behavioral disorders in educational settings: A review of the literature. *Journal of Rational-Emotive & Cognitive Behavior Therapy, 27,* 51–65.

Bauer, M. (2011). Expressive art therapy for children. Retrieved from http://www.livestrong.com/ article/209497-expressive-art-therapy-for-children/

Bernard, M.E., Ellis, A., & Terjesen, M. (2006). *Rational-emotive behavioral approaches to childhood disorders: History, theory, practice and research.* New York, NY: Springer.

Butler, S., Guterman, J. T., & Rudes, J. (2009). Using puppets with children in narrative therapy to externalize the problem. *Journal of Mental Health Counseling, 31,* 225–233.

Canfield, B. S. (2012, May, 7). ACA provides feedback on the ASCA National Model revision [Electronic mailing list message]. Retrieved CESNET- L@LISTSERV.KENT.EDU

Carey, M., Walther, S. A., Russell, S. (2009). The absent but implicit: A map to support therapeutic enquiry. *Family Process*, 48, 319–331.

Carlson, T. D. (1997). Using art in narrative therapy: Enhancing therapeutic possibilities. *American Journal of Family Therapy*, 25, 271–283.

Corey, G. (2009). *Theory and practice of counseling and psychotherapy* (9th ed.). Belmont, CA: Brooks/Cole.

Enea, V., & Dafinoiu, I. (2009). Motivational/solution-focused intervention for reducing school truancy among adolescents. *Journal of Cognitive and Behavioral Psychotherapies*, 9, 185–198.

Eppler, C., Olsen, J. A., & Hidano, L. (2009). Using stories in elementary school counseling: brief, narrative techniques. *Professional School Counseling*, 12, 387–391.

Fearrington, J. Y., McCallum, R. S., & Skinner, C. H. (2011). Increasing math assignment completion using solution-focused brief counseling. *Education and Treatment of Children,* 34, 61–80.

Frey, A. J., Cloud, R. N. Lee, J., Small, J. W., Steeley, J. R., Fell, E. G., Walker, H. M., & Golly, A. (2011). The promise of motivational interviewing in school mental health. *School Mental Health*, 3, 1–12. doi: 10.1007/s12310–010–9048-z

Gladding, S. (2005). *Counseling as an art: The creative arts in counseling* (3rd ed.). Alexandria, VA: American Counseling Association.

Glasser, W. (2001). *Counseling with choice theory*. New York, NY: Harper Collins.

Hall, T. M., Kaduson, H. G., & Schaefer, C. E. (2002). Fifteen effective play therapy techniques. *Professional Psychology: Research and Practice*, 33, 515–522.

Ingram, M. A. (2003, July/August). Rhyme with reason. *School Counselor*. Alexandria, VA: ASCA.

Ivey, A. E., D'Andrea, M. J., & Ivey, M. B. (2012). *Theories of Counseling & Psychotherapy: A Multicultural Perspective* (7th ed.). Los Angeles, CA: Sage.

Jones, C. N., Hart, S. R., Jimerson, S. R., Dowdy, E., Earhart, J. Renshaw, T., & Eklund, K. (2009). Solution-focused brief counseling: Guidelines, considerations, and implications for school psychologists. *California School Psychologist*, 14, 111–122.

Khalsa, S. B., Hickey-Schultz, L., Cohen, D., Steiner, N., & Cope, S. (2011). Evaluation of the mental health benefits of yoga in a secondary school: A preliminary randomized controlled trial. *Journal of Behavioral Health Services & Research*, 39, 80–90. doi10.1007/s11414–011-9249-8

Koshland, L., & Wittaker, J. W. & Wilson, B. (2004). PEACE through dance/movement: Evaluating a violence prevention program. *American Journal of Dance Therapy*, 26, 69–90.

Lambie, G. W., & Milsom, A. (2010). A narrative approach to supporting students diagnosed with learning disabilities. *Journal of Counseling & Development*, 88, 196–203.

Landreth, G. L., Ray D. C., & Bratton, S. C. (2009). Play therapy in elementary schools. *Psychology in the Schools,* 46, 281–289. doi:10.1002/pits.20374

Ledger, A. & Edwards, J. (2011). Arts-based research practices in music therapy research: Existing and potential developments. *The Arts in Psychotherapy*, 38, 312–317.

Lee, S. M., & Yang, E. (2013). Counseling in South Korea. In T. H. Hohenshil, N. E. Amundson, & S. G. Niles (Eds.), *Counseling around the world: An international handbook* (pp. 137–144). Alexandria, VA: ACA.

Locke, D. C., & Bailey, D. F. (2014). *Increasing multicultural understanding*. Los Angeles, CA: Sage.

Loyd, B. D. (2005). The effects of reality therapy/choice theory principles on high school students' perception of needs satisfaction and behavioral change. *International Journal of Reality Therapy*, 25, 5–9.

Mikhemar, S. (2013). Counseling in Egypt. In T.H. Hohenshil, N.E. Amundson, & S.G. Niles (Eds.), *Counseling around the world: An international handbook* (pp. 275–283). Alexandria, VA: ACA.

Miller, N. H. (2010). Motivational interviewing as a prelude to coaching in healthcare settings. *Journal of Cardiovascular Nursing*, 25, 247–251.

Miller, W. R., & Rose, G. S. (2009). Toward a theory of motivational interviewing. *American Psychologist,* 64, 527–537. doi: 10.1037/a0016830

Mpofu, E., Makuane, M. R., Richards, K. A., Mhaka-Mutepfa, M. M. Mpofu, J., Zebron, S., & Clever, M. N (2013). Counseling in Zimbabwe. In T.H. Hohenshil, N.E. Amundson, & S.G. Niles (Eds.), *Counseling around the world: An international handbook* (pp. 65–76). Alexandria, VA: ACA.

Murphy, S. N. (2010, February). Remembering play. *Counseling Today*. Alexandria, VA: ACA.

National Institutes of Health (2013). MedlinePlus. Retrieved from http://www.nlm.nih.gov/medlineplus/news/fullstory_136915.html

Olson-McBride, L. & Page, T. F. (2012). Song to self: promoting a therapeutic dialogue with high-risk youths through poetry and popular music. *Social Work with Groups*, 35, 124–137. doi.org/10.1080/01609513.2011.603117

Paterson, J. (2011, June). Bullies with byte. *Counseling Today*. Alexandria, VA: ACA.

Pehrsson, D.E., & McMillen (2003). Competent bibliotherapy: Preparing counselors to use literature with culturally diverse clients. VISTAS. Alexandria, VA: ACA. Retrieved from http://counselingoutfitters.com/Pehrsson.htm

Rosenthal. H. G. (2001). *Favorite counseling and therapy homework assignments* (pp. 82–84). Philadelphia, PA: Routledge.

Saginak, K. (2012, May, 1). ACA provides feedback on the ASCA National Model revision [Electronic Mailing List Message]. Retrieved CESNET-L@LISTSERV.KENT.EDU

Schofield, M. J. (2013). Counseling in Australia. In T. H. Hohenshil, N. E. Amundson, & S. E. Nikes (Ed.), *Counseling around the world: An international handbook* (pp. 335–348). Alexandria, VA: American Counseling Association.

Selekman, M., & Gil, E. (2010). *Collaborative brief therapy with children*. New York, NY: Guilford Press.

Semmler, P. L., & Williams, C. B. (2000). Narrative therapy: A storied context for multicultural counseling. *Journal of Multicultural Counseling & Development*, 28, 51–62.

Shallcross, L. (2010, November). The power of play. *Counseling Today*. American Counseling Association, 26–30.

Strasser, J. (2013). Couneling in Germany. In T. H. Hohenshil, N. E. Amundson, & S. E. Nikes (ed.). *Counseling around the world: An international handbook* (pp. 203–214). Alexandria, VA: American Counseling Association.

Substance Abuse and Mental Health Services Administration (2008, December). Mental Health Settings: New Data. Retrieved from http://www.samhsa.gov/samhsaNewsletter/Volume_16_Number_6/MentalHealthSettings.aspx

Thompson, C. L., Rudolph, L., & Henderson (2004). *Counseling children* (6th ed.). Belmont, CA: Thomson.

United States Department of Education (2010-2011). Student to school counselor ratio. Retrieved from http://www.schoolcounselor.org/asca/media/asca/home/Ratios10-11.pdf

VanVelsor, P. (2013, February). Thinking creatively: Expressive arts for counseling youth in the schools. *Counseling Today*, 55, 52–55.

Vernon, A. (2011). Rational emotive behavior therapy: The past, present, and future. *Journal of Rational-Emotive Cognitive-Behavior Therapy*, 29, 239–247. Doi 10.1007/s10942–011–0147-z

White, M., & Epston, D. (1990). *Narrative means to therapeutic end*. New York, NY: Norton.

Williams, R. (2007). To tell or not to tell: The question of informed consent. *ASCA School Counselor.* Alexandria, VA: ASCA.

Williams, R. (2009). Parent permission: A pain or an invitation. *ASCA School Counselor.* Alexandria, VA: ASCA.

Wright, R. J. (2012). *Introduction to school counseling*. Thousand Oaks, CA: Sage.

Wubbolding, R. E. (2000). *Reality therapy for the 21st century*. Muncie, IN: Accelerated Development.

Chapter 7

THE SCHOOL COUNSELOR'S ROLE IN CRISIS COUNSELING

*CACREP Standards

FOUNDATIONS

A. *Knowledge*

  7. Understands the operation of the school emergency management plan and the roles and responsibilities of the school counselor during crises, disasters, and other trauma-causing events.

COUNSELING, PREVENTION, AND INTERVENTION

C. *Knowledge*

  6. Understands the potential impact of crises, emergencies, and disasters on students, educators, and schools, and knows the skills needed for crisis intervention.

D. *Skills and Practices*

  4. Demonstrates the ability to use procedures for assessing and managing suicide risk.

ASSESSMENT

G. *Knowledge*

  1. Understands the influence of multiple factors (e.g., abuse, violence, eating disorders, attention deficit hyperactivity disorder, childhood depression) that may affect the personal, social, and academic functioning of students.

  2. Knows the signs and symptoms of substance abuse in children and adolescents, as well as the signs and symptoms of living in a home where substance abuse occurs.

CACREP

COLLABORATION AND CONSULTATION

M. *Knowledge*

> 7. Knows school and community collaboration models for crisis/disaster preparedness and response.

> *I was called to help at the middle school in our district when the news was shared that a student died in a zipline accident. Students and parents had just learned this news through text messages, which created disruption in the classrooms. As I made my way down the hallways I realized that learning the news and the uncertainty of its accuracy were creating a ripple of emotions among the students and faculty. Students who didn't even know this student were upset as they witnessed the emotional responses of their friends. When an announcement was made on the public address system I learned how difficult it is for administrators to make decisions without time to prepare or anticipate reactions. This experience helped me realize the importance of having a crisis intervention plan in place.*

> —Intermediate School Counselor

Depression, abuse, eating disorders, suicide, poverty, and substance use are just a few of the issues impacting today's school-age youth. Across the world crises happen every day—some make headlines and others are local, devastating situations that are smaller in impact, but critical to those who are personally influenced by these incidents. When a traumatic event occurs, an understanding of self and his/her world is interrupted and attempts are made to activate resources to reduce personal stress and regain a sense of equilibrium (Abernathy, 2008).

The school counselor is often the only mental health professional in the educational environment with the training and skills to work with students in crisis, yet few school counselors have received pre-service training in crisis intervention. Allen et al. (2002) revealed that only one-third of experienced school counselors in their study had received any training in crisis intervention. Understanding different types of crises youth encounter and strategies for helping them gain understanding and mastery over these events is an essential part of our role as school counselors. However, it is not enough to provide succor to devastated youth. You also have a responsibility to self-reflect on your attitudes and beliefs about youth who engage in risky behaviors, who contemplate harm to self or others, who live in appalling conditions, or indicate abuse or other horrific situations that have the potential of putting them at risk. This personal contemplation could create insight on whether or not your personal attitudes could contribute to additional student stress, or student recovery with an arsenal of coping strategies.

A definition of the various types of crises in schools, a crisis intervention model, and essential skills for the school counselor who works with students and families in crisis are discussed in this chapter. In addition, a critical incident management plan for the school and the role of the school counselor in that plan, various crises situations that are common in school settings, and counselor interventions are also included in this chapter.

YOUTH IN CRISIS

A crisis is a situation that occurs suddenly, unexpectedly, without warning, and surpasses a person's ability to cope (James & Gilliland, 2005). People who have been in crisis report feelings of helplessness, fear, tension, and confusion with physical reactions that include insomnia or nightmares, appetite changes, and/or psychosomatic complaints. Each of these reactions contributes to an inability to concentrate, higher absenteeism, and lowered academic performance (Walz & Kirkman, 2002).

At times, school counselors wonder why some students who experience the same event go into crisis and others do not. Children, like adults, react to stressful situations differently. Variables such as existing mental health problems, previous stressors, lack of support from family and significant others, reactions of parents and other close adults, prior warning of the event, personal characteristics, and direct exposure to the situation may place an individual at greater risk for traumatization (Bauman, 2008).

Type 1 and Type 11 Trauma are two categories of childhood trauma (Terr, 1995, as cited in James & Gilliland, 2005). Type 1 trauma occurs as a result of one sudden, distinct traumatic situation such as a car accident, whereas Type 11 trauma is longstanding, repeated ordeals such as child abuse. Youth who have experienced Type 11 traumas may be diagnosed as having conduct disorders, attention deficits, depression, or dissociative disorders (Terr, as cited in James & Gilliland, 2005). Without knowledge of situations that influence school-age youth and/or characteristics of youth in crisis, students may not get the help that is desperately needed. There is also some evidence that suggests an unrecognized trauma (Bauman, 2008) may lead to mental health disorders such as borderline personality disorder. Furthermore, some students who have experienced a traumatic event and have not received treatment have mistakenly been placed in special education classes due to the impaired cognitive ability that often accompanies a crisis.

TYPES OF CRISES

Developmental, situational or traumatic, and existential crises are not necessarily discrete and at times overlap with one another. These crises, even though they may be anticipated and expected, serve as a critical point for our understanding of how we view the world, with the potential to disrupt how we see ourselves (Abernathy, 2008) and others. For instance, a situational crisis such as a tornado could impact the individual's developmental growth and also create an existential crisis.

Developmental

Erik Erikson identified psychosocial stages in which developmental crises or tasks need to be accomplished at different stages throughout the lifecycle. These epigenetic stages require that each task in the previous stage needs to be accomplished before going on to the next developmental task. For instance, competence is to be accomplished during the school-age years of 6–12. In addition to the stages identified by Erikson, events such as divorce or retirement serve as catalysts of a developmental crisis.

Traumatic or Situational Crisis

A situational or traumatic crisis is a sudden, unexpected event that is unpredictable and uncontrollable (James & Gilliland, 2005). Natural or environmental disasters include such events as a hurricane, tsunami, tornado, school shootings, terrorist attacks, or toxic chemical spills. Although any of these events has the potential to put people in crisis, evidence suggests that man-made crises put people in a more vulnerable state than do those that are natural disasters (James & Gilliland, 2005).

Existential Crises

Loneliness, a lack of purpose in life, work, or death are existential crises that accelerate the contemplation of the meaning of life. An existential crisis often precipitates death, suicide, or major illness, whereas connections with others, participation in activities, establishment of educational goals including jobs, and involvement in the community contribute to resiliency among adolescents who experienced multiple crises (Flom & Hansen, 2006).

Whatever type of crisis the student is experiencing, crisis situations are time limited and usually last a maximum of six to eight weeks (James & Gilliland, 2005), with the precipitating event (the crisis) occurring usually 10–14 days before help is sought (Aquilera, 1998). An intervention is most effective when you see the student whenever and however often is necessary (Smith, n.d.), which could mean that a student will need to be seen several times during the week, and then again at a later date to assess problem resolution.

As the counselor, we are responsible for helping the student return to a state of normalcy with better coping skills than were in existence pre-crisis, or to a state of equilibrium. Successfully solving a crisis situation has the potential to promote a positive outcome that may include enhanced coping skills, a more complex understanding of life, a sense of competency (Abernathy, 2008), or an improved self-concept. Figure 7.1 illustrates the crisis process and resolution.

As illustrated in Figure 7.1, a state of *equilibrium* exists when the physical, behavioral, cognitive, and affect aspects of self are balanced and in harmony. When a crisis incident occurs, attempts are made to solve the problem (as depicted by the spiked lines in the illustration). As coping skills are activated without successful results, anxiety increases. When the crisis has been resolved, the student will experience a "new normal" that is hopefully at a higher level of functioning (new state of normalcy) due to the newly acquired coping skills. However, there are times when the crisis situation is so overwhelming that the student is at a lower level of functioning, and when this occurs, harmful responses could be a consequence.

Figure 7.1 Crisis Stages and Resolution

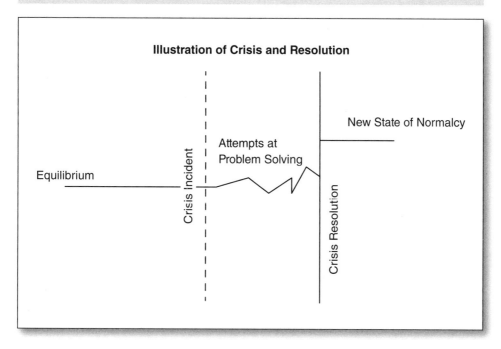

Illustration of Crisis and Resolution

In order to help you understand how a crisis situation is different from other difficult life situations, complete Conceptual Application Activity 7.1.

CONCEPTUAL APPLICATION ACTIVITY 7.1

Think of a time you were in crisis. If you are unable to think of a specific situation, think in terms of how you felt when you heard about or experienced events such as Hurricane Katrina or 9/11. How was this time of your life different from other times in your life? Physically? Cognitively? Behaviorally? Discuss your reactions with a classmate.

As may have been evident from Conceptual Application Activity 7.1, there are numerous affective, physical, cognitive, and behavioral responses expressed in crisis situations with a belief that no one has ever felt as you do when involved in the situation. When this occurs, individuals believe their feelings are somehow abnormal, and that something obviously must be wrong with them. Expressing, validating, and recognizing emotions is a type of self-disclosure associated with crisis reduction and resolution (Granello, 2010).

Behavior is impaired when a traumatic event occurs, and anxiety increases when multiple unsuccessful attempts are made to solve the problem using typical coping skills. Crisis may also be expressed as psychosomatic complaints in the form of headaches or sleeplessness, particularly among children with a limited vocabulary. As a school counselor you may want to check with the school nurse to determine the frequency a child has visited his/her office to complain about symptoms, or you may want to verify the child's attendance/tardiness record to determine absences.

Cognitively, people in crisis are incapacitated and unable to trigger rational thought. It is not unusual for traumatized students to repeat their story over and over, or for the student to have a problem accurately recalling specific parts of the event. This difficulty is a result of thoughts and emotions travelling through different parts of the brain (Echterling, Presbury, & McKee, 2005).

Crisis symptoms among individuals who have been part of a community disaster such as a flood or hurricane are similar to those who have directly witnessed traumatic situations. Too often teachers do not understand the characteristics of trauma and the impact on their students, and likewise school counselors may dismiss and not validate the reactions of those who were not directly impacted by an event. These indifferent reactions could lead to greater traumatization (Honos-Webb, Hart, & Scalise, 2009). In recognizing the different types of crises and the impact on student wellness, many school counselors wonder, "How do I work with students in crisis?" and "What is my role when my school is impacted by a crisis?" Box 7.1 contains common stress responses among students and can be used as a guide for instructing teachers about trauma reactions.

BOX 7.1 COMMON STUDENT STRESS RESPONSES

Physical

- Agitation
- Hyper-alertness
- Erratic Heartbeat
- Breathing problems
- Gastrointestinal Distress
- Sleep problems—excessive sleepiness or inability to sleep
- Tension-aches & pains
- Headaches

Cognitive

- Negative Outlook
- Anxiety in problem-solving
- Disorganized with inability to concentrate
- Sluggish or hyperactive thought processes
- Inability to see a different perspective
- Egocentrism

Emotional

- Generalized distress
- Anger or hostility
- Depression
- Anxiety, fear, or panic
- Powerlessness
- Undirected or directed guilt
- Shame or self-disgust

Social/Behavioral

- Substance abuse
- Eating disorders
- Constriction of activities (doing nothing)
- Inability to perform routine functions
- Restricted social contacts
- Deterioration of spiritual faith
- Rigid adherence to or rejection of perceived cultural values

A CRISIS INTERVENTION MODEL

A major difference between traditional and crisis counseling is that the goal of traditional counseling is to increase personal and interpersonal functioning, whereas the goal of crisis counseling is to decrease anxiety and increase coping with the intention of returning a person to a state of normalcy (Jackson-Cherry, & Erford, 2010). The LAPC Model of Crisis Intervention (Cavaiola & Colford, 2011) is a comprehensive guide for crisis counseling which includes the steps of Listen, Assess, Plan, Commit. These steps are not discrete but integrally related, as the counselor listens and collaboratively helps the student create a plan to which the student commits.

Listen

Listen, understand, validate (LUV) is a useful mnemonic devised by Echterling, et al. (2005), to remember while the student shares his/her distress. Using these skills while communicating to the student that he/she is in a place in which he/she can be heard, is in control, and is safe validates the student's pain (Honos-Webb, et al., 2009). In addition, listen for the student's needs while remembering that what he/she identifies as a need may not necessarily be what you believe to be essential to the student's recovery. For instance, I counseled an 18-year-old high school female who only had enough credits to be considered a freshman because a few years earlier she had dropped out of school, gotten married, and was raising two young children. She decided to return to school to finish her degree despite the protests of her husband, who wanted her to stay at home. One morning she stopped in my office sporting a black eye that her husband had given her when she announced she was going to school that morning. Naturally, I was concerned about such things as her health and safety, her children, where she would stay, and so on. However, her priority concern was about missing a party she wanted to attend that weekend. We were obviously concerned about entirely different needs at this time.

Trauma influences each person individually and cultural differences play a role when providing crisis support (Bauman, 2008). Knowledge of the beliefs, values, and experiences of culturally diverse individuals facilitates crisis resolution. For instance, individuals from war-torn countries who have immigrated to a new country have already faced pain and suffering due to the devastation of war, and additional stress could be a result as they try to acculturate themselves to a new country. Furthermore, many cultural groups have additional conflict as they experience discrimination and racism (Amri, Nassar-McMillan, Amen-Bryan, &

Misenhimer, 2013). In some cases, it may be necessary to collaborate with leaders from the student's cultural group to ensure that the student and his/her family receive appropriate support.

Assess

Some distressed students need to "tell their story" repeatedly, without interruptions, with the likelihood that the student may need assistance in finding the right words to accurately reflect his/her feelings. Through reflection of feelings and validation, the student may begin to recognize that his/her feelings do not mean that he or she is "crazy" but rather that he/she is having normal reactions to an abnormal situation. Determining the student's perception of the event, significant others in the student's life, and coping skills are balancing factors that can restore normalcy (Aquilera, 1998).

Perception of the Event. Cognition is the meaning a person puts on a stressful event and how the threat is perceived as a disruption to goals, values, or coping styles (Aquilera, 1998). In some cases, the significant event may be denied and avoided, whereas a realistic view of the event facilitates successful problem-solving. In other cases the student may attempt multiple, established problem-solving strategies, and as each attempt fails, anxiety increases. Determining what the event means to the person and how goals are influenced aid in assessing the student's perception of the incident.

Situational Supports. Situational supports are the individuals who can be counted on to nurture and provide support when self-esteem is threatened (Aquilera, 1998) as a result of a distressing event. Coping is influenced by the ability or inability of others to provide assistance and affirmation, and to identify these individuals school counselors can ask the question, "Who are the people in your life to whom you can go when you need help?" Student Activity 7.1 *Who Are My Supports?* is an activity to answer this question.

STUDENT ACTIVITY 7.1. WHO ARE MY SUPPORTS?

Give the student a blank sheet of paper and ask him/her to make a circle that represents him/herself. The student can decide where to place the circle on the paper as well as the size of the circle, and writes his/her name in the middle of the circle. Then,

(Continued)

(Continued)

ask the student to think of different people in his/her life, and without censoring any-one, ask him/her to draw a circle representing each of these individuals and that person's name in the circle. Again, it is the student's decision as to the size and placement of these circles.

When the student is finished, ask the student to draw solid lines from the circle that represents self and the individuals with whom he/she feels there is a strong relationship. For the individuals with whom there is a tenuous relationship, the student draws a dotted line, and for those in which there is a tense relationship, a jagged line is to be drawn.

Next, ask the student about the size and distance of circles from one another, including his or her circle, and to identify people who are missing from the diagram. A discussion of these significant individuals and their relationship to the student can be followed by a conversation of how the student would prefer his/her relationships to appear, and what steps need to be taken to make this goal occur. Finally, the student is instructed to put the names and contact information of those with whom he/she feels a strong relationship in a safe place so that they can be reached in an emergency situation. An example is below:

Example of Student Activity 7.1

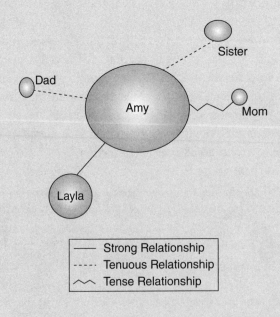

——	Strong Relationship
- - - -	Tenuous Relationship
∿∿	Tense Relationship

Coping Mechanisms. Coping skills range from either consciously or unconsciously expressed cognitive, affective, spiritual, or behavioral responses (Aquilera, 1998; James & Gilliland, 2005). Coping includes having feelings that are unpleasant but normal in an atypical situation. When a person believes he/she has the skills to overcome a situation, his/her world appears more meaningful and understandable, and the coping skills that are utilized lead to a sense of confidence, strength, and self-efficacy (Abernathy, 2008). Other individuals respond by denying the event, and in doing so unresolved issues could resurface and exacerbate a future dilemma. There are other individuals who lack appropriate coping skills to confront a crisis that potentially erodes their confidence and ability to seek mental health assistance (Smith, n.d.).

Because crisis events usually occur 12–14 days prior to the student seeking counseling (Aquilera, 1998), ask the student the reason he/she decided to seek help from you at that particular time. For example, I met with a ninth-grade student who spoke with me about her parents' impending divorce. During these sessions I was impressed with her thoughtful appraisal of the situation and her ability to handle some of the expected events. A few days after our last meeting I was surprised when she arrived in my office in tears, and between sobs she choked out, "My parents are getting a divorce!" This statement perplexed me because this was something we had discussed on several occasions. When I asked her if something recently occurred that she decided to see me at that time, she sorrowfully blurted out, "I saw my dad at the coffee shop holding hands with another woman!" It was obvious that it was this event that served as the catalyst to her crisis.

People in crisis often have an impaired time orientation with difficulty thinking about and telling their story in a logical manner. Listen for how the student talks about the traumatic incident. If there is a reference to past issues, this indicates a sense of loss. If the student talks about the incident in the present, this is often indicative of a transgression, whereas references to the future indicate a perception of a threat (Myer, 2001). Furthermore, use a direct intervention if you perceive that the student is sensitive and vulnerable with an inability to resolve the problem. For instance, make instructional statements with the use of the pronoun "I" such as, "*I* want you to. . . ." However, if you believe the student has the ability to mobilize resources for problem resolution, use an indirect approach with the use of the pronoun "you," such as, "What are some of the things *you* can do make yourself feel better?" A collaborative approach is recommended if you believe the student is capable of activating coping skills but needs additional support. In these cases, the pronoun "we" is used. For instance, "*We* can brainstorm ways to cope with stress." Table 7.1 is a guide for assessing the student's ability to resolve issues in the affective, cognitive, and behavioral areas.

Table 7.1 Interventions for Responding to Students in Crisis

	Direct	*Indirect*	*Collaborative*
Affect	I want you to focus on what you are feeling right now	You sound as if you are sad	We can discuss how you are feeling
Cognitive	I want you to stop thinking about this for a moment and take a deep breath	You need help figuring this out	We can brainstorm some ideas together
Behavioral	I want you to call your mom	You can continue exercising to relieve some of your stress	We can talk to your parents together

Planning

While you are actively listening and assessing the student, help the student create long- and short-term goals while supporting the student in finding words to describe his/her terror, pain, or sadness. Furthermore, you can also help the student gain a sense of control and empowerment while explaining that what used to be considered "normal" no longer exists, but a new "normal" will emerge (Riethmayer, n.d.). Provide structure while encouraging the student to resume a daily routine as quickly as possible. Homework assignments such as journaling or exercising in addition to art, music, dance, or other creative techniques aid students' return to normalcy.

Commit

The intention of this final step is to empower the student while collaborating and committing to a plan of action. Several meetings may be needed to modify the plan, and a follow-up meeting at some point in the future provides an opportunity to assess student progress.

Most people will display symptoms such as shock, distress, fear, or disbelief when exposed to a trauma. If the symptoms continue for at least two days and a maximum of four weeks following the event, these indicators meet the criteria for acute stress disorder (ASD). If these symptoms continue after this period of time, the student could meet the criteria of post-traumatic stress disorder (PTSD) (Jackson-Cherry & Erford, 2010).

POST-TRAUMATIC STRESS DISORDER (PTSD) AND ACUTE STRESS DISORDER (ASD)

The symptoms of PTSD and ASD are similar but differ in the length of time the symptoms persist. Symptoms such as a) hyperarousal, including such reactions as hypervigilance, concentration difficulties, heightened responses, and sleep disorders; b) re-experiencing the event by flashbacks, nightmares, or disturbing thoughts; and c) avoidance of reminders of the devastating situation, inability to recollect details surrounding the event, detachment, dissociation, or restricted affect (Jackson-Cherry & Erford, 2010) are characteristics of both PTSD and ASD.

As discussed earlier, many traumatized individuals have difficulty remembering details of the debilitating event and react to triggers on an unconscious level. The parts of the brain known as the amygdala and hippocampus are responsible for event recall difficulties. The amygdala is the part of the brain that is responsible for the formation of emotional memories, whereas the hippocampus is a part of the brain that plays an essential role in cognitive memory. When these two parts of the "nose brain" work collaboratively, the individual is able to appropriately process the event. Yet, there are times when the amygdala captures stimuli before the hippocampus is able to recall the event. When this occurs, the individual anxiously reacts to unconscious triggers while not being able to coherently recall the event (Echterling, et al., 2005). Figure 7.2 is a picture of the parts of the brain that are impacted during a crisis.

Your role as a school counselor is essential in returning the school environment to a pre-crisis level of functioning, which includes an awareness of the symptoms displayed by traumatized school-age youth and knowledge of your role in critical incident planning. The following section provides information on critical incident management.

Figure 7.2 The Parts of the Brain That Are Impacted During a Crisis

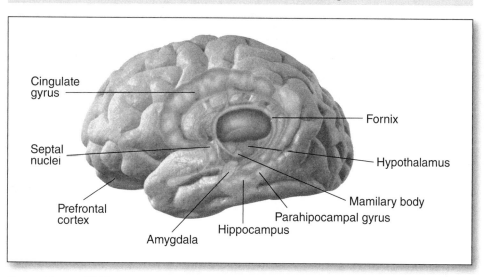

Source: Garrett (2011).

CRITICAL INCIDENT MANAGEMENT

A critical incident in the schools could include situational or environmental crises such as an explosion in the chemistry lab, school shootings, hurricanes, or floods, yet identifying all of the crises that may impact the school is nearly impossible. For instance, one school counselor reported the devastation of the school community when a beloved principal died suddenly and unexpectedly in his sleep. As teachers and students were learning about this tragic event, she recognized that with this death there was no leadership in the building. She quickly made the decision to convene a faculty/staff meeting to discuss the facts that were known and how to handle the day. She was relieved when a crisis team arrived at the school about an hour later, and it wasn't until that afternoon that she recognized how emotionally drained she was due to this stressful incident.

Situations such as this have the potential to impact the performance of youth and negatively influence their developmental stages and growth. According to ASCA's position statement on crisis response in the schools, "the professional school counselor serves as a leader in safe school initiatives and a vital resource in the creation, development and implementation of response plans before, during, and after a crisis. A crisis or an act of violence thrusts professional school counselors into positions of responsibility to ensure the safety and well being of all students and staff" (ASCA, 2013, para. 1). Despite this endorsement, research suggests that there is little evidence of the most essential roles or successful strategies in crisis management (Adamson & Peacock, 2007). In fact when crises did impact schools, tension and strained relations occurred between school counselors and building administrators when school counselors assumed roles that administrators perceived were "beyond their authority level" (Wiger & Harowski, 2003). To avoid this type of conflict, a succinct crisis intervention plan that distinguishes roles, intervention/prevention training procedures, response to crisis, debriefing and defusing activities, and a consistent evaluation is necessary. In addition, efforts that are sensitive to the diversity of students, the family, and community are all elements in critical incident planning.

Crises have the potential to impact the entire community, negatively impact the school's reputation, and create conflict among stakeholders (Gainey, 2010). Although most school personnel have developed crisis plans for their school, some have not responded to security and emergency planning, and still others have only designed a perfunctory strategy without any real foundation and no consideration for evaluating or practicing the plan. Critical incident plans vary from school to school, with some having significant gaps and problems including: a) outdated guidelines; b) failure to include aspects of the community safety personnel; c) lack of training; d) deficits in conducting practice drills; and, e) inattention to preventive activities (Cornell & Sheras, 1998).

The National Organization for Victim Assistance (NOVA) Community Crisis Response is a crisis response protocol with three main tasks of crisis intervention, including: 1) restoring safety and security (addressing physical safety and medical concerns); 2) ventilation and validation (listening to the survivor's story); and 3) prediction and preparation (providing the survivor with information about what may occur in the future). The PREPaRE model (Prevent, Reaffirm, Evaluate, Prevent and Respond, Examine (Brock, Nickerson, Reeves, Jimerson, Lieberman, & Feinberg, 2011) was designed as another prototype for schools to customize a critical incident plan. Whatever model is chosen as a template for crisis management and planning, a board-approved critical incident plan includes attention to the components of training, planning, responding, de-briefing/defusing, and evaluating.

Training

Plan considerations include continual training on issues of grief, developmental issues of children, suicide prevention, trauma, organizational matters, knowledge or crises, and role assignments. In addition, the plan is strengthened through revisions after evaluating the strategy following a drill or actual event.

Grief. Children and adolescents grieve differently than do adults, and youths' developmental level, ability to process abstract reasoning, and understand feelings play a part in how reactions are expressed. Counselors can work with parents/guardians to encourage their child to maintain a normal routine, and help them understand how their reactions provide cues for appropriate or inappropriate ways to cope with loss (Slate & Scott, 2009). Signs and symptoms of traumatic grief in youth are difficult to recognize as some display symptoms in the first few months, whereas others do not show grief until many years later. Grief responses could include emotional reactions such as sadness, guilt, or anger, impaired behavior and social interactions, irrational thoughts, transformed perception, and impaired academic functioning (NCTS, 2000). The relationship between grief, personal values, and beliefs needs further exploration, particularly as the cultural community in which the child belongs influences how grief is expressed. These beliefs could serve as a source of hope and support or as a foundation that fosters additional depression.

BOX 7.2 DIVERSE EXPRESSIONS OF GRIEF

A wide spectrum of grief reactions is expressed among cultures and individuals. In Turkey, many Muslims display their emotions of grief openly and are encouraged to cry, as this act is believed to cleanse the soul. Conversely, many Asians are stoic about grief and do not openly express their emotions. Retrieved from http://griefspeaks.com/id90.html

Developmental Issues of Children. Children are part of a cultural community that influences development and growth, as well as reactions to difficult situations. Traumatized youth have difficulty problem-solving and display lower academic performance (James & Gilliland, 2005), impaired attachment to others, social regression, and school avoidance, which are exacerbated when caregivers are having difficulty coping with the traumatic incident (James & Gilliland, 2005). As a school counselor, learn to understand what emotions and behaviors are considered normal in the child's culture and be aware of anniversary dates that could serve as catalysts to anxiety (Slate & Scott, 2009).

Suicide Prevention. Suicide is the third leading cause of death among youth between the ages of 15–24 (Suicide.org, n.d.). This mental health problem (National Institute of Mental Health [NIMH], 2010) is preventable, particularly when stakeholders are educated on the signs and symptoms of suicidal ideation and put into practice newly understood skills for intervention. In addition, teachers and other school personnel such as bus drivers, cafeteria workers, and custodians who see students on a daily basis are resources for alerting others of student behaviors that may indicate suicidal ideation. In fact, several states require in-service training on suicidal behavior on a yearly basis, and school counselors are key individuals to provide these training sessions. For example, in Case Study 7.1, training that was provided by the school counselor served as a source of knowledge for a high school receptionist who took action to help a student at risk for suicidal ideation.

CASE STUDY 7.1

A receptionist at the front desk at our high school read a letter that was dropped off by a mother of one of our students. The letter explained that the reason her daughter had been absent from school was due to two concurrent stays in a local psychiatric unit. This student was new to our school and there was no history in her file to indicate mental illness or concerns. Later, we found out that this student's parents had recently divorced after her dad returned home from Iraq and expressed no interest in the family, including his three children. Since the divorce, this student had five admissions to a psychiatric unit due to multiple suicide attempts, with the last attempt being the reason for her most recent stay in the hospital. Approximately 6 years ago a cousin physically abused her, which served as a catalyst for self-mutilating behaviors. As her counselor, I had spoken with her on two previous occasions but our conversations concerned her credits from her other schools and her current course selections. I had no idea that she was having personal issues in her life, as teachers never reported any behavior incidents, nor did she indicate any problems to me. It was due to the receptionist taking the action to bring these incidents to my attention that we were able to provide her the additional support she needed at school.

— High School Counselor

School-age youth are more likely to talk with their peers when they are upset or having suicidal thoughts, and peer helping has been a successful component of an effective school-based suicide prevention strategy (Stuart, Waalen, & Haelstromm, 2003). Although some individuals believe that talking to youth about suicide promotes this behavior, evidence does NOT support this belief (Shallcross, 2010). Under the leadership of the school counselor, peer helpers are able to receive the training, knowledge, and skills to understand the signs and symptoms of suicidal ideation and take the designated steps to aide peers who are displaying these challenging behaviors or attitudes. Supplementary information on suicide assessment is found in a later part of this chapter.

Trauma. As discussed earlier, if trauma is not treated, PTSD (James & Gilliland, 2005) could result. Traumatized youth may develop such symptoms as character difficulties, anxiety disorders, impaired thinking, and/or eating disorders. Furthermore, traumatic stress is related to significantly lower academic achievement scores, and in some instances these students are mistakenly placed in classes for students with learning disabilities, or labeled with a behavior disorder (Goodman, Miller, & West-Olatunji, 2012). Unfortunately, when students are misdiagnosed, appropriate services that are so badly needed may not be received, and mental, emotional, and behavioral problems could continue throughout life.

BOX 7.3 DID YOU KNOW? IMPROVING YOUR KNOWLEDGE OF CULTURE AND TRAUMA

When a cultural group responds to stressors differently from the dominant culture, these responses are likely to be labeled as "abnormal." Sensitivity to culture facilitates recovery. For example, Latino children who have been traumatized could manifest PTSD symptoms as "susto" or the belief that the soul is not longer part of their physical body. Native Americans, especially after the death of a loved one develop "ghost sickness" that manifests as weaknesses, loss of appetite, and nightmares.

Organizational Issues. Too often school personnel will adapt a generic plan that doesn't adequately address the unique needs of the specific school and community. Critical incident planning is an opportunity for a team of school and community members to consider distinctive strategies for the preparation, prevention, response, management, and evaluation of crises that could transpire (Gainey, 2010). A primary concern is to address the physical safety and emotional health of school-age youth when planning a crisis intervention plan, including a consideration of the types of crises that have the potential to disrupt the achievement of students. Although it is impossible to predict every emergency, plans can be adapted when any critical incident occurs. For instance, none of the personnel at a rural elementary school anticipated that a truck would hit and kill a 7-year-old boy as he ran through a hole in the fence to chase a stray ball during recess, nor the aftermath of devastated students, teachers, and parents who questioned how this event could occur, and what could have prevented it. Triage includes planning for primary, secondary, and tertiary plans.

Primary intervention activities, also known as the pre-impact period, include prevention programs that are designed to avert problems from developing such as the implementation of conflict resolution skills and knowledge of suicide signs and symptoms (Aspiranti, Pelchar, McCleary, Bain, & Foster, 2011; Jimerson, Brock, & Pletcher, 2005). *Secondary intervention activities* include medical and psychological first aid and screening, which occur during or immediately after the crisis to prevent further problems from developing. *Tertiary intervention,* or the post-impact period, are designed to assist in long-term counseling and follow-up activities such as making referrals, monitoring, or supporting those who need the additional assistance (Aspiranti, et al., 2011). Finally, the *recovery* or *reconstruction* phase includes an assessment of the plan, anniversary preparedness, and memories of the people hurt or deceased in the crises (Jimerson, et al., 2005). (*Note that in the case of suicides, memorials are to be avoided.*) Figure 7.3 is a checklist school personnel can adopt for critical incident planning.

Figure 7.3   Checklist for Crisis Intervention Planning

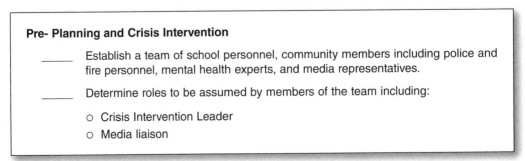

Pre- Planning and Crisis Intervention

_____   Establish a team of school personnel, community members including police and fire personnel, mental health experts, and media representatives.

_____   Determine roles to be assumed by members of the team including:

   o Crisis Intervention Leader
   o Media liaison

- o Parent contact
- o Scheduler of events (e.g., parent meetings, services)
- o Website observer to monitor reports, discussion boards, etc.
- o Medical coordinator
- o Psychological services coordinator
- o Security/safety coordinator

_____ Train team members

_____ Create relationships with media outlets

_____ Develop positive relationships between the school and community agencies

_____ Create means of communication such as through blogs, e-mails, hotline

_____ Schedule times for crisis drills

_____ Mandate school employee safety plan

_____ Determine an advance signal to warn individuals of impending danger

_____ Establish a plan to follow for crisis occurring on weekends or holidays

_____ Brainstorm different situations (e.g., hostage, fire, fights) that could occur

_____ Develop a list of resources at the local, state, and national level

_____ Establish emergency funds to assist victims and survivors.

_____ Develop procedures to inform students, parents, and the community of crisis

_____ Identify facilities for counseling, team meetings, and so on

_____ Fill a chest with crisis information and materials such as: aerial photos of school, rosters, keys, alarm turn off/on procedures, utility locations, and so on

_____ Identify appropriate alternative sites for school in the event the building is damaged or unsafe

_____ Create materials for crisis responders

_____ Develop a plan for dealing with possible deaths of students/faculty/staff

_____ Plan for counseling and follow-up procedures

_____ Create a plan for monitoring at-risk students/faculty members

_____ Define postvention plans including de-briefing/de-fusing

_____ Create procedures for communicating with family following a loss

_____ Identify procedures for evaluating plan

_____ Determine procedures for handling student belongings in the case of a death

In addition to the planning checklist, post-planning includes debriefing/defusing and evaluation.

Postvention

Follow-up events include defusing and debriefing, systematic screenings, counseling interventions, parent meetings, and plan assessment and revisions. Culturally grounded approaches are also essential to include in the plan. For instance, attention to the beliefs of the community members may include contacting local community cultural leaders, incorporating traditional healing methods with postvention strategies, and understanding the cultural/community standards for restoring individuals and families to at least a pre-crisis level of functioning.

Defusing/Debriefing. Critical incident stress defusing and debriefing are group interventions designed for the prevention of post-traumatic stress disorder (PTSD). Debriefings usually occur within 2 to 7 days after the crisis, whereas defusing, an abbreviated form of debriefing, occurs the same day or within 24 hours of the incident. The goal of defusing is to provide coping strategies to expedite a return to a state of equilibrium and to possibly eliminate the need for a debriefing (Everly, Flannery, & Mitchell, 2000). Although there are several defusing/debriefing models, the seven stage cognitive-emotional Mitchell model is described in Figure 7.4.

Figure 7.4 The Mitchell Model of Defusing/Debriefing

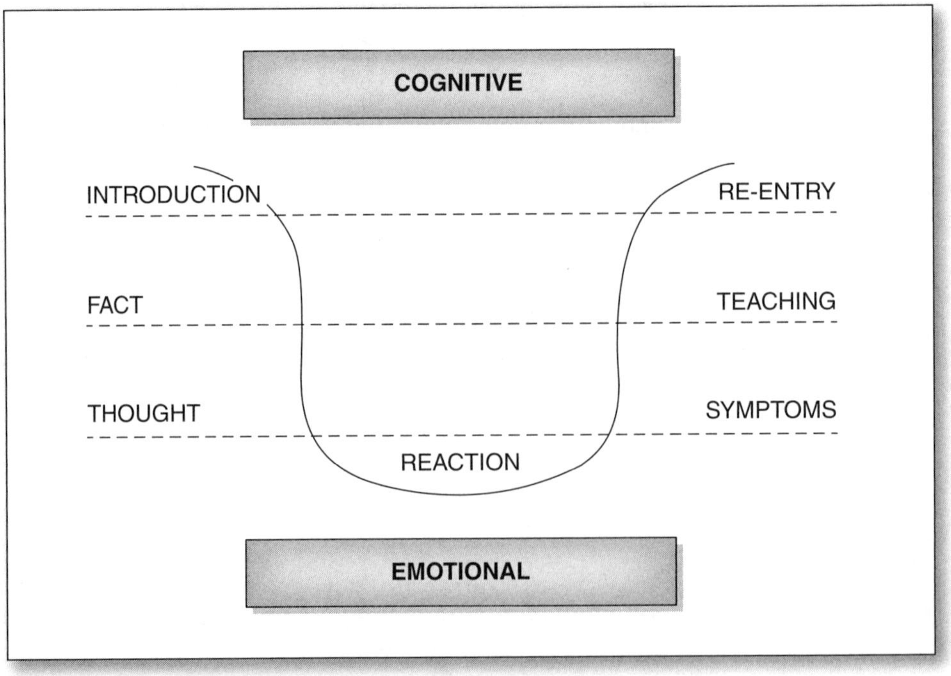

1. *Introduction.* This step includes informing the group members about the group members, the model process, goals, format, rules, a discussion of confidentiality, and expected outcomes.

2. *Fact Phase.* In this phase the facts, roles of members, the thoughts at the time of the event, and each individual's interpretation of the event are shared. The details are relayed and rumors are dismissed.

3. *Thought Phase.* During this phase each member reveals his/her most vivid thoughts at the time of the incident. From here, there is a transition to an emotional level.

4. *Reaction Phase.* At this time members identify their emotions and affective responses in addition to their perceptions of the worst part of the experience.

5. *Symptom Phase.* At this phase there is a shift back to a cognitive level. Members identify symptoms and reactions they are experiencing such as stomachaches, flashbacks, or nightmares.

6. *Teaching Phase.* In this phase members are taught about thoughts, feelings, and physiological reactions that are normal during a crisis event. In addition, coping skills are discussed to teach members appropriate skills to utilize to facilitate a return to normalcy.

7. *Re-entry Phase.* This final phase of the model is intended to give members necessary skills to activate when stressed as well as resources for assistance.

Source: Everly, Flannery, & Mitchell (2000).

Evaluation is a final component of a critical incident plan, and is also one that is often overlooked. This particular phase provides the planning team with an opportunity to revisit the plan.

Evaluation

There are several techniques that could be used to evaluate a critical incident plan. A fishbowl evaluation technique is recommended for use with a group of individuals to discuss or evaluate sensitive topics such as a critical incident. Using this strategy a group of five to eight individuals sit in a circle, with a larger group of individuals who are not allowed to talk sitting in a larger circle around them. The individuals in the inner circle discuss their perceptions of the plan, issues that went well, areas for improvement, and suggestions for improvement. This phase lasts approximately 10 minutes while the discussion is recorded. Observers in the outer circle can change places with inner circle members at any time to express opinions. After the time ends observers will switch with inner circle members until everyone has had an opportunity to express oneself. Following this process, the crisis team meets to revise and rewrite the school crisis intervention plan.

School personnel are usually adept at dealing with developmental crises that occur, but less capable of knowing how to respond to situational crises (James & Gilliland, 2005). The following section includes a discussion of various crisis situations, including youth living in poverty, child/abuse and neglect, violence and bullying, eating disorders, drug abuse, self-mutilation, grief, and homelessness.

MULTIPLE STRESSORS IMPACTING SCHOOL-AGE YOUTH

Youth Living in Poverty

According to the U.S. Census Bureau (2010) more than 1 in 5 U.S. children live in poverty. Poverty in America has been, and continues to be, a very serious yet not always fully visible issue in which youth and their families exist at levels below what is needed for human decency. Unsuitable housing, lack of medical care, insufficient food, or not having basic needs met are just a few of the daily struggles impoverished youth face. Youth living in poverty confront more stress, chaos, cognitive and behavioral disabilities, unemployment, and receive less education than do youth who do not grow up in impoverished families (Macartney, 2011).

School counselors sometimes hold the mistaken notion that these youth are under-prepared and unmotivated, a belief that has the potential to create an additional strain on the difficulties these students and their families already suffer. Instead, support is built when disadvantaged youth are connected to resources to fulfill their basic needs. You can serve as an advocate and resource for improving conditions by recognizing students who have insufficient food and poor nutrition, safety needs, and/or teachers who reject or disrespect them (Harper, Harper, & Stills, 2003). In addition, you can teach these youth adaptive social functioning and advocacy skills such as demonstrating assertiveness competencies, making appropriate requests, starting conversations, and requesting information (Manso, Sanchez, Alonso, & Romero, 2012). The National Center for Youth in Poverty is a resource that presents resources on children in poverty and can be accessed at http://www.nccp.org/profiles/

Child Abuse and Neglect

The United States leads the industrialized countries in the number of child abuse and neglect cases, with an average of five child fatalities reported every day in America (ChildHelp, 2012). The association between child maltreatment in all forms is associated with deleterious behaviors, delayed socio-emotional growth, and communication difficulties (Manso, et al., (2012). As a mental health professional you are a mandated reporter. It is not our job to investigate the report, but we are required to report the abuse. As stated in the ASCA position statement (2003), "ASCA recognizes it is the absolute responsibility of professional school counselors to report suspected cases of child abuse/neglect to the proper authorities" (para. 4). The National Child Abuse Hotline number (1–800–4ACHILD or 800–422–4453) is one resource for reporting suspected abuse/neglect.

School counselors can help students develop cognitive skills in which the student recognizes and learns to dispute irrational thoughts, practices deep breathing, and demonstrates relaxation techniques to cope with the anxiety that accompanies abuse (Bauman, 2008). Signs and symptoms of neglected, abused youth are found in Table 7.2

Table 7.2   Common Signs and Symptoms of Physical Abuse, Neglect, and Sexual Abuse

Signs of Physical Abuse

- Unexplained burns, bites, bruises, broken bones, or black eyes
- Appears frightened of parents/caregivers and is upset when reunited with them
- Appears scared of other adults

Signs of Neglect

- Excessive absences or tardiness
- Appears hungry
- Lacks medical or dental attention
- Clothing is dirty and child has severe body odor
- Does not have sufficient clothing for weather
- Abuses drugs and/or alcohol
- No one at home to provide care

Signs of Sexual Abuse

- Child has difficulty walking or sitting
- Declines to change clothing for gym or other activities
- Appears to have an unusual knowledge of sexual behaviors
- Nightmares
- Bedwetting
- Change in appetite
- Has a sexually transmitted disease or becomes pregnant, particularly under age 14
- Running away behavior
- Dresses provocatively or wears baggy clothing to cover body

Substance Use

CACREP

Extreme use of drugs such as tobacco, marijuana, and alcohol are capable of putting students at risk academically, physically, and behaviorally (Sznitman,

Dunlop, Nalkur, Khurana, & Romer, 2012). Today, there is an array of services for substance abusing youth, yet only about 10% of the adolescents who need this treatment actually receive it (Winters, Fahnhorst, Botzet, Lee, & Lalone, 2012). The school is an ideal setting for reaching these individuals; however, even though schools have a long history of developing prevention programs for substance use, these programs have not been effective (Sznitman, et al., 2012).

Despite the lack of success for substance use prevention programs, brief intervention counseling groups have shown success in schools. In a study by Winters et al. (2012), drug-abusing adolescents who were mildly to moderately involved with drugs were placed in either a two-session adolescent-only group using brief interventions, a two-session brief intervention group with adolescents that included one-session with parents, or a control group in which participants did not receive an intervention. Adolescents in the brief intervention groups displayed significant improvements at a six-month follow-up, with those involved in the parent session intervention showing even greater recovery. This study supports brief interventions as a viable option for working with substance abusing youth, and the value of including parents. Furthermore, less substance abuse and better mental health are found in schools in which staff and faculty create a positive climate and demonstrate respect for students and their needs. The National Institute on Drug Abuse offers additional information on drug use and is accessed through the website: http://www.drugabuse. gov/publications/drugfacts/high-school-youth-trends

---

BOX 7.4 FACTS ABOUT ADOLESCENT DRUG USE

Marijuana use by teens declined in the late 1990s but is now increasing, with 6.5% of twelfth graders reporting marijuana use on a daily basis, However, inhalant and alcohol use are at lower levels than in previous years. Retrieved from the National Institute on Drug Abuse, December 2012, http://www.drugabuse.gov/publications/drugfacts/high-school-youth-trends

---

Homelessness and Unaccompanied Youth

Homeless children and adolescents are also known as runaways, throwaways, street youths, or systems youth. Regardless of the term, homelessness is difficult to define (Edidin, Ganim, Hunter, & Karnik, 2012). Unaccompanied youth are those in which there is no physical presence or custody of a parent or guardian, such as a runaway or a child forced out of the home. The McKinney-Vento Act was passed in 1987 and reauthorized by NCLB in 2001 for the purpose of providing services to people experiencing homelessness, including all school-age youth up to the age of 21. School counselors are able to obtain assistance for these youth through knowledge of this law. For instance, youth who are homeless are able to remain in his/her present school even when temporary housing is located in a different school district. In addition, the school has a responsibility to provide transportation, and these youth are able to attend school even without appropriate documents such as birth certificates and immunizations.

Financial instability, a decline in mental and physical health, greater risks for being victims of violence, sexually transmitted diseases, and substance abuse are a few of the repercussions of homelessness. Impaired cognition that influences decision-making, problem-solving, and lower academic achievement are also associated with transient youth as they transfer from one school to another (Edidin, et al., 2012). Furthermore, similar to youth who live in poverty, homeless youth are sick more often than are other youth, go hungry at twice the rate of their peers, and have higher rates of obesity due to deficits in nutrition (Agnes & Elizondo, 2012). Unfortunately, homeless youth are often mistakenly either placed in special education classes due to their poor academic achievement, or if legitimately diagnosed with a disability, often do not receive special educational services because of their enrollment and withdrawal from school to school (Edidin, et al., 2012).

School counselors are key individuals to nonjudgmentally communicate (Agnes & Elizondo, 2012) and coordinate with community agencies to provide the resources homeless youth and their families desperately lack. However, partnering can be frustrating due to the mistrust homeless youth and their families have toward human service workers. School counselors may consider the use of alternative methods for sending information home to inform parents/guardians of special school events, particularly when these families do not have access to technology or postal services due to their transient lives. Cognitive behavioral therapy, life skill development, and peer interventions are shown to facilitate healthy development in homeless youth (Edidin, et al., 2012). The National Association for the Education of Homeless Children and Youth (www.naehcy.org) is a resource dedicated to assisting homeless families.

Youth Who Self-Harm

Self-mutilating behaviors, deliberate self-harm, non-suicidal self-injury, and parasuicide are all terms used to describe youth who deliberately harm themselves (Dixon-Gordon, Harrison, & Roesch, 2012). Cigarette burns, carving in skin, head banging, inserting needles, and applying acid are common forms of self-harming behaviors. According to Malikow (2006), "self-mutilation is a positive act performed to promote relief from greater pain or recover from mental illness: (Cutters) deliberately harm themselves to feel better, to get rapid respite from distressing thoughts and emotions, and to regain a sense of control" (p. 46). The term "positive" is not used to refer to a constructive act, but rather in reference to a desired outcome of regulating mood by exchanging emotional pain for physical pain (Malikow, 2006).

Although self-harm is often mistaken as a suicide attempt, it is not; it is actually an attempt to prevent suicide by stopping painful emotions. Specific associations with self-harm behaviors include avoidant coping styles, relationship difficulties, negative emotions connected to shame, and childhood trauma (Dixon-Gordon et al., 2012). In reality, self-injury is often a result of negative situations that impact the child in his/her first 6 years of life (Coy & Simpson, 2002). As a school counselor, take time to reflect on your own feelings regarding self-harm, and recognize that this behavior is NOT an attempt to gain attention or to commit suicide, but rather that these students are making their best effort to deal with unbearable pain. The Mayo Clinic furnishes an Internet resource on self/injury and cutting and is accessible at http://www.mayoclinic.com/health/self-injury/DS00775.

Bullying

The media frequently reports incidents of bullying and its deleterious impact on school-age youth, with approximately anywhere from 10–30% (Nansel, Haynie, & Simons-Morton, 2003) school-age youth who report being bullied. Bullying is a subtype of aggression and is characterized as an unequal relationship between the bully and the target of bullying (Olweus, 1993), consists of a series of repetitive behaviors as opposed to a specific, isolated incident (MacNeil & Newel, 2004), and is intentional. For instance, the bully's intention is to hurt another by repetitively engaging in harmful behaviors based on a perception of greater power (Kowalski & Limber, 2007).

Physical, verbal, relational, and cyber bullying compose the various types of bullying. Physical bullying is comprised of hitting, punching, threatening acts, and kicking, whereas verbal bullying includes such actions as name-calling or teasing. Relational bullying (also known as social aggression) involves spreading rumors or excluding someone from others or events (Espelage & Swearer, 2003), ignoring others, spreading nasty rumors, leaving hurtful messages on desks, making prank phone calls, and/or giving "death stares." Finally, cyber bullying is using technology to harass, exclude, or degrade another through such means as instant messaging, e-mail, chat rooms, and videos, through cell phones, social networking sites, and so on (Espelage, 2004). Targets of bullying, bullies themselves, victim-bullies, witnesses, and cyber-victims are all negatively affected by this aggressive behavior.

Typical bullies often have negative opinions of others, difficulty resolving problems, come from a hostile family associated with poor parental monitoring (Cook, Williams, Guerra, Kim, & Sadek, 2010), and/or authoritarian discipline styles.

Bullies who observe their parents/guardians engaging in violent actions tend to accept these behaviors as normal and are inclined to view violence positively. Targets of bullying often have an inability to form relationships, exhibit emotional, physical, and behavioral signs of being mistreated, do not feel accepted, have difficulty with problem solving (Cook et al., 2010), display lowered self-esteem, and show signs of depression, all of which could lead to suicidal ideation (Nansel et al., 2003).

Bully-victims are those who both bully others as well as being targeted by their peers (Pollasstri, Cardemil, & O'Donnell, 2010). These individuals do not do well in school, regularly display behavioral problems, and are isolated from peers (Diamanduros, Downs, & Jenkins, 2008). They are both rejected by and negatively influenced by peers (Cook, et al., 2010).

Bully witnesses are also impacted as they stand silently by and witness the aggressive situation. Witnesses sometimes realize that anyone can be a target of bullying and often take a safe, observer position to avoid being the next target (Jeffrey, 2004). Others may also serve as the bully's assistant, encourage the bullying behaviors because of the entertainment, and/or enjoy the acts of defiance.

Cyber bullying is also referred to as online aggression, Internet harassment, and electronic aggression. Although cyber bullying is largely believed to be similar to offline aggression, the content of messages on the Internet lives forever in that it can be re-read, uploaded, and posted, which may provide opportunities for the experience to be re-lived (Law, Shapka, Hymel, Olson, & Waterhouse, 2012) and lead to re-victimization.

BOX 7.5 THE ASSOCIATION BETWEEN BULLYING AND MENTAL ILLNESS

There is some controversy regarding mental illness and bullying. Some researchers state that youth who are bullied between the developmentally critical ages of 8–10 are twice as likely to develop symptoms of psychosis later in life. Other researchers state that it is possible that youth are bullied because they are exhibiting early signs of mental illness. Source: The Week/Health Secrets (2010).

A parent/guardian/community partnership with school personnel is essential to reducing school violence. Some schools elicit the support of paraprofessionals such as parents/guardians to monitor the halls or to serve as recess aides. School counselors can form a partnership with teachers and other education personnel to facilitate skill development to combat the negative effects of bullying. These curricular and counseling responses are aimed at changing attitudes and beliefs toward aggressive behaviors and teaching all students adaptive life-long skills. Social-cognitive training including the theoretical models of Rational Emotive Behavioral Therapy (REBT) and Solution-Focused Brief Counseling (SFBC), and strategies such as mentoring, emotional awareness, and bibliocounseling are effective in reducing bullying behaviors and responses to this aggressive behavior. The government website http://www.stopbullying.gov imparts additional information on the social issue of bullying.

Suicide

CACREP

Suicide is one of the most stressful situations all counselors will confront at some point in their career. Suicidal gestures are considered as a form of communication and when a safe environment is provided for students to talk about incidents that are adversely affecting them, suicidal ideation is likely to be lessened. Talking about suicide is actually shown to decrease the actual risk, with approximately 80 percent of individuals who contemplate or commit suicide who actually have told someone of their intention. Unfortunately, in most cases these confessions are often met with derision and silence (Shallcross, 2010).

Risk factors for children and adolescents include helplessness (feeling as if they have no control over stressful life situations), hopelessness (having no future goals), haplessness (having a number of worrying events occurring in life), and loneliness (the perception that a support system is unavailable). In addition, approximately 90 percent of people who died by suicide had been diagnosed with a mental health disorder such as depression or bipolar disorder. Additional factors associated with suicidal behaviors include a rigid thinking style leading to poor coping skills, perfectionism, loss, impulsivity, previous trauma, history of suicide in the family or among peers, and substance abuse.

Your job as a school counselor is to determine whether a student is at risk for suicide, and if you believe there is a possibility that the student is thinking of self-harm, the parents/guardians need to be contacted, and this action needs to be documented. The best method of assessing risk of suicide is to ask the student. A direct, simple question such as, "Are you thinking of suicide?" can bring about relief in that the student feels that there is a caring individual with whom he/she can discuss the depth of his/her pain, known as *psycheache*. If the student affirms that he/she is contemplating suicide, the SLAP method of suicide assessment (shown in Figure 7. 5) is a helpful acronym to determine the extent of the risk, including previous attempts. If the SLAP assessment indicates that there had been a previous attempt, the acronym DIRT is an additional aid to assess the seriousness of the present risk based on past attempts (see Figure 7.6).

Additional questions I sometimes ask students when assessing suicide risk are: "Whom besides yourself would be most affected by your suicide?" or, "On a scale from 1 to 10, with 10 meaning you want to die, and 1 meaning you want to live without the pain you are currently feeling, where are you now?" The first question helps me figure out whom I need to contact to provide succor to the student, and the second question gives me an idea of the seriousness of the suicidal intention. The Jason Foundation is dedicated to the prevention

Figure 7.5 The SLAP Suicide Assessment

S = Specifics of the plan. Ask about the details of the plan. The more detail the student has provided in the plan to commit suicide, the higher the student's risk for suicide is. For instance, if a student says to you, "I am going to drive my car off the bridge on Saturday evening," the risk is considerably higher than someone who states, "I think I may take some pills."

L = Lethality of plan. The more lethal the means of the suicide plan, the higher the risk. Guns or jumping from high places or in front of moving vehicles are among the most fatal means of committing suicide; however, overdosing and carbon monoxide attempts, although also lethal, can be reversed or interrupted.

A = Availability of the method. If the student indicates the use of a weapon, determine if that particular means is available and assessable. For instance, at one time I was counseling with a male student who stated that he was considering suicide through the use of a gun. When I asked him whether he had guns in his house he replied, "We have several guns that my father locked in a gun case, but I know where he has hidden the key." In this case I knew that his father needed to be called.

P = Proximity to helping resources. A suicidal individual feels lonely and has tunnel vision, meaning that he/she believes there is no way out of the existing situation. Stressed individuals are difficult to be with, and it could be that the significant people in his/her life have become disconnected. Determine who is available in the student's life to provide the support, encouragement, and assistance that is needed and mobilize these individuals. As an example, a female student with whom I worked discovered she was pregnant, and the father of the child decided to leave the relationship when she revealed her pregnancy to him. Distraught about this turn of events, she asked her mother to pick up a sandwich for her at a local drive-thru restaurant. While her mother was gone, she took a handful of her mother's medication, and when her mother returned the student told her mother what she had done. Her mother immediately called the emergency squad and she was rushed to the hospital for treatment. Fortunately, both she and her baby survived this attempt, but if her mother had not returned in the short period of time that it took to get the sandwich, the student could have been a victim of lethality.

Figure 7.6 DIRT Assessment of Previous Attempt

D = Dangerousness. Assess the dangerousness of the method that was previously used.

I = Impression of dangerousness. Determine whether the student perceived that the suicide attempt method was dangerous. For example, one 6-foot-2-inch male I worked with tried to hang himself from the showerhead. In his mind, he believed that he would die. From my perspective, this method did not seem to be as deadly as other means; however, his *impression* was that it was a viable means.

R = Rescue. Did the student attempt suicide at a time where there was a high probability of being discovered? Another student I worked with attempted suicide by turning on his car in a closed garage. Fortunately, he was aware of the time his mother would arrive home from work, and his attempt was interrupted when she arrived.

T = Timing. When did the attempt occur? The more recently the attempt was made, the higher the risk.

of suicide and increasing awareness of suicide and is accessed at http://jason foundation.com.

It is obvious from the types of crises discussed above that students face numerous issues which negatively impact their well-being. Crisis counseling entails immediate attention to making certain that the student's basic physiological needs are being met and providing tools to assist in managing the detrimental emotions that accompany disquieting situations. A collaboratively constructed safety plan arms students with the skills and resources to assist in coping with future disturbing incidents. An example of a safety plan that can be adapted to meet the needs of the student and the situation is found in the Figure 7.7 Safety Plan.

Figure 7.7 Safety Plan

Name _____

I understand this plan will help me cope with my current situation, and I realize this is an initial plan and can be revised at any time. This plan is designed to help me by recognizing some of the cues that may create difficulties for me, and identifying certain actions I can take to prevent me from feeling constant worry.

Risk Factors:

Physical Factors: (These are situations I must avoid)

1. _____
2. _____
3. _____

Emotional Factors: (These are feelings that indicate that I am not doing well and might need some help)

1. _____
2. _____
3. _____

Cognitive Factors: (These are examples of negative ways of thinking that indicate I need to reframe my thinking)

1. _____ Reframe _____
2. _____ Reframe _____
3. _____ Reframe _____

Physiological Factors: (These are physical reactions indicating that I need to seek help—e.g., sleeplessness, not eating)

1. _____
2. _____
3. _____

Strategies for Making Myself Feel Better:

If I recognize these or any other factors in my life, I will do the following specific things to help me deal with the situation better.

1. _____
2. _____
3. _____

_____   _____
Signature of Student   Signature of Counselor

CONCLUSION

Students are impacted by developmental, traumatic or situational, and existential crises, and respond to crisis physically, cognitively, emotionally, and socially/behaviorally. The school counselor is a key individual trained in crisis and intervention to facilitate a new sense of "normalcy," with the intention of aiding the student with new, effective coping skills and attitudes.

The LAPC model of crisis intervention is highlighted as a template for working with youth in crisis, with attention given to the perception of the event, significant supports, and coping mechanisms as balancing factors that aid in trauma recovery. Critical incident management in schools includes attention to children's development, suicide prevention, trauma responses, and organizational issues. School counselors are instrumental team members in plan development that meets the needs of a specific school. Finally, youth living in poverty, child abuse and neglect, substance abuse, homelessness, self-mutilation, bullying, and suicide are some of the crises situations that have the potential of restricting growth and success. School counselors at all levels have the skills to intervene to avert potentially devastating and sometimes fatal situations that challenge youth on a daily basis.

REFERENCES

Abernathy, B. E. (2008). Who am I now? Helping trauma clients find meaning, wisdom, and a renewed sense of self. In G. R. Walz, J. C. Bleur, & R. K. Yep (Eds.), *Compelling counseling interventions: Celebrating VISTAS' fifth anniversary* (pp. 199–208). Ann Arbor, MI: Counseling Outfitters.

Adamson, A. D., & Peacock, G. G. (2007). Crisis response in the public schools: A survey of school psychologists' experiences and perceptions. *Psychology in the Schools, 6,* 96–102.

Agnes, N., & Elizondo, J. (2012, February). Helping homeless youth. *ASCA School Counselor,* 28–31.

Allen, M., Burt, K., Bryan, E., Carter, D., Orsi, R., & Durkan, L. (2002). School counselors' preparation for and participation in crisis intervention. *Professional School Counseling, 6,* 96–102.

American School Counselor Association (2003). The professional school counselor and child abuse and neglect prevention. Retrieved from http://www.schoolcounselor.org/content.asp?contentid=178

American School Counselor Association (2013). *The professional school counselor and safe schools and crisis response.* Retrieved from http://www.schoolcounselor.org/asca/media/asca/PositionStatements/PS_SafeSchools.pdf

Amri, S. Nassar-McMillan, S., Amen-Bryan, S., & Misenhimer, M. M. (2013). Counseling Arab Americans. In L. Lee (ed.), *Multicultural Issues in Counseling* (4th ed.). Alexandria, VA: American Counseling Association.

Aquilera, D. C. (1998). *Crisis intervention: Theory and methodology.* St. Louis, MO: Mosby.

Aspiranti, K. B., Pelchar, T. K., McCleary, D. F., Bain, S. K., & Foster, N. (2011). Development and reliability of the comprehensive crisis plan checklist. *Psychology in the Schools, 48,* 146–155. doi:10.1002/pits.20533

Bauman, S. (2008). *Essential topics for the helping professional.* Boston: Pearson.

Brock, S. E., Jimerson, S. R., Hart, S. R., Nickerson, A. B. (2002). Preventing, preparing for, and responding to school violence with the prepare model. In Jimerson, S. R., Nickerson, A. B., Mayer, M. J., & Furlong, M. J. (Eds.), *Handbook of school violence and school safety: International research and practice* (2nd ed.), (463-474). New York, NY: Routledge.

Brock, S. E., Nickerson, A. B., Reeves, M. A., Savage, M. A., & Woitaszewski, S. A. (2011). Development, evaluation, and future directions of the prepare school crisis prevention ad intervention training curriculum. *Journal of School Violence, 10,* 34–52.

Cavaiola, A. A., & Colford, J. E. (2011). *Crisis intervention case book.* Belmont, CA: Cengage Learning.

ChildHelp (2012). *National Child Abuse Statistics.* Retrieved from http://www.childhelp.org/pages/statistics/

Cook, C. R., Williams, K. R., Guerra, N G., Kim, & Sadek, S. (2010). Predictors of bullying and victimization in childhood and adolescence: A meta-analysis investigation. *School Psychology Quarterly, 25,* 65–83. doi:10;10.10371a0020149

Cornell, D. G., & Sheras, P. L. (1998). Common errors in school crisis response: Learning from our mistakes. *Psychology in the Schools, 35,* 297–307.

Coy, D. R., & Simpson, C. (2002). Adolescents who cut. *ACSA School Counselor,* 40, 16–19.

Diamanduros, T., Downs, E., & Jenkins, S. J. (2008). The role of school psychologists in the assessment, prevention, and intervention of cyberbullying. *Psychology in the Schools, 45,* 693–704. doi: 10.1002/pits.20335 Published in Wiley Interscience.

Dixon-Gordon, K., Harrison, N., Roesch, R. (2012). Non-suicidal self-injury within offender populations: A systematic review. *International Journal of Forensic Mental Health, 11,* 33–54. doi: 10.1080/1499013.2012.667513

Echterling, L. G., Presbury, J. H., & McKee, J. E. (2005). *Crisis intervention: Promoting resilience and resolution in troubled times.* Upper Saddle River, NJ: Pearson.

Edidin, J. P., Ganim, Z., Hunter, S. J., & Karnik, N. S. (2012). The mental and physical health of homeless youth: A literature review. *Child Psychiatry Human Development, 43,* 354–375. doi 10.1007/s10578–011–0270–1

Espelage, D. L., (2004). An ecological perspective to school-based bullying prevention. *The Prevention Researcher, 11,* 3–6.

Espelage, D. L., & Swearer, S. M. (2003). Research on school bullying & victimization: What have we learned and where do we go from here? *School Psychology Review, 32,* 365–383.

Everly, G. S., Flannery, R. B., & Mitchell, J. T. (2000). Critical incident stress management (CISM): A review of the literature. *Aggression and Violent Behavior, 5,* 23–40.

Flom, B. L., & Hansen, S.S. (2006). Just don't shut the door on me: Aspirations of adolescents in crisis. *Professional School Counseling, 10,* 88–92.

Gainey, B. (2010). Crisis management in public school districts. *Organization Development Journal, 28,* 89–95.

Garrett, B. L., (2011). *Brain & behavior: An introduction to biological psychology.* Thousand Oaks, CA: SAGE.

Goodman, R. D., Miller, M. D., & West-Olatunji, C. A. (2012). Traumatic stress, socioeconomic status, and academic achievement among primary school students. *Psychological Trauma: Theory, Research, Practice, and Policy, 4,* 252–259.

Granello, D. H. (2010). A suicide crisis intervention model with 25 practical strategies for implementation. *Journal of Mental Health Counseling, 32,* 218–235.

Harper, F. D., Harper, J. A., & Stills, A. B. (2003). Counseling children in crisis based on Maslow's hierarchy of basic needs. *International Journal for the Advancement of Counselling, 25,* 11–25.

Honos-Webb, L. S., Hart, S, & Scalise, J. T. (2009). How to help after national catastrophes: Findings following 9/11. *The Humanistic Psychologist, 34,* 75–97.

Jackson-Cherry, L. R., & Erford, B. T. (2010). *Crisis intervention and prevention.* Boston, MA: Pearson.

James, R. K., & Gilliland, B. E. (2005). *Crisis intervention strategies.* Belmont, CA: Thomson.

Jeffrey, L. R. (2004). Bullying bystanders. *The prevention researcher, 11,* 7–10.

Jimerson, S. R., Brock, S. E., & Pletcher, S. W. (2005). An integrated model of school crisis preparedness and intervention. *School Psychology International, 26,* 275–296.

Kowalski, R. M., & Limber, S. P. (2007). Electronic bullying among middle school students. *Journal of Adolescent Health, 41,* S22-S30. doi.10.1016/j.jadohealth.2007.08.017

Law, D. M., Shapka, J. D., Hymel, S., Olson, B. F., & Waterhouse, T. (2012). The changing face of bullying: An empirical comparison between traditional and internet bullying and victimization. *Computers in Human Behavior, 28,* 226–232.

Macartney, S. (2011). Child poverty in the United States 2009 and 2010: Selected race groups and Hispanic origin; American community Survey Briefs. Retrieved from http://www.resourcelibrary.gcyf.org/node/3884

MacNeil, G.A., & Newel, J.M. (2004). School bullying: Who, why, and what to do. *Prevention Researcher, 11*(3), 15–17.

Malikow (2006, April). When students cut themselves. *Education Digest,* 45–50. Retrieved from www.eddigest.com

Manso, J. M. M., Sanchez, M. E., Alonso, M. B., & Romero, J. M. P. (2012). Pragmatic-communicative intervention strategies for victims of child abuse. *Children and Youth Services Review, 34,* 1729–1734. doi: 10.10.1016/j.childyouth.2012.05.003

Myer, R. A. (2001). *Assessment for crisis intervention: A triage assessment model.* Belmont, CA: Wadsworth.

Nansel, T. R., Haynie, D. L., & Simons-Morton, B. G. (2003). The association of bullying and victimization with middle school adjustment. In Elias, M J., & Zins, J. E. (Eds.), *Bullying, Peer Harassment, and Victimization in the Schools: The Next Generation of Prevention* (pp. 45–61). New York, NY: Haworth.

National Child Traumatic Stress Network (2000.). *The typical grieving process.* Retrieved from http://www.nctsn.org/trauma-types/traumatic-grief/typical-grieving-process

National Institute of Mental Health (2010). Suicide in the U.S.: Statistics and Prevention. Retrieved from http://www.youtube.com/watch?v=-f_007QCuq0

Olweus, D. (1993). *Bully/victim problems among schoolchildren: Long-term consequences and an effective intervention program.* Thousand Oaks, CA: Sage.

Pollassri, A. R., Cardemil, E. V., & O'Donnel, E. H. (2010). Self-esteem in pure bullies and bully/victims: A longitudinal analysis. *Journal of Interpersonal Violence, 25,* 1489–1502.

Riethmayer, J. (n.d.). *Dealing with the impact of trauma.* Retrieved from http://www.counseling .org/PressRoom/NewsReleases.aspx?AGuid=b8890bed-5842–4c52–8719-eeb4fcbbd562

Shallcross, L. (2010, July). Confronting the threat of suicide. *Counseling Today.* Alexandria, VA: American Counselor Association.

Slate, C. N., & Scott, D. A. (2009, March). *A discussion of coping methods & counseling techniques for children and adults dealing with grief and bereavement.* Paper based on a program presented at the American Counseling Association Annual Conference and Exposition, Charlotte, N. C.

Smith, H. B. (n.d.). Providing mental health services to clients in crisis or disaster situations VISTAS (article 3). Retrieved from http://www.counseling.org/

Stuart, C., Waalen, J, K., Haelstromm, E. (2003). Many helping hearts: An evaluation of peer gatekeeper training in suicide risk assessment. *Death Studies, 27,* 321–333. doi.org/10/1080 /07481180302906

Suicide.org (n.d.). Suicide statistics. Retrieved from http://www.suicide.org/suicide-statistics.html

Sznitman, S. R., Dunlop, S. M., Nalkur, P., Khurana, A., & Romer, D. (212). Student drug testing in the context of positive and negative school climates: results from a national survey. *Journal of Youth Adolescence, 41,* 146–155. doi 10.1007/s10964-011–9658–2

Tennessee Schools: *PREPARE* (2007). Vanderbilt Community Mental Health Center.

U.S. Census Bureau (2010). U.S. Department of Commerce. Retrieved from http://www .census.gov/#

Walz, G. R, & Kirkman, C. J. (2002). *Helping people cope with tragedy and grief.* Greensboro, NC: CAPS.

Wiger, D. E., & Harowski, K. J. (2003). *Essentials of crisis counseling and intervention.* Hoboken, NJ: John Wiley & Sons Inc.

Winters, K. C., Fahnhorst, T., Botzet, A., Lee, S., & Lalone, B. (2012). Brief intervention for drug-abusing adolescents in a school setting: Outcomes and mediating factors. *Journal of Substance Abuse Treatment, 42,* 279–288.

Chapter 8

THE SCHOOL COUNSELOR AND CAREER COUNSELING

Aaron H. Oberman

*CACREP STANDARD

COUNSELING, PREVENTION, AND INTERVENTION

C. *Knowledge*

4. Knows how to design, implement, manage, and evaluate transition programs, including school-to-work, postsecondary planning, and college admissions counseling.

ACADEMIC DEVELOPMENT

L. *Skills and Practices*

2. Implements strategies and activities to prepare students for a full range of postsecondary options and opportunities.

> *What is the recipe for successful achievement? To my mind there are just four essential ingredients: Choose a career you love, give it the best there is in you, seize your opportunities, and be a member of the team.*
>
> Source unknown

An individual's career development is a lifelong, constantly changing process with the professional school counselor playing an integral part in facilitating career choices (Ginzberg, Ginzburg, Axelrad, & Herma, 1951; Super, 1957). Our professional foundation was originally conceived as a career emphasis and eventually expanded to include academic and professional/social growth. With the rapid societal shifts, the emphasis on vocational choice continues as a fundamental school counselor responsibility. This belief is clearly articulated in the American School Counselor Association's position statement, *The Professional School Counselor and Academic and Career Planning*:

> Professional school counselors recognize that each student possesses unique interests, abilities, and goals that will lead to many future opportunities. Collaborating with students, parents, educational staff, and the community, the professional school counselor works to ensure that all students develop an academic and career plan that reflects their interests, abilities, and goals and includes rigorous, relevant coursework and experiences appropriate for the student (ASCA, 2012a para. 1).

In this chapter I will discuss theoretical orientations relevant to the career counseling process and the essential role of the school counselor in relationship to the career development of K–12 students. In all likelihood you have a separate career counseling course in your school counseling program curriculum. It is not my intention to duplicate the concepts you will learn in this class, but instead my goal is to supplement the concepts identified in your career development class as they apply to school-age youth. The chapter information will assist you in understanding the different career responsibilities assumed by school counselors at all levels and how this professional is able to integrate program standards to the academic curriculum through teacher collaboration. Examples of developmentally appropriate guidance websites and activities that complement career development theories that you can use in your role as a school counselor are provided. See Table 8.1 for a list of ASCA's Career Development Student Standards.

Table 8.1   ASCA National Standards for Career Development

ASCA National Standards for career development guide school counseling programs to provide the foundation for the acquisition of skills, attitudes and knowledge that enable students to make a successful transition from school to the world of work, and from job to job across the life span.

Standard A: Students will acquire the skills to investigate the world of work in relation to knowledge of self and to make informed career decisions.

(Continued)

Table 8.1 (Continued)

C:A1 Develop Career Awareness

C:A1.1 Develop skills to locate, evaluate and interpret career information

C:A1.2 Learn about the variety of traditional and nontraditional occupations

C:A1.3. Develop an awareness of personal abilities, skills, interests and motivations

C:A1.4 Learn how to interact and work cooperatively in teams

C:A1.5 Learn to make decisions

C:A1.6 Learn how to set goals

C:A1.7 Understand the importance of planning

C:A1.8 Pursue and develop competency in areas of interest

C:A1.9 Develop hobbies and vocational interests

C:A1.10 Balance between work and leisure time

C:A2 Develop Employment Readiness

C:A2.1 Acquire employability skills such as working on a team, problem-solving and organizational skills

C:A2.2 Apply job readiness skills to seek employment opportunities

C:A2.3 Demonstrate knowledge about the changing workplace

C:A2.4 Learn about the rights and responsibilities of employers and employees

C:A2.5 Learn to respect individual uniqueness in the workplace

C:A2.6 Learn how to write a résumé

C:A2.7 Develop a positive attitude toward work and learning

C:A2.8 Understand the importance of responsibility, dependability, punctuality, integrity and effort in the workplace

C:A2.9 Utilize time- and task-management skills

Standard B: Students will employ strategies to achieve future career goals with success and satisfaction.

C:B1 Acquire Career Information

C:B1.1 Apply decision-making skills to career planning, course selection and career transition

C:B1.2 Identify personal skills, interests and abilities and relate them to current career choice

C:B1.3 Demonstrate knowledge of the career-planning process

C:B1.4 Know the various ways in which occupations can be classified

C:B1.5 Use research and information resources to obtain career information

C:B1.6 Learn to use the Internet to access career-planning information

C:B1.7 Describe traditional and nontraditional career choices and how they relate to career choice

C:B1.8 Understand how changing economic and societal needs influence employment trends and future training

C:B2 Identify Career Goals

C:B2.1 Demonstrate awareness of the education and training needed to achieve career goals

C:B2.2 Assess and modify their educational plan to support career

C:B2.3 Use employability and job readiness skills in internship, mentoring, shadowing and/or other work experience

C:B2.4 Select course work that is related to career interests

C:B2.5 Maintain a career-planning portfolio

Standard C: Students will understand the relationship between personal qualities, education, training and the world of work.

C:C1 Acquire Knowledge to Achieve Career Goals

C:C1.1 Understand the relationship between educational achievement and career success

C:C1.2 Explain how work can help to achieve personal success and satisfaction

C:C1.3 Identify personal preferences and interests influencing career choice and success

C:C1.4 Understand that the changing workplace requires lifelong learning and acquiring new skills

C:C1.5 Describe the effect of work on lifestyle

C:C1.6 Understand the importance of equity and access in career choice

C:C1.7 Understand that work is an important and satisfying means of personal expression

C:C2 Apply Skills to Achieve Career Goals

C:C2.1 Demonstrate how interests, abilities and achievement relate to achieving personal, social, educational and career goals

C:C2.2 Learn how to use conflict management skills with peers and adults

C:C2.3 Learn to work cooperatively with others as a team member

C:C2.4 Apply academic and employment readiness skills in work-based learning situations such as internships, shadowing and/or mentoring experiences

Source: ASCA National Standards for career development. Reprinted with permission.

THE ELEMENTARY SCHOOL COUNSELOR AND VOCATIONAL AWARENESS

Although there are some who believe that career development is to be reserved for older students, research is clear that elementary-age students benefit from knowledge of careers. One of the main roles of the professional school counselor at the

elementary level is to increase the career awareness of all students (ASCA, 2012; Auger, Blackhurst, & Wahl, 2005). During these early years, students should be exposed to a full array of career possibilities. Professional school counselors generally conduct regular classroom guidance lessons with all elementary grades and are able to build an awareness of careers through such activities as word searches, coloring pages, costumes or other dress-up clothing, collages, and interactive websites. These lessons fit with the "fantasy stage" (birth to 11 years) proposed by Ginzberg, et al. (1951), in which children can try out, role-play, and imagine themselves in different work environments. Children may also begin to think about a future career path as their play becomes more work oriented. Donald Super's (1990) life-span, life-space approach is another career theory created with the premise that self-concept serves as a means to career expression. Super believed children at the elementary and middle school levels are in the growth stage, a time when children are beginning to develop their attitude and interests related to one's view of self. A developmental framework is helpful for elementary counselors as they conduct individual and group career counseling interventions; however, most career counseling interactions at this level are conducted through classroom guidance lessons and reinforced by classroom teachers.

Helping students set goals for future occupational choices starts with an awareness of options that may not have been previously viewed as viable options, including college readiness. College is not for everyone, and there are many successful individuals who have excellent and lucrative careers without the benefit of a college education. For instance, Steve Jobs started college and eventually lost interest in his studies and dropped out, but he did create Apple computer and became one of the world's most successful businesspeople.

College readiness includes providing educational supports so that if students choose to do so, they will have the knowledge to make the transition to higher education. No Excuses University is the name of a program adopted by Los Penasquitos Elementary School in San Diego, CA, to promote college readiness. This comprehensive program promotes college readiness for every student regardless of socioeconomic status (Hjalmarson, 2007). Students participate in such activities as an annual college/career day, discussions about college planning, and exposure to vocabulary words related to college. Parents are encouraged to spend time with their child to discuss academic success and readiness, and to ask their child questions such as, "What did you do today to help achieve your student goal?" The philosophy behind this program is that college readiness needs to start early, as elementary-age children need to think about possibilities for themselves early in life. Waiting to start until high school to develop career awareness and readiness is too late.

In addition to career/college awareness, the school counselor assists students with the transition to middle school. Students will likely be anxious about moving up to a new school, locating classes in an unfamiliar building, having more than one teacher, and the increasing academic work load. The school counselor can alleviate students' stress by organizing times for middle school teachers and/or students to visit the elementary school to share their tips and strategies for being successful in middle school (NEA, n.d.), or even schedule time for elementary students to visit the middle school and practice traveling to classes using a mock schedule. Other helpful activities might include a parents' night, classroom guidance lessons about the changes to expect in middle school, and related guidance events to help everyone feel comfortable with this transitional process.

CONCEPTUAL APPLICATION ACTIVITY 8.1

To help you better understand the role of the elementary school counselor, take a minute and think back to when you were eight years old. List three careers you can remember telling family members you wanted to have. Now think about your current career path. What similarities and differences do you notice when you reflect on these different career opportunities?

Website for Career Awareness

The website Paws in Jobland—http://paws.bridges.com/cfnc1.htm is a great interactive tool for elementary students to learn about different career paths. Paws is the puppy that leads young students through Jobland. The four main subsections of the website are Jobland, Job Finder, Quiz, and ABC Search. Jobland is a city of interactive buildings found in the community in which people with different occupations work. Students can click on a building that leads to an associated career, and information is provided regarding the details of this job. The Job Finder function asks the student to respond to 26 age-appropriate questions related to school subjects and personal interests, and the student's answers are used to direct the student to particular buildings in Jobland that match their career interests. The Quiz function allows students to view pictures of individuals working in various occupations and to respond to multiple-choice questions about the career shown in the picture. For instance, three pictures of workers are provided and the student will select a worker to answer questions such as, "Which of these people uses water in their job?" These questions also help students expand awareness of alternative career paths that they may not have previously considered. The ABC Search provides additional information about a particular career path.

Examples of Career Activities for Elementary-Age Students

There are many good books available to help students explore different jobs. Bibliocounseling is one way to share career awareness and development with elementary-age children and provides an excellent opportunity for the school counselor and classroom teacher to partner in meeting curricular standards. *Mama's New Job* from the Berenstain Bears series is a story that could be used to begin a discussion with young students about the types of careers about which they already are familiar, such as jobs held by family members or neighbors. After allowing time to discuss various careers the counselor reads the book to the students and asks follow-up questions such as, "What was mama's new job?" or, "What did she like about her job?" or "What are some of the skills needed to perform this job?" In addition to the book about mama's job and those identified by the students from the introductory discussion, students can draw a picture of the job that most interested them from the reading. Additional books related to careers are included below.

- Rockwell, A. (2000). *Career day.* New York: Harper Collins Publishers.

  This book describes a typical career day that takes place in an elementary school where each of the 10 children in Mrs. Madoff's class brings a family member to the classroom to discuss his/her career path. Colored pictures, as well as the adults enjoying their careers make this an engaging book for children to explore and learn about a variety of potential careers.

- Scarry, R. (1968). *What do people do all day.* New York: Random House Children's Books.

  This is a classic book in which many different potential careers and their interrelationships are discussed. The story helps children learn about what their parents do at work all day, and includes age-appropriate pictures to help elementary-age children understand each career path.

- Geisel, T. (Dr. Seuss) (2000). *Oh! The places you'll go.* New York: Random House Children's Books.

  This book provides a window into the journey of life. The story helps children to optimistically think about the future and reach for the stars in making a career selection. The illustrations are eye-catching and encourage young children to explore the world.

A word search or word puzzles are other developmentally appropriate activities that introduce elementary students to careers. You could create a career word search using the *SuperKids Word Puzzle Creator* found at http://www.superkids .com/aweb/tools/words/search/

Through this website the counselor is able to key in several different careers and then a ready-made word search is immediately created. The counselor could also develop a word scramble by identifying a career, such as TEACHER, mixing up the letters such as CRTEAHE, and giving the student blanks to fill-in (_ _ _ _ _ _) the unscrambled career term. For younger elementary students, it may also be helpful to include a picture of the career to assist them in unscrambling the word. After the students have completed the word search or puzzle they could be given the homework assignment of investigating a career, which could be linked to an academic subject such as English.

THE MIDDLE SCHOOL COUNSELOR AND CAREER EXPLORATION

One of the tasks of middle school counselors is to facilitate the career exploration and development of students (Zunker, 2006). In the middle school years, students begin to orient themselves to different career paths and think in greater depth about their career interests. Ginzberg et al. (1951) referred to this developmental time frame as the "tentative stage." This stage is when the student is in a period of transition, and in the process of developing a greater understanding of abilities, values, and interests. The school counselor can help the students navigate this developmental milestone by introducing career assessments, interviewing or job shadowing an employer, or conducting career research projects using the Internet. While the middle school counselor still focuses on classroom guidance, there is an increased focus on individual student planning in which the student develops career, educational, and personal/social goals (ASCA, 2012).

John Holland's Typology provides the framework for many of the more commonly used career assessments, with the focus on the match between one's personality and the work environment. This belief is central to his theory that our career choice is an extension of our personality, in that a sense of occupational congruency will usually lead to job satisfaction and self-fulfillment (Zunker, 2006). Holland identifies six categories that include: realistic (hands on), investigative (problem solvers), artistic (creators), social (helpers), enterprising (influencers), and conventional (detail-oriented) (see Figure 8.1). Based on these six categories, Holland believes we search out an environment (career path) allowing us to express our skills, abilities, and values, which eventually leads to job satisfaction. Some of the assessments based on this theory include the *Self-Directed Search, Strong Interest Inventory, Campbell Interest and Skills Inventory, and the Kuder Navigator.* In these assessments the student is asked to complete a series of questions related to Holland's six career environments, and based on responses, results related to two or three of the categories are provided, or students are given a list of careers to consider based on his/her answers. With the supervision and guidance of the school counselor, students are able to explore different career options.

As students transition from the middle to high school, the school counselor's role is to foster and support student growth and achievement. Organizing visits with teachers and administrators at each of the "feeder" schools helps alleviate anxiety related to this process. As a school counselor at the middle school level, you may also consider the opportunity for middle school students to shadow one of the high school students for a more in-depth look at the daily high school schedule. Beginning this process early in the eighth-grade year could increase student success and decrease drop-out rates in high school (Graber & Brooks-Gunn, 1996).

Figure 8.1   Holland's Hexagon Model

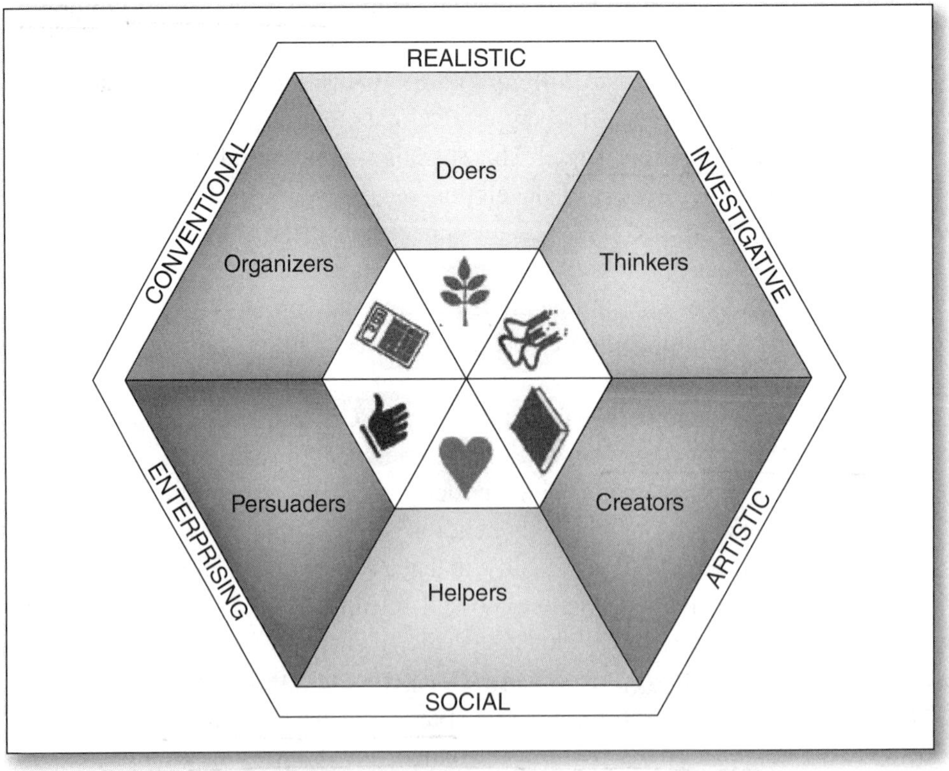

Source: www.career.utk.edu/holland.php

Teachers and parents/guardians should also be involved in the process of transitioning to high school. The school counselor can hold meetings and workshops and provide information regarding psychological preparation for the transitional process to high school (Turner, 2007). It may also be helpful to have one-on-one sessions with parents/guardians to discuss the academic and career-related skills needed to help their student experience success in high school. Overall, school counselor collaboration with other stakeholders helps students prepare for not only the increased career and academic challenges they will face, but also the personal/social needs of developing healthy and supportive relationships with peers.

CONCEPTUAL APPLICATION ACTIVITY 8.2

Stop and take a minute to think about each of the Holland codes (realistic, investigative, artistic, social, enterprising, conventional) that most closely fits with your career personality. Pick two to three of the six codes that best represent you. Then, go to http://www.123test.com/career-test/ and take a quick 16-question career assessment to see if the results match up with your self-perceptions. Were the results what you expected? Note any similarities and differences.

Website for Career Exploration

The Occupational Outlook Handbook (K–12 website)—http://www.bls.gov/k12/ is a kid-friendly version of the *Occupational Outlook Handbook,* and is similar to the original site published by the Bureau of Labor Statistics; however, it is geared to helping the middle school student explore different career paths. One important difference is that the student is able to research career paths based on subjects he/she enjoys or excels in. Some of these topics include math, helping people, social studies, and computers. As you review the list of topics, you may notice that many of these connect to Holland's six career categories. After clicking on one of the school academic subjects or areas of interest, students will be taken to a screen with six different careers where they can learn more about a sampling of career paths related to that topic. This link to academic subjects facilitates the career exploration process, as students make the connection between academic achievement and career development. Understanding how academics and careers are linked increases student attitudes and interest in school success (Lapan, 2004). Once selecting a career path to research, students are taken to a different screen that gives answers to common questions such as: "What is the job like?" "How do you get ready?" "How much does the job pay?" "How many jobs are there?" "What about the future?" "Are there other jobs like this?" and, "Where can you find more information?" Answers to these questions offer enough information to help the student determine if this career path is one he or she would like to explore in more detail. Or, if students are looking for a particular career, they can click on the A-Z index to locate a specific career of interest. While this site is good for exploration, some students are likely to have a more defined career path than others. If the career the student is exploring is not contained on this website, he/she could explore the website http://www.bls.gov/oco for a more detailed listing of career paths.

Examples of Career Activities for Middle School Students

The website *This Could Be Your Life*—http://ctbyl.icsps.ilstu.edu/illinoisntc//index.asp is designed for students to develop a more realistic picture about their career and life choices and to learn how these decisions can impact their future. Although this activity is developed with data from the state of Illinois, students can make connections that relate to their region of the country with the guidance and support of their school counselor. Students will first enter their name, gender, and desired level of education. Next, students will answer a brief series of multiple-choice questions regarding their interests, and based on these responses the students are given a few potential careers to consider. After choosing a career path of interest, students are informed of potential salary, and from here the student answers more specific questions such as a region of the state of Illinois in which to live, and how much money he or she will need for housing, food, taxes, transportation, and so on. After making a selection, the student is able to determine whether or not he/she will have enough money to live comfortably in his/her preferred life style based on the chosen career path.

Through the website *Drive of Your Life*—http://www.driveofyourlife.org/launch.html students learn about themselves and the career planning process. After completing the log-in procedure, students answer a series of questions that are related to Holland's theory. Once students complete these questions they are able to select a model car, color, wheels, personalized license plate, and so on. Next, students are able to review a summary of their results and receive a selection of different careers they can select to "test drive." During this phase, students' personalized car drives along the highway to their selected career path, where they can learn more about the identified career and what a typical day might be like in this profession. If the student decides he or she is no longer interested in a particular career path, another choice can be made. Although this information has been developed by the state of Indiana, it provides students with the opportunity to think about their career path and to arouse their curiosity about the world of work in the state where they live. In addition, the school counselor can work cooperatively with a classroom teacher to meet both school counseling program and academic objectives to develop students' speaking skills as they present information to their peers about a career path that interests them.

THE HIGH SCHOOL COUNSELOR AND CAREER PLANNING

As students transition to high school, so does the role of the school counselor. At this level the career development focus is working with students to plan and prepare for a range of post-secondary options and opportunities (ASCA, 2012; CACREP, 2009). For some students career development may include furthering their education at a college or trade school, while other students may decide to enter the work force upon graduation, join the military, or choose to get married. Ginzberg et al. (1951) referred to this developmental time frame as the "realistic stage." According to Ginz-

Photo 8.1 Students Exploring Careers in Science

Source: © JuiceImages/iStockphoto.com

berg et al. (1951) this stage begins around age 17 and continues into adulthood, with an emphasis on the integration and further development of occupational choices.

While high school counselors have many different responsibilities as they work within a comprehensive, developmental school counseling (CDSC) program, the guidelines within ASCA National Model (2012a) indicate that high school counselors should spend approximately 25–35% of their time with individual student planning. A graduation or four-year plan for all students is one major school counselor responsibility. These plans have a variety of names in different states; however, regardless of the defining term, the goal of helping students to graduate and move on to future careers is the same.

The four-year plan provides direction for post-secondary options for all students based on a list of required courses and elective course selections for each of the high school years. Students are required to take a set number of classes and subjects in areas such as math or language arts, with flexibility for students to take coursework relevant to future career plans (see Table 8.2).

Table 8.2 Four-Year Plan Worksheet

Name: _____	Class: _____
Plans: _____	Date Initialed: _____
Grade 9	**Grade 11**
English 9th _____	English Elective _____
World History _____	Social Studies Elective _____
Science _____	Science _____
Math _____	Math _____
Physical Education _____	Elective _____
Elective _____	Elective _____
Elective _____	Elective _____
_____	_____
Total Credits _____	Total Credits _____
Grade 10	**Grade 12**
English 10th _____	English Elective _____
U.S. History _____	Social Studies Elective _____
Science _____	Math or Science Elective _____
Math _____	Elective _____
Elective _____	Elective _____
Elective _____	Elective _____
Elective _____	Elective _____
_____	_____
Total Credits _____	Total Credits _____
Cumulative Credits _____	Cumulative Credits _____

Source: http://www.lruhs.org/program-of-studies/57-4-year-plan-worksheet

Parents/guardians are an essential part of career planning and are strongly encouraged to attend annual course selection meetings with their child and school counselor to discuss class options for the following academic year. When including parents/guardians in this process, the student benefits as conversations about future career and post-secondary possibilities take place.

Super's life-span, life-space approach (1990) also plays an important role in the high school students' career development. His theory posits that beginning around the age of 14, individuals go through a series of stages that include growth (self-concept development), exploration (learning about career opportunities), establishment (starting out in a career path), maintenance (confirm the career choice), and decline (reducing work hours and preparing for retirement). The focus of high school counselors is based on the adolescent years; however, Super provides different expectations as we transition through the life stages of early adulthood (25–45), middle adulthood (45–65), and late adulthood (65+). The high school student would be in the exploration phase, as he or she is trying out and investigating different career options through coursework, job shadowing experiences, summer jobs, or internships. For example, students may want to pursue a career in medicine but struggle in many of the math and science courses. In this instance, the counselor should not discourage their interest; however, he or she might consider sharing other options within the medical field for the student to explore. As students get closer to graduation (junior and senior year), for the students who choose post-secondary options the counselor continues to support these choices by helping them with the college application process, including letters of reference, scholarships, and financial aid forms. However, students who choose to enter the workforce after high school graduation also need the continued support of the counselor to find internships, job shadowing experiences, or other work-related opportunities. For students who are choosing a career in the military, the school counselor is able to link these students with representatives from the various armed forces and discuss the value of the ASVAB in selecting a career within the military.

Overall, the high school counselor is helping students make the best possible decision for their career futures based on their interests, skills, and values as they relate to the world of work, yet at times this assistance may be misinterpreted. For instance, a male junior was discussing career options with his school counselor, and indicated that he was interested in aeronautical engineering. The counselor assisted him in a computer career search that included information on academic subjects related to this occupation, including higher levels of math and science. The school counselor discussed the importance of academics and other career-related skills, and pointed out that because he had difficulty passing his lower-level math class that year, he could experience difficulty with this subject in college. The next day the young man's mother arrived at the school and demanded that her son be allowed to change counselors since his counselor obviously was not being very encouraging about her son's career decision.

It is obvious that school counselors are vital resources to promote school to life plans. However, many school districts are concerned that school counselors are ill-prepared for this task. For instance, in a misguided attempt to help students facing difficult situations, too many school counselors have excused students from taking rigorous classes that would bolster a college curriculum. By limiting life options there are destructive consequences (Hines, Lemons, & Crews, 2011). In fact, 40% of high school graduates revealed that they wished they had chosen different courses in high school (Hines, et al., 2011).

Lent, Brown, and Hackett's Social Cognitive Career Theory (SCCT) is particularly helpful for the high school counselor, in that this approach focuses on how learning shapes future career behaviors (Brown & Lent, 1996). SCCT also emphasizes that individuals develop interests based on their perceived level of confidence. Therefore, if students are able to have experience in a particular career path and/or feel success in related academic areas, they are more likely to consider a related future career path in a given area. As national statistics indicate, about half of the students who enter college do not graduate within six years. Yet a large percent of our high school seniors feel obligated to attend college, in part due to the myth that when you do not enter post-secondary education you are considered as unmotivated (King & Welch, 2007).

CONCEPTUAL APPLICATION ACTIVITY 8.3

Adrian is a soft-spoken 16-year-old male with the following concerns. He wants to find a job. He is on the verge of flunking out of school and has very little work experience. Adrian lacks the skills to make appropriate decisions, and he is heavily influenced by his family, who is pushing him to drop out of school and get a job. What steps would you take to help Adrian? Take into account theoretical approaches and the school counselor's role in career decision making.

Example of a Website for Career Planning

My Future.com—Figure out what's next—http://www.myfuture.com is a comprehensive website to help high school students process the career decision-making procedure based on the options of entering the workforce, going to college, or joining the military. If a student would like to pursue a career after high school, he or she is able to search through job links that are sorted by industry, field of study, type of work, or Holland's codes. Based on these categories, students are able to click on different career paths and learn more about the day-to-day details of the job, education required, average salary, and job growth statistics. The college section provides students with a wealth of information on topics such as planning for college, entrance exams, choosing a college, the application process, and campus life. Also included are a series of checklists and timelines to help students in planning for the college experience. The military section shows students the benefits of being employed by one of the military branches, the programs that can help the student pay for college, and links to information about the different career opportunities available through the military. Students are also able to register with the site and create a user name and password they can save the materials in which to return at a later time. One unique feature about the site is called "My Pathway," which helps students navigate the website and locate the career development resources that may meet their needs.

Rather than engaging in an electronic job search, the school counselor may wish to design a card sort related to a career of interest. For instance, if a student is interested in several careers within Holland's Realistic/Investigative area, occupations within this area are printed on small index cards. Other cards are labeled Would Choose, Wouldn't Choose, or Possibly Choose printed on them to serve as headers. The student could then sort through the various occupations within the Realistic/Investigative areas and place each card under one of these headings. From here, the student could use the careers placed under the Would Choose pile and start a more in-depth computer search on the job qualifications. Next, the student could select a career and engage in a self-search to further eliminate, or continue the original career search. For instance, a dental laboratory technician is one career that falls within the Realistic/Investigative area. If this is an area of interest, the student can complete the following chart with this career in mind:

Requirement Some college or associate degree required	Do I have these skills?	Is this something which I am strongly interested in pursuing?
Critical Thinking Reading Comprehension Operation Monitoring Communication Skills		
Good Vision Inductive and Deductive Reasoning Finger Dexterity Attention to Detail		

(Continued)

(Continued)

Requirement Some college or associate degree required	Do I have these skills?	Is this something which I am strongly interested in pursuing?
Decision making Ability to analyze information Evaluating Compliance Standards Organizing and Prioritizing Work		
Dependability Initiative Self-Control Independence Persistence		

Examples of Career Activities for High School Students

Values are additional components that influence high school students as they clarify their career choices. Students can complete a values checklist that would include topics such as job security, freedom, independence, excitement, creativity, supervision, and so on. The Quintessential Careers website http://www.quintcareers .com/workplace_values.html can also be used as a values checklist for students to reflect on what is most important when selecting a career path and work environment.

Resume writing and mock interviews are two other beneficial activities as students apply for internships, college scholarships, or summer jobs. The school counselor has an opportunity to conduct classroom guidance lessons by detailing the basics of resume writing, formatting, and assisting the student with interview preparation. Topics could include interview attire, behavior, and common interview questions. In addition, the counselor can conduct mock interview sessions for students to practice their skills. The resumes, or a personal information sheet, that are written due to the guidance lesson are useful resources for high school counselors to review when they write letters of recommendation.

CONSIDERATIONS FOR WRITING LETTERS OF REFERENCE

Reference letters written by the school counselor can make the difference for scholarship selection, or when colleges are making admission decisions between two academically similar students. Based on 2011 data from the

National Association for College Admission Counseling, two-thirds of all colleges and universities gave significant attention to these letters when making an admissions decision (College Board, 2012a).

Since these letters of recommendation are valuable to the student in admission, it is vital that the counselor gather as much information about the student as possible. The student's teacher, parents/guardians, coaches, club advisors, and others are valuable sources of information, in addition to asking the student for a detailed list of their responsibilities, accomplishments, and extracurricular activities in and out of school environment (College Board, 2012a). An example of a personal information sheet that offers school counselors in-depth information about students for the purpose of writing letters of recommendation is in Table 8.3.

Table 8.3 Senior Brag Sheet

Name _____ Class of _____

1. What do you plan to study in college and why?

2. Describe specific extracurricular and after school activities and organizations in which you have participated during your high school years. You may also attach a resume. Include leadership roles, if applicable. Consider both school and community activities.

3. Which of the activities described in #2 have been the most meaningful to you and why?

4. Describe any community service/volunteer work in which you have been involved during your high school years.

5. What is important to you? What is your "passion"?

6. Describe what you believe are your academic strengths and why.

7. What are your academic weaknesses? Describe any problems or reasons which interfered with your academic achievement.

8. Is your high school academic record an accurate measure of your ability and potential? If not, what do you consider the best measure of your potential?

9. If applicable, tell about an obstacle you have overcome and how that experience changed you.

10. What sets you apart from other students in your graduating class?

11 What three words would you use to describe yourself?

12. What is something that most people don't know about you?

13. List 3–5 faculty members you would select to make recommendations to your future school.

Student Signature _____ Date _____

Source: Permission provided by Sarah Bast, Professional School Counselor, West High School, Knoxville, Tennessee.

Once these data are gathered, the school counselor has an overall picture of the student, and from this information the next step is to give special attention to the details that make this student stand out from equally capable applicants. Additionally, the school counselor should also discuss his/her opinion of the applicant's potential for future success and the "goodness of fit" at the chosen college/university (College Board, 2012a).

As school counselors, we also have ethical codes and legal issues to consider, such as the Family Education Rights and Privacy Act (FERPA), when writing letters of recommendation. While school counselors can include information that is widely known (such as the need for a service dog as a specific accommodation), it is a good idea to get student and parent/guardian approval before including any sensitive information that could negatively impact the student (Stone, 2004).

As part of a CDSC program, the professional school counselor meets the needs of all students (ASCA, 2012). Therefore, the professional school counselor works to ensure that there is no discrimination toward students based on their gender, ethnicity, or sexual orientation. Gottfredson's (1981) Theory of Circumscription, Compromise, and Self-Creation is applicable to this concept.

WORKING WITH DIVERSE POPULATIONS

CACREP

Gottfredson (1981) believes that students go through four stages in which they reflect on, think about, and gradually eliminate viable career choices. In early childhood (ages 3–5) students begin to eliminate potential careers based on power. In other words, does the occupation seem strong and important, or weak and unimportant? As students continue through childhood (ages 5–8), they also eliminate careers based on the perceived gender roles; for instance, is the career seen as gender appropriate for males or females? When children progress into adolescence (ages 9–13), Gottfredson believes we become more aware of social status and eliminate careers that do not seem prestigious enough or are not valued by society. Lastly, as individuals continue to progress through adolescence (ages 14+), career exploration is a process of discarding or retaining certain occupations, defined as *circumscription*. Gottfredson believes that many individuals will settle for what she has termed a "zone of acceptable alternatives" (Gotttfredson, 1981, as cited in Leung & Harmon, 1990). This zone develops over time because the individual has slowly eliminated many potential career choices that he/she believes are not viewed highly within society. Therefore, the individual does not consider all career choices as acceptable or accessible, and may choose a career path he or she enjoys, but was not necessarily the "best fit." This theory is applicable to all students; however, it is particularly relevant to students from diverse backgrounds. Regardless of the background of the student with whom you are working, taking time to self-reflect on attitudes that have the potential to negatively impair the counseling relationship is necessary. Questions to ask yourself include (Tollerud, 2003):

- Am I willing to discuss nontraditional career plans?
- Do I discuss employment and discrimination laws with students so that they can be prepared if bias occurs in the workplace or school?
- When I discuss course selections with students do I discuss careers with a gender-neutral attitude?
- When students decide to take a nontraditional class, do I discuss potential problems and how to address these issues?

Developmental issues impact all students, but students from diverse backgrounds encounter additional issues that could impact their plans for a college or career-ready agenda. First-generation students, gay, lesbian, bisexual, transgendered, and questioning (GLBTQ) students, and students with special needs require additional encouragement and information as they navigate the career selection process.

First-Generation College Students

First-generation college students often need more assistance in planning for post-secondary education because they do not have a family member who has earned a college degree, and may not have a supportive home environment that encourages their plans for higher education. First-generation college students are more likely to be African American or Hispanic American students from families of lower socioeconomic status (Pike & Kuh, 2005). In particular, as the number of Latinos/Latinas grows, school counselors have a responsibility to respect the cultural values that Latinas confront when examining post-secondary options. Latinas are overly represented in low-paying jobs such as sales and service, partially due to gender roles, expectations, and beliefs that attending college could drain their family's resources. School counselors can include the student's family in the process to address questions and concerns that they may have regarding post-secondary choices (Rivera, 2007).

Some of the dissimilarities noted in first-generation students compared with other college students include: a) parents' experience with college applications; b) academic and personal preparation for college; c) decision-making process for going to college; d) personal experiences; and e) overall personality traits such as lowered self-esteem and less creativity (Gibbons & Shoffner, 2004). In order to help first generation college students navigate the college process, it is important to identify these students as early as possible and to work with the families to understand the potential benefits of higher education (College Board, 2012b) while understanding cultural views that may preclude advanced education.

One beneficial resource is Component 8 (Transition from High School Graduation to College Enrollment) of the National Office for School Counselor Advocacy (NOSCA) http://nosca.collegeboard.org/eight-components/transition-high-school-graduation, which helps connect students and families to school and community resources. The four-year plans mentioned in the high school counselor section are of particular importance to first-generation college students because their parents have not experienced the procedures associated with college, such as the application process, scholarships, financial aid, and college visits, and without prior experience navigating these related areas can be frustrating and overwhelming.

Non-College-Bound Students

In today's world, it seems as if the increased push for college as the best and only option continues to increase (Schlack, 2011); however, attending college may not be the best alternative for all students. School counselors have a responsibility to advocate for students who are not on a post-secondary career path, and to help them make the best decision for their personal career goals. The Bureau of Labor Statistics, reveals that college graduates have higher salaries than those with less education, or a 61% increase in median salary for those with a bachelor's degree compared to high school graduates. Yet, salary is not the only consideration in career aspirations as the job market, the type of degree, experience and skill are also influential in career determinations (Crosby & Moncarz, 2006). Some students may benefit from entering the world of work, military service, or other non-profit opportunities. Schlack (2011) recommends that knowledge of strengths, a handful of career interests, and potential life goals help college-bound students with choosing a major. If students are unclear on their future career plans, it may be a good idea to hold off on going to college and to explore options in the work force.

CONCEPTUAL APPLICATION ACTIVITY 8.4

Tom is a high school senior who grew up on his family's Midwest farm. He has average grades and is unclear on his future career path. Tom goes to his school counselor and asks for help "picking a good job." Discuss how you would help Tom and what options are available for him.

Lesbian, Gay, Bisexual, Transgendered, and Questioning Youth

Gottfredson's (1981) theory is applicable to the professional school counselors' role in working with lesbian, gay, bisexual, transgender, and questioning (LGBTQ) students and their career development needs. As LGBTQ students are trying to determine their own sexual identities, this difficult process may be compounded as these students attempt to navigate through the career development process (Schmidt & Nilsson, 2006). LGBTQ students are especially challenged because they are not only dealing with questions about traditional career-related gender roles, but their self-concept is influenced as they search for a career identity. LGBTQ students are frequently the source of bullying and conflict in the school setting; therefore, the school counselor requires an awareness of the stereotypes and discrimination that could influence the occupational choices and career goals of LGBTQ students (Chung, 2003). For example, a gay male student with an interest in working as a hair stylist may not pursue his interests and talents because this career path could be viewed as a stereotypically gay male or female oriented profession. If this student is already bullied or teased at school, he may feel that choosing this career path may increase the school torment. As the school counselor, we not only need to help this student cope with the bullying taking place at school, but also to help the student select the best possible career for him or herself. Savickas' Constructivist Career Theory (2002) emphasizes the uniqueness of each person as an active participant in his/her career development, and each student is viewed as the "expert" on his or her own career development..

CONCEPTUAL APPLICATION ACTIVITY 8.5

Sally, a 17-year-old high school student, came to the career office stating she "did not know what to major in at college." She is a very capable student and has good relationships with students and teachers. She seems to have stereotypical views about careers for men and women. At one time she was interested in architecture but decided it was for men only. List three factors that would be important for you to consider as her school counselor. Discuss your responses with your classmates.

Students With Special Needs

The professional school counselor must also ensure he/she meets the career development concerns of students with special needs (Ljubicic, 2011), particularly because these students often require more assistance as they transition to careers (Murray, 2003). Legislation such as the Individuals with Disabilities Education

Improvement Act of 2004 (IDEIA) focuses on improving the academic achievement of students with special needs and the post-secondary transition process. Some changes to the law have included an emphasis on results-oriented activities, starting the transition plan at age 14, developing practical post-secondary goals, and a statement of transition services (Cortiella, n.d.). These changes help ensure that students with special needs are receiving adequate help with the progression into a variety of post-secondary options.

In addition, many of the guidance activities discussed in career planning for high school students would also be applicable for students with special needs. Some of the activities may need to be modified, depending upon the population being served by the counselor, and conducted in a developmentally appropriate framework. The school counselor may wish to collaborate with the special education teacher, who may be better able to help students focus on specific strengths related to their career development (Milsom, 2007).

CONCEPTUAL APPLICATION ACTIVITY 8.6

Lily is a high-functioning student but has received special education services due to her learning disability. She has spent the majority of her time in the general education classes and receives assistance from a tutor, which has enabled her to maintain average to above-average grades. She took the ACT and was disappointed that her scores were not high enough for admission into the state university, but she is motivated and willing to do "whatever it takes" to succeed. Discuss how you would work with Lily in her transition to post-secondary education.

THE CHANGING WORKPLACE

Technology is in center stage of our changing society and a mobile workforce. The world has become a place that desires the next, greatest technological advancement and wants it yesterday. The Internet has placed a wealth of information at students' fingertips, including information related to career development such as online assessments and the impact of social media on the career search process. Furthermore, technological advances usher in new careers such as social media managers, mobile application developers, robotics technicians, cyber security specialists, and simulation engineers (Farrell, 2011). Therefore, of necessity the school counselor must be cognizant of the continuous improvements in technology that impact the career development process.

The mobile work force is a new aspect of the changing workplace. Some jobs and career paths no longer exist due to changes in technology, while new careers such as genetics counselors, stem cell researchers, and medical records administrators are created as a result of these advances (Farrell, 2011), and more individuals work from home or other locations. Instead of commuting into the office or flying across the world for a business meeting, the workforce has embraced face-to-face videoconferencing. Workers can now complete many of their daily tasks and meetings from their bed, at a local coffee shop, or even at the beach. While these changes can bring about a positive work environment such as having greater flexibility, there are also seemingly undesirable consequences, such as not having a relationship with office mates. It is also difficult to predict the career opportunities that will be available in the next few decades; however, Table 8.4 indicates the career paths that are expected to show the most growth through the year 2020.

Table 8.4   Fastest-Growing Occupations Projected Through 2020

Matrix Code	Occupation	Number of new jobs added	Percent change	Wages (May 2010 median)	Entry-Level Education	Related Work Experience	On-the-job Training
29–1111	Registered Nurses	711,900	26	$64,690	Associate's degree	None	None
41–2031	Retail Salespersons	706,800	17	20,670	Less than high school	None	Short-term on-the-job training
31–1011	Home Health Aides	706,300	69	20,560	Less than high school	None	Short-term on-the-job training
39–9021	Personal Care Aides	607,000	70	19,640	Less than high school	None	Short-term on-the-job training
43–9061	Office Clerks, General	489,500	17	26,610	High school diploma or equivalent	None	Short-term on-the-job training
35–3021	Combined Food Preparation and Serving Workers, Including Fast Food	398,000	15	17,950	Less than high school	None	Short-term on-the-job training

(Continued)

Table 8.4 (Continued)

Matrix Code	Occupation	Number of new jobs added	Percent change	Wages (May 2010 median)	Entry-Level Education	Related Work Experience	On-the-job Training
43–4051	Customer Service Representatives	338,400	15	30,460	High school diploma or equivalent	None	Short-term on-the-job training
53–3032	Heavy and Tractor-Trailer Truck Drivers	330,100	21	37,770	High school diploma or equivalent	1 to 5 years	Short-term on-the-job training
53–7062	Laborers and Freight, Stock, and Material Movers, Hand	319,100	15	23,460	Less than high school	None	Short-term on-the-job training
25–1000	Postsecondary Teachers	305,700	17	62,050	Doctoral or professional degree	None	None
31–1012	Nursing Aides, Orderlies, and Attendants	302,000	20	24,010	Postsecondary non-degree award	None	None
39–9011	Childcare Workers	262,000	20	19,300	High school diploma or equivalent	None	Short-term on-the-job training
43–3031	Bookkeeping, Accounting, and Auditing Clerks	259,000	14	34,030	High school diploma or equivalent	None	Moderate-term on-the-job training
41–2011	Cashiers	250,200	7	18,500	Less than high school	None	Short-term on-the-job training
25–2021	Elementary School Teachers, Except Special Education	248,800	17	51,660	Bachelor's degree	None	Internship/ residency
43–4171	Receptionists and Information Clerks	248,500	24	25,240	High school diploma or equivalent	None	Short-term on-the-job training

Matrix Code	Occupation	Number of new jobs added	Percent change	Wages (May 2010 median)	Entry-Level Education	Related Work Experience	On-the-job Training
37–2011	Janitors and Cleaners, Except Maids and Housekeeping Cleaners	246,400	11	22,210	Less than high school	None	Short-term on-the-job training
37–3011	Landscaping and Groundskeeping Workers	240,800	21	23,400	Less than high school	None	Short-term on-the-job training
41–4012	Sales Representatives, Wholesale and Manufacturing, Except Technical and Scientific Products	223,400	16	52,440	High school diploma or equivalent	None	Moderate-term on-the-job training
47–2061	Construction Laborers	212,400	21	29,280	Less than high school	None	Short-term on-the-job training

Source: BLS Occupational Employment Statistics and Division of Occupational Outlook

The Internet's capabilities in career exploration are growing, and awareness of the validity of these profilers, sorters, finders, tests, or quizzes is essential as their use could harm students. For instance, a student could conduct a career search and erroneously believe that the highlighted career is the career path to follow even when it is unsuitable for their skills or personality. School counselor credibility could be impacted (Jones, 2007) if appropriate counseling is not provided to this student. The school counselor can sort out inappropriate inventories and be aware of website evaluation criteria that answer the questions, Who? What? When? Where? Why? and How?

Who?	is the author?
	sponsors the page?
What?	is the purpose of this site?
	are the qualifications and credentials of the author or publisher?

(Continued)

(Continued)

When?	was the website published?
	was the website revised?
Where?	can you contact the author or publisher?
	is the url domain .gov, .edu, .com, .net?
Why?	was the website published?
How?	accurate is the information?
	accurate is spelling and grammar?
	current are the hyperlinks?
	correct are the citations?
	easy is it to discern the information from advertisements?
	can the information be viewed without the limitation of fees or software requirements?

A few reliable career websites are listed below to provide students with the knowledge and awareness that are needed in the career journey.

Bureau of Labor Statistics	http://bls.gov/
Military Careers	http://www.military.net/
Job Finder	http://www.careerbuilder.com/
Jobs in Government	https://help.usajobs.gov/index.php/Main_Page
Part-time jobs	http://www.snagajob.com/part-time-jobs/?refi d=affcjpt&afsrc=1&ref=affcj

CONCLUSION

The professional school counselor plays a critical role in the career development needs of all students at all grade levels. Although the career focus and developmental tasks in grades from K-12 are different, each is important in shaping the career paths of today's youth. As students begin elementary school they start to show an interest and awareness in careers by inquiring about their parents or other family members' career paths. In middle school, students begin to develop their own ideas about a potential career path and explore different options. Finally, in high school and beyond students are evaluating all of the possible career options, and selecting the best career path based on their interests, abilities, and values. In addition, the school counselor has a responsibility to be aware of the increasingly diverse population and how the constantly changing world of work is impacting the students of the 21st century. Gottfredson's Theory of Circumscription and Compromise is a valuable theory to implement with diverse populations of students. A discussion of career strategies for work with first-generation college students, non-college-bound students, LGBTQ students, and students with special needs are included in this chapter.

REFERENCES

American School Counselor Association (2012). The *ASCA b Model: A Framework for School Counseling Program* (3rd ed.). Alexandria, VA: Author.

American School Counselor Association (2012a). *The professional school counselor and academic and career planning.* Retrieved from www.schoolcounselor.org

Auger, R., Blackhurst, A., & Wahl, K. (2005). The development of elementary aged children's aspirations and expectations. *Professional School Counseling, 8,* 322–329.

Brown, S., & Lent, R. (1996). A social cognitive framework for career choice counseling. *The Career Development Quarterly, 44,* 355–367.

Chung, Y. B. (2003). Career counseling with lesbian, gay, bisexual, and transgendered persons: The next decade. *The Career Development Quarterly, 52,* 78–86.

College Board (2012a). How to write effective college recommendations. Retrieved from: http://professionals.collegeboard.com/guidance/applications/counselor-tips

College Board (2012b). First-Generation students. Retrieved from http://professionals.collegeboard.com/guidance/prepare/first-generation

Cortiella, C. (n.d.). IDEA 2004: Improving transition planning and results. Retrieved from http://www.ncld.org/disability-advocacy/learn-ld-laws/idea/idea-2004-improving-transition-planning-results?start=1

Council for the Accreditation of Counseling and Related Programs (2009). *CACREP 2009 Standards.* CACREP: Washington, D.C.

Crosby, O., Moncarz, R. (2006, Fall). The 2004–14 job outlook for college graduates. *The Occupational Outlook Quarterly.* Retrieved from http://nosca.collegeboard.org/eight-components/transition-high-school-graduation

Farrell, R. (2011). *10 jobs of the future.* Retrieved from http://www.careerbuilder.com/Article/CB-2088-Job-Info-Trends-10-jobs-of-the-future

Gibbons, M., & Shoffner, M. (2004). Prospective first-generation college students: Meeting their needs through social cognitive career theory. *Professional School Counseling, 8,* 91–97.

Ginzberg, E., Ginzburg, S. W., Axelrad, S., & Herma, J. L. (1951). *Occupational choice: An approach to general theory.* New York: Columbia University Press.

Gottfredson, Linda S. (1981). Circumscription and compromise: A developmental theory of occupational aspirations. *Journal of Counseling Psychology* (Monograph) *28,* 545–579.

Graber, J. A., & Brooks-Gunn, J. (1996).Transitions and turning points: Navigating the passage from childhood through adolescence. *Developmental Psychology, 32,* 768–776.

Hines, P. L., Lemons, R. W., & Crews, K. D. (2011). Poised to lead: How school counselors can drive college and career readiness. *The Education Trust.* Retrieved from http://www.edtrust.org/dc/press-room/news/school-counselors-key-to-preparing-students-for-college-career

Hjalmarson, F. (2007, Nov./Dec.). College readiness: It's elementary. *ASCA School Counselor.* *21–25.*

Jones, L. K. (2007, Nov/Dec). Testing the test. *ASCA School Counselor,* 44–48.

King, J. & Welch, D. (2007, Nov/Dec). Success and satisfaction. *ASCA School Counselor,* 27–30.

Lapan, R. T. (2004). *Career development across the K–16 years: Bridging the present to satisfying and successful futures.* Alexandria, VA: American Counseling Association.

Leung, S.A., & Harmon, L. W. (1990). Individual and sex differences in the zone of acceptable alternatives. *Journal of Counseling Psychology, 37,* 153–159.

Ljubicic, L. (2011). *Empowering students with hidden disabilities to achieve career success.* Retrieved from National Career Development Association: http://www.ncda.org/aws/NCDA/ pt/sd/news_article/50358/_PARENT/layout_details_cc/false

Milsom, A. (2007). School counselor involvement in postsecondary transition planning for students with disabilities. *Journal of School Counseling, 5*(23). Retrieved from http://www.jsc .montana.edu/articles/v5n23.pdf

Murray, C. (2003). Risk factors, protective factors, vulnerability, and resilience: A framework for understanding and supporting the adult transitions of youth with high-incidence disabilities. *Remedial and Special Education, 24,* 16–26.

National Education Association (n.d.). Transition to middle school. Retrieved from www.nea.org/ tools/16657.htm

Pike, G. R., & Kuh. G. D. (2005). First- and second-generation college students: A comparison of their engagement and intellectual development. *Journal of Higher Education, 76 (3),* 276–300.

Rivera, L. M. (2007, Nov./Dec.). Career counseling for Latinas. *ASCA School Counselor.* 33–35.

Savickas, M. L. (2002). Career construction: A developmental theory of vocational behaviour. In D. Brown & Associates (Eds.), *Career choice and development* (4th ed.), (pp. 149–205). San Francisco, CA: Jossey-Bass.

Schlack, L. (2011). Not going to college is a viable option. Retrieved July 12, 2013, from: http:// www.education.com/reference/article/Ref_Going_College_Not/

Schmidt, C. K. & Nilsson, J. E. (2006). The effects of simultaneous developmental processes: Factors relating to the career development of lesbian, gay, and bisexual youth. *The Career Development Quarterly, 55,* 22–37.

Stone, C. (2004). *Legal and ethical complications in letters of recommendation.* ASCA School Counselor.

Super, D. E. (1957). *The psychology of careers.* New York, NY: Harper & Row.

Super, D.E. (1990). A life-span, life-space approach career development. In D. Brown, L. Brook, & Associates (Eds.), *Career choice and development: Applying contemporary theories to practice* (2nd ed.), (pp. 197–261). San Francisco, CA: Jossey-Bass.

Tollerud, T. R. (2003, May/June). Examining your own gender bias. *ASCA School Counselor,* 34–41.

Turner, S. L. (2007). Preparing inner-city adolescents to transition to high school. *Professional School Counseling, 10,* 245–252.

Zunker, V. (2006). *Career counseling: A holistic approach* (7th ed.). Belmont, CA: Brooks Cole.

SECTION III

ENHANCING ACADEMICS THROUGH A POSITIVE SCHOOL CULTURE

Chapter 9

THE SCHOOL COUNSELOR'S ROLE IN ACADEMIC ACHIEVEMENT

DEBORAH BUCHANAN

*CACREP STANDARDS

ACADEMIC DEVELOPMENT

K. *Knowledge*

  3. Understands curriculum design, lesson plan development, classroom management strategies, and differentiated instructional strategies for teaching counseling- and guidance-related material.

L. *Skills and Practice*

  1. Conducts programs designed to enhance student academic development.

  3. Implements differentiated instructional strategies that draw on subject matter and pedagogical content knowledge and skills to promote student achievement.

COLLABORATION AND CONSULTATION

M. *Knowledge*

  6. Understands the various peer programming interventions (e.g., peer meditation, peer mentoring, peer tutoring) and how to coordinate them.

N. *Skills and Practices*

  4. Uses helping strategies in the school counseling program

Aschool's culture and the accompanying climate are the most influential contributors to students' academic performance in that these concepts shape students' social, emotional, and academic development. School culture and school climate are often used interchangeably; however, there are a few distinctions between the two. *School culture* is broadly defined as the norms, values, rituals, and moral codes that shape the behavior and relationships of a school's constituency. Peterson and Deal (2002) believe

> Culture exists in the deeper elements of a school: the unwritten rules and assumptions, the combination of rituals and traditions, the array of symbols and artifacts, the special language and phrasing that staff and students use, the expectations for change and learning that saturate the school's world. (p. 9)

Basic assumptions and beliefs unconsciously influence the daily operation of the school, and are often more powerful in governing what people think and do than the actual management system of the school (Sergiovanni, 1991). *School climate,* on the other hand, can best be described as the *affective* manifestation of school culture. It is the current tone of the school—the expressed feelings and overall morale of the students and staff.

How do we assess a school's climate? Start by looking at the physical environment. Is it welcoming and conducive to learning? Is the building aesthetically pleasing? Does it showcase students' accomplishments, creativity, and achievement? Are classrooms and instructional materials substantive and supportive of multiple learning styles? Secondly, look for evidence that the social environment promotes communication and positive interaction. Does the school culture support a high degree of quality interactions between adults and students within and outside of its walls? Does it invite collaboration, parent and community involvement? Third, ask yourself, does the environment foster a feeling of safety and trust? Does it promote a sense of belonging and self-esteem? Are democracy, respect, and responsibility encouraged? Lastly, what can you tell about the academic environment? Does it promote learning and self-fulfillment? As a school counselor, you are in a unique position to promote and foster these essential ingredients to create a healthy school. Your knowledge and expertise in a variety of cognitive and affective domains and your perspective allows you to implement a comprehensive, developmental school counseling (CDSC) program that is integral to a positive school climate.

CONCEPTUAL APPLICATION ACTIVITY 9.1

Fly on the Wall

Keeping in mind the characteristics of a healthy school culture, spend a day in a school just observing the physical surroundings, the activities and interactions that take place. Pay attention to your own feelings about the school. Answer the following questions:

- How are you welcomed when you enter the school?
- Are doors locked and a doorbell used to announce your presence?
- Do you need to sign in at the central office and wear a name tag?
- How do teachers, students, and staff interact with each other?
- What observable artifacts are present, and do they support or detract from a positive school climate?
- How does the physical structure of the school influence the climate?
- Give examples of how classrooms and instructional materials support a healthy school climate (give examples).
- What is your sense of the social, affective, and academic environment of the school?

Share your findings with your classmates.

A discussion of your role as a school counselor and your contributions to a positive school culture and students' academic achievement are included in this chapter. In addition, the discussion includes your involvement in Professional Learning Communities (PLCs), collaborative efforts with parents, teachers, students, and staff, the programs you implement, and the delivery of a school guidance curriculum as fundamental components of a CDSC program that reflects the standards and outcomes of the ASCA National Model.

IMPROVING ACADEMIC ACHIEVEMENT THROUGH PROFESSIONAL LEARNING COMMUNITIES

The *Professional Learning Communities* (PLCs) concept has been around for several decades, but it wasn't until Richard DuFour and Robert Eaker's publication of *Professional Learning Communities at Work: Best Practices for Enhancing Student Achievement* (1998) that professional learning communities thrived as an educational reform initiative with the promise of increasing students' academic achievement. Since then, research has confirmed the effectiveness of PLCs in improving academic performance. Essentially, the PLC is a collaborative professional development model that recognizes ongoing staff development as critical to improving students' learning. In a PLC teachers meet on a regular basis, usually weekly, to reflect on teaching practices and their relationship of these practices to student learning, and discuss ways to improve teaching and learning for the students in their classes. Best practices in teaching, collaborative planning, curriculum study, and learning assessment are common topics of discussion in a PLC (Servage, 2008). Though PLCs can vary in form, DuFour (2004) established three core principles of effective professional learning communities: 1) the core mission of formal education is to ensure that students are learning; 2) a culture of collaboration is critical to achieving the common goal of "learning for all"; and 3) a PLC's effectiveness is judged on results. Effective PLCs mirror the ASCA National Model® in that they both center on student growth, focus on results, and encourage the collection of student data. These data are analyzed to improve student learning. In addition, PLCs are action oriented and team members seek systemic changes that improve the academic achievement of all students. According to Dufour and Eaker (1998), effective PLCs are characterized by members who:

- collectively pursue a shared mission, vision, values, and goals
- work interdependently in collaborative teams focused on learning
- engage in ongoing collective inquiry to ensure best practice based on the "current reality" of student achievement and the prevailing practices of the school
- demonstrate an action orientation and experimentation
- participate in systemic processes to promote continuous improvement
- maintain an unrelenting focus on results

There are two ways school counselors can be involved in professional learning communities. One is by participating in school-based teacher professional learning communities, and the other is by creating and participating in district-wide school counselor professional learning communities.

School-Based Teacher Professional Learning Communities

Your involvement in the PLCs within the school is probably one of the most efficient methods of implementing your CDSC program, in that you are able to play a significant role in the academic success of all students by forming and sustaining collaborative relationships with teachers. The PLC provides opportunities for you to support teachers' efforts and to advocate for students' needs. During PLC meetings you may learn about a student who is falling behind in his/her academic progress. This knowledge can serve as a catalyst to initiate a variety of activities such as arranging for peer-tutoring, implementing weekly check-ins to assess student progress, or introducing an after-school study group. You may also discover a need for social and emotional support activities such as the implementation of a girls' group that addresses relational aggression, or classroom guidance lessons that focus on improving social skills. By spending time in collaborative relationships with school faculty, you are better positioned to take a leadership role in advocating for systemic change that ensures "equity and access to a rigorous curriculum" for every student (ASCA, 2005, p. 25).

District-Wide School Counseling Professional Learning Communities

School districts are endorsing the development of PLCs among school psychologists, school health personnel, school social workers, and school counselors. School counselors involved in a district-level PLC are able to provide consistent monitoring and counseling throughout grade levels and school transition to enhance students' physical, social and emotional, and academic success.

District-wide school counselor PLCs are similar to school-based teacher PLCs in that school counselors within a school district meet regularly to share, reflect, and work together on essential student outcomes, counseling issues, and best practices. Opportunities to learn from each other, develop and use research-based school counseling practices, collaborate on ways to address broader district-wide concerns, and implement district-wide programs are invaluable benefits of school counselor PLCs. Adapting ideas and attending to comprehensive programming from preK–12 grades assist in delivering a consistent classroom guidance sequence.

IMPROVING ACADEMIC ACHIEVEMENT THROUGH THE GUIDANCE CURRICULUM

The implementation of a school guidance curriculum is a vital component of the Delivery System within the ASCA National Model. School counselors provide classroom instructional activities intended to promote the knowledge, attitudes, and skills that address the academic, social/emotional, and career development of all students (ASCA, 2005). The implementation of a guidance curriculum requires a specific set of skills, which include planning, designing, implementing and evaluating classroom lessons, as well as implementing classroom management strategies.

The time you will spend in delivering classroom guidance instruction will differ based on the school district and grade level in which you work (see Table 9.1). However, the ASCA National Model suggests the time spent in delivering a guidance

Table 9.1 ASCA Recommended Time Spent Delivering
Classroom Guidance Lessons

Grade Level	Percentage of Time
Elementary School	35%—45%
Middle School	25%—35%
High School	15%—25%

Source: ASCA, 2012

curriculum ranges from as much as 45% at the elementary school level and as little as 15% at the high school level. You will notice that at the elementary school level ASCA recommends the greatest percentage of a school counselor's time is to be spent delivering classroom guidance lessons, with less time at the high school level.

Vying for classroom time with the classroom teacher is sometimes difficult, particularly as mastery of identified standards is expected at the end of each academic year. Yet, when you are able to demonstrate your contributions to academic growth, teachers will be more willing to share classroom time with you. The following studies are examples of how the school counseling curriculum is able to facilitate academic growth while addressing personal/social issues.

Steen (2011) conducted a study to determine the effectiveness of a group counseling intervention on the personal development and academic success among fifth-grade students at risk for academic growth. Students who met the criteria for group intervention (low GPA in math and language arts, unsuccessful efforts to pass identified tests, and teacher referrals) were randomly divided into a group counseling intervention or a wait-listed control group that was to receive the intervention at a later time. In this study, pre- and post-tests were given to both groups to determine the effectiveness of the group counseling intervention. The school counselor led an *Achieving Success Everyday* (ASE) group based on the premise that academic growth can be addressed while focusing on personal concerns. Post-test results between the groups revealed a significantly higher GPA in language arts in the group intervention, but no differences were revealed in math growth, learning behaviors, or social skills. Although these results did not reach the anticipated results, the group results did provide valuable information for future groups, particularly as there is a paucity of research that addresses the importance of group counseling interventions in schools. As more research is conducted on counselor interventions that impact school achievement, counselors will have a greater knowledge base on which to design their involvement in school achievement (Steen, 2011).

The link between mental health issues and academic achievement has become particularly pronounced due to the stress that accompanies the emphasis on tests mandated by No Child Left Behind. Child-centered play therapy is one strategy for providing mental health services in schools as it is a means for youth to express themselves emotionally (Landreth, 2002, as cited in Blanco & Ray, 2011) in a safe, nonjudgmental environment, with the added benefit of improving academics. Elementary-school youth between the ages of 4–7 considered at risk for academic achievement were randomly placed in either the play therapy groups led by a counseling professional or placed in a wait-listed control group. All participants were given the *Young Children's Achievement Test* to measure academic achievement levels. At the end of the 8-week, 16-session play therapy group, the participants in the play therapy groups showed significant academic gains compared with those in the control groups (Blanco & Ray, 2011).

When school counselors present the outcomes of studies such as these, there will be greater interest and support in partnerships between the school counselor professional and educators at all grade levels. With consistent monitoring of academic needs and increased understanding of how the school counseling curriculum is able to address these needs, students will be the beneficiaries. The Common Core State Standards were designed for the purpose of ensuring that students leave high school with the ability to achieve in post secondary school or the workforce. The ASCA Student Standards can be integrated with these common core standards to further demonstrate how school counselors are able to assist in student success beyond high school.

THE COMMON CORE STATE STANDARDS

Standards serve as building blocks to learning with increasing complexity in building knowledge and viewing different perceptions. The National Governors Association (NGA) and Council of Chief State School Officers (CCSSO) were instrumental in leading an initiative to develop core state standards for the purpose of articulating high, consistent standards that are clearly understood. This initiative was developed due to high school graduates lacking basic skills, with American students ranked 25th in math, 17th in science, and 14th in reading compared to other industrialized countries (*The Week,* 2013). At the present time 45 states and the District of Columbus have adopted these standards and are in the process of developing assessments to measure attainment (Shallcross, 2013). Language arts and math are the core subjects chosen for standard development due to the foundation these subjects provide for all other curricular areas. The language arts standards include reading, writing to develop logical arguments, speaking, and listening to understand information presented through auditory means, language to increase vocabulary and meaning, and media and technology to critically analyze information presented electronically. More information is found at www .corestandards.org. In mathematics there are 8 standards that range from problem solving and adaptive reasoning, to being able to carry out procedures efficiently and accurately (www.corestandards.org/Math/Practice). School counselors are able to cross-walk the ASCA Student Standards with the common core standards as they collaborate with teachers in reaching academic success. For instance, the academic domain of the ASCA Student Standards—A:B: Students will complete school with the academic preparation essential to choose from a wide range of substantial post-secondary options, including college; Competency A:B1 Improve learning; and Indicator A:B1.2 Learn and apply critical thinking skills—integrates with the goals outlined in the Common Core Standards.

CONCEPTUAL APPLICATION ACTIVITY 9.2

Examine the ASCA Student Standards and identify the standards, competencies, and indicators that you believe most integrate with the goals of the Common Core Standards Initiative. With a classmate discuss the areas you have identified and the method you believe would best address these areas (e.g., group guidance, individual counseling, consultation).

As indicated in Chapter 1, many states historically required teaching experience to enter the school counseling profession, and as educational changes occurred many states dropped this prerequisite teaching requirement. An unfortunate outcome was that school counselors lacked the training and experience that was needed to design, deliver, and evaluate lesson plans. In addition, they did not have a background in classroom management, which resulted in professional stress and frustration, particularly when they were responsible for classrooms with difficult students.

DELIVERING CLASSROOM GUIDANCE LESSONS

Lesson plans are created from the domains, competencies, and indicators identified from those within the ASCA Student Standards. Good instruction requires advance planning. Instructional planning requires the identification of the knowledge and skills you want students to acquire, the sequence in which you will teach these outcomes, and activities that you will use to maximize learning and keep students motivated and on task (Ormrod, 2011). A *lesson plan* is a written guide of how you will carry out a class lesson. A typical lesson plan includes the following:

- Goal(s) and objective(s) of the lesson
- Instructional materials and equipment that will be used
- Instructional strategies and the sequence in which they will be presented
- Assessment method(s) to be used in assessing student learning

In writing lesson plans, *goals* refer to the long-term outcome of instruction and *objectives* refer to the specific desired outcome of a unit or lesson. One way to look at an instructional goal is to think of it as a standard as outlined in the ASCA Student Standards. Three standards are in each of the academic, career, and personal/social domains, and competencies and indicators are found within each of the standards that more specifically define appropriate skills to be acquired (American School Counselor Association, 2012). For example, a sample lesson plan in Figure 9.1 within the personal/social domain is *Acquire Self-Knowledge.* In association with this competency there are several indicators that more specifically identify the attitudes, behavior, or knowledge the student is to demonstrate. The competencies and indicators are written as objectives that can be evaluated.

Well-written lessons include four key components, sometimes referred to as the ABCDs of learning (Erford, 2010). First is the audience (A) for whom the objective is being directed; in most cases the students. The second is a statement of the expected behavioral (B) outcome(s) that will result from the lesson. Thirdly, is the condition(s) (C) under which the learning will occur, and lastly, lesson objectives should include the degree (D) of the expected performance, or the frequency with which students will demonstrate the competency (Goodnough, Pérusse, & Erford, 2011). The sample guidance lesson plan includes a cross-walk with the ASCA Student Standards.

It is important to remember that a lesson plan is merely a guide and not a strict "recipe" in which there has to be rigid adherence to achieve a desired outcome (Ormrod, 2011). As you progress through a lesson you may find that students have less prior knowledge than you originally thought, and you might have to review a concept that you expected students to have already mastered. You may also find that the students will show particular interest or curiosity about a particular topic that could mean spending more time than you originally intended in teaching that topic. The thing to remember in conducting a classroom lesson is to be flexible. The ultimate goal is to reach a desired outcome; how you and the students get there is a journey. You want the journey to be engaging, challenging, and rewarding for both you and the students.

Figure 9.1 Sample Lesson Plan

Classroom Guidance Lesson

Audience: 4th , 5th, & 6th Grade

Lesson Title: Fran and Nan's Lesson on Friendship

ASCA Domain: Personal/Social

Competency: Acquire Self-Knowledge

Indicators: PS:A1.1, PS:A1.2, PS:A1.6, PS:A1.9, PS:A1.10, PS:A2.3, PS:A2.4, PS:A2.8

By the end of the lesson students will be able to:

- Demonstrate how to interact and work cooperatively by working in pairs to complete the activities in the lesson (PS:A1.9)
- Identify the value, attitudes, beliefs, and behaviors that characterize a good friend and contrast these characteristics with someone who does not act like a good friend (PS:A1.2, PS:A1.6)
- Identify and discuss the personal values, attitudes, beliefs and behaviors that make them a good friend,and those characteristics they would like to change in order to become a better friend (PS:A1.1, PS:A1.10, PS:A2.8)
- Recognize that individual and/or ethnic and cultural differences are not influencing factors of friendship (PS:A2.3, PS:A2.4)

Materials:

Fran and Nancy's Friendship Activity Sheet

Whiteboard or Flip Chart

Markers

Procedures:

1. Introduce the topic for the day and explain to students that they are going to "create a friend" by examining the traits that make up a good friend and comparing them to the traits of someone who behaves in ways uncharacteristic of a good friend.

2. Divide students into pairs and provide each student with the Fran and Nancy Friendship Activity Sheet.

3. Have students fold the Fran and Nancy activity sheet in half so that only one friend is showing. Have one student brainstorm all the traits of a "good" friend under the column headed "Fran A Friend" and the other brainstorm all the traits of someone that does not behave like a good friend under the column "Nancy Not a Friend."

(Continued)

Figure 9.1 (Continued)

4. Ask students to avoid traits such as "smart," "good-looking," "athletic" and have them rephrase these as "does their best in school," "takes care of him/herself," "likes to play . . ."

5. Once lists are completed, have the pairs compare their lists and identify the differences between "Fran" and "Nancy" and add any other traits they come up with.

6. Assign a student helper, if you can, and have students share their ideas, as you or the helper write students responses under the appropriate heading on the whiteboard/flip chart.

7. Address any statements that may allude to individual, ethnic, or cultural differences as negative traits and discuss how these are not things that influence friendship.

Evaluation:

Ask students to reflect on the traits they have identified as those of a good friend and those of someone who does not behave like a good friend.

- Students will identify some of the traits they possess that are characteristic of a good friend.
- Students will identify traits that they would like to change in order to be more of a good friend.
- Students will identify ways in which peers may treat them differently if they have all the good traits of "Fran A Friend."
- Students will write one trait on which they would like to work to be more of a good friend.

Time Needed: (30–40 minutes)

Although school counselors primarily deliver their classroom guidance curriculum through direct instruction, they also collaborate with teachers to integrate the guidance curriculum with content area curricula. They may work collaboratively as part of an interdisciplinary team in the planning and implementation phases of curriculum development by integrating the guidance curriculum with other subject matter. For example, a school counselor may work with a social studies teacher who is delivering a unit on the Civil War to include lessons on conflict resolution (ASCA Student Indicator PS:B1.6) or tolerance for differences (ASCA Student Indicator PS:A2.4). Another school counselor may collaborate with an elementary school teacher in delivering a guidance lesson on acting responsibly (ASCA Student Indicator PS:A1.6) and the classroom teacher may deliver the lesson during reading time, or through a writing assignment. Yet another school counselor may team teach with the gym teacher in conducting a lesson on teamwork and cooperation (ASCA Student Indicator PS: A1.9) through an adventure learning activity.

DEVELOPING LEARNING OBJECTIVES

School counselors are trained to take a holistic approach to student learning and CDSC programs reflect this approach. As such, school counselors take into consideration the intellectual, emotional/psychological, physical, and social developmental needs of all children when creating learning objectives. In doing so, it is useful to consider the *cognitive, affective,* and *psychomotor* domains of learning when developing lesson plans. The *cognitive domain* (knowledge) refers to the mental skills you want students to be able to perform. These skills can range from the lowest level of simple recall to the highest level of cognitive processing, such as evaluating and creating. Bloom's taxonomy is a useful tool in creating lesson plans that vary in cognitive complexity. Table 9.2 provides a recent revision of Bloom's taxonomy with verbs that reflect each category of cognitive processing.

Table 9.2   Revised Bloom's Taxonomy

Level of Cognitive Complexity	*Associated Verbs*
Remembering	Tell, list, describe, relate, locate, write, find, state, name, identify, label, recall, define, recognize, match, reproduce, memorize, draw, select, recite
Understanding	Explain, interpret, outline, discuss, distinguish, predict, restate, translate, compare, describe, relate, generalize, summarize, paraphrase, convert, demonstrate, visualize
Applying	Solve, show, use, illustrate, construct, complete, examine, classify, choose, interpret, make, put together, change, apply, produce, translate, calculate, manipulate, modify, put into place
Analyzing	Analyze, distinguish, examine, compare, contrast, investigate, categorize, identify, explain, differentiate, subdivide, deduce
Evaluating	Judge, select, choose, decide, justify, debate, verify, argue, recommend, rate, prioritize, determine, critique, evaluate, criticize, weigh, value, estimate, defend
Creating	Create, invent, compose, predict, construct, design, imagine, propose, devise, formulate, combine, hypothesize, originate, add to, forecast

Source: Anderson & Krathwohl (2001)

Do you want your students to recall facts? Compare ideas or make inferences? In choosing the level of difficulty, a determination is made as to the level of knowledge you want your students to master.

The *affective domain* of learning refers to the attitudes and values you want students to learn. Although this domain is more difficult to conceptualize and demonstrate, Krathwohl, Bloom, and Masia (1964) developed a system for affective learning that includes receiving, responding, valuing, organizing, and characterizing. The lowest level of affective learning is receiving, where students passively pay attention to what is being taught. In contrast, at the most complex level of characterizing, students have adopted a value or belief to the extent that it influences their behavior. The *psychomotor domain* (skills) of learning refers to the skills and behaviors you want students to learn that primarily relate to moving, manipulating, communicating, and creating (Harrow, 1972).

It is unrealistic to expect that a single guidance lesson will include learning activities that attend to each level of each learning domain; however, a well-designed guidance unit should include a range of activities that address the three domains of learning. Students learn in different ways, and school counselors attend to these various learning styles to create and deliver guidance lessons for all students to learn and demonstrate their knowledge in meaningful ways.

Learning Styles

A variety of learning styles have appeared in the field of educational psychology since the early 1970s; however, the most common and widely used model in education is Neil Fleming's VAK/VARK model (Fleming, 2011) based on the concept that the learning process starts with the input of sensory stimuli from three major sensory systems: visual, auditory, and kinesthetic/tactile. Although people use all three sensory systems to learn, people exhibit preferences for learning. This is not to say that if you are an auditory learner that you cannot learn through tactile or visual means; it simply means you prefer, and learn more easily through auditory means. In fact, educators are encouraged to engage students in learning activities that use all three sensory systems, so students are able to utilize and strengthen all three areas for greater learning opportunities.

Visual learners learn through seeing and visualizing. Visual learners tend to sit at the front of the classroom where they can see the teacher's body language and facial expressions and avoid visual obstructions such as people's heads. There are two subchannels for visual learning—*spatial* and *linguistic*. *Visual-spatial* learners think in pictures and use their imagination, and although these learners often have difficulty with the written language, they tend to learn best from charts, graphs and diagrams, illustrated textbooks, demonstrations, and videos. *Visual-linguistic* learners prefer to learn through written language, such as reading and writing tasks, and tend to remember what they have written down, even if they have only read it once. Visual-linguistic learners like to write down directions and instructions, take detailed notes, and they pay better attention when they can watch the instructor.

Auditory learners learn best through listening, including such means as lectures and discussions. They interpret underlying meanings through listening to tone of voice, pitch, speed, and other nuances of speech, often have difficulty with reading and writing tasks, and do best when talking with others.

Kinesthetic/tactile learners learn best through moving, doing, and touching. These learners learn best through hands-on approaches and tend to lose concentration when there is little external stimulation or movement. They often find it difficult to sit still for long periods of time and become easily distracted by their need for activity and exploration. Kinesthetic/tactile learners may take notes during a lecture just for the sake of moving their hands, prefer scanning before looking for the details in written material, and they often use colored highlighters, doodle, and draw pictures during lectures. These learners prefer to engage in hands-on activities that allow them to explore the physical world around them.

CONCEPTUAL APPLICATION ACTIVITY 9.3

Think in terms of how you learn best. Are you a visual learner? Auditory? Kinesthetic? How did you adapt to instruction that was presented differently from your preferred mode? Discuss the learning strategies that assisted you in your classes with those of your classmates.

As a school counselor you will want to become familiar with how to put into practice a variety of learning activities that engage all the different learners you will encounter in today's diverse classrooms. Learning styles impact traditional lesson delivery, and although it is difficult to adapt a lesson to meet individual learning styles for each student in a classroom, a variety of strategies, exercises, and aids provide diverse learning opportunities for all students.

TYPES OF INSTRUCTION

Good classroom guidance lessons involve a variety of instructional strategies and attend to the developmental levels of students. Varying instruction offers students an opportunity to learn new information in a manner consistent with their learning style, thereby creating a more meaningful and relevant learning experience.

School counselors employ several instructional techniques in delivering classroom guidance lessons, such as didactic instruction, collaborative learning, role-play, and the use of technology.

Didactic

Didactic teaching is a form of *expository instruction* in which the teacher is at the center of the learning process through lectures (Ormrod, 2011). This type of teaching tends to be viewed negatively because the teacher is an active disseminator of information while the students are passive recipients of knowledge. Although students may appear to be inactive during didactic instruction, they may be mentally active, depending on the extent to which they are paying attention and focusing on meaning. Good didactic instruction involves the presentation of a new idea, concept, or model whereby both the students and the teacher can mutually consider, explore, and analyze a concept.

Collaborative Learning

This type of instruction, also referred to as *cooperative learning,* puts students at the center of the learning process. Students at various performance levels work together in small groups toward a common goal. In collaborative learning, the students are responsible for one another's learning as well as their own. Therefore, each student helps other students achieve. Collaborative learning increases academic performance, improves problem-solving skills, enhances critical thinking skills, and fosters communication skills. Furthermore, students who engage in collaborative learning activities such as group discussions, peer-reciprocal teaching, and problem solving tend to have more positive attitudes toward the subject matter, retain the information better, and are more motivated to learn. Several collaborative learning organizational techniques are listed below.

Think-Pair-Share *(appropriate for any grade level)*

This strategy is used for a quick discussion whereby the instructor poses a question and gives the students a few minutes to individually formulate a response. Students are then paired and share their responses with a peer. Students then build on each other's ideas and create a joint response, or if they disagree they explain their reasoning.

Fishbowl *(most appropriate for grades 5–12)*

This technique is used for reciprocal teaching, where students sit on the outside of a small inner circle of students who engage in an in-depth

Photo 9.1 Collaborative Learning Assists in Motivation and a More Positive Attitude Toward School.

Source: © Stockbyte/ThinkStock.com

discussion. While the discussion in the inner circle takes place, the students in the outer circle consider what is being said and how it is stated. When a person in the outside circle wants to make a point based on the conversation in the inner circle, he/she taps an inner circle member on the shoulder and the two peers trade places. This technique is good for providing structure to in-depth discussions and provides an opportunity for students to model or observe group processes.

Case Study *(most appropriate for grades 5–12)*

This approach is used for problem-solving and applying new skills to real-life scenarios. Typically the "case" includes a brief history of how the situation developed with a dilemma that a key character within the scenario is facing. Small group members work to resolve the problem in the case by applying newly learned concepts, and each group then discusses their problem solving strategies and resolution with the entire class. Case studies help bridge the gap between theory and practice and improve analytic and decision-making skills.

Role Play

Children look to significant individuals in their lives as models to observe, mimic, and practice behaviors. Lessons that address personal/social development through role play allow students to practice new behaviors in a safe setting before trying them in a real-life situation. In role play students are provided a scenario in which they deliberately assume a character or identity they would not normally assume. In this new role students actively apply knowledge, skill, and understanding to successfully speak and act according to the assigned perspective. Role play also involves the critical thinking skills of analyzing and problem solving, and teaches perspective-taking, cooperation, and empathy. Active involvement appeals to students with a kinesthetic/tactile learning style.

Technology

Technology is proliferating at a rapid rate and with the newest developments school counselors are able to adapt a multitude of teaching and learning possibilities in delivering a guidance curriculum. School counselors use DVDs as common technological tools and several companies such as *Sunburst, Live Wire Media,* and *Human Relations Media* have an array of resources on common student concerns. School counselors also use short clips from full-length movies to illustrate a particular concept or lesson, which appeals to visual-spatial and auditory learners.

Computers also provide access to numerous career exploration activities, including career inventories and a variety of websites through which students can research possible careers. Programs such as *Kuder, Career Choice,* and *Virtual JobShadow.com* provide students with the opportunity to explore careers, assess their interests, skills, and abilities, and match them to careers to plan their education. Teachers and school counselors look for ways to incorporate Web 2.0 applications such as Facebook, Google Docs, and Twitter in their instruction (Kennedy, 2011; Kurtz, 2009; Matterson, 2010; Taranto & Abbondanza, 2009). Twitter is used as a forum for collective writing assignments, checking for understanding, conducting live discussion feeds, and conducting quick online polls with the use of a Web service like *Polleverywhere.com.* Educators are also using Twitter to help students to connect to the people and causes that inspire them (Matterson, 2010). Google Docs, for online collaborative writing activities, and Facebook are used to post class assignments and communicate with students and their parents, though this requires that all students and their families/guardians have access to and understand how to use these Internet resources.

Students' varying learning styles and intellectual strengths are considerations in planning and creating school guidance curriculum units and lesson plans. When school counselors vary their instruction to meet the diverse learning and developmental needs of their students they engage in the process of differentiating instruction.

DIFFERENTIATED INSTRUCTION

Creating and implementing a guidance curriculum that responds to students' varying developmental levels, intellectual strengths, learning styles, and individual interests is referred to as *differentiating instruction.* Differentiated instruction is not a particular instructional technique but rather the process of "ensuring that what a student learns, how he/she learns it, and how the student demonstrates what he/she has learned is a match for that student's readiness level, interests, and preferred mode of learning" (Tomlinson, 2004, p. 188). Instruction can be differentiated through content, process, product, and learning environment based on the individual learner (Anderson, 2007).

Differentiating content refers to providing multiple options for learning information such as breaking lessons into smaller more manageable parts with specific instructions for each apart, and selecting broad instructional concepts and skills that allow for understanding at various levels of complexity. For example, you may develop a middle school guidance lesson that addresses the ASCA Career Standard A: *Students will acquire the skills to investigate the world of work in relation to knowledge of self and to make informed decisions* competency C:A1 *Develop Career Awareness* in which you focus on indicator C:A1.2 *Learn about the variety of traditional and nontraditional occupations* (ASCA, 2005). Through the use of differentiated instruction, some students could read a book on service industry careers, other students might research medical careers on the Internet, and still others could watch a video on careers in the construction field. Additional students may spend an afternoon job shadowing at a local manufacturing plant or government building. All of these methods address the specified career standard. In addition to differentiating content, you want to consider differentiating the learning process and product.

Differentiated learning process includes providing access to a variety of materials that target diverse learning preferences and reading abilities, creating activities that target different learning styles, generating activities that encourage inquiry, or establishing flexible grouping strategies to group and regroup students based on factors such as subject content, student ability, and assessment results. In the example above, not only is the content varied but the lesson incorporates several learning processes, such as reading, watching videos, researching, and job shadowing, so it reaches students with differing learning styles and ability levels.

Differentiating product refers to the variety of ways students demonstrate their understanding of the content learned during a lesson or unit. In the previous example, one student may choose to write a report on a career he/she job-shadowed, while another may give an oral report on a career that was highlighted in a book, another could create a poster or diagram of the daily activities of the career researched on the Internet, or another may chronicle his/her job-shadowing experience in a YouTube production. Finally, the learning environment impacts the type of instruction, in that space limitation could influence the magnitude of a project, or monetary issues could impact project complexity or sophistication. A creative, resourceful school counselor is able to facilitate learning and accommodate diverse learning needs.

CONCEPTUAL APPLICATION ACTIVITY 9.4

Designing a Guidance Lesson

Develop a lesson plan for a classroom guidance lesson choosing a standard, competency, and indicator within the ASCA student standards and design a lesson plan that includes differentiated instruction, content, and process. In addition, include a differentiated product to assess students' knowledge, attitudes, or skills from an array of options. Deliver the lesson to your class, having them act as students for which the grade-level lesson is designed.

CLASSROOM MANAGEMENT

As discussed in Chapter 1, school counselors were originally teachers, and for decades those entering the profession were required to have had teaching experience. Most states have dropped this requirement, and the majority of school counselors entering the field have little to no teaching experience. Although this change has been beneficial for the school counseling profession in some respects, novice school counselors are at a disadvantage in that they have not had much training in classroom management. Effectively managing a classroom is a vital skill, as it has the greatest impact on students' achievement (Marzano & Marzano, 2003). Key elements to a classroom management plan include: establishing rules, routines, and procedures; managing the classroom space; managing behavior to prevent discipline issues; and managing disruptive behavior. Each of these elements is discussed below.

Rules, Routines, and Procedures

Every democratic society has rules and procedures that govern people's behavior. In doing so, everyone has an opportunity to exercise his/her rights, take responsibility for his/her actions, and feel safe. In a democratic society people have the opportunity to pursue their goals and reach their greatest potential. The same holds true in the classroom. A classroom without rules and procedures is a place of chaos and uncertainty, and students are unable to learn and achieve to their greatest potential.

School counselors establish a brief set of rules and procedures when in the classroom, and if you are lucky enough to have your own classroom space these can be of your own design. However, most school counselors visit regular classrooms to deliver their guidance lessons. In this case it is important to consult the classroom teacher before deciding on the rules and procedures you want to include in your classroom management plan.

Rules should be clear, concise, and positive with expectations that state what you want rather than what you don't want. For example, rather than saying "Don't touch others" instead say, "Keep your hands to yourself" or, "Listen when others are talking." It is best to have few rules (no more than five) that are simple and easy to remember and expressed in an age-appropriate manner. Stating "Be respectful to others" may work well with older students, but students in their early elementary school years will need more specific rules, such as "Raise your hand before you speak" or "Listen when others are talking."

School counselors create a democratic and equitable classroom environment through collaboration with their students in the rule-making process. Including students in the process of establishing classroom rules assists students in being more invested in the ownership of these rules and less likely to break them. You will also want to determine what routines and procedures to put into place for such things as getting students' attention, transitioning from one space or activity to the next, and managing resources. For instance, careful planning to answer the questions: How will the students move from their desks to the reading rug? Will they line-up first? Will they be dismissed by table or by row? How will they retrieve and put away learning resources? How will supplies be allocated? How will the students move from the classroom to the gym or the school-yard for an adventure learning activity? Some of the simpler methods for gaining attention include flicking the lights off and on, clapping hands with the instruction that each student is to copy this action to get the attention of everyone, or raising your hand with the understanding that every child will raise his/her hand the moment your hand is spotted in the air. If you have your own guidance classroom, post the rules in a prominent place and review them at the beginning of each lesson. Remind students of what is expected as they transition from one space or activity to another, as well as how they are to manage and handle any classroom resource they may use.

Managing Space

The layout of the classroom is also an important consideration in classroom management. Student seating and resource arrangements will not only reflect your teaching style, but will also determine how students interact with each other and how you will move around the room. Figure 9.2 depicts the various seating arrangements used in classrooms.

Each arrangement has its advantages and disadvantages. *Row seating* is more conducive to lecture style teaching and independent work. The disadvantage to row seating is that it limits your visibility of what is going on in the back rows, restricts students' interactions, and impedes your ability to move around the classroom. *U-Shaped seating* and *circle seating* are two excellent arrangements in terms of visibility for you and others. Students are able to interact with you and speak directly to each other when sharing, and these arrangements provide you with space to move toward and away from students. A circle arrangement allows you to put yourself and the students at an equal level. The disadvantage of these arrangements is that students have greater access to gain the attention of all their classmates, and disruptive students who seek attention can distract the entire class very easily. Smaller groups of four to six students work well with this format; however, a disadvantage is that students can easily get off-task without an awareness of doing so. *Table seating* and *grouping* desks in two or four desks to a group

Figure 9.2 Classroom Seating Arrangements

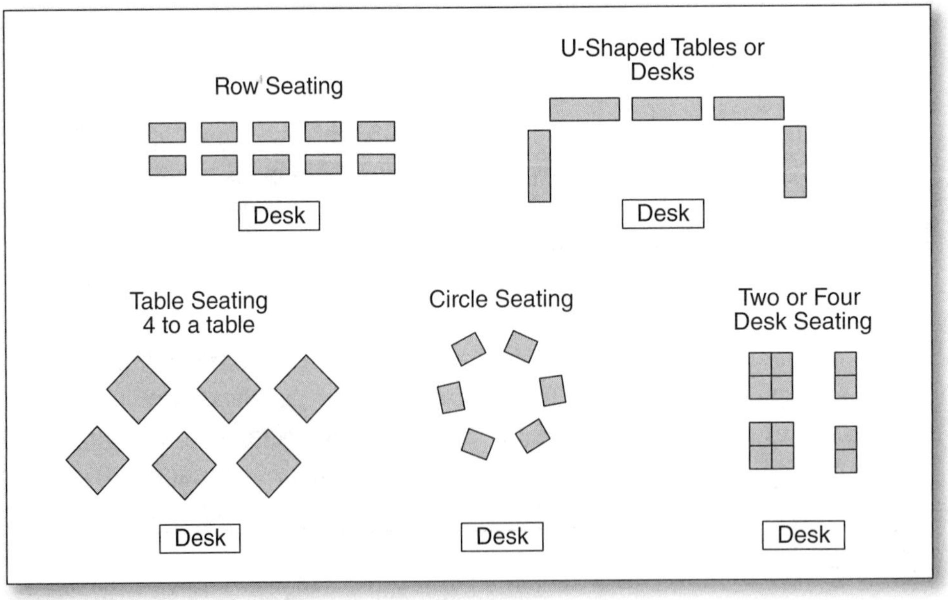

promotes collaborative learning and the active exchange of ideas. These arrangements also provide added space for hands-on creative activities that are more difficult to accomplish on a single desk surface. A disadvantage of this arrangement is cross-talk that sometimes occurs when you are giving instructions or when other students are sharing. Visibility can also be an issue with this arrangement; however, this can usually be avoided by staggering the tables and placing them at a 45% angle, with plenty of room between groupings for you to have adequate access to each group.

As with classroom rules, if you have your own classroom, you can create a space that reflects your teaching style and the learning environment you want to create. However, if you travel to regular classrooms to teach your guidance lessons, you will have little control over the arrangement of classroom space. If you have a lesson or activity that would be more effective with a different seating arrangement from that of the teacher, you may want to ask permission to rearrange the room with the understanding that everything will be put back in its place at the end of the guidance lesson.

Managing Behavior

School counselors who implement the CDSC program are naturally proactive and employ preventive measures for managing behavior. As such, classroom management plans include strategies for preventing discipline issues from arising. Building positive relationships with students, being prepared with well-planned and engaging lessons, keeping students' attention, moving around the room, employing group contingencies, and managing time and transitions so they occur with fluidity are preventive measures school counselors employ to manage student behavior.

The single most impactful way to prevent discipline issues in any setting is by building rapport and maintaining positive relationships with students. You will likely have already developed these relationships with many of the students you will see during classroom guidance lessons, but it is equally likely that a relationship has not yet been developed with many others. If this is the case, there are several ways school counselors connect with students on a personal level during guidance lessons. One of the first things you can do, if you have your own classroom, is greet the students at the door as they enter the classroom and acknowledge each one individually with a kind word or compliment. Call each student by name if you know it, and for those whose name you don't know, make an effort to get to know them. If you are traveling to regular classrooms, take a minute and go around the room and greet each student individually. Name tents on the desk are also helpful.

When students are encouraged to participate and you acknowledge the importance of their participation with praise and encouragement, they are more likely to be attentive with reduced behavioral concerns. You can encourage participation by using open-ended questions to draw out more information from the students. Examples of open-ended questions include: "How does . . . relate to this concept?" "What is another way of thinking about this?" or "What evidence to you have to support your statement?"

When reinforcing participation you want to limit evaluative responses such as "Great," "Wonderful," or "Excellent." Although these comments are intended to show appreciation for a student's contribution, they also suggest that there is only one best or correct response (Myrick, 2003) and may have the inadvertent effect of limiting students' responses who feel less secure about the quality of their ideas. Instead, consider using facilitative responses that acknowledge and thank students for their participation (Myrick, 2003). Use specific statements of praise to the entire class. When we make statements such as, "You all did great today" or "I'm proud of all of you," the students may not be exactly clear what warranted the praise. Did they listen attentively? Did they follow directions well? Did they demonstrate cooperative behavior when working in groups? By being specific, you are reinforcing the behavior you want students to repeat and students are clear on the behavior that is expected.

There are fun ways to engage students and prevent behavior problems while delivering your lesson. Consider dressing up in a costume and making a grand entrance, or start the class off with a relevant song, role-play, or surprising visual aid. For example, a middle school counselor with whom I worked would start off the first class of each year by playing Tina Turner's song "R.E.S.P.E.C.T." then a conversation would ensue on respectful behaviors and rules. An elementary school counselor could dress up as a character that appeared as the hero/heroine in a story from which she was teaching a lesson. A high school counselor could also start a lesson using an appropriate and relevant pop or rap song. I used Michael Jackson's "Man in the Mirror" when working with high school students from a low socioeconomic neighborhood where crime was prevalent. I also used cartoons at the opening of guidance lessons, and used creative and silly activities when teaching middle school students. If you choose to use bibliocounseling as a guidance activity, find a book such as those by Dr. Seuss and read it with a dramatic tone, modulating your pace and rate of speech. Students enjoy games, and lessons could be put into the form of a *Jeopardy* or *Wheel of Fortune* game. The possibilities are endless.

Discipline issues can also be prevented by maintaining *momentum*. Maintaining momentum means keeping a lesson moving smoothly by managing transitions with minimal lag time, and having resources readily available and in sufficient supply. When there are inadequate resources, the flow of the lesson becomes compromised and disruptive behavior may result (Goodnough, et al., 2011). The best way to manage behavior is by limiting opportunities for misbehavior to occur in the first place; however, there will be times when a student behaves in ways that disrupts the class no matter how creative and engaging a guidance lesson may be. Therefore, a good classroom management plan includes strategies for managing disruptive behavior.

CLASSROOM MANAGEMENT MODELS

School counselors are aware of the potential for conflicting dual relationships that could occur with students when working in the classroom. There are likely to be students you have counseled or will counsel, and dealing with disruptive behavior in the classroom could damage the rapport you have developed with students in the counseling office. For this reason, it is essential to have a plan for addressing disruptive behavior that is grounded in democratic principles. Understanding the reasons students misbehave can better prepare school counselors for handling disruptions in a democratic manner. Dreikur's Social Discipline Model and Glasser's Quality Classroom, and Contingency Group Contracting are common paradigms that are adopted for classroom management

Social Discipline Model

Dreikurs (1968) developed a Social Discipline model founded in the four basic principles of Adler's social theory, including: 1) humans are social beings and their basic motivation is to belong; 2) all behavior is purposeful; and 3) humans' perception of reality may be mistaken or biased. Based on these principles, Dreikurs (1968) believed that all children seek to find their place within the group. Well-adjusted children will conform to the requirements of the group in order to be accepted and "fit in," whereas a child who misbehaves does so in an attempt to gain or maintain social status. Whether it is through conformity or misbehavior, the main purpose will be to gain social acceptance. Dreikurs (1968) believed that there are four main goals of misbehavior. These goals and appropriate intervention strategies are listed in Table 9.3 (p. 312).

A Quality Classroom

Although William Glasser is known for Reality Therapy, he extended his ideas into the classroom through the creation of a competency-based quality classroom.

Table 9.3   Misbehavior Goals

Attention Seeking	Minimize the attention. Ignoring the behavior, use proximity (standing close), cues such as "the look." Recognize appropriate behavior. Thank students when they display appropriate behavior or give them a written note of congratulations. Move the student. Ask the student to move to a different seat or a "chill out" spot.
Power/Control Seeking	Make a graceful exit. Remove the audience; table the matter for later discussion. Use a time out or chill out spot. Apply the pre-stated consequence.
Seeking Revenge	Use the same strategies as those listed above for power seeking behaviors.
Displaying Inadequacy	Modify instruction and/or break instruction into smaller parts. Teach positive self-talk and that mistakes are okay. Focus on past successes. Recognize achievement.

Source: Adapted from Dreikurs, Grunwald, & Pepper (1982)

Glasser believed that students are able to meet their basic needs for belonging, power, fun, and freedom when taught in a safe, caring classroom environment. According to Glasser, it is the educator's responsibility to teach and model appropriate decision making because all behavior is a matter of choice that can only be accomplished when students are able to see the results of their choices (Charles, 1989). Successful classroom management occurs when the following strategies are implemented:

1. Stress Student Responsibility. A caring, respectful bond will be developed when classroom meetings are provided for students to discuss topics surrounding choices and resulting behaviors. For instance, discussions can include social problem solving for issues within the school environment, educational concerns such as learning strategies, or open-ended meetings that pertain to any topics students bring up.

2. Develop Rules. Jointly determined classroom rules facilitate achievement and ownership.

3. No Excuses. When classroom rules are not enforced, students get the impression that classroom rules are unimportant and easily dismissed.

4. Evaluate. When a student disobeys, he/she is asked to give a value judgment about the behavior. In other words, the student is asked to judge how this behavior influenced his/her commitment to the rules. If the student continues to misbehave, a "time out" from the group is given until the student is able to commit to the classroom rules.

5. Provide Options. A misbehaving student is provided two reasonable consequences and is asked to choose one of the options as an outcome for not following the rules.

6. Persistence. Consistency in enforcing these steps aids students to commit to acceptable courses of action.

School counselors realize that when directly addressing misbehaviors, they must do so as quietly and unobtrusively as possible, not only saving the student from embarrassment but to preserve the relationship.

Contingency Group Contracting

A *group contingency* is a "situation in which everyone in a group must make a particular response before reinforcement occurs" (Ormrod, 2011, p. 304). For example, if the class is particularly unruly you may want to divide them into two teams. Each time a student in a team is disruptive that team receives a mark on the board. A privilege or reward would be given to the team with the fewest marks. Group contingencies can be very effective in managing disruptions because members of the group are encouraged to change the disruptive student's behavior through the opportunity to earn privileges and rewards.

BOX 9.1 EXAMPLES OF REWARDS FOR CONTINGENCY CONTRACTING

Elementary Grades

Stickers	Certificates
Crayons	Inexpensive "Treasure Chest" items
Pencils	Sundae for class reward
Markers	Movie for entire class

Older Students

A song for an MP3 player

A CD

Cards

Coupons for food items at local fast food restaurant

Certificates

Pizza party for class

Some behaviors may best be extinguished by ignoring them. If you absolutely must discipline a student, make every effort to repair your relationship with the student by meeting with him/her in your office. Let the student know that he/she is valued and that his/her participation in the group is important to you. Discuss the reasons the behavior occurred and plan for ways the two of you can work together to avoid problems in the future.

CONCEPTUAL APPLICATION ACTIVITY 9.5

How Do Teachers Do It?

Visit one or two classrooms and observe the classroom management style of the teacher.

- How is the classroom space laid out? How is student seating arranged? Does the seating arrangement encourage student participation? Are resources in ample supply and readily available?
- Are classroom rules, routines, and procedures made explicit?
- Do students appear to be engaged and on task?
- How does the teacher prevent misbehavior and how does he/she manage disruptive behavior?

Compare your findings with those of your classmates and discuss how you may or may not do things differently.

In addition to managing the classroom, consider the variety of intellectual strengths that students possess within an academic environment through a strength-based approach to support their talents and skills that enhance learning.

GARDNER'S THEORY OF MULTIPLE INTELLIGENCES

Howard Gardner's Theory of Multiple Intelligences (1983) has been enthusiastically embraced by many educators. Unlike many theories of intelligence that are relatively one-dimensional, Gardner's theory developed in the late 1970s and early 1980s suggests that people possess eight distinctly different abilities or "intelligences" that are relatively independent of one another. Each individual possesses all of these intelligences to some extent, and he/she utilizes them individually and collectively to create products and solve-problems (Gardner, 1983, 2006). Unlike traditional theories that state intelligence is a set of relatively fixed, inherited traits that cannot be changed or improved upon, the Multiple Intelligences

Theory conceives intelligence to be a combination of inherited potentials and skills that are developed through relevant experiences (Gardner, 1983, 2006). For example, a person may possess a high degree of logical-mathematic intelligence and easily solve complex mathematical equations, while another person may have difficulty solving the equation without extensive practice. Both of these students are capable of becoming skilled mathematicians; however, the amount of time and effort, and the means by which this will occur may vary significantly.

Gardner's theory originally included seven intelligences: *linguistic, logical-mathematical, spatial, musical, bodily-kinesthetic, interpersonal,* and *intrapersonal.* In later years Gardner included an eighth intelligence—*naturalistic*—and suggested the possibility of a ninth—*existential* intelligence, dedicated to spiritual and philosophical intelligence (Gardner, 2006). This last is not included in the discussion. The characteristics of each type of intelligence are presented in Table 9.4.

Table 9.4 Characteristics of Gardner's Eight Multiple Intelligences

Type of Intelligence	*Characteristics*
Linguistic	An ability to analyze and create products using oral and written language. Generally have highly developed auditory skills and excellent speakers. Are skilled listeners, speakers, storytellers, teachers, and writers.
Logical-mathematic	An ability to use reason, logic, and numbers. Are skilled at problem-solving, working with abstract concepts, classifying/categorizing information, doing experiments, and performing complex mathematical equations. Generally possess a curiosity about the world around them and ask lots of questions.
Spatial	An ability to recognize, interpret, and manipulate large-scale and fine-grained spatial images. Tend to think in pictures and create vivid mental images to retain information. Are skilled at building puzzles, reading and writing, understanding charts and graphs, drawing, painting, constructing, fixing and designing particular objects. Enjoy looking at maps, charts, pictures, videos, and movies.
Musical	An ability to produce, remember, and make meaning out of different patterns of sounds. Tend to think in sounds, rhythms, and patterns and respond to music. Can be extremely sensitive to environmental sounds. Are skilled at singing, playing musical instruments, composing music, remembering tonal patterns and melodies, and understanding the structure and rhythm of music.

(Continued)

Table 9.4 (Continued)

Type of Intelligence	Characteristics
Bodily-kinesthetic	An ability to use one's own body to create products and solve problems, and handle objects skillfully.
	Generally has a good sense of balance, and hand-eye coordination.
	Are able to remember and process information through interacting with the space around them.
	Are skilled at dancing, sports, hands-on experiments, crafts, acting, using body language, and using their hands to create or build.
	Tends to express emotions through the body.
Interpersonal	An ability to recognize and understand other people's moods, desires, motivations, intentions, and see things from others' point of view.
	Tend to be great organizers and generally try to maintain peace in group setting and encourage cooperation.
	Are skilled at verbal and non-verbal communications, understanding multiple perspectives, listening, using empathy and understanding, co-operating in groups, establishing positive relationships with others, and resolving conflicts peacefully.
Intrapersonal	An ability to recognize and understand one's own moods, desires, motivations, and intentions.
	Generally try to understand their inner feelings, dreams, strengths and weaknesses, and their relationships with others.
	Are skilled at reflecting, analyzing, and reasoning with themselves, evaluating their thinking patterns, and understanding their role in relationship to others.
Naturalistic	An ability to identify and distinguish between different types of plants, animals, and weather formations.
	Tends to have a profound love for the outdoors, plants, animals, and most natural objects.
	Are skilled at recognizing different flora and fauna, species discernment, and the ability to recognize, appreciate, and understand the natural environment around them.
	Generally enjoy zoos, farms, gardens, nature walks, and museums.

Gardner's theory of Multiple Intelligences appeals to school counselors because of its optimistic view of human potential that supports a strengths-based perspective.

School counselors improve the academic performance of students by enhancing the school's climate, working collaboratively with administrators, teachers, and others. Counselors also pay careful attention to the guidance curriculum that responds to students' varying learning styles and developmental levels with knowledge and skill in maintaining a democratic classroom based on respect enhances skill and knowledge acquisition. Additionally, school counselors collaborate with students to improve academic performance through a variety of peer programming interventions.

IMPROVING ACADEMIC PERFORMANCE THROUGH PEER FACILITATION PROGRAMS

The school counselor is able to reach all students (Kracher, 2009) through the leadership of a school counselor-led CDSC program. Peer interventions are an additional means to reach students. As stated in the ASCA position statement on peer helping: "ASCA believes that peer-helping programs are one means of helping students reach a higher level of maturity and accepting responsibility. Peer-helping programs are implemented to enhance the effectiveness of school counseling programs by increasing outreach and the expansion of available services" (2008, para. 1).

There are numerous benefits of a peer facilitation program for both the students delivering the service (Helper) and those receiving the service (Helpee). A few of these benefits include:

<u>For Helper</u>

- Improved self-concept.
- Opportunities to interact with students different from themselves.
- Improved social skills.
- Development of personal values, interpersonal acceptance, and friendship.

<u>For Helpee</u>

- Learning and practicing new skills with a trusted "friend."
- Multiple examples of appropriate behaviors modeled by the helper.
- Multiple experiences with students of different backgrounds.
- Improved social skills.
- Interpersonal acceptance and friendship.

Not only do peer program interventions have the benefits mentioned above, they have the potential to improve students' overall attitude toward the school environment, enhance the school's climate, and reduce dropout rates. Peer facilitation programs vary from school to school and the exact role of the participants varies from program to program. There are generally four types of student facilitation programs: peer helpers, peer tutors, peer mentors, and peer mediators. The various programs are often used interchangeably but there are some distinctions among them.

Peer Helpers

Peer helpers are an effective way to assist classroom teachers in effectively helping students with disabilities, and also with others who typically have a difficult time "fitting in" with their peers. Peer helpers can be assigned to a student who requires additional assistance either because the helpee has a learning disability, is struggling with a particular concept or subject matter, or is having difficulty with social interactions. The helper could interact with the helpee in social settings such as the classroom, gym, lunchroom, library, or bus. Tasks could include assisting with such activities as getting and cleaning up his/her lunch, obtain school supplies and educational resources, participating in gym and extracurricular activities, or accompanying the helpee to the office, library, school nurse, bus, and so on. At times student helpers will spend time in a special education classroom working with students with severe physical or mental handicaps.

Peer Tutors

Peer tutoring programs are intended to help students with academic achievement, and may involve same-grade tutoring where the tutor and student are in the same grade level, or cross-grade level programs. In cross-grade level tutoring programs, older students with more knowledge work with younger grade level students to obtain mastery in a given subject area. Tutoring programs typically occur outside of the academic classroom before or after school; however, there are also programs where older students work inside the classroom with the teacher during classroom instruction.

Peer Mentors

Peer mentoring programs typically are developed to help students with school transitions. In these programs upper-grade level students are assigned to a lower-grade level student who is transitioning to a new school environment. For example, high school mentors work with eighth-grade students who will be entering the high school the following year, or middle school students could be assigned to fifth graders transitioning into middle school. Typically, mentors and mentees get to know each other at the end of the previous school year and communicate with one another throughout the summer to discuss school life at the entering grade level, answer questions, provide information about school programs and activities, and offer support and encouragement. The mentor/mentee assignment usually lasts throughout the academic year to assist with pivotal issues throughout the year. Peer mentors could also be assigned to new students entering the school.

Peer Mediators

Peer mediation programs are intended to help students resolve conflicts. Peer mediators are students who are trained in mediation, negotiation, and conflict resolution skills. Peer mediators may be effective in helping students resolve minor conflicts but should not be used for serious, potentially dangerous conflicts. Typically, the school counselor will have trained several peer mediators, and when the word of a conflict arises the disputing students will meet with a peer mediator in a designated location with a school counselor available to handle any difficulties the mediator may encounter. The peer mediators referee a peaceful resolution to the problem between the two disputants.

The ASCA (2008) provides guidelines for school counselors as they design, implement, and evaluate peer programs.

1. Assess the needs of the school population and design a program that will meet those needs.

2. Gain support for the program through positive public relations efforts with faculty, staff, parents, and community.

3. Select peers who will be compatible with the population to be served.

4. Coordinate an appropriate training program that includes effective communication and helping skills as well as the necessary skills to meet the needs of the population served.

5. Schedule adequate time for training and supervision.

6. Monitor, evaluate, and adjust the program and training to meet the needs of the population the program serves.

7. Evaluate and report the results of the program to the population served and other school stakeholder (e.g., students, teachers, administrators, parents, and community).

Peer program interventions are invaluable outreach services provided as part of a comprehensive school counseling program. These programs provide school counselors who have limited time and resources to efficiently apportion their time and energy, help school counselors meet the needs of a range of students, and serve as role models (Kracher, 2009).

CONCLUSION

School counselors play an integral role in improving academic performance through their involvement in creating a positive school culture that nurtures and promotes the academic, social/emotional, and career development of all students. School counselors contribute to a positive school culture by participating in school-based and system-wide professional learning communities (PLCs). These collaborative teams meet to assess curricular school counselor objectives that address school-wide concerns. School counselors develop and deliver a classroom guidance curriculum that aligns with the ASCA Student Standards and they support and encourage professional endeavors while being mindful of learning styles, multiple intelligences, and the developmental levels of the students they serve. In addition, differentiated instructional strategies address the unique learning styles and needs of their students.

A well-thought-out and executed classroom management plan—including rules, routines, and procedures that are established within the available space—assists in managing disruptive behavior and is an essential component of effective delivery of a guidance curriculum. Dreikurs' Social Discipline model, Glasser's Quality World model, and Behavioral Contingency Contracting serve as prototypes for effective classroom management. In addition, effectual school counselors create lessons that are engaging and relevant to students, with instructional strategies that address the student's individual needs. Peer programs also support academic performance, and school counselors contribute to a positive school culture by developing, implementing, supervising, and evaluating peer program interventions that meet the needs of the school population.

REFERENCES

American School Counselor Association (2005). *The ASCA national model: A framework for school counseling programs* (2nd ed.) Alexandria, VA: Author.

American School Counselor Association. (2008). *Position Statement: The Professional School Counselor and Peer Helping.* Retrieved from: http://www.schoolcounselor.org/files/PS_Peer Helping.pdf

American School Counselor Association (2012). *The ASCA national model: A framework for school counseling programs* (3rd ed.). Alexandria, VA: Author.

Anderson, K. M. (2007). Tips for teaching: Differentiating instruction to include all students. *Preventing School Failure, 51*(3), 49–54.

Anderson, L.W., & Krathwohl, D. R. (eds.) (2001). *A taxonomy for learning, teaching, and assessing: A revision of Bloom's Taxonomy of educational objectives.* New York: Longman.

Blanco, P. J., & Ray, D. C. (2011). Play therapy in elementary schools: A best practice for improving academic achievement. *Journal of Counseling & Development, 89,* 235–243.

Charles, C. M. (1989). *Building classroom discipline: From models to practice* (3rd ed.). New York: Longman.

Dreikurs, R. (1968). *Psychology in the classroom.* New York: Harper & Row.

Dreikurs, R. Grunwald, B. B., & Pepper, F. C. (1982). *Maintaining sanity in the classroom* (2nd ed.). New York: HarperCollins.

DuFour, R. (2004). Schools as learning communities. *Educational Leadership,* 61(8), 6–11.

DuFour, R., & Eaker, R. (1998). *Professional learning communities at work: Best practices for enhancing student achievement.* Bloomington, IN: National Education Service.

Erford, B. T. (2010). How to write learning objectives. In B. T. Erford (Ed.), *Professional school counseling: A handbook of theories, programs and practices* (2nd ed.), (pp. 279–286). Austin, TX: Pro-Ed.

Fleming, N. (2011). Introduction to VARK. Retrieved from: http://www.vark-learn.com/english/page.asp?p=introduction.

Gardner, H. (1983). *Frames of mind: The theory of multiple intelligences.* New York: Basic Books.

Gardner, H. (2006). *Multiple intelligences: New horizons.* New York: Basic Books.

Goodnough, G. E., Pérusse, R., & Erford, B. T. (2011). Developmental classroom guidance. In B. T. Erford (Ed.), *Transforming the school counseling profession* (3rd ed.), (pp.154–177). Upper Saddle River, NJ: Pearson.

Harrow A. (1972). *A taxonomy of the psychomotor domain.* New York: McKay.

Kennedy, M. (October 2011). Facing the future. *American School and University.*

Kracher, M. (2009). Increases in academic connectedness and self-esteem among high school students who serve as cross-age peer mentors. *Professional School Counseling,* 12(4), 292–299.

Krathwohl, D.R., Bloom, B.S., and Masia, B.B. (1964). *Taxonomy of educational objectives: Handbook II: Affective domain.* New York: David McKay Co.

Kurtz, J. (Summer 2009). Twittering about learning: Using Twitter in an elementary school classroom. *Horace,* 25(1).

Marzano, R. J., & Marzano, J. S. (2003). The key to classroom management. *Building Classroom Relationships,* 6(1), 6–13.

Matterson, A. (2010, September-October). Tweacher (n): The Twitter Enhanced Teacher. *School Library Monthly,* 27(1).

Myrick, R. A. (2003). *Developmental guidance and counseling: A practical approach.* Minneapolis, MN: Educational Media Corporation.

Ormrod, J. E. (2011). *Educational psychology: Developing learners* (7th ed.). Boston, MA: Allyn & Bacon.

Peterson, K. D., & Deal, T. E. (2002). *The Shaping School Culture Fieldbook.* San Francisco, CA: Jossey-Bass.

Sergiovanni, T. J. (1991). *The principalship: A reflective practice perspective.* Boston, MA: Allyn & Bacon.

Servage, L. (Winter 2008). Critical and transformative practices in professional learning communities. *Teacher Education Quarterly.*

Shallcross, L. (2013, August). Counselors and the common core. *Counseling Today,* 56, 36.

Steen, G. (2011). Academic and personal development through group work: An exploratory study. *Journal for specialists in group work, 36,* 129–143, doi: 10.1080/01933922.2011.562747

Taranto, G., & Abbondanza, M. (December 2009). Powering students up. *Principal Leadership* 10(4), 38–42.

The Week (2013, June 14). *Education: The Common Core Backlash,* 19.

Tomlinson, C. A. (2004). Sharing responsibility for differentiating instruction. *Roeper Review,* 26, 188.

Chapter 10

DEVELOPMENTAL AND MULTICULTURAL ISSUES OF SCHOOL-AGE YOUTH

 *CACREP STANDARDS

FOUNDATIONS

A. *Knowledge*

> 6. Understands the effects of (a) atypical growth and development, (b) health and wellness, (c) language, (d) ability level, (e) multicultural issues, and (f) factors of resiliency on student learning and development.

DIVERSITY AND ADVOCACY

E. *Knowledge*

> 1. Understands the cultural, ethical, economic, legal, and political issues surrounding diversity, equity, and excellence in terms of student learning.

> 2. Identifies community, environmental, and institutional opportunities that enhance—as well as barriers that impede—the academic, career, and personal/social development of students.

> 3. Understands the ways in which educational policies, programs, and practices can be developed, adapted, and modified to be culturally congruent with the needs of students and their families.

> 4. Understands counseling issues, as well as the impact of ability levels, stereotyping, family, socioeconomic status, gender, and sexual identity, and their effects on student achievement.

F. *Skills and Practices*

> 1. Demonstrates multicultural competencies in relation to diversity, equity, and opportunity in student learning and development.

ASSESSMENT

H. *Skills and Practices*

> 1. Assesses and interprets students' strengths and needs, recognizing uniqueness in cultures, languages, values, backgrounds, and abilities.
>
> 5. Assesses barriers that impede students' academic, career, and personal/social development.

COLLABORATION AND CONSULTATION

N. *Skills and Practices*

> 1. Works with parents, guardians, and families to act on behalf of their children to address problems that affect student success in school.

> *If teachers and counselors do not recognize the influence of cultural group membership, students and clients can be expected to profit only minimally from our interactions with them.*
>
> (Locke & Bailey, 2014)

When the Puritans first arrived in America, debates regarding the best way to educate youth were at the center of these discussions. Free public education was established, and parents were responsible for the basic education and literacy of their children for the purpose of reading and understanding basic laws and the Bible. However, not all colonists agreed with the concept of state supported schools. In particular, some from the South believed that education was not a government concern but rather a private, family matter. In addition, some held the belief that each race had certain physical and mental characteristics, with white men having a superior ability to learn, whereas other racial groups perceived as lacking this ability were denied access to any type of formal education.

Schools in early America were reserved for elite, white males, and teachers prepared these individuals primarily for the fields of law, medicine, or the clergy. As industrialization created more jobs, an increasing number of migrants from Europe were entering the United States and enrolling in schools, and teachers were faced with a host of students from diverse backgrounds. Although mandatory education laws were in place, they were loosely enforced (Tolnay & Bailey, 2006). Social and legislative issues were instrumental in recognizing the rights of individuals, yet educational systems were slow in adapting to diverse classrooms. Understanding diversity and developing the attitudes, skills, and knowledge to competently meet the needs of youth and families from divergent backgrounds facilitates school counselors' abilities to influence behaviors and achievements.

Too often, school personnel work with individuals from a narrow perspective and fail to consider human, contextual experiences and perceptions, and societal influences that impact growth and development. Race, ethnicity, gender, and other factors contribute to definitions of who we are and how to interact with others based on these variables (Cook, 2012).

Developmental psychology concepts make efforts to answer the question, "How does the behavior of humans change across the life span?" (Woods, 2001). Urie Brofenbrenner's *Ecology of Human Development,* Erik Erikson's *Theory of Psychosocial Development,* Jean Piaget's *Theory of Cognitive Development,* and Robert Havighurst's *Theory of Personality Development* aid in our understanding of human growth and development.

DEVELOPMENTAL THEORIES

Brofenbrenner's Ecology of Human Development Theory

Urie Brofenbrenner's ecological approach explains the interactional factors that influence human behaviors (Tang & Bashir, 2012). The structure (shown in Figure 10.1) depicts the significant forces of experiences, behaviors, and thoughts of each individual (Newman & Newman, 2012) from the microsystem, mesosystem, exosystem, macrosystem, and chronosystem (Brofenbrenner, 1977).

The *macrosystem* is the largest, most remote institutional pattern of the culture or subculture and includes attitudes and beliefs, values, laws, and customs. Each of these invisible components influences the child through direct or indirect interaction. Conceptual Application Activity 10.1 is designed to get you to start thinking about how these various systems have influenced your life.

CONCEPTUAL APPLICATION ACTIVITY 10.1

Think in terms of your beliefs and values and how they are similar or different from other members of your community. Next, interview people who are different from you (e.g., culturally, ethically). How do your beliefs/values differ? How are they the same?

Figure 10.1   Brofenbrenner's Ecology of Human Development Model

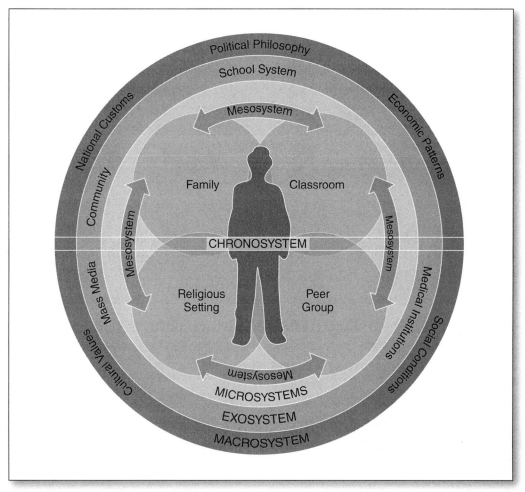

Source: http://clarityrising.wordpress.com/

The *exosystem* includes the impact of people and places on the individual's perceptions and behaviors even when there is no direct interaction. Behavior is considered from a contextual (Cook, 2012) viewpoint. For instance, a business that employs a majority of the people within the community suddenly shuts down and forces families to move and schools to lay off teachers. This event may necessitate that a child move from a familiar neighborhood and community. As another example, in one community the increasing population created a need for a new school, yet this elementary school created zoning issues and families who had children who attended one elementary school were now re-zoned to another. This change necessitated some of the siblings to attend one school while other siblings attended a different school. This change has influences on each family member as school rules, teachers, and curriculum are different, with dissimilarities among school cultures.

CONCEPTUAL APPLICATION ACTIVITY 10.2

Think about the influences of the institutions, media, and so on in the community in which you attended school. What were some of the interactions among these? Was there a significant community event that influenced the members of the community? Discuss your answers with a peer.

The *microsystem* is defined as "the complex of relations between the developing person and environment in an immediate setting containing that person [e.g., home, school, workplace, etc.]." (Brofenbrenner, 1977, p. 514). The setting provides an opportunity for the individual to carry out roles such as daughter, mother, worker, and so on, with specific purposeful tasks.

CONCEPTUAL APPLICATION ACTIVITY 10.3

Think about some of the roles you play in various settings. For instance, one of your roles is a student. How does this role impact some of the other roles you play? How are your present roles different from those of five years ago?

The *mesosystem* consists of related microsystems of interrelationships between the settings such as the school, family, peer group, church, workplace (Brofenbrenner, 1977). For example, a mesosystem could be the linkage between the child's parents and the family church.

CONCEPTUAL APPLICATION ACTIVITY 10.4

Identify some of the mesosystem interactions in your environment. For instance, school athletics play a role in grade attainment, practice times, scheduling time for other activities, and so on.

The *chronosystem* refers to the individual's life experiences, transitions, and sociohistorical events that influence all people (Santrock, 2008). For example, military duty is one example of a sociohistoric event in that a military spouse may be called to active duty and leave behind a family who needs to reorganize as a result of this departure. Or, 9/11 influenced families when lives were lost, families were disrupted, and income was lost.

CONCEPTUAL APPLICATION ACTIVITY 10.5

Identify some of the significant life events you have had that have shaped who you are. Next, interview a person from a different generation and ask this person about significant life events that shaped how he/she views the world.

As an example of how these systems are interrelated, a school counselor may be working with Sherilyn, a high school junior from a rural, Appalachian community, who is thinking of attending college. However, Sherilyn discloses that she is afraid of leaving home because her father regularly "beats up" her mother (microsystem). She states that she has thought of talking to the family minister on several occasions but is fearful that this may make the situation worse for her mother (mesosystem). If Sherilyn decides to see the counselor, the counselor may direct Sherilyn to resources in the community that could guide her and her mother to sources of assistance (exosystem). In addition, the counselor could direct Sherilyn to the laws that are directly aimed at intervention and prevention (macrosystem). It is possible that with this support, Sherilyn and her mother could mobilize these resources to move to a safe place and begin a new way of living (chronosystem).

BOX 10.1 ABOUT URIE BRONFENBRENNER

Urie Bronfenbrenner (1917–2005) was born in Moscow and came to the United States when he was six years old. He was influenced by the struggles of his father, who was frustrated by the juvenile courts, where it was assumed that institutionalized children needed to be placed in a home with developmentally disabled youth (Brendtro, 2006). As a result of his father's beliefs, Urie became an ardent advocate for providing children and their families with resources that would better meet their needs.

Developmental stages and the various emotional, cognitive, and physiological changes that occur at each stage of growth provide a framework to assist counselors in working with youth. Development is viewed as the interaction between people, events, physiology, and cultural interactions that become increasingly complex as the individual matures. This maturity places more and more demands on each individual (Cook, 2012).

Erikson's Theory of Psychosocial Development

Erik Erikson proposed eight stages of psychosocial development based on biological and cultural influences rather than looking at growth from a chronological perspective (Newman & Newman, 2012). According to Erik Erikson, each individual progresses through life stages in which a specific task is to be mastered before moving to the next stage of development, also known as the *epigenetic principle*. Successful or ineffectual resolution of the task/crisis creates favorable or adverse outcomes. Physical and emotional growth, social relationships, cognitive abilities, and culture all impact the mastery of developmental tasks (Newman & Newman, 2012), in addition to the social meaning attached to these events (Weigert & Gecas, 2005).

This theoretical approach is limited and has been criticized by some, in that the foundation for this theory was based on males from a Western culture (Dunkel & Sefcek, 2009). School counselors use these stages as guidelines while assessing students for developmental issues that are essential to their chronological and/or developmental age.

Table 10.1 Psychosocial Developmental Tasks

Age	Task	Description	Basic Strength
Infancy Ages birth-2	Trust vs. Mistrust	The child develops a sense of trust when provided with consistent affection by caregivers. Mistrust occurs when not given constant care.	Hope
Early Childhood Ages 2-3	Autonomy vs. Shame and Doubt	The child develops a sense of control and autonomy. A sense of doubt results about abilities if encouragement is not received.	Will
Preschool Ages 3-5	Initiative vs. Guilt	The child observes and imitates adults and takes the initiative to create play situations. The child also begins different types of activities.	Purpose

Age	Task	Description	Basic Strength
School Age Ages 6-12	Industry vs. Inferiority	The child is able to create, learn, and accomplish new skills. Success leads to feelings of competence while failure leads to a sense of inferiority.	Organization and Competence
Adolescence Ages 12-18	Identity vs. Role Confusion	At this stage the individual tries to find his/her own identity while struggling with social relationships and contending with moral issues.	Sense of integration and self-understanding
Young Adulthood Ages 18-35	Intimacy vs. Isolation	The person seeks companionship through marriage and friends. If this stage is reached successfully intimacy is experienced; otherwise, there is a sense of loneliness.	Love and intimate relationships
Middle Adulthood Ages 35-55/65	Generativity vs. self-absorption	During idle-age, individuals are occupied with work and family, and the perpetuation of values to the family. People are concerned with the betterment of society and others.	Production and Care for Society and Others
Late Adulthood 55/65 to Death	Ego Integrity vs. Despair	At this stage people look over their lives with happiness and contentment, with a sense of contribution to life, Or, adults may feel that they have not lived up to their expectations and have a sense of despair and hopelessness	Wisdom

BOX 10.2 A GLIMPSE OF ERIK ERIKSON

Erik Erikson's theory and the concept of identity confusion may have arisen as a result of his own experiences. Erikson never met his biological father and was raised by his Jewish mother, who was single until she married Dr. Theodor Homberger, whom Erik believed was his birth dad. When he learned the truth about his father, he experienced confusion regarding his identity. His identity crisis was further exacerbated by the teasing he received from his classmates due to his Nordic features and Jewish background.

Piaget's Theory of Cognitive Development

Jean Piaget, another prominent developmentalist, was interested in how we learn, partly as a result of his experiences in the Binet institution. During these years he recognized that young children responded to questions much differently than did older children. From this observation, he recognized that it was not that younger children were less intelligent but that their thinking processes were different from their older peers. Piaget posited that as children develop, their thinking becomes more structured due to biological maturation. Piaget's four stages of cognitive development are represented in Table 10.2.

Many school program curricula are developed from this theory, yet empirical evidence reveals that not all cultures follow this progression of cognitive development. Furthermore, data from adolescent populations reveal that only 30–35% of high school seniors within the United States have actually reached the formal operational stage, which indicates that perhaps abstract thinking does not develop until much later than Piaget originally indicated. This finding could shed light on curriculum decisions, particularly since Piaget believed children should not be taught concepts until they have reached the appropriate cognitive developmental stage. Table 10.3 represents the various classroom strategies that facilitate cognitive development at each of the four stages.

Table 10.2   Piaget's Stages of Cognitive Development

Stage	Approximate Age	Characteristics
Sensorimotor Stage	Infancy 0–2 years of age	Children learn through their senses. Language development occurs at the end of this stage.
Preoperational Stage	2–7	Intelligence is developed through the use of symbols and language progresses. Egocentrism is prominent.
Concrete Operational Stage	7–11	Operational thinking develops. Learning occurs through the manipulation of objects to solve problems. Egocentrism lessens, which allows children to take another person's perspective.
Formal Operational Stage	11–Adult	Abstract thinking is prevalent. Egocentrism returns at the beginning of this stage. Person is capable of reflective thought.

Table 10.3 Cognitive Developmental Theory and Classroom Applications

Theoretical Concept	*Classroom Applications*
Piaget's Stages of Cognitive Development	
Preoperational	Use props and visual aids Use picture books Use actions and words to give instructions Use hands-on activities
Concrete operational	Use actions, props, hands-on activities Use role-plays Use brain teasers, mind maps, and riddles
Formal operational	Use hypothetical questions Debates Use songs and lyrics to reflect topics Teach broad concepts Use Socratic questioning

BOX 10.3 A GLIMPSE OF JEAN PIAGET

The Binet Institute employed Jean Piaget to translate intelligence test questions from French to English. It was this job that was the catalyst for his investigation of how children think. Piaget's work is criticized because he did not consider the influences of the social setting or culture on cognitive development. Furthermore, Piaget's work was often based upon observation of his own children and experiments conducted with them at home, rather than working with a large cohort of subjects and developing a data-set based on controlled experiments.

Havighurst's Theory of Personality Development

Robert Havighurst's Theory of Personality Development extended the developmental tasks identified within Erikson's psychosocial stages to other age-related arenas. Similar to Erikson, Havighurst believed that bio-psycho-social task confrontation and achievement begins in infancy and continues throughout the lifespan. Tasks are attempted 1) as a result of physical growth such as learning to walk, talk, relate to others, and so on; 2) due to intrapersonal resources such as values, personality, and skill acquisition; and 3) as a result of societal pressures from laws, policies, and so on.

When tasks are successfully completed there is a sense of personal and social adjustment, satisfaction in accomplishing previous tasks, happiness and success, or unhappiness and difficulties if not achieved (Havinghurst, 1972, as cited in Stringer, Kerpelman, & Skorikov, 2012). As school counselors, awareness of and the provision of experiences to tackle these tasks fit with the student competencies in the academic, career, and personal/social domains inherent in the ASCA National Model. Elementary school counselors are able to integrate the nine developmental tasks identified by Havighurst to the ASCA Student Standards to facilitate task completion. The nine tasks identified by Havighurst include:

1. Learning physical skills for games

2. Building healthy attitudes toward self

3. Building socialization skills for relating to peers

4. Learning gender roles

5. Developing skills in reading, writing, and arithmetic

6. Acquiring everyday living skills

7. Developing a sense of right and wrong

8. Achieving autonomy

9. Developing attitudes about social groups and institutions

School counselors are also able to partner with teachers to ensure that students develop these skills and attitudes. For example, teaching perspective-taking activities, personal dilemmas, or social skills in a group format augments skills students may have already developed, or for others these concepts may be an entirely new learning experience. Student Activity 10.1 is an example of a perspective-taking technique that can be used to address the tasks Havighurst identified.

STUDENT ACTIVITY 10.1.
STEPPING INTO ANOTHER PERSON'S SHOES

Develop a list of different scenarios such as the one below, and ask students to distinguish how various individuals could respond to the incidents cognitively, emotionally, and behaviorally.

Situation: School was cancelled because of a major snowstorm

	What might this person be thinking?	What might this person be feeling?	What might this person do?
Student	Hooray! I get to stay home!	Happy	Build a snowman
	Rats! I studied hard for that test and I want to get it over with.	Frustrated	Continue studying
Grandmother	Oh, no! I am afraid to drive in snow.	Worried	Call a taxi
	Yippee! I get to watch my grandkids.	Content	Make cookies
Street Cleaner	What a mess! People never seem to be able to drive in this mess.	Aggravated	Obtain additional salt and brine for roads
	Hurrah! I will get overtime pay.	Enthusiastic	Pack a snack for the long hours on the road

Likewise, Havighurst identified 9 developmental tasks for adolescents including:

1. Identifying with a gender orientation

2. Maintaining mature friendships with males and females

3. Accepting body structure and maintaining a healthy lifestyle

4. Achieving emotional autonomy

5. Selecting and preparing for a career

6. Preparing for marriage and family life

7. Behaving in a socially acceptable manner

8. Acquiring intellectual skills and civic engagement

9. Developing values and ethical guidelines

Adolescents can be assisted in developing the tasks identified by Havighurst through Student Activity 10.2, which is designed to help students recognize various self-identities and how these characteristics have impacted self and others. (Note: this exercise can also be used to introduce the concepts of oppression, defined as the social and institutional power of policies, practices, norms, and traditions that exploit a target group by the privileged group [Locke & Bailey, 2014].) It is also a useful strategy for students to begin thinking about civic engagement and values.

STUDENT ACTIVITY 10.2. MY VARIOUS IDENTITIES

A list of group/cultural identities are below. In a group guidance class, have students complete the first column and then ask students to decide whether or not this characteristic is viewed as socially disadvantaged or "oppressed" or socially advantaged or "privileged." Have students use the following scale: 1 = oppressed and 5 = privileged. In the third column students describe unique experiences they have had in each area. When students are finished, lead a class discussion on these characteristics.

Describe your identity in each area	Use the following scale 1 = Oppressed 5 = Privileged	Describe the experience
Gender		
Age		
Race		
Ethnicity		
Skin color		
Weight		
Height		
Religion		
Social class		
Language		
Appearance		
Nationality		
Health		
Gender typical interests		

> ## BOX 10.4 A GLIMPSE OF ROBERT HAVIGHURST
>
> Robert Havighurst had two distinctly different careers. He obtained a PhD in chemistry from the Ohio State University and worked in the fields of physics and chemistry for many years, until he decided to enter the field of experimental education. As a professor of education he was instrumental in developing educational theory and contributing to the field of international and comparative education.

Social Cognitive Theory of Development

Lev Vygotsky posited that social interaction is essential to cognitive development. In his social cognitive theory, he stated that learning occurs when there is an interaction between an individual who has a better understanding of a concept than the learner; known as the *zone of proximal development*. This concept is defined as the range of tasks that a learner cannot yet perform on his/her own, but can accomplish with the assistance and support of someone more knowledgeable (Ormrod, 2011). For this reason, collaborative learning activities where students of varied ability levels work together, or programs in which those with more knowledge are able to be peer tutors are effective.

The sociocultural context in which individuals interact is essential to learning. According to Vygotsky the child's language serves as a tool for intellectual assimilation and adaptation, and the culture teaches the child both the context and content of their thinking.

> ## BOX 10.5 A GLIMPSE OF LEV VYGOTSKY
>
> Lev Vygotsky was born in Russia and received a law degree from Moscow State University, where he studied a range of subjects, including psychology and sociology. He published a wide variety of books primarily on the topic of child development. Although his ideas were controversial in Russia, they were well received in the West. He died of tuberculosis at the age of 38.

Each of these developmental theories provides a foundation for thinking about our work with students and their families; yet these views could be inappropriate or insensitive to the experiences of some students. For instance, if a 12-year-old is having difficulty with abstract thinking, which is a characteristic of Piaget's formal operational stage, or has not demonstrated the ability to initiate assigned homework, a skill within Erikson's industry vs. inferiority stage, this does not mean that this individual has developmental concerns that would imply a diagnostic label. These developmental theories are simply guides that are not necessarily appropriate for all individuals. As you work with students, consider how culture, beliefs, and experiences are essential to a productive counseling relationship. People from different backgrounds and histories differ with respect to: 1) their view of life's difficulties; 2) their description of these difficulties; 3) methods of communicating; 4) their view of the causes of distress; 5) views of the counselor, and 6) views of counseling (McGoldrick & Giordano, 1996, as cited in Locke & Bailey, 2014).

DEVELOPMENTAL ISSUES AND MULTICULTURALISM

Mental health fields have traditionally trained students from a Eurocentric perspective with white European-American attitudes and values as the standard, without consideration to other worldviews, gender differences, or culture. Unfortunately, there is a lack of research with diverse students in the school milieu to determine the effectiveness of counseling strategies with diverse students (D'Andrea & Daniels, 1995). Compounding the problem is the fact that most graduates and students in the mental health professions have been white, sometimes with little understanding of

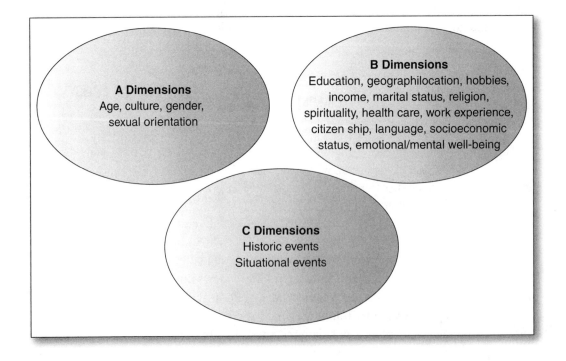

systemic oppression and social justice. The ABCs of racial dimensions provide a context for viewing our students and family.

- A dimensions are the more visible characteristics upon which stereotypes are often based
- B dimensions may not be visible to others but impact view of self and others.
- C dimensions include the historical events that influence lives such as hurricanes, acts of terrorism, or a disease outbreak (Robinson-Wood, 2003).

When the school counselor acknowledges the association between ethnic identity and emotional well-being, there is a greater opportunity to facilitate cultural exploration and the influence of perceived discrimination. Furthermore, assisting students with identity affirmation contributes to increased well-being, less stress, and higher academic achievement (Syed, Walker, Lee, Umana-Taylor, & Zamboanga, 2013).

Students with diverse backgrounds and experiences are more prevalent in our schools today than several decades ago. Statistics reveal that America's racial and ethnic minorities now comprise about half of the under-five age group. This is a historic population shift as it is projected that whites will become a minority in the next generation (Yen, 2013). Imagine a child from a different country with limited English attending school in the United States, while trying to navigate the educational system with a goal of academic achievement. Even students who are verbally fluent may be confused as to the regional language dialects and colloquialisms. Not understanding customs may also be overwhelming, particularly when their peers are discussing celebrations such as the 4th of July, Halloween, or Thanksgiving. In addition, students from families who have lived in countries in which daily violence and killings were witnessed may be enduring tremendous emotional losses as well as post-traumatic stress disorder (PTSD). In many cases these individuals will often not seek out counseling as a first resource, and if counseling is sought, the school counselor needs to take an opportunity to explore the reasons for seeking counseling at that time.

Whatever the presenting problem, spending some time in learning about the culture of the individual is essential. A productive counseling relationship includes working in partnership with the value system of the student and his/her family rather than taking a stance based on your own personal belief system. This includes critically examining your own cultural values and biases, recognizing your cultural background, and learning about cultures and skills to select appropriate counseling strategies.

At times we need to educate students about racial terms that are hurtful. For example, an elementary-age African American student told his school counselor, who is also African American, that his best friend called him the "N" word. This counselor had many thoughts and feelings racing through her mind as she considered how she was going to handle the situation. When she called the young man to her office and confronted him, he readily admitted that he used that word and acknowledged that he learned the word from his grandfather. The counselor's feelings ranged from anger and disgust, to sympathy and understanding as she recognized that this student loved his grandfather, and to berate him for the use of this word would be harmful to a working relationship between her and the student's family. Instead, she asked him if he knew what the word meant. He said he did not and when she explained that it was an offensive term, he replied that he like his friend didn't know it was a bad word. The counselor was able to turn this situation into a learning opportunity for this young man, and rather than having the student leave her office feeling belittled, angry, and insulted, he left more educated with a promise to not use the word again.

Teachers from diverse backgrounds can also have difficulty fitting into a school environment. For instance, a high school counselor worked in a school in which a chemistry teacher from Nigeria was hired. Not only was this a difficult transition for the teacher due to the differences between schools in Nigeria and the United States, she replaced a well-respected chemistry teacher who retired the previous school year. A student who was doing well in other academic classes but was not successful in this chemistry class came to the school counselor for advice on how she could make better grades in this class. When the school counselor spoke with the teacher, she learned that the teacher felt that the students were disrespectful when they asked questions and further relayed that she felt students were questioning her authority when they made inquiries. Through this consultation the chemistry teacher realized that it was "ok" to be more human and have fun with the students in her classes.

The ACA Multicultural Competencies Table 10.4 serves as a self-assessment checklist for identifying areas in which additional knowledge is needed.

CONCEPTUAL APPLICATION ACTIVITY 10.6

Read through the multicultural competencies in Table 10.4 and place a check next to the competencies that you feel you have mastered. For the areas you did not mark, identify strategies for gaining these needed attitudes, knowledge, and skills. Discuss your plans with your classmates.

Table 10.4 ACA Multicultural Counseling Competencies

I. Counselor Awareness of Own Cultural Values and Biases

A. Attitudes and Beliefs

I believe that . . .

_____1. cultural self-awareness and sensitivity to one's own cultural heritage is essential.

_____2. I am aware of how my own cultural background and experiences have influenced my attitudes, values, and biases about psychological processes.

_____3. I am able to recognize the limits of my multicultural competency and expertise.

_____4. I am able to recognize my sources of discomfort with differences that exist between myself and students in terms of race, ethnicity and culture.

B. Knowledge

I am knowledgeable of . . .

_____1. my own racial and cultural heritage and how it personally and professionally affects my definitions and biases of normality/abnormality and the process of counseling.

_____2. and understanding about how oppression, racism, discrimination, and stereotyping affect me personally and in my work. This allows me to acknowledge my own racist attitudes, beliefs, and feelings. Although this standard applies to all groups (for white counselors) it may mean that I understand how I may have directly or indirectly benefited from individual, institutional, and cultural racism as outlined in White identity development models.

_____3. my social impact upon others. I am knowledgeable about communication style differences, how my style may clash with or foster the counseling process with persons of color or others different from me based on the A, B, and C Dimensions, and how to anticipate the impact it may have on others.

C. Skills

I am able to . . .

_____1. seek out educational, consultative, and training experiences to improve my understanding and effectiveness in working with culturally different populations. Being able to recognize the limits of my competencies, I (a) seek consultation, (b) seek further training or education, (c) refer out to more qualified individuals or resources, or (d) engage in a combination of these.

(Continued)

Table 10.4 (Continued)

_____2. constantly seek to understand myself as a racial and cultural being and am actively seeking a non racist identity.

II. Counselor Awareness of Client's Worldview

A. Attitudes and Beliefs

I believe that . . .

_____ 1. I am aware of my negative and positive emotional reactions toward other racial and ethnic groups that may prove detrimental to the counseling relationship. I am willing to contrast my own beliefs and attitudes with those of my culturally different clients in a nonjudgmental fashion.

_____2. I am aware of my stereotypes and preconceived notions that I may hold toward other racial and ethnic minority groups.

B. Knowledge

I am knowledgeable of . . .

_____1. specific knowledge and information about the particular group with which I am working. I am aware of the life experiences, cultural heritage, and historical background of culturally different students. This particular competency is strongly linked to the "minority identity development models" available in the literature.

_____2. how race, culture, ethnicity, and so forth may affect personality formation, vocational choices, manifestation of psychological disorders, help seeking behavior, and the appropriateness or inappropriateness of counseling approaches.

_____3. sociopolitical influences that impinge upon the life of racial and ethnic minorities. Immigration issues, poverty, racism, stereotyping, and powerlessness may impact self-esteem and self concept in the counseling process.

C. Skills

I am able to . . .

_____1. familiarize myself with relevant research and the latest findings regarding mental health and mental disorders that affect various ethnic and racial groups. I actively seek out educational experiences that enrich my knowledge, understanding, and cross-cultural skills for more effective counseling behavior.

_____2. become actively involved with minority individuals outside the counseling setting (e.g., community events, social and political functions, celebrations, friendships, neighborhood groups, and so forth) so that my perspective of minorities is more than an academic or helping exercise.

III. Culturally Appropriate Intervention Strategies

A. Beliefs and Attitudes

I believe that . . .

_____1. I respect students' religious and/or spiritual beliefs and values, including attributions and taboos, because they affect worldview, psychosocial functioning, and expressions of distress.

_____2. I respect indigenous helping practices and respect helping networks among communities of color.

_____3. I value bilingualism and do not view another language as an impediment to counseling (monolingualism may be the culprit).

B. Knowledge

I am knowledgeable of . . .

_____1. and understand the generic characteristics of counseling and therapy (culture bound, class bound, and monolingual) and how they may clash with the cultural values of various cultural groups.

_____2. institutional barriers that prevent minorities from using mental health services.

_____3. the potential bias in assessment instruments and use procedures and interpret findings keeping in mind the cultural and linguistic characteristics of the students.

_____4. family structures, hierarchies, values, and beliefs from various cultural perspectives. I am knowledgeable about the community where a particular cultural group may reside and the resources in the community.

_____5. relevant discriminatory practices at the social and community level that may be affecting the psychological welfare of the population being served.

C. Skills

I am able to . . .

_____1. engage in a variety of verbal and nonverbal helping responses. I am able to send and receive both verbal and nonverbal messages accurately and appropriately. I am not tied down to only one method or approach to helping, but recognize that helping styles and approaches may be culture bound. When I sense that my helping style is limited and potentially inappropriate, I can anticipate and modify it.

_____2. exercise institutional intervention skills on behalf of my clients. I can help students and their families determine whether a "problem" stems from racism or bias in others (the concept of healthy paranoia) so that students and their families do not inappropriately personalize problems.

_____3. seek consultation with traditional healers or religious and spiritual leaders and practitioners in the treatment of culturally different clients when appropriate.

(Continued)

Table 10.4 (Continued)

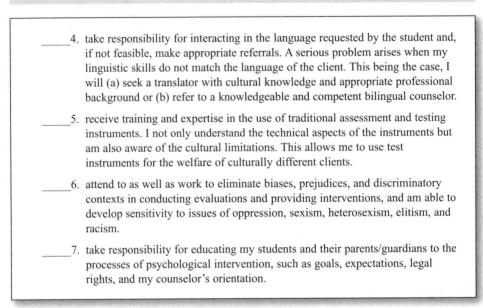

_____4. take responsibility for interacting in the language requested by the student and, if not feasible, make appropriate referrals. A serious problem arises when my linguistic skills do not match the language of the client. This being the case, I will (a) seek a translator with cultural knowledge and appropriate professional background or (b) refer to a knowledgeable and competent bilingual counselor.

_____5. receive training and expertise in the use of traditional assessment and testing instruments. I not only understand the technical aspects of the instruments but am also aware of the cultural limitations. This allows me to use test instruments for the welfare of culturally different clients.

_____6. attend to as well as work to eliminate biases, prejudices, and discriminatory contexts in conducting evaluations and providing interventions, and am able to develop sensitivity to issues of oppression, sexism, heterosexism, elitism, and racism.

_____7. take responsibility for educating my students and their parents/guardians to the processes of psychological intervention, such as goals, expectations, legal rights, and my counselor's orientation.

Source: Adapted from: Sue, D. W., Arredondo, P. M., & McDavis, R. J. (1992). Multicultural counseling competencies and standards: A call to the profession. *Journal of Counseling & Development, 70,* 477–486. The American Counseling Association. Reprinted with permission. No further reproduction authorized without written permission from the American Counseling Association.

A discussion of developmental theories and multicultural concepts were discussed. Conceptual Application Activity 10.7 gives you an opportunity to systematically apply these ideas and to think about your work with a diverse student body as a school counselor.

CONCEPTUAL APPLICATION ACTIVITY 10.7

Tomika is a 17-year-old student, first-generation Japanese, who arrived in the United States with her parents seven years ago. Tomika was referred to your office because she was not completing her homework assignments, which had resulted in failing grades in three of her five classes. Prior to this year she had excelled in her classwork, particularly in art classes. Tomika has a younger sister and an older brother, who is attending a prestigious university in a different part of the country. Tomika's teachers reported that she recently appeared sullen in class, does not seem to pay attention, and could not be depended upon to complete homework assignments. One teacher even commented that she thought she smelled alcohol on Tomika's breath one morning, which Tomika vehemently denied when confronted. There were other occasions when she skipped school or was tardy to class.

When you met with Tomika she seemed reticent and unwilling to talk, but she did indicate that she did not have many friends, and she relayed that on one occasion she heard some of her classmates talking, laughing, and pointing at her when she was changing classes. Tomika stated, "I just lost it—I haven't done anything to any of these students, and they make me feel as if I am not worth their time. I didn't even want to face them in class so I just ran out of the building and didn't return that day."

You decide to call Tomika's parents in for a conference, and despite their limited English, you learn that they have also noticed a change in their daughter. Up until a few months ago she seemed energetic, happy, and a "normal teenage girl." They also stated that she and her older brother had a close relationship until he left for college several months ago. They did disclose, however, that they were struggling financially and that they both put in long hours at work.

With a classmate, discuss the issues that you think may be affecting Tomika. Apply the developmental theories and multicultural concepts in your discussion. What factors may be at work in this case? How would you address them? How would you develop a counseling plan with Tomika?

WORKING WITH A DIVERSE STUDENT BODY AND THEIR FAMILIES

Social concerns throughout the decades have led to legislative mandates and these, in turn, influence the school culture and policies. Some sixty years have passed since the pivotal case of *Brown v. the Board of Education* (Smith & Kozleski, 2005) that invalidated educational segregation in public schools. This 1954 law created an opportunity for all educators to assess their beliefs and values regarding their role in educating all individuals equally and respectfully. Likewise, prior to the decade of the 1950s, children with low IQs were excluded from schools and families had to establish classrooms in church basements and community centers for these marginalized youth. In reaction to this egregious act of isolation, the National Association for Retarded Citizens (NARC) was established. Just as *Brown v. Board of Education* established equitable educational opportunities, the Education for All Handicapped Children Act of 1975 (PL 94–142) was passed (later known as the Individuals with Disabilities Education Act [IDEA]), and in 2004 was changed to the Individuals with Disabilities Education Improvement Act (IDEIA). These acts ensured that students with disabilities had access to a free, appropriate public education in the least restrictive environment (Smith & Kozleski, 2005).

These initiatives and others created conversations to transform the educational system for students of all abilities, ethnicities, races, gender orientations, experiences, and socio-economic levels. In addition, they are designed to address equality for all students in a welcoming and inclusive school milieu. School counselors are instrumental professionals in leading this mission that is also one of the greatest challenges facing the profession (Holcomb-McCoy, 2004). As stated in the ASCA Professional School Counselor and Cultural Diversity position statement, "Professional school counselors are expected to "specifically address the needs of every student, particularly students of culturally diverse, low social-economic status, and other underserved or underperforming populations" (American School Counselor Association, 2009, para. 3). Despite these guidelines, discriminatory practices and policies are still evident in regard to students with exceptional needs, English-Language Learners, youth with mental health disorders, students who are gifted, and those with gender differences.

STUDENTS WITH EXCEPTIONAL NEEDS

Imagine being a parent/guardian who has been asked to attend a meeting at the school to discuss teachers' educational concerns regarding his/her child. Notification of this meeting alone is enough to create trepidation, but imagine what it would be like to enter a room full of people whom you don't know, who are focused on your child's deficits, and using educational jargon that you don't understand. Meetings such as this are often problem focused in that the student's areas of weakness are often the purpose for convening the meeting. School counselors are able to make a difference by creating more inviting meetings for parents/guardians through advanced information on who will be attending the meeting, what will be discussed, where it will be held, and the purpose behind the conference. As a school counselor, focusing on student strengths and viewing the parents/guardians as experts about their child provides a more balanced perspective of the student and contributes to a more successful outcome.

Students with special needs often require modifications, accommodations, personal aides, or other support services for academic success (Nichter & Edmonson, 2005). At times teachers do not understand some of the mental health issues that impact student behaviors and criticize school counselor interventions that are sometimes viewed as enabling the student. For instance, a second-grade teacher had a student in her class who was diagnosed as autistic. This student would get frustrated when he transferred from one task to another and expressed his aggravation by rolling up into a ball and hiding under his desk. The school counselor asked the teacher to contact her when he displayed this behavior so she could come to the classroom and walk him to her office. The teacher was displeased with this idea because she believed that this plan was reinforcing the student's bizarre behavior. In response, the school counselor decided to provide in-service training to the faculty and staff on characteristics of students with autism and strategies for assisting these students. At the end of the school year the student displayed these bizarre behaviors less frequently due to the trusting relationship between the teacher and the school counselor and the knowledge she shared.

The Individuals with Disabilities Education Improvement Act (IDEIA) that was passed in 2004 includes provisions such as eligibility requirements, funding, service evaluations, educational placements, judicial process, discipline stipulations, and Individualized Education Programs (IEPs). To familiarize you with common terms used in special education programs, the IEP, transition, and 504 plans are discussed below.

The Individualized Education Plan (IEP)

The IEP is a contract written in consultation with the student's parents/guardians and a team of professionals. This legal mandate requires a statement of goals and objectives, the student's current levels of educational achievement, and the impact of the disability on the student's educational progress. In addition, this document outlines annual educational goals, the types of services and program accommodations available to the child, time to be spent in the general education program, dates for receiving services and evaluation of these services, testing modifications (if appropriate), and transition services for students (Olson & Platt, 2004). School counselors may also be requested to provide such services, including individual or small group counseling if this intervention is determined to be appropriate.

Transition

School counselors are instrumental in providing transition assistance. The transition mandate for students with exceptional needs occurs at four pivotal levels: from elementary to middle school, middle school to high school, high school to postsecondary options, and from regular and special education classrooms. Transition services must be addressed in the IEP at the earliest appropriate age, but for each student with a disability, a statement regarding the student's transition services must be on the IEP beginning no later than the age of 14. Beginning at age 16, or younger if appropriate, the IEP must include a statement of the types of transition services that are needed, including inter-agency responsibilities, if necessary (Parent Brief, 2002). Of all these transitions, the transition from elementary to middle school is considered as the most significant transition for students with disabilities (Milsom, 2007). School counselors can systematically approach these transitions through collaboration with educators, parents/guardians, and school/community institutions, leading psychoeducational groups, and teaching assertiveness and social skills (Milsom, 2007).

504 Plans

The 504 Section of the Rehabilitation Act of 1973, now covered under the Amendments to the Americans with Disabilities Act (ADA) of 2008, broadened the definition of disabilities and services for students. This legislation mandates that any individual with a disability cannot be denied participation in any program receiving federal funding if the disability limits at least one major life activity (Turnbull, Turnbull, Shank, Smith, & Leal, 2002). However, students covered under the 504 plan are not required to have an IEP, unlike the students covered by IDEIA. Most schools assign one school person to be responsible for the 504 plans, and a multidisciplinary team meets to decide whether or not the student is eligible for accommodations under this mandate. A physical or mental disability that substantially impairs at least one major activity such as walking, breathing, seeing, hearing, learning, taking care of oneself, or has a documented impairment, is regarded as having a disability. (A child or adolescent with HIV or attention deficit/hyperactivity is protected under Section 504 and ADA.) For instance, Lisa, a pregnant 15-year-old who is having a difficult pregnancy that could impair her health or the well-being of her baby, would be eligible for accommodations on the 504 plan, such as a supplemental tutor to assist with her assignments and school work (MentalHelp.net, 2010). Table 10.5 lists conditions that are covered under the 504.

Table 10.5   Some of the Common Conditions Covered by 504 Plans

Diabetes	Pregnancy-related concerns
Epilepsy	Poor hearing
Allergies	Heart disease
Poor vision	Chronic illnesses such as kidney disease, ulcers
High blood pressure	Attention deficit disorder

A disturbingly disproportionate number of students from diverse backgrounds and limited English skills are diagnosed as having a learning disability and placed into special education classrooms. For instance, Black, non-Hispanic students, and American Indians are overly identified for services in special education classrooms. Hispanic students, particularly those from Puerto Rico, are often seen as displaying more body movements, facial expressions, and gestures and are more frequently and incorrectly labelled as hyperactive (Bauermeister, 1995, as cited in Turnbull, Turnbull, Shank, Smith, & Leal, 2002). In contrast, Asian/Pacific Islanders that could qualify for special education services are underrepresented in disability categories.

School counselors have an opportunity to work with parents of students with special needs through advocacy, explaining the IEP process, and understanding the parents'/guardians' perspective (Taub, 2006) regarding their child's behavior. It is possible that parents/guardians may have difficulty accepting a recommendation for special education services. In some instances parents may be overly protective of their child, worry about safety concerns such as bullying, the attitudes of other parents and peers, and fear that school personnel do not acknowledge their child's abilities (Taub, 2006). An example of how parents/guardians may react is in Case Study 10.1.

CASE STUDY 10.1

A female fifth-grade student was difficult to be around in that she was quick to insult and criticize others, which her parents viewed as typical reactions to remarks other students made to her. Her mother insisted that her daughter be switched to a different class, due to her perception that she was receiving poor treatment from her peers, and expressed displeasure that the school personnel were not able to "control" the peers in her class. The school counselor was finally able to convince the mother that there were patterns to her daughter's behavior, and she finally consented to psychological testing in which the daughter was diagnosed with Asperger's syndrome. The mother had difficulty accepting this diagnosis, including the information that her daughter would be placed in special education classes. She also insisted that this diagnosis not be shared with anyone because she was embarrassed about the label placed on her daughter. If the mother had been able to accept the diagnosis, the school personnel would have been able to provide services that the fifth-grader so desperately needed.

—Intermediate School Counselor

ENGLISH-LANGUAGE LEARNERS (ELL)

English language learners (ELLs) are projected to represent approximately 30% of the school population by the year 2015 (Capps, et. al, 2005, as cited in Moughamian, Rivera, & Francis, 2009). ELL refers to students who are either not proficient in English, or students who adequately converse in English but have difficulty with language within coursework.

Provisions under No Child Left Behind (NCLB) provide support for ELLs, in that school personnel are compelled to create effective instructional practices and demonstrate that these students are making Adequate Yearly Progress (AYP) (Moughamian, et al., 2009). Prior to 1974 schools did not provide ELLs with assistance in learning English, when the U.S. Supreme Court ruled this was a violation of civil rights (Crawford, 2004, as cited in Moughamian, et al., 2009). The Bilingual Education Act passed in 1968 requires schools to provide equal educational opportunities to students who do not speak English as a first language. Although the Office of Civil Rights (OCR) enforces the law and specifies that students are to read, write, and comprehend English proficiently enough to participate in the school's curriculum, there is debate as to the most effective method for teaching English language learners (Olson & Platt, 2004). The English-Language only and Bilingual models are common instructional methods found in schools.

English Language Instructional Programs

In the English-only model (known as English as a second language [ESL] or English language development [ELD] program), students are either placed in general classrooms with support provided by a specialist in the classroom, or students are placed in content-based subjects in which structured immersion, or individually designed instruction is offered in English. The goal is to teach both academic concepts and English while teachers use strategies such as gestures, or visual aids, and adjust their rate and tone while communicating.

The Bilingual Model

In this type of program, instruction is provided in English and the student's native language. The *Dual Language Programs* and *Transitional Bilingual Programs* are two types of bilingual models practiced in schools and are more easily facilitated when there are a large number of students who speak the same language. Dual Language Programs (also known as bilingual immersion, two-way bilingual, two-way immersion, and dual immersion) develop language skills in two languages to reinforce the native language and to accelerate English language development. Transitional bilingual programs use native language instruction that eventually tapers off while students learn English (¡Colorín Colorado! 2011).

School counselors are usually not prepared to work with ESL students (Burnham, Mantero, & Hooper, 2009). Unfortunately, not many have had meaningful interactions with ESL students outside of behavior, scheduling, or academic concerns that most commonly bring most school counselors and these students together. For example, as a practicing school counselor I met a student who arrived from Hong Kong to enroll in our high school. He spoke primarily Cantonese with little English ability. Imagine how difficult it had to have been for this young man to leave behind his friends and family, enter a new culture in which he had no friends, and try to keep up academically. To make things worse, I found myself talking in a loud voice in an effort to be understood. We can be instrumental in creating collaborative environments to reach underserved students who have limited interactions with school counselors (Burnham, et al., 2009). These students are excellent resources for teaching their peers about their culture, values, and beliefs.

STUDENTS WITH GIFTEDNESS

Think about a person you know who is considered "gifted and talented." Does this individual show talent in academics? Creativity such as in music, art, or dance? Or, perhaps this person excels in leadership. Some individuals are "double-gifted," in that they have learning difficulties as well as outstanding talent in certain areas. Giftedness includes exceptional general intellectual characteristics, specific academic acumen, creativity, leadership ability, visual/performing art capabilities, musical characteristics, or drama traits. The definition of giftedness fluctuates among schools and states, with great variation of characteristics and criteria for inclusion. Students who are talented are found in all cultural, racial, and socioeconomic groups. The Jacob K. Javits Gifted and Talented Students Education Act Title V, Part D, Subpart 6 of the No Child Left Behind Act of 2001 was created for youth who have exceptional talent in intellectual, creative, artistic, leadership, or specific academic fields. A major focus of this program is to identify students who are underrepresented in gifted and talented programs, such as those who are disadvantaged or who have limited English skills. This legislation does not require states to establish programs for students who meet these criteria (Turnbull, et al., 2000; U.S. Department of Education, 2012), and this results in a wide variability between states, as well as gifted youth not getting the services that facilitate educational opportunities.

Most adolescents experience stress and turmoil during adolescence, but for youth who are gifted there are additional challenges that compound the stress. For instance, anxiety over high parental expectations could contribute to a perfectionist attitude accompanied by a sense of being different from peers (Freeman, 2001, as cited in McQueen, Reynolds, & Rinn, 2011). As such, these individuals may need greater emotional and academic assistance. A study by McQueen et al. (2011) revealed that adolescents who were gifted perceived their classmates as providing little support but did view adults and/or older peers as a source of succor. School counselors could facilitate small group counseling strategies with these youth, with the goal of teaching social skills to create better connections with same-age peers.

BOX 10.6 FAMOUS "DOUBLE-GIFTED" PEOPLE

Giftedness appears differently behaviorally, emotionally, and intellectually, with many historic figures who were considered "gifted" displaying variations in development. It is not uncommon for an individual to have a label of both "learning disabled" and "gifted," also known as "double-gifted." The following list is of some of the famous people who may have been "double-gifted."

1. Walt Disney was fired as a news reporter because he "had no good ideas" and as a child was labeled as being "slow."

2. Cher is a well-known entertainer who was diagnosed with dyslexia.

3. Tom Cruise is a talented actor with a diagnosis of dyslexia, which he has accommodated by learning his lines by listening to a tape.

4. George Patton, a successful field commander, had a reading deficiency his entire life but was talented in his ability to memorize speeches.

Source: http://dyslexiamylife.org/who_els.html

STUDENTS WITH MENTAL HEALTH OR DISABILITY DISORDERS

Mental health disorders manifest in approximately 20% of adolescents; many of these are first identified during adolescence (National Institute of Mental Health, n.d.). Approximately 8.0% of youth between the ages of 12–17 are diagnosed with a major depressive episode, with suicide identified as the third leading cause of death in adolescents (Substance Abuse and Mental Health Services Administration, 2012).

The Diagnostic and Statistical Manual of Mental Disorders (DSM) is used to diagnose mental health disorders. The DSM aligns with the categories established by the World Health Organization, (WHO), *International Classification of Diseases, 11th edition* (ICD-11), which was developed for consistent diagnosing around the world. The newest edition was released in May 2013, but with this latest release many counseling professionals are divided regarding the legitimacy of this newest revision and how it will affect diagnoses. However, the DSM-5 does contain a new dimensional approach to assessment that many practitioners believe will improve the diagnostic sensitivity because the new guidelines make provisions to rate the presence, frequency, and duration of the symptoms (Rollins, 2013).

The newest edition (DSM-5) was revised from a multiaxial system to three sections. Section 1 provides an introduction to the DSM-5 with information on use. Section 2 presents an outline of the diagnoses, and section 3 includes conditions about which more research is needed, cultural considerations, and a glossary of terms.

School counselors and other members of the professional child study team are often the first to recognize youth with disorders. Although school counselors do not typically take a class in diagnosis and treatment, understanding common terms assists in collaborating with other mental health professionals, and having knowledge of the diagnosis aids in helping students. Despite the controversy surrounding this manual, school counselors and teachers express concern with their lack of training in working with students diagnosed with mental or emotional disorders, particularly as individuals with mental health issues are entering schools in greater numbers.

Cultural bias needs consideration when evaluating behaviors since disorders cannot be separated from cultural considerations or contexts, and practitioners are not behaving ethically when strictly using the characteristics or symptoms that are presented in the DSM without consideration of sociological and cultural factors (Erk, 2008). With more and more youth in schools with a diagnosis on the autism spectrum disorder scale, as well as attention deficiencies and hyperactivity disorders, a discussion of these disorders follows.

Autism Spectrum Disorders

Prior to the latest edition of the DSM, youth were diagnosed with four distinct disorders: autistic disorder, Asperger's disorder, childhood disintegrative disorder, and pervasive developmental disorder, not otherwise specified. The DSM-5 now places these syndromes on an autism spectrum disorder (ASD) continuum, with some individuals displaying mild symptoms and others showing severe symptoms. According to the Centers for Disease Control and Prevention, approximately 1 in 88 youth is identified with ASD, with boys 5 times more likely to have this diagnosis than girls (CDC, 2013). Youth with ASD often have communication difficulties such as responding appropriately in conversations, misreading nonverbal cues, or difficulty in making friends. Furthermore, youth with ASD may be dependent on routines, with sensitivity to changes in their schedule, or intensely focused on ill-chosen items (APA, 2012). For instance, one student with ASD would spend hours watching the swirling motion of the cleaning device in his family's swimming pool, despite his mother's requests to stop.

Despite mandates stipulated in IDEIA, educational programs and treatment considerations have not kept up with the increased numbers of children diagnosed with these disorders, and general educators often feel unprepared for successful integration of these students into their classrooms. Students with ASD may exhibit anxiety or acting out behaviors to sensory stimuli, such as the ringing school bell to announce a change in class schedule. The school counselor is able to assist these students by discussing schedule changes such as a planned assembly. Weekly meetings with the student and concretely identifying events that are placed on a personal calendar is one method to prepare for changes that could disrupt a daily routine. Figure 10.2 is an example.

Figure 10.2   Calendar With Daily Representations of Schedule Changes

Sun	Mon	Tues	Wed	Thurs	Fri	Sat
6 Church	7 School	8 Tutoring	9	10 SCHOOL ASSEMBLY	11 Leave for weekend	12

Counselors are also able to teach communication skills through group counseling strategies, in which students with ADS and their peers can practice making eye contact, shaking hands, practicing appropriate greetings, and saying goodbye. Watching these skills on a DVD, watching a peer group member, and then practicing with a partner while receiving feedback are helpful instructional strategies.

BOX 10.7 UNDERSTANDING MORE ABOUT AUTISM

Children are usually diagnosed with autism by the age of 3, due to noticeable differences with other children at this age. More recently, there has been evidence that a simple name test at the age of 1 could present a clue of potential difficulties. When a

1-year-old consistently does not respond to the sound of his/her name, it is possible that this signals a developmental difficulty.

With continued research in detecting clues associated with developmental delays or deficits, greater opportunities exist for more timely interventions. (Detecting autism, 2013).

Attention-Deficit/Hyperactivity Disorder

The percentage of individuals with ADHD has changed over the years, with approximately 3–7% of today's students diagnosed as having this disorder (CDC, n.d.). Attention-deficit disorder (ADD) /hyperactivity (ADHD) criteria defined in the DSM-5 are similar to those that were found in the DSM-IV-TR. Changes in diagnoses include a greater clarity across the life span, the inclusion of additional symptoms across multiple situations, and the onset of several symptoms prior to age 12 (previously 7 years of age was the minimum age for diagnosis). ADHD is divided into three types, with symptoms found in two categories of inattention and hyperactivity and impulsivity or both. Symptoms include the inability to attend to details, difficulty with organization, excessive talking or fidgeting, and trouble sitting still (APA, 2012). Children must exhibit at least six symptoms from either (or both) the inattention group in several settings for a diagnosis.

BOX 10.8 UNDERSTANDING MORE ABOUT ADHD

Hyperactivity is generally associated with boys. Boys (13.2%) were more likely than girls (5.5%) to be diagnosed with ADHD (CDC, 2013). Although boys who exhibit this characteristic generally get treatment and outgrow their energy and restlessness, girls with hyperactivity may become more troubled with age. Girls with ADHD are often misdiagnosed as anxious and/or depressed and tend to conform to teachers' expectations more than do boys. These girls tend to show social deficits at an early age, were twice as likely to become addicted to tobacco and enter into mentally abusive relationships. In addition, those who exhibited aggression along with their hyperactivity were more likely to get pregnant early in life and to live on welfare (BBCnews.com; Nadeau, 2004).

Researchers state that the disorder is difficult to treat due to its link to genetics rather than environmental factors. Nonetheless, school counselors are able to assist these students in managing their behaviors (Webb & Myrick, 2003) through various counseling strategies, with group counseling often recommended over individual counseling (Braswell & Bloomquist, 1991, as cited in Webb & Myrick, 2003). For instance, a group approach in which the sessions were associated with a journey was implemented for elementary-age students diagnosed with ADHD. The group began by teaching students about the feelings, thoughts, and actions linked to this diagnosis. From there, the group expedition related trip planning as similar to class organization, focusing on attention by recognizing and remembering cues that were likened to road signs, and identifying obstacles to school success, similar to detours. Students were taught to name these signs that serve as cues and to identify strategies for managing their "journey" through school. A significant improvement in student success resulted from this concrete, visual intervention.

Working with a diverse student body also requires that the school counselor have an awareness of gender attitudes and beliefs. Gender identity is influenced by the culture and context judgments regarding femininity and masculinity (Stone & Dahir, 2006).

GENDER EQUITY

Gender Issues

Before 1972, educational policies excluded girls from participating in athletics and some academic courses. When Title IX Education Amendments of 1972 became law, academic and athletic opportunities became available for girls. Before this time girls were required to take "home economics" and boys to enroll in "shop" classes. College entrance examination scores were separated into male and female categories, and chances for success in post-secondary institutions were evaluated based on these gender specific scores. Girls were not encouraged to enter math and science arenas as these were considered fields for males only, but instead were encouraged to enter nursing, teaching, or secretarial fields. Boys were encouraged to enter pre-med, engineering, and the clergy. There was little awareness of sexual harassment, and when boys (and men) made sexual comments or unwanted advances to girls, these were laughed off or dismissed with the attitude that "boys will be boys."

Although over 40 years have passed since the passage of Title IX, deep-rooted attitudes and beliefs are difficult to change. In the 1990s when I was a practicing school counselor, I worked with a female student who was at the top of the class. She had taken all the college preparation and honors classes that the school had to offer in addition to taking classes at the local college. Due to her impressive achievements, she was selected to receive a large scholarship from a local business to attend a college of her choice. Although she wanted to attend college, her parents were firm believers that girls should not attend college, as this privilege was reserved for the males in the family. Although I strongly believe in the importance of women receiving higher education, this decision represented a family value. Instead of resisting and sharing my beliefs with the family, I realized that I needed to work with the family to assist in a smooth transition from high school.

In 1992 the American Association of University Women (AAUW) published a landmark study that revealed girls were ignored in the classroom and the curriculum, particularly in math and sciences. Six years later, the gap between girls and boys in these courses narrowed but a large disparity continued, with boys taking more advanced math and science courses than girls. This difference was reflected in the National Assessment of Educational Progress (NAEP), in which boys' scores in math, science, history, and geography were higher than girls', whereas girls outperformed boys in reading and writing. These results continued to reinforce traditional stereotypes. Although women have made strides, a 2010 study by the AAUW revealed that women's progress in the STEM occupations (science, technology, engineering, and mathematics) continues to be slow. Although school counselors are burdened with large caseloads, concerted efforts to educate others about gender issues are necessary to create a gender equitable environment.

A multiculturally competent school counselor has an awareness of personal gender bias that may impair a counseling relationship. This means continued self-assessment regarding your own gender biases to assure equitable treatment of all students is essential. Introducing your students to nontraditional career options, informing students of the barriers and risks of entering these careers, and providing support for those who do enter these nontraditional career paths are school counselor responsibilities (Tollerud, 2003). Figure 10.3 (p. 356) is a self-reflection checklist to help you think about your gender attitudes and implications for working with all students.

CONCEPTUAL APPLICATION ACTIVITY 10.8

After completing the checklist in Figure 10.3 discuss your answers and reasons for your beliefs. Have your attitudes changed after this conversation? If you are able to see different perceptions, what made a difference in this changed viewpoint?

Gender equity also includes attention to lesbian, gay, bisexual, transgendered, and questioning/queer youth (LGBTQ), due to the fact that these individuals need support and assistance (Fish, 2009). There is a positive difference in student well-being when students are aware of at least one individual in their school who is supportive of their lifestyle. This individual could be you.

Figure 10.3   Gender Self-Reflection Checklist

_____ I think every student should make career, academics and personal choices based on individual interests, abilities, aptitudes, and values rather than gender.

_____ I believe every student has the right to pursue his or her career aspirations and dreams even if they are dominated by the opposite gender.

_____ I believe it is important to talk about nontraditional careers with all of the students, both the boys and girls.

_____ I think it is important to use examples and resources on nontraditional careers in my school, including role models, guest speakers, mentors, bulletin board displays, and in reading materials.

_____ I believe in discussing job salaries with all my students, pointing out that typical male-dominated jobs mean higher salaries and typical female jobs mean lower salaries in the workplace.

_____ I believe it is important to talk about nontraditional options with all students, even if they already have a tentative career decision planned.

_____ I believe that I need to talk with students about employment rights and discrimination laws in the workplace so they will be informed when the enter the workforce.

_____ I think it is important to speak to all students about barriers preventing them from choosing nontraditional occupations.

_____ I believe that when students discuss taking courses that are composed mostly of students of the opposite gender, I need to discuss the barriers that may be encountered (e.g., sexual harassment) and how these issues can be addressed.

_____ It is important that when students take a nontraditional course, I should meet with them and discuss the problems they may be encountering.

_____ I feel it is important to discuss traditional attitudes that parents/guardians may have that could prevent their child from entering into a nontraditional career.

_____ I believe that it is my responsibility as a school counselor to discuss nontraditional careers with teachers so that they can reinforce these ideas in their classes.

SEXUAL MINORITY YOUTH

Lesbian, gay, bisexual, transgendered, and questioning/queer (LGBTQ) students have often been invisible in the educational arena, though this has been changing in recent years, especially in certain areas Although legal mandates offer protection for LGBTQ students, marginalization of these students continues, often with the complicity of school officials. According to the ASCA position statement:

The professional school counselor works with all students through the stages of identity development and understands this process may be more difficult for LGBTQ youth. School counselors provide counseling and individual student planning services to LGBTQ students . . . Professional school counselors are committed to the affirmation of all youth regardless of sexual orientation, gender identity and gender expression and work to create safe and affirming schools (ASCA, 2013, para. 3).

When misinformed school personnel (Bidell, 2012) make decisions that adversely affect sexual minority students, addressing sexual orientation in the schools can be difficult as tenure, dismissal, or retribution are possible outcomes. Check the written school policies regarding antiharassment and antidiscrimination and whether there is an appropriate process for responding to policy abuses (Dugger & Carlson, 2012). The website http://www.aclu.org/lgbt-rights_hiv-aids/model-policy-schools serves as a template for designing an inclusive school policy (Dugger & Carson, 2012). Resources from the Safe Schools Coalition are also helpful in writing policies, available at http://safeschoolscoalition.org/

Rather than taking a passive stance and avoiding these issues, you need to have a conversation with decision-makers and share lawsuits that have been filed when discriminatory practices negatively impact LGBTQ youth. For instance, the ACLU filed lawsuits against schools in Kentucky and Texas when administrators banned the formation of a Gay-Straight Alliance (GSA) club (ACLU, 2003). School counselors are able to facilitate a supportive, safe environment, such as making certain anti-bullying policies that specifically mention LGBTQ youth are in place, advising or developing a GSA group, and/or putting up safe space stickers such as a rainbow flag to let all students know that your office is one that is supportive of all students (Jackson, 2011).

There is debate regarding the appropriate age to discuss sexuality issues. In fact, the state of Tennessee is considering legislation known as the "Don't Say Gay Bill" that would disallow talk about sexual orientation in public schools (Shahid, 2011). This is a short-sighted view because elementary-age students are not too young to discuss topics surrounding respect and differences. Consider Ella, a seven-year-old who lives with her two lesbian mothers. Ella has come home crying on numerous occasions due to her peers making derogatory comments about her "two moms." Or, consider Carter, a ten-year-old boy who has been suspended from school due to physical fights with his peers who bullied him because his father is gay. School counselors can take opportunities to discuss respect and differences in guidance classes, assume a leadership role in character education classes, and/or educate teachers and parents with information on developmental issues including sexuality and gender orientation. Several resources are available for school counselors to provide support for sexual minority youth and their families.

RESOURCES FOR SEXUAL MINORITY YOUTH

The Gay, Lesbian, and Straight Education Network (GLSEN)

This organization was founded to improve the school climate for all students, no matter what sexual orientation or identity (GLSEN, 2012). GLSEN sponsors Gay Straight Alliances (GSA), an organization that is composed of lesbian, gay, bisexual, and transgender students. According to the 1984 Federal Equal Access Act, GSAs are legally permitted. http://www.glsen.org

COLAGE

This is a network organization for children, youth, and adults with one or more lesbian, gay bisexual, transgender, and/or queer parent or guardian (COLAGE, n.d.). Resources such as books, camps, guides, and activities are available for parents/guardians and children. http://www.colage.org

Gender Education and Advocacy (GEA)

GEA is a national organization focused on the needs, issues, and concerns of gender variant people in society. GEA educates and advocates for all individuals who suffer from gender-based oppression. www.gender.org.

The It Gets Better Project

This project was developed for young LGBTQ individuals to educate about how happiness, potential, and positivity can be part of living. The project is designed to remind LGBTQ adolescents that they are not alone and there are supportive individuals available (www.itgetsbetter.org). It was formed in response to a series of suicides among gay teenagers who had been bullied, and the growing recognition that LGBTQ students were at a higher risk for suicide, bullying (including cyber bullying), and serious harassment because of their gender orientation.

Bibliocounseling

School counselors are able to contribute to a safe, equitable school environment through education, self-reflection, and connecting with diverse community members. Bibliocounseling is a strategy for recognizing ing diversity and fostering respect in the school environment. A list of children's books that celebrate diversity is below.

David's Drawings (Cathryn Falwell)

A young African American boy works on a drawing with the help of his classmates.

How My Parents Learned to Eat (Ina R. Friedman)

A story of different customs of a Japanese mother and an American father

I Love My Hair! (Natasha Tarpley)

A celebration of a little girl's naturally curly hair and individual beauty

Stinky the Bulldog (Jackie Valent)

A story about not pre-judging others

Jack and Jim: Picture Book (Kitty Crowther)

Two diverse birds with messages of friendship and acceptance

CONCLUSION

School counselors work with youth at all developmental levels and attend to issues of diversity in supporting school-age youth and their families. Too often we take a restricted approach when assisting youth by focusing solely on individual attributes, behavior, or attitudes, without attention to other external influences on the child's growth. Urie Brofenbrenner's Ecology of Human Development Theory, Erik Erikson's Theory of Psychosocial Development, Jean Piaget's Cognitive Development Theory, and Robert Havighurst's Theory of Personality Development serve as developmental foundations for understanding children and adolescents. However, the sensitive school counselor is one who understands and works with the cultural values and diversity of the student and family, self-examines views surrounding various cultures, and establishes a collaborative, trusting relationship by viewing students from numerous dimensions.

School counselors assist students with exceptional needs, and an awareness of legal requirements to accommodate these youth—including knowledge of the IEP, transitioning, and the 504 plan—is necessary. Increasing numbers of English-language learners, students who are gifted, and students with mental health or disability disorders are in our schools, and the effective school counselor is responsible for understanding the needs of these individuals and training other educators about methods for enhancing their academic, career, and personal/social growth. School counselors are also aware of gender biases that impair successful academic growth, as well special issues for those who are Gay, Lesbian, Bisexual, Transgender, or Questioning/Queer, as these students have often been marginalized in schools. School counselors are leaders in working with administrators in advocating for students to eliminate barriers that prevent optimal growth, and in providing equal opportunities for all students.

REFERENCES

American Association of University Women (2010). *Breaking through the barriers.* Washington, D.C. Author. Retrieved from http://www.aauw.org/searchResults.cfm?cx=008426594581391 752977%3Apovjlwdjwlq&cof=FORID%3A10&ie=UTF-8&q=whysofew_execsummary .pdf++++++&sa=Search&siteurl=www.aauw.org%2F&ref=us.yhs4.search.yahoo.com%2Fy hs%2Fsearch%3F%26hspart%3DFreeCause%26hsimp%3Dyhs-shopathome_001%26type% 3D100973%26p%3Damerican%2520association%25200f%2520university%2520women&s s=7j49j2

American Civil Liberties Union (2003, January 13). *ACLU files lawsuits against schools in KY and TX for discrimination against gay-straight alliances.* Retrieved from http://www.aclu .org/lgbt-rights_hiv-aids/aclu-files-lawsuits-against-schools-ky-and-tx-discrimination-against-gay-straig

American Psychiatric Association: Diagnostic and Statistical Manual of Mental Disorders (2012). *DSM-5: The future of psychiatric diagnosis.* Retrieved from http://www.dsm5.0rg/Pages/ Default.aspx

American School Counselor Association (2006). *The professional school counselor and equity for all students. Gender gaps. Where schools still fail our children.* Alexandria, VA: Author.

American School Counselor Association (2009). *Professional School Counselor and Cultural Diversity.* Alexandria, VA: Author.

American School Counselor Association (2013). The professional school counselor and LGBTQ youth. *Position Statement.* Alexandria, VA: Author.

Bidell, M. P. (2012). Examining school counseling students' multicultural and sexual orientation competencies through a cross-specialization comparison. *Journal of Counseling & Development, 90,* 200–207.

Brendtro, L. K. (2006). The vision of Urie Bronfenbrenner: Adults who are crazy about kids. *Reclaiming Children and Youth, 15,* 162–166.

Bronfenbrenner, U. (1977). Toward an experimental ecology of human development. *American Psychologist, 32,* 513–531. doi: 10.1037/0003–066X.32.7.513

Burnham, J. J., Mantero, M., & Hooper, L. M. (2009). Experiential training: Connecting school counselors-in-training, English as a second language (ESL), and ESL Students. *Journal of Multicultural Counseling and Development, 37,* 2–14.

Centers for Disease Control and Prevention (n.d.). Attention-deficit/hyperactivity disorder (ADHD). Retrieved from http://www.cdc.gov/ncbddd/adhd/data.html

Centers for Disease Control and Prevention (2013, June). *Autism spectrum disorders* (ASDs). Retrieved from http://www.cdc.gov/ncbddd/autism/data.html

COLAGE (n.d.). People with a lesbian gay bisexual transgender or queer parent. Retrieved from http://www.colage.org/

¡Colorín Colorado! (2011). *Helping children read . . . and succeed!* Retrieved from http://www .colorincolorado.org/educators/background/programs/

Cook, E. (2012). Behavior is interactional. In E. Cook (Ed.), *Understanding people in context: The ecological perspective in counseling.* Alexandria, VA: ACA.

D'Andrea, M., & Daniels, J. (1995). Promoting multiculturalism and organizational change in the counseling profession: A case study. In J. G. Ponterotto, J. M. Casas, & L. A. Suzuki (Eds.), *Handbook of Multicultural Counseling.* Thousand Oaks, CA: Sage.

Detecting autism at age 1 (2013). Health Secrets. *The Week Magazine*, p. 29.

Dugger, S. M., & Carlson, L. A. (2012). Sexual minority youth: The case of Donald Wilson. In S. H. Dworkin & M. Pope (Eds.), *Casebook for counseling: Lesbian, gay, bisexual, and transgender personals and their families* (pp. 7–22). Alexandria, VA: American Counseling Association.

Dunkel, C. S.& Sefcek, J. A. (2009). Eriksonian lifespan theory and life history theory: An integration using the example of identity formation. *Review of General Psychology, 13,* 13–23.

Erk, R.R. (2008). *Counseling treatment for children and adolescents with DSM-IV-TR disorders.* Upper Saddle River, NJ: Pearson.

Fish, J. (2009). Invisible no more? Including lesbian, gay and bisexual people in social work and social care. *Practice: Social Work in Action, 14,* 47–64. Retrieved from http://dx.doi.org/10.1080/09503150902746003

Gender Education and Advocacy (2005). *About GEA.* Retrieved from http://www.gender.org/

GLSEN (2012). *About Gay Straight Alliances (GSA).* Retrieved from http://www.glsen.org/cgi-bin/iowa/all/library/record/2342.html?state=what

Holcomb-McCoy, C. (2005). Investigating school counselors' perceived multicultural counseling competence. *Professional School Counseling, 8,* 414–423.

Jackson, K. (May/June, 2011). Safe and Sound. *ASCA School Counselor,* 17–19.

Locke, D. C., & Bailey, D. F. (2014). *Increasing multicultural understanding* (3rd ed.). Los Angeles, CA: Sage.

Martines, D. (2008). *Multicultural school psychology competencies: A practical guide.* Los Angeles, CA: Sage.

McQueen, K. S., Reynolds, M. J., & Rinn, A. N. (2011). Perceived social support and the self-concepts of gifted adolescents. *Journal for the Education of the Gifted, 34,* 367–396.

MentalHelp.net (2010). *504 Plans.* Retrieved from http://www.mentalhelp.net/poc/view_doc.php?type=doc&id=36233&cn=1275

Milsom, A. (2007). Interventions to assist students with disabilities through school transitions. *Professional School Counseling, 10,* 273–278.

Moughamian, A. C., Rivera, M. O., & Francis, D. J. (2009). *Instructional models and strategies for teaching English language learners.* Portsmouth, NH: RMC Research Corporation, Center on Instruction.

Nadeau, K.G. (2004). *High school girls with AD/HD.* Retrieved from http://www.addvance.com/help/women/high_school.html

National Institute of Mental Health (n.d.). *Any disorder among children.* Retrieved from http://dyslexiamylife.org/who_els.html

Newman, B. M., & Newman, P. R. (2012). *Development through life: A psychosocial approach.* Belmont, CA: Cengage Learning.

Nichter, M., & Edmonson, S. L. (2005). Counseling services for special education students. *Journal of Professional Counseling: Practice, Theory, & Research, 33,* 50–62.

Olson J. L., & Platt, J C. (2004). *Teaching children and adolescents with special needs* (4th ed.). Upper Saddle River, NJ: Pearson.

Ormrod, J. E. (2011). *Educational psychology: Developing learners* (7th ed.). Boston, MA: Allyn & Bacon.

Parent Brief (2002, July). *Promoting effective parent involvement in secondary education and transition.* Retrieved from http://www.ncset.org/publications/viewdesc.asp?id=423

Robinson-Wood, T. I. (2003). *The convergence of race, ethnicity, and gender multiple identities in counseling.* Upper Saddle River, NJ: Pearson.

Rollins, J. (2013, May). The dawn of a new DSM. *Counseling Today.* Alexandria, VA: ACA.

Santrock, W. J. (2008). *Life-span development* (11th ed.). New York, NY: McGraw Hill.

Schwarz, S. W. (2009). Adolescent mental health in the United States: Facts for policy makers. *National Center for Children in Poverty.* Retrieved from http://nccp.org/topics/healthydevel opment.html

Shahid, A. (2011, May). 'Don't say gay' bill passes Tennessee senate, would ban teachers from discussing homosexuality. Retrieved from http://www.nydailynews.com/news/national/don-gay-bill-passes-tennessee-senate-ban-teachers-discussing-homosexuality-article-1.145355

Smith, A., & Kozleski, E. B. (2005). Witnessing Brown: Pursuit of an equity agenda in American education. *Remedial and Special Education, 26,* 270–280. Retrieved from http://rse.sagepub .com/content/26/5/270. doi:10.1177/07419325050260050201

Stone, B. C., & Dahir, C. A. (2006). *The transformed school counselor.* Boston: Lahaska Press.

Stringer, K., Kerpelman, J., & Skorikov, V. (2012). A longitudinal examination of career preparation and adjustment during the transition from high school. *Developmental Psychology, 48,* 1343–1354.

Substance Abuse and Mental Health Services Administration (2012). *Results from the 2010 National Survey on Drug Use and Health: Mental health findings,* NADUH Series H-42, HHS Publication No. (SMA) 11–4667. Rockville, MD: Substance Abuse and Mental Health Services Administration.

Syed, M., Walker, L. H.M., Lee, R. M., Umana-Taylor, A. J. & Zamboanga, B.L. (2013). A two-factor model of ethnic identity exploration: Implications for identity coherence and well-being. *Cultural Diversity and Ethnic Minority Psychology, 19,* 143–154.

Tang, M., & Bashir, H. (2012). Diversity from the ecological perspective. In E. Cook (Ed.), *Understanding people in context: Ecological perspectives in counseling.* Alexandria, VA: ACA.

Taub, D. J. (2006). Understanding the concerns of parents of students with disabilities: Challenges and roles for school counselors. *Professional School Counseling, 10,* 52–57.

Tollerud, T. R., (2003, May & June). Examining your own gender bias. *School Counselor.* Alexandria, VA: American School Counselor Association.

Tolnay, S. E., & Bailey, A. K. (2006). Schooling for newcomers: Variation in educational persistence in the northern United States in 1920. *Sociology of Education, 79,* 253–279.

Turnbull, R., Turnbull, A., Shank, M., Smith, S., & Leal, D. (2002). *Exceptional lives: Special education in today's schools* (3rd ed.). Upper Saddle River, NJ: Merrill Prentice Hall.

U.S. Department of Education (2012). *Jacob K. Javits Gifted and Talented Students Education Act.* Retrieved from http://www2.ed.gov/programs/javits/legislation.html

Webb, L. D., & Myrick, R. D. (2003). A group counseling intervention for children with attention deficit hyperactivity disorder. *Professional School Counseling, 7,* 108-115.

Weigert, A. J., & Gecas, V. (2005). Symbolic interactionist reflections on Erikson, identity, and postmodernism. *Identity: An International Journal of Theory & Research, 5,* 161–174. doi:10.1207/s1532706xld0502_5

Woods, N. S. (2001). Life span development: Is teaching developmental psychology obsolete? In R. S. Feldman (Eds.), *Development Across the Life Span* (pp. 286–288). doi:10.1037/002496

Yen, H. (2013, June 13). Census: White majority in U.S. gone by 2043. *U.S. News on NBCNews .com.* Retrieved from http://www.ncda.org/aws/NCDA/pt/sd/news_article/50358/_PARENT/ layout_details_cc/false

Chapter 11

THE SCHOOL COUNSELOR AS AN ADVOCATE AND LEADER

*CACREP Standards

DIVERSITY AND ADVOCACY

F. *Skills and Practices*

> 2. Advocates for the learning and academic experiences necessary to promote the academic, career, and personal/social development of students.
>
> 3. Advocates for school policies, programs, and services that enhance a positive school climate and are equitable and responsive to multicultural student populations.

LEADERSHIP

O. *Knowledge*

> 1. Knows the qualities, principles, skills, and styles of effective leadership.
>
> 2. Knows strategies of leadership designed to enhance the learning environment of schools.
>
> 4. Understands the important role of the school counselor as a system change agent.
>
> 5. Understands the school counselor's role in student assistance programs, school leadership, curriculum, and advisory meetings.

> *A student is denied an educational accommodation in class because the teacher feels this adjustment is unfair to the rest of the students in class*

A student is unfairly graded and you believe it is due to her ethnicity

A student is bullied due to physical impairments

The principal assigns student discipline to you as a daily responsibility

The examples above are only a few of the types of situations in which school counselors apply their advocacy and leadership skills. School counselors advocate at multiple levels in regards to students and their families, the need for student groups, increasing resources for programs, ending school policies that discriminate, and gaining professional acknowledgment. Through these advocacy efforts we are also campaigning for our profession (Hof, Dinsmore, Barber, & Suhr, 2009).

Unfortunately, many school counselors do not support the concepts of advocacy, due to the belief that it is "just another task" to an already full job description (King, 2011). Some researchers state that the counseling profession criticizes social justice and advocacy due to the lack of research to support its effectiveness (Smith, Reynolds, & Rovnack, 2009, as cited in Locke & Bailey, 2014). However, in reviewing the history of the profession, basic listening skills, communication, and mediation skills that facilitate advocacy have traditionally been a part of the counselor's role (Lewis, et al., 2011). Furthermore, Frank Parsons and Jesse B. Davis, pioneers of our profession, advocated for disenfranchised youth and created programs to expand vocational awareness for these youth. Clifford Beers, another pioneer in the counseling profession, was instrumental in advocating for an awareness of mental health issues in the early 1900s. Consequently, advocacy has been a part of our professional story, and we need to continue to challenge existing laws, institutional policies, procedures, or uninformed attitudes that serve as obstacles to student opportunity. Regrettably, educational institutions have traditionally not done well interceding for students who struggle (Kennedy, 2008) or addressing inequalities that exist among students (Griffin & Steen, 2011).

Responding to social institutions that disenfranchise school-age youth promotes a shift in how students are treated in the school (Green & McCollum, 2004). "Social justice in counseling means that [stakeholders] have access to resources, determining whether systemic barriers stand in the way of . . . optimal psychological health and sometimes using advocacy to change those oppressive environmental barriers" (Shallcross, 2010, p. 30). Furthermore, the American School Counselor Association (ASCA) ethical standards are clear in regard to school counselors' ethical responsibility to advocate for equal opportunity and social justice for their students within schools and the larger community. The ethical standards state:

> [School counselors] monitor and expand personal multicultural and social justice advocacy awareness, knowledge and skills . . . develop competencies in how prejudice, power and various forms of oppression . . . affect self, students, and all stakeholders . . . acquire educational, consultation and training experiences to improve awareness, knowledge, skills and effectiveness in working with diverse populations . . . advocate for equitable school and school counseling program policies and practices for every student and all stakeholders . . . and provide regular workshops and written/digital information to families. . . . to promote increased student achievement (ASCA, 2010, E.1.).

CASE STUDY 11.1

Shawna transferred to a new high school in the middle of the academic year, which meant that she would need to be enrolled in classes that were similar to, but different from those she took at a previous school. When the school counselor first met Shawna, her height, beauty, and fashionable clothes stood out in contrast to the appearance of the majority of the students in the school. As the counselor was working with Shawna on her class schedule, Shawna announced that she was born a male but was in the process of living as a female in preparation for her sex change surgery that would occur when she was 18 years of age. The counselor was uncertain how to proceed with Shawna without the assistance of the school principal; even registering her into the computer was an issue since she had to note Shawna's gender. Naturally, Shawna and her grandmother, who had custody, wanted this information to be confidential.

When the principal arrived in the office, he was adamant that this student did not belong in the school as he believed that it would create an unworkable educational environment. Furthermore, he was concerned about Shawna in physical education classes and the restrooms that she would use. The school counselor conveyed to him that an alternative plan could be worked out for the physical education class, and that Shawna could have access to a restroom down a hall in which there were few students. Despite the principal's opposition, the school counselor was able to advocate for Shawna and a workable plan was arranged.

Mental health issues are associated with oppression. Disadvantaged youth often confront more prejudice and discrimination, leading to problems such as depression and anxiety, stress, lowered self-esteem, and impaired self-identity (Greenleaf

& Williams, 2009). Racial discrimination is associated with lower socioeconomic status, lower educational attainment, and lower employment and wages. The question is, "How can school counselors advocate?"

BOX 11.1 CHECK YOUR CULTURAL AWARENESS

School counselors can act as change agents for Japanese Americans by recognizing the needs of individual students rather than assuming that these students are only suited for the math and science fields. In addition, many school counselors incorrectly assume that Japanese American students do not need financial assistance for postsecondary institutions.

CACREP

ADVOCACY

Both social justice advocacy and multicultural concepts have philosophical commonalities and use similar strategies to change inequities among disenfranchised groups, individuals (Trusty & Brown, 2005), and programs. Advocacy is described as a compass to intentionally navigate power structures, create bonds, teach self-advocacy skills, and use data to educate others as to how the school counselor works to close the achievement gap (Locke & Bailey, 2014). Social justice advocacy can be thought of as active behaviors to transform institutions that have policies in place that impede opportunities for marginalized students and families (Gerstein & Toporek, 2006, as cited in Locke & Bailey, 2014).

Advocacy may be regarded as a tool for achieving social justice (Murray, et al., 2010) and includes developing the skills that are needed to promote access to opportunities for all students, as well as teaching students how to self-advocate. Social justice concepts provide students with support as school counselors raise awareness about disenfranchised youth (Locke & Bailey, 2014). Self-advocacy includes setting meaningful goals, developing a sense of self-efficacy, gaining knowledge and competence, and putting concepts into action (Cattaneo & Chapman, 2010).

Both the Transforming School Counseling Initiative (TSCI) and the ACA Advocacy Competencies support advocacy skills for counselors, the individual, school/community, and the public at various levels. The mission of TSCI is to "promote a new vision of school counseling . . . by [transforming] school counselors into powerful agents of change . . . to close the gaps in opportunity and achievement . . ." (Education Trust, 2009, para. 1). The ACA Advocacy

Competencies were developed for counselors in all specialty areas to apply on behalf of diverse individuals at the community or public arena, or to teach others skills for self-empowerment.

At the individual level the counselor works with the student and/or family to advocate for self, such as teaching assertiveness skills, or to practice strategies to address barriers. At the school or system level, the counselor may either bring unfair policies to the attention of the administration or use community groups to facilitate the removal of obstacles that impede success. For instance, a school counselor concerned about students who were bullied due to their sexual orientation could identify community members to develop and lead a group exclusively for these students. At social/political levels, school counselors could address legislators and other policymakers to inform them as to how policies may discriminate against certain groups (Marbley, et al., 2011). Conceptual Application Activity 11.1 identifies advocacy domains as endorsed by the ACA Governing Council.

CONCEPTUAL APPLICATION ACTIVITY 11.1

Advocacy Competencies

Directions: Look at the list of advocacy competencies below, and check those skills where you feel confident in your ability to perform the skill.

Empowerment Counselor Competencies

I am able to:

_____ Identify strengths and resources of students

_____ Identify social, political, economic and cultural factors that affect the student

_____ Recognize the signs indicating that an individual's behavior and concerns reflect responses to systemic or internalized oppression

_____ Help the student identify the external barriers that affect his or her development

_____ Train students in self-advocacy skills

_____ Help students develop self-advocacy action plans

_____ Assist students in carrying out action plans

(Continued)

(Continued)

Student Advocacy

I am able to:

_____ Negotiate relevant services and education systems on behalf of students

_____ Help students gain access to needed resources

_____ Develop an initial plan of action for confronting these barriers

_____ Identify potential allies for confronting the barriers

_____ Carry out the plan of action

Community Collaborative Counselor Competencies

I am able to:

_____ Identify environmental factors that impinge upon students' development

_____ Alert community or school groups with common concerns related to the issue

_____ Develop alliances with groups working for a change

_____ Use effective listening skills to gain an understanding of the groups' goals

_____ Identify the strengths and resources that the group members bring to the process of systemic change

_____ Communicate recognition of and respect for these strengths and resources

_____ Identify and offer the skills that I can bring to the collaboration

_____ Assess the effect of my interaction with the community

Systems Advocacy Counselor Competencies

I am able to:

_____ Identify environmental factors impinging on students' development

_____ Provide and interpret data to show the urgency of change

_____ Collaborate with other stakeholders to develop a vision to guide change

_____ Analyze the sources of political power and social influence within the system

_____ Develop a step-by-step plan for implementing the change process

_____ Develop a plan for dealing with probable resistance to change

_____ Recognize and deal with resistance

_____ Assess the effect of my advocacy efforts on the system and constituents

Public Information Counselor Competencies

I am able to:

_____ Recognize the impact of oppression and other barriers to healthy development

_____ Identify the environmental factors that are predictive of healthy development

_____ Prepare written and multi-media materials that provide clear explanations of the role of specific environmental factors in human development

_____ Communicate information in ways that are ethical and appropriate for the target population

_____ Disseminate information through a variety of media

_____ Identify and collaborate with other professionals who are involved in disseminating public information

_____ Assess the influence of public information efforts I have undertaken

Social/political Advocacy Counselor Competencies

I am able to:

_____ Distinguish those problems that can best be resolved through social/political action

_____ Identify the appropriate mechanisms and avenues for addressing those problems

_____ Seek out and join with potential allies

_____ Support existing alliances for change

_____ Prepare convincing data and rationales for change with the help of my allies

_____ Lobby legislators and other policymakers with the help of my allies

_____ Maintain open dialogue with communities and students to ensure that the social/political advocacy is consistent with the initial goals

Source: Permission granted from the American Counseling Association: Lewis, J. A., Arnold, M. S., House, R., & Toporek, R. L. (2002). ACA advocacy competencies. Retrieved from http://counseling. org/Resources/Competencies/Advocacy_Competencies.pdf

Despite a greater awareness of multiculturalism, generally described as the right of all individuals to be respected regardless of differences (Locke & Bailey, 2014), our society's institutions, including our schools, continue to encourage and attend to some groups and identities while marginalizing others on the basis of constructs such as gender, race, sexual orientation, socioeconomic level, disabilities, and so on (Locke & Bailey, 2014). School personnel state that all students are treated equally, yet this practice may not always be fair. For instance, is it fair to expect a student who has a bladder infection to wait to use the restroom when the rest of the classroom students are granted permission? In another example, consider the plight of undocumented students, who for the most part have been ignored though no fault of their own and have not received the assistance that they deserve. School counselors can learn about these individuals and they can use social justice principles to advocate for these individuals.

BOX 11.2

Undocumented children and adolescents account for 15% of the immigrants living in our country, and are sometimes referred to as the 1.5 generation because they fit somewhere between the first and second generation. They aren't second generation, but they are also not first generation because much of their childhood was spent in the United States. Although these children were not born in this country, they have received much of their education here, but without a method for legalizing their status they have difficulty going on to higher education or to seek work legally. Furthermore, they have the fear of deportation on a daily basis.

The Development, Relief and Education for Alien Minors (DREAM) Act was first introduced to Congress in 2001 and reintroduced in 2011, and when it failed to pass, an executive memorandum known as the Deferred Action for Childhood Arrivals (DACA) was issued by President Barack Obama in June 2012. The U.S. Customs and Immigration Service (part of the Department of Homeland Security) administers the program and invites those eligible to apply. The DACA offers 2-year protection from deportation to undocumented immigrants who arrived in the United States before the age of 16, have not committed a serious crime, have lived here for five years, are either currently enrolled in school, graduated from high school, or earned a GED, or have served in the military (Gonzalez, 2013; Gonzales & Terriquez, 2013).

Advocating for Social Justice from a Broader Perspective

Too often, we view problems from an intrapersonal perspective without considering the bio-psycho-social influences that pertain to genetic, intrapersonal, and interpersonal influences on the lives of the individuals with whom we work. Targeting students' needs without considering internal and external factors limits how we can build resiliency among students and their families. A social justice perspective represents a shift from traditional Western-based counseling theories (Zalaquett, 2011) to an expanded vision. This broader view, as depicted in Urie Brofenbrenner's Ecological Systems model contributes to a greater repertoire of techniques and interventions to more successfully work with marginalized students. Barriers to achievement and personal growth include such factors as poor teacher quality, negative school climate, policies that negatively impact academic achievement, and biased teacher attitudes. Levels of advocacy occur from the microlevel of intervention to the macrolevel as we intervene with the client/student, the school or community, or the public arena. Figure 11.1 illustrates the various domains and areas of advocacy focus that were developed by Lewis, Arnold, House, & Toporek, 2002, and endorsed by ACA in 2003.

Knowledge of advocacy domains is not sufficient; one must have particular strategies to employ to address these areas. School counselors are able to aid students through awareness and implementation of five fundamental components of culturally proficient practices. These areas include evaluating cultural

Figure 11.1   Advocacy Competency Domains

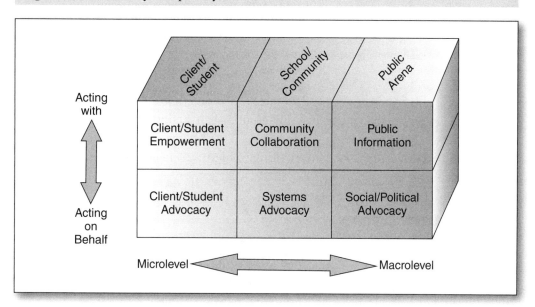

Source: Permission granted from the American Counseling Association: Lewis, J. A., Arnold, M. S., House, R., & Toporek, R. L. (2002). ACA advocacy competencies. Retrieved from http://counseling.org/Resources/Competencies/Advocacy_Competencies.pdf

knowledge, valuing diversity, managing differences, knowledge of diverse cultures, and instituting cultural change (Stephens & Lindsey, 2011). Table 11.1 describes these components.

Table 11.1 Fundamental Components of Cultural Proficiency

Evaluating Cultural Knowledge	Understanding the community and groups within the community, evaluating the attitudes and biases of educators, and recognizing the efforts that have been made to respond to needs
Valuing Diversity	Establishing an advisory board composed of various members of the community, which reflects the school demographics while valuing their views, opinions, and problem-solving initiatives
Managing Differences	Initiating conflict-mediation strategies and educating students, parents, and faculty/staff about cultural issues and diverse student needs
Knowledge of Diverse Cultures	Constantly assessing personal knowledge, values, and attitudes regarding cultural differences and updating knowledge about cultural groups
Instituting Cultural Change	Assessing the school climate and policies that may inadvertently discriminate, and advocating for change

Source: Adapted from Stephens & Lindsey (2011)

As an advocate, you can collaborate with various social systems while respecting advocacy domains and instituting cultural diversity proficiencies to prevent barriers to social, academic, and vocational well-being. Through these conscious efforts the needs of the student are recognized to prevent contributing to additional stress. As an example, read Case Study 11.2

CASE STUDY 11.2

An elementary school counselor served as an advocate for one of his students when the school secretary received a phone call from a detective in a neighboring town. The detective requested that the secretary call the mother of one of the fourth-grade students and ask her to come to the school for a meeting, and he further relayed that when she arrived he would place the mother under arrest. The principal was not in the building at the time and because the secretary felt uncomfortable with this request, she asked the school counselor what she should do. The school counselor replied that it was not the responsibility of the school to entrap parents and have them arrested in front of the students, and with this advice the secretary called the detective back and told him that she would not be making the call. Not happy with this response, the detective claimed that he would come to the school to speak with the fourth-grader instead. The school counselor called the principal, explained the situation, and requested that he return to the building. When the detective arrived at the building, he stated that there was evidence that the mother had stolen a pair of shoes and some jewelry from a store in the detective's precinct, and he wanted to talk with the student and see if he was wearing the shoes that were allegedly stolen. The principal and the counselor explained to the detective that they would not allow him to meet with the student, and after a heated discussion the detective retorted that they were "interfering with an investigation." The school officials were able to reach the mother and after explaining the situation to her she agreed to meet the detective at a different location, so her son would not be involved or embarrassed because of the allegations.

In this example, the school counselor worked in the best interests of the student to protect him from incidents that were beyond his control.

Working as a Social Justice Advocate

It is easier to talk about social action than to achieve it or even to take concrete action toward its achievement (Marbley, et al., 2011). As school counselors we have a responsibility to work with *all* students with the intention of creating meaningful changes in the school. School counselors view the school from a different lens than do most school administrators, and this perspective sometimes necessitates challenging existing inequities that have the potential to negatively impact individual students. School administrators determine policy based on what is in the best interests of the majority of the students and the school as a whole, whereas school counselors advocate for individual students when school policies unfairly impact access to opportunities that others enjoy. For instance, a student with diabetes may need to be dismissed from class during certain times of the day to check his/her sugar level. This sometimes requires approximately 15 minutes, particularly if a snack such as crackers or juice is needed to regulate low blood sugar. These items may also need to be refrigerated, which could mean a designated refrigeration area within the school. Or, a student with Crohn's disease may be

Photo 11.1   Children Actively Engaged in Learning

Source: © Stockbyte/ThinkStock.com

reluctant to tell teachers about the need for frequent, urgent bathroom privileges. In this case, you may need to advocate on the student's behalf by notifying the teachers, and developing a plan for the student to leave the classroom without delay, when necessary.

When we question authority about policies or rules that we believe are discriminatory toward students, we challenge the status quo, which has the potential of creating tension and conflict between professionals, as well as burnout from these efforts and the conflict. To prepare for these times, some preventive strategies include: a) identifying personal coping skills to cognitively reframe the situation; b) engaging in behavioral supports such as running or hobbies; and c) participating in enjoyable activities (Trusty & Brown, 2005).

As a school counselor, be sure to take time to reflect on your personal and professional role and your beliefs regarding those who are different. Agents of social change have an awareness of personal views and biases with a desire to become more multiculturally competent (Griffin & Steen, 2011). Hayes, Dean, and Chang (2007) revealed that although counselor education students endorsed beliefs surrounding advocacy, identifying advocacy strategies was more difficult. Community asset mapping and grant writing may be considered as methods for resource identification and collaboration.

Community Asset Mapping. Asset mapping is a tool for identifying community resources. Needs assessments are often used to identify issues within the school and community, yet an unfortunate outcome of these tools is that when problems or needs are identified, there could be a perception that the community has numerous inadequacies. Instead, asset mapping is an optimistic strategy that refocuses from a deficit view to one in which individual, organizational, and institutional resources and talents that exist in the community are identified. This is a large task that cannot be undertaken by a single individual, but rather one in which the school counselor, advisory board, and community members can partner to identify and locate assets. Table 11.2 is an example of a community/school asset map.

Table 11.2   Community Asset Chart

Individual	*Institutional*	*Governmental*
Skills	Churches	State/City/Local government
Talents	Colleges and universities	Federal government agencies
Experiences	Elderly care facilities	Bureau of Land Management
Professional	Police/Fire department	Economic development
Personal	Hospitals and clinics	Military facilities
Resources	Mental health facilites	Small Business
Leadership	Libraries	Administration
Networks	Schools	State education agency
	Transportation	Telecommunications
Organizational	*Physical/Land*	*Culture*
Small and large businesses	Utility companies	Historic/Arts council groups
Citizen groups/Clubs	Parks and recreational facilities	Council for cultural affairs
Community centers	Real estate agencies	Tourism
Home-based enterprises	Waste management facilities	City council
Radio/TV stations	Chamber of Commerce	Museums
Nonprofit organizations		

Source: Retrieved from U.S. Department of Housing and Urban Development Office of Multifamily Housing Programs. http://portal.hud.gov/hudportal/HUD?src=/program_offices/housing/hsgmulti

Note: HUD uses the term "Churches" to refer to religious institutions of all kinds.

CONCEPTUAL APPLICATION ACTIVITY 11.2
With a partner, choose one of the areas identified in the community map and begin to identify the various resources in your community. Bring your list to class and share the assets you have identified, and as a group add other potential assets of which group members may be aware. Be sure to include names, phone numbers, websites, and so on to this list. This will serve as a beginning list of resources that you could use when you begin your career as a school counselor.

If community asset mapping is not an option, collecting a list of community agencies, resources, and individuals, and annually revising the list is a valuable resource for making referrals and connecting students and their families with essential sources of help.

Grant Writing. Writing grants to obtain needed resources for students provides visibility, generates needed materials for resources, and promotes advocacy for the profession. School counseling programs rarely have a budget, and monies for supplies and materials are often at the discretion of the school board. You may want to check out organizations such as the PTA for funding, and with a cogent proposal that includes objectives and projected outcomes, monies may be obtained to meet program goals. Grant writing also has the potential to generate even greater resources and publicity.

Public and private funds available through federal and state government and local agencies are primary sources for grant money. These resources include organizations such as foundations, philanthropic organizations, voluntary agencies, and community groups. A guide to funding resources can be found at http://www.nal.usda.gov/ric/ricpubs/fundguide.html#fdatabase

Various funding agencies have different requirements to procure available money, but the first step is to look for a Request for Proposal (RFP) that lists the necessary grant requirements. Generally, the following information is required: a) summary or abstract, b) introduction, c) problem statement, d) objectives, e) method, f) evaluation, and g) budget for project consideration. Table 11.3 defines the various proposal components

Table 11.3   Elements of Grant Writing

Abstract	This is a one-page summary of the grant proposal. The RFP usually specifies the length of the abstract.

Introduction	The reader is given background information about the individuals carrying out the project, the demographics of the school and community, and the purpose of the project. The larger the numbers of individuals impacted by the project, the more it helps in having the proposal selected over others that are submitted. Also, providing information about local and national trends helps convince the grant reviewers that this project is worthy of consideration.
Problem Statement	The grant writer provides a persuasive rationale for the project. Rational, factual, and logical information that gives evidence of the need for the monies is more convincing than applications based on emotional or political appeals.
Objectives	Objectives, sometimes called *aims*, *goals*, or *purposes*, are measurable and tied to evaluation. They are written using action-oriented verbs such as "demonstrate," "identify," or "define."
Methodology	The grant reviewer wants to know who will be implementing the project, who will be impacted, what will happen, when it will occur, and where it will be conducted. Since this is the most carefully read part of the grant, it should be written logically, with all professional jargon carefully explained. More likely than not, someone outside of your profession, with limited knowledge of professional terms, will be reading this proposal.
Evaluation	Both formative (assessment during the project) and summative evaluation (assessment after the completion of the project) are addressed. Include who will be evaluating the project and the types of data that will be collected. The program objectives serve as the basis of the evaluation.
Budget	The budget is often considered as a monetary basis of the project. Considerations include: a) salary for personnel, if needed; b) fringe benefits; c) travel expenses; and d) price of equipment, supplies, software, and so on, including model numbers.
Follow-up	Funders of the grant sometimes provide suggestions for obtaining the money. Or, if the grant is not funded, an explanation is usually provided giving the reason for not funding the grant. These suggestions provide helpful feedback in that you can rewrite and resubmit the proposal when the next Request for proposal (RFP) is announced.

Generally, reasons for not funding a grant proposal include:

- Failure to follow grant instructions (in some cases even a missing signature is a reason for not funding the proposal)
- Not addressing specific requests in the RFP such as staffing or organizational issues
- Use of excessive "flowery" language that is based on emotion rather than fact
- Lack of measurable objectives and evaluation procedures

CONCEPTUAL APPLICATION ACTIVITY 11.3

Talk with a school counselor about some of the resources that the school counseling program needs to benefit students in the school. Research funding options and assist in writing a grant to address the identified issue.

In addition to community mapping and grant writing, Griffin and Steen (2011) provide supplemental strategies for systemic change and advocacy:

- Develop an understanding of cultural differences between and within populations
- Brainstorm ideas to meet with stakeholders when and where needed. For example, if a parent/guardian is unable to come to the school, arrange to meet in their home or another place that is mutually agreeable (keeping personal safety in mind).
- Create strong partnerships in the community in which roles, services, and resources are understood. Many counselors complain about the rapid attrition of caseworkers that impair strong alliances. Find a person within a social service agency who will provide long-range services and develop a sustained relationship with students and their families.
- Engage in direct two-way conversations in which your role is clearly understood and in which your understanding of the roles of other community resources is evident. Too often social service workers do not understand our education and training, and we also misinterpret their role, which leads to collaboration misconceptions. For instance, when I was a practicing school counselor I was concerned about one of our students, who talked about coming to school with a loaded gun to "take out" some of the teachers whom he believed treated him poorly. He stated that when he was finished he was going to go home and "take care" of his father as well. I called the Department of Children's Services and tried to get in touch with his father. A woman from DCS arrived at the school within the hour and asked to speak with this young man. When she was finished interviewing him she asked to speak with his brother, who happened to be sitting outside the principal's office for disciplinary purposes. When she was finished interviewing both of the brothers, she announced she was leaving. I was surprised at her nonchalant demeanor and asked her about her plan of action. She replied, "Obviously, the student had been provoked," and she didn't feel she needed to take any action. I was alarmed at her casual approach to what I felt was something

that was an immediate and serious situation, particularly because I had been an experienced school counselor for about 15 years at the time this incident occurred. She, on the other hand, was a novice caseworker who had been on the job for less than four months. I believe that if we had the opportunity to collaborate on successfully resolving this situation that this young man would not have dropped out of school a few weeks later and would not have been arrested by the police for holding a girlfriend at gunpoint several months later. At this point, I needed to go a step further by engaging my advocacy skills to get this student the assistance that I felt we denied to him.

- Encourage students to join with peers experiencing similar issues and channel efforts to influence policy-makers (Green & McCollum, 2004) to support these organizations.
- School counselors can work with administrators and other decision-makers to address institutional racism and heterosexism (Green & McCollum, 2004).

THE T.R.A.I.N.E.R. ADVOCACY MODEL

The T.R.A.I.N.E.R. acronym is a 7-step advocacy training model that could also be used as a problem-solving paradigm to begin the advocacy process (Hof, et al., 2009), and to facilitate systemic change.

Targeting refers to identifying a particular issue that is negatively affecting an identified group. A needs assessment will identify issues, or priorities can be identified by looking at the school report card, disaggregating data, and determining students within a group who need assistance. For instance, if you notice a large number of students coming to see you due to bullying, you may want to address this issue at the individual level, or provide classroom guidance on pro-social behaviors using a team-teaching model. In identifying a problem, determine where the problem arises. Is it a student issue? Family? School? Environment? Too often we have a tendency to look at a problem stemming from the individual without identifying other possible sources or system interactions (Trusty & Brown, 2005).

Responding to an identified inadequacy involves looking at the student, system, or political levels. Data collection that clearly specifies the extent of the problem makes a stronger statement (e.g., 28% of students who are bullied are Freshmen).

Articulating involves planning the process to address the issue. It could mean looking at existing policies for the school board to reconsider, or it could mean selecting aspects of school rules or procedures that need revision.

Implementing creates an action plan in which the questions of "who" will implement the plan, "where" it will occur, "when" it will take place, and "how" the plan will be most effective through the use of data.

Networking results in partnership initiatives in which members of the school and community initiate personal action plans to address an issue. It could mean providing a district-wide program that is comprehensive and developmental to address the problem, and/or asking community members to volunteer time and expertise to address an issue such as bullying.

Evaluating the event(s) may include pre/post tests or looking at discipline referrals for bullying before the plan was put into effect and later after the plan was initiated. A follow-up report to the school board at a future date with community members who have volunteered time to the project will make the effort more visible.

Retargeting by reviewing the evaluation data helps to determine the next steps or plan revisions. This step includes connecting with stakeholders to evaluate how individual and systemic advocacy plans are meeting the targeted goal, and making revisions for the areas that were not as successful.

CONCEPTUAL APPLICATION ACTIVITY 11.4

If you are in your clinical experiences of practicum or internship, look at the school data and determine a need that could be addressed through an advocacy competency. Using the T.R.A.I.N.E.R. model, develop a plan to address this issue. If you are not yet assigned to a school, identify a school and look at the school report card to determine a need to address, and implement the T.R.A.I.N.E.R. model.

Initiating skills to systematically transform the school environment and community is one level of advocacy. Teaching students to self-advocate is another level of advocacy.

TEACHING SELF-ADVOCACY SKILLS

Learning to advocate for self is a vital life-long skill for individuals. Although self-advocacy and self-determinism are sometimes considered to be the same skill, others consider them as complementary skills (*Self-determination Resource Handbook*, 2001). Self-advocacy can be thought of as the ability to express and fulfill personal needs. On the other hand, self-determinism incorporates the attitudes and beliefs including self-esteem (how the individual feels about his/herself), self-efficacy (belief in ability to be successful), and determination (the amount of responsibility the student takes for his/her actions) (*Self-determination Resource Handbook*, 2001).

Attention to individual factors that contribute to resiliency promote self-assertiveness. For instance, students who view themselves from a deficit perspective can be encouraged to recognize personal strengths to promote personal growth, self-awareness, and empowerment. Primary skills for teaching self-determination include:

1. self-awareness, including strengths, needs, and interests
2. problem-solving and decision-making
3. goal-setting
4. communication skills

(*Self-determination Resource Handbook*, 2001)

In addition, self-awareness and connections with others can be learned through role-playing in which suitable skills are viewed and practiced. In a study by Mishna, Muskat, Farnia, and Wiener (2011), sixth- and seventh-grade students who were diagnosed with a learning disability participated in a group intervention designed to teach self-advocacy. Group members were taught to recognize personal strengths, as well as understand strategies for completing school work, deal with bullies, ask for help with school work, learn to relax, and solve problems. The results of this study indicated a significant improvement in self-advocacy skills among group members. Student Activity 11.1 *My Personal Sketch* is an example of a self-advocacy strategy to use with students.

STUDENT ACTIVITY 11.1. MY PERSONAL SKETCH

Ask students to complete the sentences below.

One of the things I enjoy doing is. . . . .

A long-term goal that I want to accomplish in the next 3 years is. . . . .

One of my skills is. . . . .

One of the helpful strategies I use to solve problems is. . . . .

One of the barriers that stands in the way of getting what I want is. . . . .

One of my biggest concerns is. . . . .

Three people I trust who can help me are. . . . .

Two things I am going to do to reach my goals are. . . . .

After the students have completed this exercise, take the time to collaboratively establish steps students could take during the week to begin the process of reaching the established goal.

As schools represent the diversity of our society, a greater need exists for school counselors to be social justice advocates and collaborate with others to lead school transformation (Curry & DeVoss, 2009). Because leadership has not been a skill that counselor education programs have traditionally emphasized, novice school counselors often lack a clear understanding of how they can serve as leaders to impact change in an already existing structure (Mason, 2011). The next section of this chapter focuses on leadership within a Comprehensive Developmental School Counselor (CDSC) program.

CACREP THE SCHOOL COUNSELOR AS A SCHOOL LEADER

CONCEPTUAL APPLICATION ACTIVITY 11.5

Think of times in which you have observed someone in a leadership position. What were some of the qualities that this leader possessed that you felt made this person effective as a leader? Share your list of characteristics with a peer and discuss similarities and differences between the lists.

Much has been written about leadership styles (Kaslow, Falender, & Grus, 2012; Knutson, Miranda, & Washell, 2005) and how leadership qualities influence the learning environment. When a school environment or program is undergoing change, a competent leader demonstrates social skills that have the power to mobilize and energize others. Transformational leaders bring about change and benefit the learning community through behaviors such as empathy, helping, sharing, confidence in others, and an ability to admit mistakes (Kaplan, 1991, as cited in Knutson, et al., 2005). Through these leadership characteristics others are focused on achieving a common goal (Kaslow, et al., 2012).

A study that examined school counselor leadership identified five leadership characteristics that were positively related to successful school counseling programs. These attributes included: 1) resourceful problem-solving to obtain needed resources and initiate services; 2) systemic collaboration or engaging stakeholders in accomplishing goals; 3) interpersonal influence in which others are motivated to support program initiatives; 4) social justice advocacy in which the counselor takes risks to respond to inequities; and 5) professional efficacy in which the school counselor is confident in personal abilities to bring about change (Young, 2013).

CONCEPTUAL APPLICATION ACTIVITY 11.6

Read the following list of characteristics and making an honest appraisal of yourself, put a check next to the areas that you feel match your personal qualities as a leader. For the areas that you did not mark, what are some of the strategies you could use to improve these areas? Discuss your responses with your classmates.

I am able to:

_____   use multiple strategies and resources for problem-solving

_____   build partnerships and engage multiple stakeholders

_____   navigate through the politics of systems

_____   advocate for equitable services for all students

_____   excel in the use of appropriate accountability techniques to confront the current status quo

_____   motivate colleagues to reach an agreement

_____   identify and reach goals with self-assurance

_____   exceed expectations when completing tasks

_____   acquire a leadership frame of mind

Adapted from Young (2013)

The ASCA recognizes "leadership skills [as] critical to the implementation of a comprehensive, developmental school counselor program that influences systemic change and advocacy for every student" (Bowers, 2004, para. 5). In addition, the *Transforming School Counseling Initiative* acknowledges and promotes leadership as a practice for engaging in equity and advocacy enterprises. Leadership also entails learning about the cultures integral to the community and taking opportunities to meet leaders of the various cultural groups to engage leadership skills and connect the school personnel with the community (Stephens & Lindsey, 2011).

Leadership in schools is often viewed as the sole responsibility of administrators; however, other school personnel also display leadership characteristics. For instance, school counselors serve as leaders of a CDSC program and assist in building a school culture based on an awareness of diversity and school/family/community partnerships (Wingfield, Reese, & West-Olatunji, 2010). Unfortunately, many school administrators do not consider school counselors as being in a decision-making position within the school milieu, which limits the school counselor's ability to effect change.

The School Administrator and School Counselor

When school counselors make decisions within the context of their responsibilities, tension and animosity could occur between the principal and the school counselor. Principals have the authority to shape the professional identity of school counselors, especially when there are no other school counselor colleagues in the building (Armstrong, et al., 2010) to aid in supporting ASCA's philosophy and vision. Principals hold power over school counselors in regard to performance evaluations, and in these situations the school counselor's voice could be silenced, with some school counselors reluctant to express their own views and required to operate according to the belief system of the principal.

Principals often determine their knowledge of the school counselor's role based on their own experiences during K–12 school, a lecture or course about school counseling, or contact with a school counselor professional. These experiences sometimes result in principals assigning quasi-administrative or clerical tasks to school counselors that do not mirror the education and training of the school counselor. Although both of these professionals value student achievement, each has a different approach for reaching this goal.

School counselors are trained in counseling, consultation, collaboration, and advocacy with ASCA guidelines that suggest that 80% of their time be spent in direct service. Yet many school counselors' contracts read that the school counselor is to do "any and all tasks assigned by the principal," which often prevents school counselors from performing tasks necessary for a CDSC program.

Historically, many school counselors adopted a "nice counselor syndrome" and engaged in tasks that were assigned just to maintain a harmonious relationship. When the principal and school counselor engage in an honest, open dialogue about responsibilities and exchange important information, principals are more likely able to listen to the school counselor's perspective and make decisions that positively impact this professional (Clemens, Milsom, & Cashwell, 2009). When a positive relationship exists, school counselors are better able to define their role, how they contribute to the growth of students, work in a setting that matches their training and education, and are less likely to seek employment elsewhere (Clemens, et al., 2009). Some of the factors that contribute to this strong relationship include eliciting the trust and respect of the principal by utilizing active listening skills, and serving on school teams such as advisory committees.

Positive relationships occur when engaging in conversations with the principal regarding troublesome situations, such as a visit from an angry parent. Through these meetings the principal can stay informed about situations that school counselors confront on a daily basis.

Armstrong, et al. (2010) investigated the perceptions of school counselors and principals regarding relationships, leadership, and professional preparation.

The results of this study revealed that perceptual differences were greater between secondary school counselors and principals than those between elementary school counselors and principals. This study was supported by Dodson (2009), who revealed that secondary school counselors perceived their relationship with their principal much more negatively than did elementary school counselors. Furthermore, principals working with school counselors who have not implemented the ASCA National Model expressed more confusion about the roles of high school counselors, with views that did not match the roles and tasks reported by their high school counselors (Carnes-Holt, Range, & Cisler, 2012).

In a separate study, Dollarhide, Smith, and Lemberger (2007) found principals appreciated the role of school counselors when they added value to the school system through competence, trustworthiness, and respect. Administrators in this study indicated that they were able to provide greater support when school counselors were able to broaden their vision of the educational process by supporting the school mission, working for changes in the school climate, and/or serving as resources to parents and teachers.

In a study by Mason and McMahon (2009, as cited in Wingfield, et al., 2010), more experienced school counselors with longevity in their schools reported engaging in more leadership practices than did their less experienced peers. This trend may be due to the evolution of leadership skills as a continuing process, or that the principal is more willing to partner with a more accomplished, seasoned school counselor. As an emerging school counselor, this finding may be discouraging, yet as a student you have the advantage of being exposed to the innovative trends in the profession, and you bring new ideas to the practice of school counseling. Advocating for students or programs will seem easier once you have had an opportunity to learn about the school structure and have demonstrated how your role as a change agent will be beneficial to them.

Leadership Strategies

Leadership involves educating and mobilizing others to support student growth and achievement. Teachers and other stakeholders will be more likely to work with school counselors when they observe administrators interacting with and affirming the role of the school counselor. Educating others about myths surrounding homelessness, LGBTQ students, or those with special needs is a form of advocacy through leadership; however, not all stakeholders will agree with school counselors who advocate for marginalized students.

Recognizing emotional reactions to change and addressing these responses will ease the transformation process, particularly when school personnel believe changes are thrust upon them with little input and they are required to engage in additional activities (Seo, et al., 2010). When a positive vision is portrayed as to how the school counselor is able to contribute to reaching school-wide goals through collaborative activities, the school counselor's leadership will more likely be recognized (Wingfield, et al., 2010). This momentum may be facilitated when copious notes are kept that reflect where time is spent on tasks, and data are available that inform how student growth improved.

In another study by Mason (2011), school counselors' perceptions of the relationship between leadership practices and the school counseling program were investigated. The results of this study revealed that school counselors who employed more leadership practices also had greater success in CDSC program implementation. When participants were asked about the practices that enhanced their leadership role, responses included following through on commitments and responsibilities, treating others with respect and dignity, and developing a cooperative relationship with others. When school counselors follow through on what they say they are going to do, others view them as being reliable and tend to seek out their expertise. Naturally, the opposite situation is also the case. A school counselor employed in a local school was responsible for such tasks as finding scholarships, writing recommendations, and assisting students with post-secondary options. When parents called her office and did not receive a return phone call or e-mail, or when letters of recommendation for scholarships or college admission materials were not submitted in a timely manner, she eventually lost her job. She wasn't seen as a responsible person with the needs of the student as a priority, nor did they feel they could work collaboratively with her.

CONCLUSION

Advocacy for marginalized students and their families promotes program awareness. Advocacy is a central competency that is part of our professional history, and is even more essential today with the diversity that is seen in our student body. When students are oppressed, lowered academic achievement and dropping out of school are often outcomes.

School counselors have the skills to advocate for social justice, with a responsibility to work with individuals from any and every background to obtain the resources that are needed. Community asset mapping is one strategy for identifying and mobilizing community strengths. Procuring needed resources or monies through grant writing is another type of advocacy that has the potential to benefit school-age youth and their families. The T.R.A.I.N.E.R. acronym can be utilized as a problem-solving advocacy model for school counselors as they strive to close the achievement gap while teaching advocacy skills to students. Self-advocacy and self-determinism are both means of achieving these goals, with self-advocacy being viewed as one's ability to express and meet personal needs, while self-determinism involves having the attitudes and beliefs to meet these needs.

Leadership requires transforming a traditional program into one that is comprehensive and developmental, while attending to the negative emotions and thoughts that accompany any change. As school counseling program leaders, we have a responsibility to build a respectful learning culture while educating our stakeholders about our training and education so support for our profession—and most importantly the students and families we work with—will increase.

REFERENCES

American School Counselor Association (2010). *Ethical standards for school counselors.* Retrieved from http://www.schoolcounselor.org/

Armstrong, S. A., MacDonald, J. H., & Stillo, S. (2010). School counselors and principals: Different perceptions of relationship, leadership, and training. *Journal of School Counseling.* Retrieved from ERIC database. (EJ885153).

Bowers, J. (2004). The power of "one vision, one voice." *ASCA School Counselor.* Retrieved from http://schoolcounselor.org/article.asp?article=716&paper=91&cat=139

Carnes-Holt, K., Range, B., & Cisler, A. (2012). *Teaching about the principal and school counselor relationship: ELCC2.1A.* Retrieved from Http://cnx.org/content/m43541/1.3/

Cattaneo, L. B., & Chapman, A. R. (2010). The process of empowerment: A model for use in research and practice. *American Psychologist, 65,* 646–659.

Clemons, E. V., Milsom, A., & Cashwell, C. S. (2009). Using leader-member exchange theory to examine principal-school counselor relationships, school counselors' roles, job satisfaction, and turnover intentions. *Professional School Counseling, 13,* 75–85.

Curry, J. R., & DeVoss, J. A. (2009). Introduction to special issue: The school counselor as leader. *Professional School Counseling, 13,* 64–67.

Dodson, T. (2009). Advocacy and impact: A comparison of administrators' perceptions of the high school counselor role. *Professional School Counseling, 12,* 480–488.

Dollarhide, C. T., Smith, A. T., & Lemberger, M. E. (2007). Critical incidents in the development of supportive principals: Facilitating school counselor-principal relationships. *Professional School Counseling, 10,* 360–369.

Education Trust (2009). *A new vision for school counseling.* Retrieved from http://www.edtrust.org/dc/tsc/vision

Gonzalez, D. (2013, August 13). A year later, immigrants face DREAM act's limits. Retrieved from http://www.usatoday.com/story/news/nation/2013/08/13/a-year-later-immigrants-face-deferred-action-programs-limits/2651235/

Gonzalez, R. G., & Terriquez, V. (2013, August, 13). *How DACA is impacting the lives of those who are now DACAmented.* Retrieved from http://www.immigrationpolicy.org/issues/DREAM-Act

Green, E. J., & McCollum, V. J. (2004, Sept.–Oct.). Empowerment through compassion. *ASCA School Counselor.* Alexandria, VA: American School Counselor Association.

Greenleaf, A. T. & Williams, J. M. (2009). Supporting social justice advocacy: A paradigm shift towards an ecological perspective. *Journal for Social Action in Counseling and Psychology, 2,* 1–28.

Griffin, D., & Steen, S. (2011). A social justice approach to school counseling. *Journal for Social Action in Counseling and Psychology, 3,* 74–85.

Hayes, D., Dean, J., & Chang, C. (2007). Addressing privilege and oppression in counselor training and practice: A qualitative analysis. *Journal of Counseling & Development, 88,* 259–268.

Hof, D. D., Dinsmore, Barber, S., & Suhr, R. (2009). Advocacy: The T.R.A.I.N.E.R. model. *Journal for Social Action in Counseling and Psychology, 2,* 15–28.

Kaslow, N. J., Falender, C. A., & Grus, C. L. (2012). Valuing and practicing competency-based supervision: A transformational leadership perspective. *Training and Education in Professional Psychology, 6,* 47–54.

Kennedy, A. (2008, Sept.). From immigrant to advocate. *Counseling Today* (48-50). Alexandria, VA: American Counseling Association.

King, J. H. (2011, Sept.). Three paradoxes of the counseling social justice movement. *Counseling Today* (46–47). Alexandria, VA: American Counseling Association.

Knutson, K. A., Miranda, A. O., & Washell, C. (2005). The connection between school culture and leadership social interest in learning organizations. *Journal of Individual Psychology, 61,* 25–36.

Lewis, J. A., Ratts, M. J., Paladino, D. A., & Toporek, R. L. (2011). Social justice counseling and advocacy: Developing new leadership roles and competencies. *Journal for Social Action in Counseling and Psychology, 3,* 5–16.

Locke, D. C. & Bailey, D. F. (2014). *Increasing multicultural understanding* (3rd ed.)*.* Los Angeles, CA: Sage.

Marbley, A. F., Malott, K. M., Flaherty, A., & Frederick, H. (2011). Three issues, three approaches, three calls to action: Multicultural social justice in the schools. *Journal for Social Action in Counseling and Psychology, 3,* 59–73.

Mason, E. (2011). Leadership practices of school counselors and counseling program implementation. *NASSP Bulletin, 94,* 274–285. doi:10.1177/0192636510395012

Mishna, F., Muskat, B., Farnia, F., & Wiener, J. (2011). The effects of a school-based program on the reported self-advocacy knowledge of students with learning disabilities. *Alberta Journal of Educational Research, 57,* 185–203.

Murray, C. E., Pope, A. L., & Rowell, P. C. (2010). Promoting counseling students' advocacy competencies through service-learning. *Journal for Social Action in Counseling and Psychology, 2,* 29–47.

Self-determination Resource Handbook (2001). A resource guide for teaching and facilitation transition and self-advocacy skills. Oregon Department of Education. Retrieved from http://www.ltschools.org/files/www/file/self-advocacy%20ResourceHandbook.pdf

Seo, M. G., Yaylor, M. S., Hill, N. S., Zhang, X., Tesluk, P. E., & Lorinkova, N. M. (2010). The role of affect and leadership during organizational change. *Personnel Psychology, 65,* 121–165.

Shallcross, L. (2010, June). Counselors taking a stand. *Counseling Today* (28-35). Alexandria, VA: ACA.

Stephens, D. L., & Lindsey, R. B. (2011). *Culturally proficient collaboration.* Thousand Oaks, CA: Corwin.

Trusty, J., & Brown, D. (2005). Advocacy competencies for professional school counselors. *Professional School Counseling, 8,* 259–265.

Wingfield, R. J., Reese, R. F., & West-Olatunji, C.A. (2010). Counselors as leaders in schools. *Florida Journal of Educational Administration & Policy, 4,* 114–128.

Young, A. (2013, July/August). Building-level leadership. *ASCA School Counselor, 50,* 35–40.

Zalaquett, C. P. (2011). Social justice counseling and advocacy: Developing new leadership roles and competencies. *Journal for Social Action in Counseling and Psychology, 3,* 5–16.

Chapter 12

THE SCHOOL COUNSELOR AS CONSULTANT AND COLLABORATOR

*CACREP STANDARD

FOUNDATIONS

A. *Knowledge*

   3. Knows roles, functions, settings, and professional identity of the school counselor in relation to the roles of other professional and support personnel in the school.

DIVERSITY AND ADVOCACY

F. *Skills and Practices*

   4. Engages parents, guardians, and families to promote the academic, career, and personal/social development of students.

ASSESSMENT

H. *Skills and Practices*

   4. Makes appropriate referrals to school and/or community resources.

COLLABORATION AND CONSULTATION

M. *Knowledge*

   I. Understands the ways in which student development, well-being, and learning are enhanced by family-school-community collaboration.

CACREP

4. Understands systems theories, models, and processes of consultation in school system settings.

5. Knows strategies and methods for working with parents, guardians, families, and communities to empower them to act on behalf of their children.

N. *Skills and Practices*

2. Locates resources in the community that can be used in the school to improve student achievement and success.

3. Consults with teachers, staff, and community-based organizations to promote student academic, career, and personal/social development.

5. Uses referral procedures with helping agents in the community (e.g., mental health centers, businesses, service groups) to secure assistance for students and their families.

LEADERSHIP

P. *Skills and Practices*

2. Plans and presents school-counseling-related educational programs for use with parents and teachers (e.g., parent education programs, materials used in classroom guidance and advisor/advisee programs for teachers).

Mr. Scherger and Mrs. McCarthy would like to implement peer-tutoring after school and they would like you, as the school counselor, to assist in developing this program.

Mr. Alvarez came to see you, the school counselor, because his 12-year-old granddaughter whom he and his wife are raising, has been acting defiant and secretive.

Betsy's father was just deployed for combat overseas. She frequently throws temper tantrums in class and refuses to do her homework. Teachers look to you for help.

Issues such as these require harmonious, working relationships so students can be the recipients of resources that will assist in academic, career, and personal/social growth. The ASCA ethical standards state: "[school counselors] recognize that teachers, staff and administrators . . . can be powerful allies in supporting student success. School counselors work to develop relationships with all faculty and staff in order to advantage students" (ASCA Ethical Standards, 2010 C.1). Yet, with the current trends promoting academic development, personal and career growth are often discounted (Van Veisor, 2009) and viewed as being less important within the school arena. With No Child Left Behind (NCLB) serving as a catalyst to the emphasis on academic achievement as measured through standardized tests, school counselors struggle to convince others of the interconnections between personal well-being, career development, and academic growth. This view is particularly evident due to the belief that a focus on areas other than academics will detract from learning (Van Veisor, 2009).

School counselors can quell these concerns and act as collaborators as well as consultants to transform this perception by demonstrating how these domains work in tandem to promote the growth of students (Pérusse & Goodnough, 2005). For instance, the reading and math achievement scores among fifth-, sixth-, eighth-, and ninth-grade students who participated in a school counselor-led Student Success Skills (SSS) program were compared to their peers who did not participate in the program. This program highlighted cognitive, social, and self-management skills in both classroom guidance and small groups. At the end of the intervention, math scores were significantly improved among members of the SSS program compared with the nonparticipants (Brigman, Webb, & Campbell, 2010). In another study, a school counselor conducted a group of African American students who were not achieving on the Georgia High School Graduation Tests at the same rates as their white peers. The school counselor conducted an eight-week group intervention that included the topics of student success, test-taking strategies, school culture, stereotypes, goal setting, interpersonal relations, and conflict resolution. Results indicated enhanced test performance at the group conclusion (Bruce, Getch, & Ziomek-Daigle, 2009).

When school counselors were asked to list tasks that they considered most essential to their role, collaboration between families and communities was ranked as a top school counselor priority (Cook & Friend, 2010). Yet, some school counselors report discomfort in initiating these processes due to concern about disrupting relationships with colleagues and the variations in role expectations (Cook & Friend, 2010).

CONCEPTUAL APPLICATION ACTIVITY 12.1

Although school counselors' duties are different from teachers, we are considered as equal partners in the educational role. What are some of the ways you could work with teachers to promote consultation and collaboration?

Collaboration and consultation are often perceived as interchangeable processes, and although they share commonalities there are also differences (Kampwirth, 2006). Interacting with others to address a problem, sharing ideas, encouraging change, and solving problems are some of the mutual factors in collaboration and consultation. Collaboration is also considered as a particular type of consultation model that is chosen to reach mutual goals (Kampwirth, 2006).

CONSULTATION

Consultation is an interpersonal relationship in which school counselors help stakeholders attend to the academic, career, and personal/social needs of students (Gysbers & Henderson, 2012). It is possible that the consultant may never have contact with the student, particularly if the teacher (or consultee) implements and evaluates the plan—a major difference between consultation and collaboration. There are five models of consultation that you may choose, depending on the people involved and the context. These include Prescription, Provision, Initiation, Collaboration, and Mediation.

MODELS OF CONSULTATION

Prescription

This model is used when a consultee (e.g., a teacher) asks a consultant (the school counselor) to assist with a problem that he/she is having with a third individual (usually a student). Using this model, the consultant would gather as much information about the problem from the perspective of the teacher or other consultee. The consultant could even choose to observe the student in multiple settings, and/or obtain additional information to understand the student better. For instance, the student's permanent school record provides sources of information as could the logs from the school nurse, social worker, or teacher. After information gathering, the consultant develops a plan for the consultee to implement (Baker, et al., 2009). This model is illustrated in Figure 12.1

CONCEPTUAL APPLICATION ACTIVITY 12.2

Brainstorm some common issues in which you would use this prescriptive consultation approach. What are some of the skills that you would consider in these cases? Discuss your thoughts with your classmates.

Figure 12.1   Prescription Consultation Model

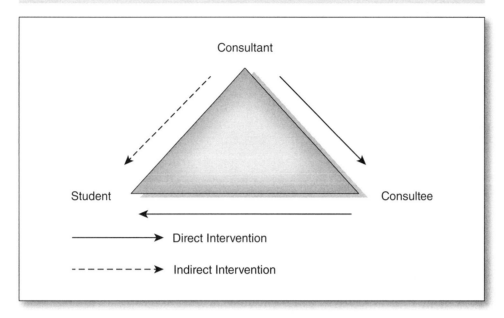

Provision

For a variety of reasons, there may be situations in which a consultee may not want to be responsible for implementing or evaluating a plan. The teacher (or other consultee) may feel that he/she doesn't have the skills that are needed to solve the problem and would feel more comfortable when a third-party, such as the counselor, provides the intervention (Baker, et al., 2009). If this is the case, it is important that the teacher's perceptions are validated. For instance, a teacher may feel uncomfortable talking with his/her class about the death of a student, and in this incident the school counselor consultant would express understanding regarding the teacher's fears and agree to come to the classroom to talk with the students about grief, signs and symptoms of sorrow, address student concerns, and answer questions. Figure 12.2 illustrates this model

CONCEPTUAL APPLICATION ACTIVITY 12.3

What are some of the issues in which a provision consultation model would be the best approach? Discuss your ideas with your classmates.

Figure 12.2 Provision Consultation Model

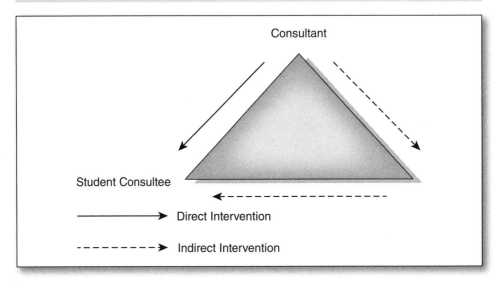

Initiation

This model would be implemented if someone needed support and assistance in order to properly fulfill responsibilities. For instance, if a teacher is having specified difficulties that the consultant has the skills to address, the consultant could teach concepts or skills that the teacher lacks. Classroom management, for example, is often a problem for novice teachers, and if students are complaining about a chaotic classroom environment, the school counselor could initiate consultation by sharing and/or demonstrating classroom management strategies with the teacher (Baker, et al., 2009). If this is the model the counselor chooses to use, it is possible that the teacher may feel threatened by the counselor's presence and resist the intervention. Reassurance with support and understanding could defuse this situation and create a more amiable relationship. For instance, the counselor-consultant could say, "I am sure that you have probably already thought about this . . . ," acknowledging efforts that may already have been tried. Or, "This may be difficult to try, but . . ." reassures that the counselor/consultant is available to help rather than criticize (Bostic, 2002). See Figure 12.3 as an example of this model.

CONCEPTUAL APPLICATION ACTIVITY 12.4

What are some common issues in which school counselors would initiate the consultation? Discuss your thoughts with those of your peers.

Figure 12.3   Initiation Consultation Model

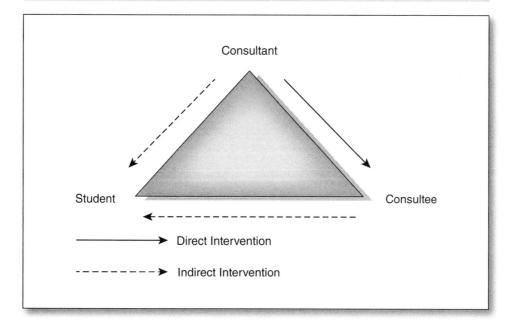

Collaboration

This type of model, sometimes referred to as collaborative-consultation (Kampwirth, 2006), is implemented when consultants and consultees partner to identify and mutually determine solutions to problems. For instance, if bullying is a school issue, school personnel may wish to partner with community members, parents, and other stakeholders to work on a solution (Baker, et al., 2009). If parties are unable to work together, it is possible that there are fears and biases that are impeding a strong relationship, and unless the underlying cause is discussed, unexpressed attitudes could lead to irrational behaviors (Bostic, 2002). See Figure 12.4 as an example of a collaborative consultation model.

CONCEPTUAL APPLICATION ACTIVITY 12.5

No single helping professional is able to address all of the issues that are evident in the school setting. What are some of the issues in which a collaborative consultative approach would be used? Discuss your thoughts with your classmates.

Figure 12.4   Collaborative Consultation Model

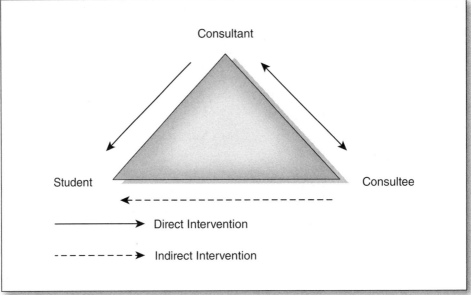

Mediation

At times there are individuals who have difficulty resolving issues among themselves. In this case, the counselor could serve as a mediator through communication and compromise (Baker, et al., 2009). For instance, if a parent and teacher are disagreeing about a child's grade, the counselor could serve as a mediator between the parent and teacher, with the goal of listening to and discussing each other's perspective and helping them reach an agreement. An acceptable compromise may be reached through active listening skills and clarifying unrealistic expectations, while focusing on common goals (Bostic, 2002) through brainstorming. See Figure 12.5 as an example of a mediation consultation model.

CONCEPTUAL APPLICATION ACTIVITY 12.6

What are some of the issues that could create conflict between stakeholders in a school setting? What skills would you need to consider if you are using this type of consultation? Discuss your responses with those of your peers.

Figure 12.5 Mediation Consultation Model

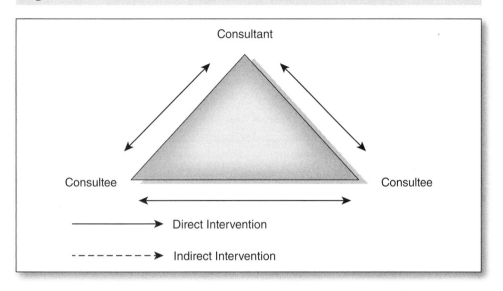

Photo 12.1 Collaborative Consultation Among Colleagues

Source: © track5/iStockphoto.com

CONSULTATION STRATEGIES TO BRING ABOUT CHANGE

CACREP

Teachers or other consultees ask for assistance when they have made attempts to solve a problem without success. It could be that they are "stuck" because of a distorted view of the problem, or perhaps they view the student based on a label such as learning disabled, or it is also possible they are too close to the issue (Hylander, 2012). Change occurs when the consultee is able to perceive the problem from a different lens. The counselor/consultee is able to facilitate this shift in thinking by assuming various positional stances (Hylander, 2012) that range from approach, neutral, to moving away.

When the counselor/consultant uses an *approach mode,* basic counseling skills such as active listening, paraphrasing, and reflecting offer an opportunity for the consultee to vent while sharing his/her affective, cognitive, and behavioral perceptions of the issue. These counseling skills facilitate a supportive, respectful position in which the consultee feels heard. The consultant assumes a *neutral* stance to give structure and focus by confirming what is heard, both positively and negatively. This stance is assisted by asking questions such as, "How long has the problem been going on?" or, "How have others been affected by this problem?" From here, the counselor/consultant is able to describe his/her understanding of the consultee's view of the problem and is able to challenge this perspective by *moving away* from a neutral position to one that challenges the view by offering an alternative explanation. This confrontation may create discomfort, particularly if the consultee does not feel enough time was given to discuss the issue. Therefore, timing in an arena of respect can pave the way for a shift in thinking. Questions such as "What would you have done if a different student had done this?" could facilitate a perception shift and a new view of the problem.

Figure 12.6 depicts the various consultant stances assumed to facilitate the consultees' perceptual change of the problem.

Consultation involves interrelated tasks and interlinked stages with specific tasks that are revisited as the process unfolds. Regardless of the type of consultation that is chosen, attention to a trusting, open relationship in an inviting environment is a requirement for successful consultation.

STAGES OF THE CONSULTATION PROCESS

Stage 1. Specify Responsibilities

Establishing rapport and identifying responsibilities of the consultant and consultee prevents disappointment when the process is not clearly defined. Who,

Figure 12.6 Consultative Modes of Interaction

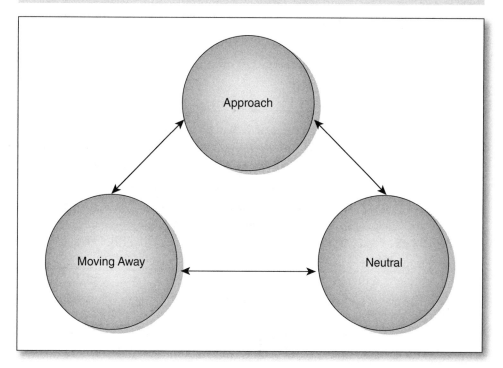

what, where, when, and how questions are addressed at this stage to clearly outline expectations and responsibilities.

As a consultant you would be interested in knowing:

- What is the issue?
- What results are expected?
- How did the problem start?
- Who is involved in the problem?
- Is the client (e.g., student) concerned about this problem?

Consultees will want to know answers to the following questions:

- Who will be involved in this process?
- What do I have to do?
- What happens if I don't participate?
- Why am I here?
- How will this benefit me?
- When will this consultation process occur? How long will it last?

The consultation process will have a greater chance for success when the process is explained, time is taken to develop rapport, and questions are clearly answered. At times it may be necessary to revisit this stage to clarify roles and expectations, particularly if anxiety, hostility, or uncertainty are evident between individuals.

Stage 2: Define and Clarify the Problem

When a problem is not clearly identified, chaos could be an outcome with the potential for unresolved issues. The desired goal should be written in an observable, measurable, objective format to gather data-driven assessment results. A global approach to identify all the influences that contribute to the problem (e.g., Brofenbrenner's Ecological Systems Model) promotes problem resolution. For instance, a teacher may be concerned about a student's poor grades and label this problem as a lack of motivation. If external forces are overlooked such as the child being homeless, his/her parents divorcing, a devastating loss, or substance abuse, the student will be shortchanged. In addition, there may be a medical condition that hasn't been considered. For instance, a parent was upset because teachers regularly called her due to her daughter's disruptive behaviors and poor grades. When she took her daughter to an eye doctor for a vision test, she realized that her daughter was not able to see clearly. Once the student received a pair of glasses, her behavior and grades immediately improved. In each situation, a wide array of influences and factors must be considered.

Stage 3. Brainstorm Strategies

When the consultant and consultee are permitted to brainstorm possible solutions, a wider range of diverse possibilities will emerge as potential resolutions. Part of the brainstorming technique is to generate, without judgment, as many interventions as possible regardless of how unusual or improbable they may seem. In fact, creativity and novelty are encouraged since solutions often appear when various suggestions are combined to form a viable alternative.

Stage 4. Choose Among Alternative Strategies

At this stage the "maximum benefit for the minimal effort" principle guides strategy choice. Since the consultee will likely be implementing the strategy as opposed to the consultant, it is the consultee who needs to choose and identify an acceptable course of action rather than deferring to the consultant's expertise.

Stage 5. Evaluation and Follow-up

At a date in the future, an evaluation of the consultation intervention will provide information as to what worked well and if any aspects of the plan need attention. In addition, the consultant should meet with all individuals who are involved to determine if other issues are to be considered or if additional follow-up is necessary.

CONCEPTUAL APPLICATION ACTIVITY 12.7

Tamika is a 17-year-old Hispanic female in her junior year of high school. Recently, her teachers have been concerned due to her poor grades and disruptive classroom behaviors. Prior to this time Tamika was a model student and received outstanding grades and accolades for her academic and athletic behaviors. You met with Tamika and she confided to you that school just doesn't seem to be worthwhile anymore because her parents are opposed to her going on to higher education. What type of consultation do you think would best meet Tamika's needs? What are some of the factors that need consideration?

Although each of these consultations is used in schools, the research on consultation effectiveness is weak. Traditionally, outcomes have been based on subjective data such as teacher attitudes rather than objective data such as improved student growth. Data-driven evidence is needed to more concretely demonstrate consultation effectiveness. Other consultant influences include:

- Establishing a comfortable atmosphere in which the consultee can express him- or herself without feeling as if there will be repercussions
- Communicating that you are working as a partner and that there are times that you will listen to the consultee to understand his/her perspective, and that the consultee will also need to listen to your point of view
- Scheduling a school-based consultation with teachers that lasts no more than 15–20 minutes at a time. Time is critical!
- Considering ongoing solutions. Data gathering and analyzing information assists in considering solutions.
- Immersing oneself in the consultee's world. Observations in the classroom, on the playground, or in the cafeteria provide a greater picture of the situation. In addition, the consultee will recognize that you are invested in the situation and interested in seeing the situation from his/her perspective.
- Following up after the consultation. Assess how well the plan is working. The first session is generally devoted to developing rapport, listening, and

learning more about the problem. Subsequent phases are allotted to devising strategies and constantly evaluating the process.

- Understanding the multiple pressures that confront the stakeholder in order to assess the barriers preventing problem resolution.

- Preparing ahead of time with research that clearly states authors, titles, dates, and so on. If you simply assert, "Research says . . . ," you may be viewed as being less credible, too "academic," and unwilling to invest in practical solutions.

- Providing practical suggestions. Using vague terms such as "use more structure" or "be more consistent" are not helpful. Instead, provide concrete strategies that can be used to be more consistent or structured.

- Using terms to which your audience can relate. Nothing is more aggravating than when words or examples are used that are outside the realm of the consultee's experience.

- Informing the consultees of your consultation plan so expectations are shared.

- Soliciting input. When others' views are not considered, investment in the process is low.

- Using counseling skills such as active listening, clarification, open-ended questions, paraphrasing, and so on.

- Dealing with individual concerns after the session.

- Using the expertise of other group members (Adapted from Kampwirth, 2006).

CONSULTATION WITH A MULTICULTURAL PERSPECTIVE

Successful consultants possess an awareness of cultural differences between themselves, the consultee, and student/client, a concept known as *cultural saliency* (Jackson & Hayes, 1993, as cited in Martines, 2008). A competent, multicultural consultant also has an awareness of his/her communication style and values, and acknowledges how these characteristics influence consultation. Such a consultant is able to assist others shift from tolerance to transformation that occurs on a continuum from *cultural destructiveness* to *cultural competence* (Stephens & Lindsey, 2011).

Cultural destructiveness encompasses actions and attitudes that range from compliance-based tolerance for diversity, in which all references to differences are rejected due to laws and policies, cultural incapacity or an indifference to diversity, to cultural blindness, in which diverse individuals are ignored (Stephens & Lindsey, 2011). Cultural competence is a process that moves from an awareness of what is not known about a diverse school setting, to advocating for the educational needs for all students (Stephens & Lindsey, 2011). This culturally proficient consultation model is an "inside-out" process in which the consultant willingly reflects on personal actions and how institutional policies and discriminatory attitudes influence school-age youth and their families. Success is also related to the consultant's cultural awareness and expectations for the consultation process.

An alternative five-stage cross-cultural consultation model created by Duncan (1995) is an "outside-in" approach, in which the consultee views the process from his/her beliefs and cultural perspective. This model includes the following stages:

- *The appraisal stage*—the ethnic minority consultee makes assumptions about the consultant based on first impressions
- *The investigative stage*—the consultee challenges the consultant's views and values
- *The involvement stage*—the consultee has a favorable impression of the consultant
- *The commitment stage*—occurs only if the consultant is sensitive to the consultee in the process
- *The engagement stage*—both the consultee and consultant work together, but only if cross-cultural concerns are considered

Similar to consultation, collaboration occurs on a continuum that ranges from individuals from two different professions discussing an issue, to the creation of a new structure when novice organizations or ideas merge. Collaboration has the potential to infuse excitement, optimism, and creativity into the organization (Conoley & Conoley, 1991).

COLLABORATION

CACREP

With the multiple influences impacting our school-age youth, no one professional can address all the issues presented by any single individual. Interdisciplinary collaboration is an interpersonal process in which various professionals meet to address problems (Bruner, 1991, as cited in Bronstein, 2002). Too often communication breaks down between school personnel, parents/guardians, and outside agencies when there is no systematic method for sharing information. The school counselor is in a central role to coordinate input and communicate issues among all stakeholders.

School counselors are vital members of the education team as they help all students in the areas of academic achievement, personal/social development, and career development to become productive, well-adjusted adults. As a team member, some of the professionals with whom you will collaborate include the school psychologist, school social worker, resource officer, school nurse, and administrator. A brief description of the role each plays in the school is summarized below.

PROFESSIONAL AND SUPPORT PERSONNEL IN SCHOOLS

School Psychologist

The National Association of School Psychologists (NASP) and division 16 of the American Psychological Association (APA) guide school psychologists. A master's degree is the minimum level of education that is needed to be a school psychologist. Similar to school counselors, school psychologists initially entered the educational setting to fulfill numerous educational needs (Braden, DiMarino-Linnen, & Good, 2001). When the first intelligence tests were developed, assessing children who were not making acceptable academic progress was a task assumed by school psychologists. As school administrators demanded services for students with special needs, this role became the benchmark of the school psychology profession, a role that has not been entirely accepted by school psychologists (Fagan, 1981). School psychologists receive training in testing and assessment, consultation and collaboration, interventions to support academics, interventions in mental health services, prevention and responsive services, diversity, and human growth and development. Although the school counselor and school psychologist professions emerged as a result of different societal needs with diverse philosophical positions, both of these professionals have similar education with training that overlaps (Rowley, 2000).

School Social Worker

A bachelor or master's degree is the minimum level of education to be a school social worker. The National Association of Social Workers is the regulating agency that standardizes the training and education of social workers. In the school setting these professionals serve as a liaison between the school, family, and community to locate needed resources. School social workers use a comprehensive approach that integrates primary prevention with evidence-based interventions to positively influence attendance, grades, and behaviors.

School Resource Officer

The National Association of School Resource Officers (NASRO) provides special training to school-based law enforcement officers to educate and protect the school community. Through partnerships with parents, students, school educators, and community police officers, school resource officers work to protect school-age youth. They serve on school safety teams to create and evaluate crisis intervention plans to promote a safe school environment. As a result of the 2012 shooting in Newtown, Connecticut, at Sandy Hook Elementary School where twenty children and six adults were killed, some individuals are requesting that more resource officers be placed in schools. Others are requesting that more school counselors be placed in schools to work on prevention and improved mental health.

School Nurse

The National Association of School Nurses, the professional organization for school nurses, is devoted to improving the education and requirements for school nurses to aid in enhancing the health and academic achievement of students (NASN, 2013). A bachelor's degree in nursing is recommended as the minimum requirement for beginning nurse practitioners. School nurses promote health and well-being and collaborate with others to promote an optimal life-style for the development and growth of all students. School nurses are excellent resources to learn about physical issues that could negatively impact school-age youth, as reflected in Case Study 12.1.

CASE STUDY 12.1

As an intermediate level school counselor, a fifth-grade girl came to my office to discuss her concerns about her fifth-grade friend, who was sexually active with a boy in the same grade. The sexually active girl was overweight with significant self-esteem issues, and she lived with her father while her mom was in prison. I realized that the school nurse would be helpful in providing support and information regarding the dangers of sexual activity, particularly at such a young age. I spoke to the school nurse and asked her if she would be willing to be present when I spoke with both the boy and the girl, and she agreed.

The boy was called to the office first and when he arrived he was visibly upset. He explained that his friends dared him to have sex at the local park with this young girl, and he did. After clarifying the type of sexual contact that occurred, the school nurse and I talked about the reality of this decision and the dangers of sexually transmitted

(Continued)

(Continued)

diseases, pregnancy, and so on. He agreed that he made a mistake and would not talk about this incident with his friends.

Next, the young girl came to the office, and instead of being humiliated or anxious, she giddily stated, "I know what you want to talk with me about." She described what happened and said that this was what love was all about. She stated that she envisioned having a baby as part of the romance, and that the boy would marry her and they would raise the child. Once again, we informed her of the dangers of sexual activity and she seemed to understand that having sex at this age was a poor decision. Next, we talked about her friends being aware of this situation, and we practiced responses she could make to students who asked her about the incident. Next, I called her father and I was surprised at the lack of surprise, concern, or disappointment. The father even went on to say, "Well, fifth-grade is a pretty tough age, you know." He responded as if he thought it was developmentally appropriate for a fifth-grade girl to have sex in the woods. I recognized the importance of having the school nurse available to support me in these conversations.

-Intermediate-grade school counselor

School Administrator

School administrators are the decision makers and leaders of the school faculty and staff; a role that includes supervision and evaluation while ensuring that resources are available to effectively work with students and their families. In addition, the administrator disciplines students, evaluates school data to determine progress toward goals, and communicates results. School leaders look for new ways to improve student learning and empower teachers to implement new strategies in teaching and learning. Principals are ultimately responsible for the continuous improvement of the school and creating a safe learning environment. They work to maintain a comfortable school environment, and in some cases this philosophy is incompatible with that of the school counselor, who may advocate for policy revisions for certain students who may be harmed by school rules.

The school counselor is not limited to work with the school professionals mentioned above. Teachers, bus drivers, secretaries, coaches, and school cooks are some of the other personnel who provide valuable information to school counselors. Communicating your role and educating the stakeholders with whom you work is crucial to a collaborative relationship, with the ultimate goal of supporting school-age youth. With the high student/counselor ratio that often exceeds the ASCA recommended ratio of 250/1, interprofessional teaming is a method in which multiple experts are able to work together to deliver more robust services than an individual, or a school or agency working alone is able to do.

Response to Intervention (RtI) is a collaborative strategy that was originally included in the Individuals with Disabilities Education Improvement Act (IDEIA) legislation, with the goal of accurately identifying and providing students with special needs the services they need. Today it is a comprehensive framework that brings concerned personnel together to identify any student who is having difficulty with academics, behavior, or social/emotional growth.

RESPONSE TO INTERVENTION

Response to Intervention (RtI) is a fluid continuum that integrates assessment, instruction, and intervention using a multi-tiered approach. A team of school personnel such as the school counselor, administrator, and teacher meet with parents/guardians to discuss academic and/or behavioral issues (Sabella & Clements, 2010). The purpose of this intervention is to reduce behavior problems while maximizing academic achievement. Therefore, students who are exhibiting poor academic achievement are identified and monitored at each stage of intervention. If the child moves up to the next tier of intervention, more intensive data-driven instruction or intervention is provided (Sabella & Clements, 2010). The three steps included in RtI are as follows:

- Tier 1 includes universal screening of all students with careful monitoring and charting of each student's progress.
- Tier 2 provides interventions for students who are not making Adequate Yearly Progress (AYP) in the general classroom. Students continue to learn through Tier 1 instruction but participate in Tier 2 interventions, which often involves small group counseling strategies. Progress is monitored and charted and if the students are still not progressing as anticipated, they move to Tier 3.
- Tier 3 provides intense one-on-one interventions for those students who have not made progress at the previous level. In this tier a student works with a designated individual to reach a targeted level of progress. The school counselor may be the designated individual to assist this student. When students do not respond to these influential strategies, the student may be eligible for special education services.

The intensity and duration of the data-driven strategies are considered in determining an appropriate educational strategy for the student (CTB/McGraw-Hill,

2011). School counselors are able to intervene at Tier 1 by providing guidance for all students through large group interventions. Small group counseling or skill development lessons can be conducted at Tier 2, and individual counseling and or agency referral are appropriate school counselor interventions at Tier 3. Response to Intervention is shown in Figure 12.7.

Figure 12.7   A Representation of RtI Intervention Phases

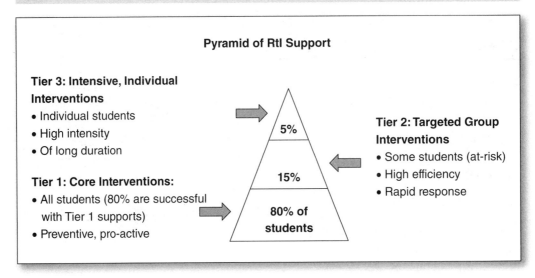

Pyramid of RtI Support

Tier 3: Intensive, Individual Interventions
- Individual students
- High intensity
- Of long duration

Tier 1: Core Interventions:
- All students (80% are successful with Tier 1 supports)
- Preventive, pro-active

5%

15%

80% of students

Tier 2: Targeted Group Interventions
- Some students (at-risk)
- High efficiency
- Rapid response

Source: http://www.aleks.com/k12/rti

School-wide Positive Behavioral Interventions and Supports (SW-PBIS) is a system similar to RtI in that instructional strategies are integrated to improve academics and behaviors. SW-PBIS is a universal method that supports appropriate behaviors and decreases unwanted behaviors.

SCHOOL-WIDE POSITIVE BEHAVIORAL INTERVENTIONS AND SUPPORTS

Educators consider classroom management as the most difficult aspect of their job, and one in which they have received little training (Reinke, Herman, & Stormont, 2013). Poor classroom management is associated with negative academic behavior and social growth (Weinstein, 2007, as cited in Reinke, et al., 2013). Historically, when students misbehaved they received adverse consequences such as paddling, which has been found to be ineffective in reducing unwanted behavior (Sprague, et al., 2001). School Wide-Positive Behavior Interventions and Supports (SW-PBIS) is a positive data-driven approach associated with behavior changes (Farkas, et al., 2012) and improved academic and behavioral outcomes, using evidence-based practices to identify the effects of interventions, as well as system support (Kay, 2005).

SW-PBIS consists of a developmentally appropriate list of classroom rules and procedures in which behaviors are positively stated, reinforced, and understood by all students and adults (Reinke, et al., 2013). Too often we tell students what we don't want but fail to tell them what is desired (e.g., "Don't run in the halls" as opposed to "Walk in the halls"). When behavior that is desired is defined, acknowledged, and rewarded, an outcome is improved behavior and academic growth. For positive rewards to be effective, researchers recommend that students receive a ratio of 4 positive contacts to 1 negative exchange (Reinke, et al., 2013).

SW-PBIS is similar to RTI in that it also consists of three tiers of prevention. Tier 1 is a universal school-wide intervention based on reinforcing positive behaviors. Tier 2 is a more intense intervention that targets small groups of students, and Tier 3 is an individualized, focused intervention for frequent or intense behavior problems (Farkas, et al., 2012). Both SW-PBIS and RTI have a goal of involving parents/guardians in implementing this collaborative, team-based approach to meet student needs. Both approaches support several ASCA National Standards for Student Competencies in the academic (A: A3 Achieve school success), career (C: C2 Apply skills to achieve career goals), and personal/social (PS:B1 Self-knowledge application) domains (Kay, 2005). Figure 12.8 (p. 410) depicts the levels of intervention.

As school systems adopt comprehensive models such as RtI and SW-PBIS for enhancing the academic, vocational, and personal/social growth of students, school counselors are essential in facilitating successful team-building through interdisciplinary collaboration.

INTERDISCIPLINARY COLLABORATION

When professionals from different areas meet, successful outcomes for this interdisciplinary collaboration include the components of interdependence, innovative strategies, flexibility, collaborative commitment to goals, and process reflection (Mellin, Anderson-Butcher, & Bronstein, 2011).

Interdependence

A common philosophy, budget, expertise, and communication style contributes to an effective collaborative relationship. Trust and reliance occur when there is a

Figure 12.8 School-Wide Positive Behavioral Interventions and Support

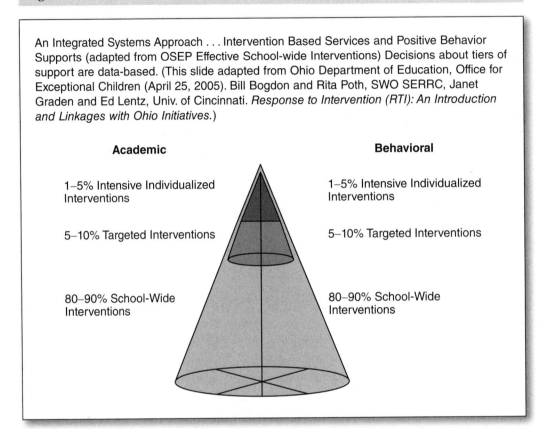

An Integrated Systems Approach . . . Intervention Based Services and Positive Behavior Supports (adapted from OSEP Effective School-wide Interventions) Decisions about tiers of support are data-based. (This slide adapted from Ohio Department of Education, Office for Exceptional Children (April 25, 2005). Bill Bogdon and Rita Poth, SWO SERRC, Janet Graden and Ed Lentz, Univ. of Cincinnati. *Response to Intervention (RTI): An Introduction and Linkages with Ohio Initiatives.*)

Academic

1–5% Intensive Individualized Interventions

5–10% Targeted Interventions

80–90% School-Wide Interventions

Behavioral

1–5% Intensive Individualized Interventions

5–10% Targeted Interventions

80–90% School-Wide Interventions

Source: http://www.pacer.org/pbis/pdf/PBISfeb08.pdf

clear understanding of roles among professionals who interact and rely on each other, time is spent together in both formal and informal arenas, respect is given for one another's opinions, and task identification and implementation occurs (Bronstein, 2002).

Innovative Strategies

Richer solutions will emerge when professionals meet to brainstorm solutions to dilemmas. As each professional contributes suggestions, a repertoire of answers that are fundamentally different and more innovative than what would be provided by an individual professional member emerges. A sense of belonging and accomplishment occurs when personal ideas and suggestions are acknowledged and considered during the process.

Flexibility

At time, professionals tend to be territorial when they believe that their knowledge and skills are superior to those of other professionals, a belief that leads to strained relationships when other professionals assume similar roles or tasks. Some may become concerned that their jobs may be eliminated, or additional tasks may be added to an already full work-load when others are involved in a project. However, when roles, strategies, and ideas are shared, compromises can be reached, new and more rewarding outcomes achieved, and greater satisfaction can result.

Collaborative Commitment to Goals

When professionals from different areas commit to goal development and achievement, each team member assumes goal failure or success. Movement toward goals includes actively listening to other members, respecting others' views in a trusting environment, and providing constructive feedback with the potential to create future collaborative efforts.

Process Reflection

Mellin, et al. (2011) revealed that results are disappointing when professionals fail to reflect and evaluate the collaborative process. When time is provided to think and talk about the collaboration, a greater understanding of strategy and process will emerge with stronger, more effective relationships as an outcome. Reserving the last five minutes of each meeting for gathering thoughts on how well the meeting went, and offering ideas to strengthen the process, or collecting interview and/or reaction statements offers an opportunity for useful evaluation.

Trusting relationships tend to be healthier and more productive, with the potential for creating a greater array of resources (Conoley & Conoley, 1991); however, not all collaborative relationships work as smoothly and productively as intended. For instance, when problems are not validated or addressed, and the seriousness of a situation is not acknowledged, teachers or other individuals will have difficulty enthusiastically working with you. Other barriers to collaboration are discussed in the next section.

Barriers to Collaboration

School principal expectations and school counselor self-efficacy influence partnerships (Bryan & Henry, 2012). Interpersonal collaboration could also be impeded when: a) professional roles in which expectations, respect, or perspectives are dissimilar, b) structural characteristics in which administration, time, or professional autonomy are not supported, c) personal characteristics such as the inability to understand or trust one another cause tension, and/or d) a negative history of inter-disciplinary collaboration is present.

Mellin et al. (2011) also emphasized the influence of physical space and sufficient time to conduct meetings. At times administrators who are focused on school achievement and improvement have difficulty understanding the need to allow time and the need for sufficient space for issues that they per-ceive do not directly contribute to this goal. School counselors can advocate for this practice by sharing studies that reveal concrete outcome data with principals. For instance, in one study when mental health practitioners and community mental health agencies assumed a partnership in suicide preven-tion and education, and worked together to identify and intervene with indi-viduals with mental health issues or suicidal ideation, a greater expansion of services resulted (Nickerson & Slater, 2009). The outcome was a cooperative endeavor in which individuals were able to receive greater resources than would be attained without this partnership.

CONCEPTUAL APPLICATION ACTIVITY 12.8

With a classmate, brainstorm ways that you could eliminate barriers to collaborative relationships.

Mistrust and frustration among professionals are created when there is a mis-understanding of terminology, training, and roles. As an example, I called the Department of Children's Services in the town in which I had been a practicing school counselor to report a student's threat that he was going to shoot his father. The social worker arrived at the school to meet with the student, and after an hour of conversing with the student she reported that she was going back to her office. When I inquired what she was going to do about the student's threats, she simply replied, "He was provoked—there is nothing I can do." Concerned about her cavalier attitude, I called the student's father to report my trepidation. Shortly after this event the student dropped out of school and a month later he was arrested for armed robbery. I often wondered if the outcome would have been different if she had understood my role as a school counselor and if we had worked collabora-tively to resolve the issue.

CASE STUDY 12.2

An elementary school counselor reported an incident of an attempt at collaboration that did not achieve the desired goals. Ten-year-old Eric (not his real name) enrolled in school as a result of being placed with his father and stepmother when his biological mother was arrested and put in jail due to drug charges. Although his father and stepmother really did not want to have custody of him, they reluctantly agreed when they were told that if they did not take him in, Eric would be placed in the foster care system. Several months later the stepmother requested to speak with the school counselor and principal due to her frustration because she suspected Eric of hurting her animals and what she termed his "manipulative attitude," even though she was unable to provide examples of these statements. The counselor empathically explained that it is not unusual for children to act out as a result of living in a home in which there was substance abuse, neglect, and being displaced from his home when his mother went to jail. The stepmother asked what the counselor was going to do to "fix him," and the counselor patiently explained that he had limits to what he was able to do. He provided the stepparent with a list of resource people whom the family could contact to receive family counseling, which she agreed to do.

Several months later, the counselor, who works at two different elementary schools, received a call from the elementary school where Eric was enrolled. The principal relayed that Eric urgently needed to talk with his counselor and asked if the counselor would be able to counsel Eric via a webcam. This technology provided an opportunity for the counselor to learn that Eric had been punished by holding his arms straight out to the side while holding soup cans, and at other times he would have his hands duct taped together while peanut butter would be smeared over his face and head as their pit bull licked it off. Eric explained that he was frightened because his stepmother threatened to "taze" him when he got home because of an argument they had that morning. The counselor contacted Children's Services, and since Eric no longer complained about his home life, it was assumed that Eric's home situation had improved until Eric had gotten into a fistfight with another student. After the counselor conducted a mediation with the two young boys, the principal called both of the boys' parents, which was the school protocol when a physical altercation occurred between students.

When Eric's stepmother was contacted she arrived at the building quite irate and stated that she was "done working with the school counselor since Eric hasn't been 'fixed' yet." The stepmother also heatedly informed the counselor that they had not gone to family counseling since Eric was the problem and obviously Eric had everyone fooled. The student transferred to a new school the next day and the counselor often lamented that the school, family, and the Department of Children's Services were not able to collaborate to give Eric the services he so greatly needed.

In this case, the school counselor desperately tried to create a supportive atmosphere in which all parties could develop rapport to acknowledge successes and reframe problems. Yet, despite these intentions, the desired outcome did not occur.

SCHOOL-PARENTAL/ GUARDIAN-COMMUNITY COLLABORATION

When all parties are willing to agree on a common goal, collaborative efforts will build a stronger appreciation for the process (Mellin, et al., 2011) and academic achievement may be enhanced. For instance, in a study by Ziomek-Daigle (2010), graduation rates increased when school/family/community interventions were implemented. This study revealed that the drop-out rate was reduced and academics were improved when the family was included in supervising and monitoring their child. Other studies suggest that collaborative schools tend to be more successful compared to traditional schools, where teachers tend to work in isolation (Cook & Friend, 2010). A better structure or outcome occurs when collaborators recognize, acknowledge, and inform others that discomfort often accompanies any type of change.

Successful school-family and community partnerships create external and internal resources for students (Bryan & Henry, 2012). School counselor partnership occurs at three levels: 1) involvement with the school and family through bridge-building to facilitate communication through workshops, home visits, and helping families access resources; 2) involvement in the school-community through such means as recruiting community mentors and tutors; and, 3) involvement on family teams through membership on community committees (Bryan & Henry, 2012).

School counselors collaborate with numerous stakeholders and in these situations student confidentiality with the provision of essential information (Iyer & Baster-MacGregor, 2010) must be balanced. Providing specific information may assist others in understanding the student's behavior, but also poses a potential ethical dilemma for the counselor in deciding how much information is too much to share. Furthermore, parent or guardian consent is necessary for information to be shared among practitioners.

When the family is invited to interact with school and/or community members, there is greater involvement with the possibility of improved academic success, attendance, and motivation, with decreased rates of suspension and substance use (Stevenson, Metz, & Snow, 2010). Yet, there are many factors that influence how parents/guardians interact with school personnel. For instance, the parent's history with school personnel, the type of experience the parent/guardian had when he/she was a student in school, and even the school atmosphere contribute to collaboration success or failure. In general, the more positive the parents'/guardians' past experiences have been, the more welcome the family will feel.

The school counselor is often viewed as a school leader who represents students' best interests, and in this role the school counselor sometimes receives parent/guardian wrath when their expectations for their child are not met. In one instance, a talented high school student was actively involved in many extracurricular activities and although he was enrolled in honors classes, he would not follow through on tasks and rarely handed assignments in on time. A team of high school teachers composed the scholarship selection committee and when this young man was not selected for a scholarship, the student's mother met with the school counselor for answers. The school counselor explained that her son did not follow through on responsibilities and additionally did not meet the ACT/SAT score criteria that were required for the scholarships. In response, this parent wrote a letter to the school board members about the school counselor's lack of assistance with her son, and as a result she stated that she would no longer be helping with school committees. Although this is a rare outcome of parent conferences, school counselors are considered as school figureheads and at times receive unjustified criticism. In these unusual circumstances, the use of basic counseling skills in which the parent/guardian can be heard without judgment has the potential to defuse uncomfortable situations.

A study by Griffin and Galassi (2010) sought to determine parental perceptions of barriers to their child's academic growth and the strategies that were helpful in overcoming these obstacles. Several themes emerged including: a) misunderstanding of their parental educational responsibilities; b) large student-teacher ratios that prevented individual attention; c) lack of communication between teachers and parents; d) educational barriers such as a lack of mentoring, complications in securing needed special education services, lack of transportation, and high-stakes testing pressures; e) lack of community programs such as before and after school programs for tutoring, affordable summer programs, and little knowledge of resources.

School/Parent/Community Collaborative Activities

CACREP

Successful collaboration is linked to family/school/and community empowerment in which there is shared decision making, ownership, and responsibility for outcomes (Bryan & Henry, 2012). These partnerships are intentional in the involvement of culturally diverse members and the cultivation and formation of mutually established goals. Griffin and Galassi (2010) suggest that school counselors consider the development of school/parent/community collaborative activities, cultivate parents as resources, facilitate a welcoming school culture, and develop a list of resources.

- **Parents as Resources.** The parent-teacher association (PTA) is a long established organization that links parents and school personnel. At times this organization does not meet the needs of the parents, and in these instances other parental programs may be needed. For instance, recognizing parents in the community who have unique talents and skills may be one strategy for initiating new programs such as mentoring programs, teaching parenting skills, providing tutoring, or helping with transportation barriers.
- **Welcoming School Culture.** Communication with a personal touch humanizes the school environment. In a study by Epstein (1986, as cited in Griffin & Galassi, 2010), 16% of parents reported not receiving any communication from teachers, 35% never had a parent/teacher conference, and 60% reported that they never had a direct phone call from teachers. Although technology has improved communication since this study occurred, school counselors can emphasize the importance of communicating with trust, support, and respect through multiple approaches.
- **Developing a List of Resources.** An updated listing of the community resources, contact information, and description of services that is accessible to community and educational personnel offers parents/guardians the services that promote success academically, vocationally, and personally/socially.

Active participation in which parent/guardian concerns are freely expressed (Bryan & Henry, 2012) in a culture of respect for diverse viewpoints assists in closing the achievement gap. When a healthy environment is created with attention to cultural differences, students will benefit.

Awareness of Diversity in Collaboration

Awareness of personal and cultural values and how they could impact ethnically diverse individuals, and vigilance to different family structures are components that also influence collaborative success. Knowledge of cross-cultural views such as non-verbal communication including lack of eye contact, time orientation, rules and norms, collectivist versus independence values, and family hierarchy are elements that create effective relationships without pathologizing the family.

It is also possible that individuals may have had negative cultural experiences in previous relationships. Individuals from some cultures believe that education is best left to the educators, whereas other families take a more active role. The school counselor could consider enlisting the support of other members within the family's culture such as a religious figure or a leader of the ethnic group, particularly if there are communication difficulties. As an example, I taught in a school counseling program in California in which there was a large Hispanic population. One of my graduate students told me that her parents had never learned to speak English and only communicated with people who spoke Spanish, even though they had lived in California for the past 30 years. She further relayed that when she was in high school her parents were called to the principal's office regarding her disruptive behavior. When this occurred she would serve as a translator, and rather than appropriately divulging the principal's concern about her disturbing classroom behavior and poor grades, she instead translated the message to be, "Your daughter is doing very well in school and we are glad she is here." Although this is a humorous anecdote, a more productive relationship would occur when translators are available for the conference rather than relying on the student's report.

It is obvious that communication is the key to parent/guardian involvement, and technology can be a useful strategy for keeping families informed of school events, yet not all families have access to this technology. We need to consider a variety of ways to keep all parents and families apprised of significant school dates, activities, and their child's progress. Stevenson, et al. (2010) tackled the issue of parents not attending school events by asking each teacher in the school to identify the top 10 parents they wished would attend a parent/teacher conference. The school counselors then personally invited these parents/guardians to a school meeting on a specific day and time, with the option to request a different appointment. Attendance was significantly increased due to this intervention that created a "personal touch." Other communication strategies to initiate a positive school/family partnership include multiple mailings, phone calls, notes sent with students, neighborhood "breakfast chats," or e-mails.

CONCEPTUAL APPLICATION ACTIVITY 12.9

Brainstorm methods with your classmates that school counselors could use to communicate with parents and some of the pros and cons of each of these methods.

Membership in families with a student with special needs, grandparents raising grandchildren, and youth from military families are households in which numbers are increasing in comparison to the numbers of these families in previous generations. The school counselor is critical in easing stressors these families confront by making a positive school milieu for students and their families.

WORKING WITH STUDENTS
AND FAMILIES WITH SPECIAL NEEDS

The Individuals with Disabilities Education Improvement Act (IDEIA) is a federal law that provides funding to schools to deliver a "free an appropriate public education" to students with identified special needs (*Special Education News,* 2012). The Individual Education Plan (IEP) is an essential component of the student's education that includes specific goals and strategies for addressing these goals. An IEP team requires that parents/guardians, at least one general education teacher, a special education teacher, and a school representative who is familiar with special education laws be present at the meeting (George, 2013). Federal law requires that parents/guardians are to be included in writing the plan. Every effort is to be made to ensure that parents/guardians are informed of the purpose of the meeting, when it will occur, the location, and who will be present. In some schools the school counselor takes a leadership role in planning, leading, or attending these meetings.

Imagine being a parent/guardian invited to a school meeting in which numerous school professionals whom you don't know are in attendance. This is a situation that can create stress accompanied by defensiveness. The school counselor can be helpful in preparing families for these meetings by giving advance notification of the individuals who will be present, their roles, the purpose of the meeting, and how long the meeting will last. School counselors are also able to express to the parents/guardians that their contributions are important components in bringing the meeting to an acceptable outcome. In addition, parents/guardians are to understand that if they have questions about terminology or other aspects of the meeting, their questions are welcome.

At one time my husband and I attended a parent/teacher conference because of our concern over our daughter's low social studies grades. Although we were well aware of the parent-teacher conference expectations, we still had some anxiety as we entered this meeting, apprehension that increased as the meeting progressed. Rather than taking time to let us introduce ourselves and our own concerns about our daughter's grades, the teacher started the conference by tossing his grade book on the table while stating, "Your daughter's grades are terrible—just terrible." This action was not only unhelpful, it created reluctance in wanting to partner with this teacher to figure out how we could work together to improve her grades.

WORKING WITH
GRANDPARENTS RAISING GRANDCHILDREN

Throughout history grandparents have raised grandchildren, but it was not until the last few decades that the numbers of grandparent-headed families have significantly increased (Glass & Huneycutt, 2002a, as cited in Edwards & Ray,

2008). Generally, these family structures are created due to crisis events designated as the "4-Ds," or more specifically known as divorce, desertion, drugs, and death (DeToledo & Brown, 1995, as cited in Edwards & Ray, 2008). More recently, with the rise of dual income households, especially when there are infants and young children, grandparents have increasingly been asked to serve as caregivers. When caregiving situations arise, grandparents need to adapt to this changing situation and in many cases may be forced to give up plans such as travel or engaging in hobbies, which could result in feelings of guilt and anger when life plans are disrupted (Strom & Strom, 2011). These changing circumstances can place children at risk for school failure and difficult life situations. However, factors such as the grandparents' age, energy level, and ability to buffer negative influences may promote resiliency among the grandchildren.

Grandparents raising their grandchildren are also confronted with additional expenses that they had not anticipated, particularly since (on average) their yearly incomes are approximately half of what nuclear families with children make (Strom & Strom, 2011). This is a genuine hardship when grandparents do not live in the same school district as their grandchildren and tuition is involved to keep them in the same district.

The school counselor is in a position to provide grandparents with a sense of community with their reacquired parenting roles. Grandparents are sometimes hesitant to attend school meetings, particularly when they are much older than the other parents. If this is the case, school counselors could assist in providing referral services for family counseling or any other needed community resource, or arranging seminars on topics such as parent/teacher conferencing, managing finances, helping children with homework, or stress and relaxation.

WORKING WITH MILITARY FAMILIES

Children from families in which one or both parents are in the military have a unique set of challenges. These children change schools frequently not only when moving off or on base, but also when a parent is deployed. Although deployment differs among military branches, the estimated length of deployment averages around 12–15 months, with approximately 2.2 deployments (Chandra, et al., 2008, as cited in Card, et al., 2011), though in recent years the number of deployments may well have risen.

Deployment has the potential to create positive experiences, particularly when youth take on new roles that have the potential of bringing about a sense of pride and accomplishment. However, there may also be negative consequences such as academic concerns (Card, et al., 2011) due to frequent school transfers.

When school counselors are aware of some of the issues that could negatively impact youth growth and achievement, they are in a unique position to provide support and serve as a resource. For instance, military children who have lived in a different country may have difficulty acclimating themselves to a new country, culture, and curriculum. Those who have lived in countries in which a language other than English was spoken may have difficulty with the English language. Further complications arise when records for those who have been in special education classes are difficult to obtain, and in some cases students could be inappropriately placed in a classroom until a copy of an IEP can be received (Rowland & Benton, 2005).

School counselors can be excellent resources for these students by creating an "ambassador program" in which an already enrolled military student can serve as a mentor to the newly enrolled student. In addition, creating a support group for students from military families to discuss concerns and give advice and information can be critical to the well-being of the group members (Rowland & Benton, 2005). The Military Child Education Coalition (MCEC) http://www.militarychild.org/ is a resource for helpful information about such things as scholarships, training, and camps.

CONCLUSION

School counselors have responsibilities as consultants and collaborators. These responsibilities are designed to assist students in achieving maximum growth in the academic, vocational, and personal/social domains. Although consultation and collaboration roles are similar, there are also differences in methodology used and responsibility for outcome. Working with others who support this mission has the potential for creating greater opportunities for students and their families than can be achieved by one professional working without the assistance of others. Empowering parents in school/community collaboration through a caring, welcoming school culture also creates a partnership for success. School counselors' collaborative efforts are especially needed when attending to students with special needs, grandparents who are raising grandchildren, and students who live in military families. Finally, the school counselor has a responsibility to be aware of ethical and legal considerations in collaboration and consultation.

REFERENCES

American School Counselor Association (2010). *Ethical standards for school counselors.* Retrieved from http://www.schoolcounselor.org

Baker, S. B., Robichaud, T. A., Westforth, V. C., Wells, S. C., & Schreck, R. E. (2009). School counselor consultation: A pathway to advocacy, collaboration, and leadership. *Professional School Counseling, 12,* 200–209.

Bodenhorn, N. (2006). Exploratory study of common and challenging ethical dilemmas experienced by professional school counselors. *Professional School Counseling, 10,* 195–202.

Bostic, J. Q. (2002). School consultation. In Jellinek, M., Patel, B.P., & Froehle, M.C. (Eds.), *Bright futures in practice: Mental Health–Volume II. Tool Kit.* Arlington, VA: National Center for Education in Maternal and Child Health.

Braden, J. S., DiMarino-Linnen, E., & Good, T. L. (2001). Schools, society, and school psychology: History and future directions. *Journal of School Psychology, 39,* 203–219.

Brigman, G., Webb, L. D., & Campbell, C. (2007). Building skills for school success: Improving the academic and social competence of students. *Professional School Counseling, 10,* 279–288.

Bronstein, L. R. (2002). Index of interdisciplinary collaboration. *Social Work Research, 26,* 113–126.

Bruce, A. M., Getch, Y.Q., & Ziomek-Daigle, J. (2009). Closing the gap: A group counseling approach to improve test performance of African-American students. *Professional School Counseling, 12,* 450–457.

Bryan, J., & Henry, L. (2012). A model for building school-family-community partnerships: Principles and process. *Journal of Counseling & Development, 90,* 408–420.

Card, N.A., Bosch, L., Casper, D. M., Wiggs, C. B., Hawkins, S. A., Schlomer, G. L., & Borden, L. M. (2011). A meta-analytic review of internalizing, externalizing, and academic adjustment among children of deployed military service members. *Journal of Family Psychology, 25,* 508–520. doi: 10.1037/a0024395

Conoley, J. C., & Conoley, C. W. (1991). Collaboration for child adjustment: Issues for school and clinic-based child psychologists. *Clinical Psychology, 59,* 821–829.

Cook, L., & Friend, M. (2010). The state of the art of collaboration on behalf of students with disabilities. *Journal of Educational and Psychological Consultation, 20,* 1–8. doi: 10.10.10 80/10474410903535398

CTB/McGraw-Hill (2011). *Response to intervention: Integrating assessment and intervention to improve student achievement.* Retrieved from http://www.ctb.com/ctb.com/control/productC ategoryViewAction?productCategoryId=362&p=products

Duncan, C. F. (1995). Cross-cultural school consultation. In C. C. Lee (Ed.), *Counseling for diversity: A guide for school counselors and related professionals* (pp. 129–141). Needham Heights, MA: Allyn and Bacon.

Edwards, O., & Ray, S. (2008). An attachment and school satisfaction framework for helping children raised by grandparents. *School Psychology Quarterly, 23,* 125–138.

Fagan, T. K. (1981). Special educational services and the school psychologist. *Journal of Learning Disabilities, 14,* 383–384.

Farkas, M. S., Simonsen, B., Migdole, S., Donovan, M. E., Clemens, K., & Cicchese, V. (2012). Schoolwide positive behavior support in an alternative school setting: An evaluation of fidelity, outcomes, and social validity of Tier 1 implementation. *Journal of Emotional and Behavioral Disorders, 20,* 275–288.

George, S. (2013). Working with families of children with exceptional needs. In K. B. Grant & J. A. Ray (Eds.), *Home, School, and Community Collaboration: Culturally responsive family engagement* (2nd ed.). Los Angeles, CA: Sage.

Griffin, D., & Galassi, J. P. (2010). Parent perceptions of barriers to academic success in a rural middle school. *Professional School Counseling, 14,* 87–100.

Gysbers, N., & Henderson, P. (2012). *Developing & managing your school guidance and counseling program* (5th ed.). Alexandria, VA: ACA.

Hylander, I. (2012). Conceptual change through consultee-centered consultation: A theoretical model. *Consulting Psychology Journal: Practice and Research, 64,* 29–45.

Iyer, N. N., & Baster-MacGregor, J. (2010). Ethical dilemmas for the school counselor: Balancing student confidentiality and parents' right to know. *NERA Conference Proceedings. Paper 15.* Retrieved from http://digitalcommonsucon.edu/near_2010/15

Kampwirth, T. J. (2006). *Collaborative consultation in the schools* (3rd ed.). Upper Saddle River, NJ: Pearson.

Kay, D. (2005, June). A team approach to positive behavior. *ASCA School Counselor.* Alexandria, VA: ASCA.

Martines, D. (2008). *Multicultural school psychology competencies: A practical guide.* Los Angeles, CA: Sage.

Mellin, E. A., Anderson-Butcher, D., & Bronstein, L. (2011). Strengthening interprofessional team collaboration: Potential roles for school mental health professionals. *Advances in school mental health promotion, 4,* 51–61. doi.org/10.1080/1754730X.2011.9715629

National Association of School Nurses (2013). About NASN. Retrieved from http://www.nasn.org/AboutNASN

Nickerson, A. B., & Slater, E. D. (2009). School and community violence and victimization as predictors of adolescent suicidal behavior. *School Psychology Review, 38,* 218–232.

Pérusse, R., & Goodnough, G. E. (2005). Elementary and secondary school counselors' perceptions of graduate preparation programs: A national study. *Counselor Education & Supervision, 45,* 109–118.

Reinke, W. M., Herman, K. C., & Stormont, M. (2013). Classroom-level positive behavior supports in schools implementing SW-PBIS: Identifying areas for enhancement. *Journal of Positive Behavior Interventions, 15,* 39–50. doi: 10.1177/1098300712459079

Rowland, K. D., & Benton, J. (2005, Nov.-Dec.). How to be a military friendly school. *ASCA School Counselor,* 17–20.

Rowley, W. J. (2000). Expanding collaboration partnerships among school counselors and school psychologists. *Professional School Counseling, 3,* 224–228.

Sabella, R. A., & Clements, K. D. (2010, May/June). Response to intervention: Make it work. *ASCA School Counselor.*

Special Education News (2012, Sept.). IDEIA—Individuals with Disabilities Education Improvement Act. Retrieved from http://www.specialednews.com/special-education-dictionary/ideia—individuals-with-disabilities-education-improvement-act.htm

Sprague, J., Walker, H., Golly, A., White, K., Myers, D. R., & Shannon, T. (2001). Translating research into effective practice: The effects of a universal staff and student intervention on indicators of discipline and school safety. *Education and Treatment of Children, 24,* 495–511.

Stephens, D.L., & Lindsey, R. B. (2011). *Culturally proficient collaboration: Use and misuse of school counselors.* Thousand Oaks, CA: Corwin.

Stevenson, R., Metz, A. J., & Snow, M. (2010, July/August). Empowered high school parents. *ASCA School Counselor.* Alexandria, VA: American School Counselor Association.

Strom, P. S., & Strom, R. D. (2011). Grandparent education: Raising grandchildren. *Educational Gerontology, 37,* 910–923. doi.org/10.1080/03601277.2011.595345

Van Veisor, P. (2009). School counselors as social-emotional learning consultants: Where do we begin? *Professional School Counseling, 13,* 50–58.

Ziomek-Daigle, J. (2010). Schools, families, and communities affecting the dropout rate: Implications and strategies for family counselors. *The Family Journal, 18,* 377–383.

INDEX

Figures and tables are indicated by an *f* or *t* following the page number.

About the Author

Jeannine R. Studer is a professor of counselor education at the University of Tennessee, Knoxville. She was previously a high school counselor at Perkins High School in Sandusky, Ohio, and later she began the school counseling program at Heidelberg University in Tiffin, Ohio, where she was an assistant and associate professor and program coordinator. Studer was also an associate professor and co-program coordinator of school counseling at California State University, Stanislaus.

Studer received her doctorate in counseling at the University of Toledo. She has written numerous journal articles on the school counselor's role, at-risk students, students with special needs, supervision of school counselors, and accountability procedures. She is the author of *The Professional School Counselor: An Advocate for Students; Supervising the School Counselor Trainee: Guidelines for Practice;* and *A Guide to Practicum and Internship for School-Counselors-in-Training.*

ABOUT THE CONTRIBUTORS

Carolyn Berger, PhD, is a graduate of the University of Florida and is presently an assistant professor at Nova Southeastern University. She is a certified school counselor and served as a school counselor for five years. She is a board member of the Florida School Counselor Association and is president for 2013–2014. She has several publications about career theory and career readiness, and the school counselor's role in bullycide.

Deborah Buchanan, PhD, is an assistant professor of psychology and counselor educator in the psychology department at Austin Peay State University (APSU) in Clarksville, Tennessee. She is currently the graduate program coordinator for the school counseling program at APSU. She received her PhD in Counselor Education in 2011 from the University of Tennessee. She has 13 years of experience in the public school setting, five as a middle school teacher and eight as a middle school counselor. She maintains her certification both as a professional school counselor and a middle school teacher in the state of Tennessee. She has published and presented on the topics of school administrators' perceptions of school counselors' roles; classroom management tips and techniques for school counselors; effective collaboration between school counselors and stakeholders; transforming counselor educators: facilitating a change in professional identity through a constructivist approach; and transforming counselors to counselor educators: doctoral students' exploration of PhD programs. Deborah's current research interests include school counselors' experiences with classroom management, school administrator and school counselor relationships, and counselors-in-training skill development.

Michael Bundy, PhD, NCC, CPC, is an assistant professor in the School Counseling Program at Carson-Newman University. For over twenty years, he served in East Tennessee as a secondary and junior high counselor in a rural school and as an elementary school counselor in a suburban setting. He earned his PhD in counselor education from the University of Tennessee. His research interests include best practices in school counseling and comprehensive developmental school counseling programs. He has published eighteen articles and three book chapters and has made numerous presentations at the regional, state, and national levels. He has been recognized numerous times for his work, most notably as Counselor-of-the-Year, Outstanding Achievement in Counselor Education, and Counselor-Educator-of-the-Year by the Tennessee Counseling Association.

Tara Jungersen, PhD, LMHC, NCC, ACS, is an assistant professor of counselor education at Nova Southeastern University. She completed her PhD in Counselor Education and Supervision at the University of Tennessee, and her M.Ed. in Community Counseling at the University of Virginia. She is a licensed mental health counselor, with both individual and group work experience in private practice, community mental health, and elementary, middle and high schools. Her research interests include clinical supervision, intimate partner violence, trauma, and treatment access for underserved populations. Jungersen is a member of the American Counseling Association, the Association for Counselor Education and Supervision, and Chi Sigma Iota.

Aaron H. Oberman, PhD, NCC, is an associate professor of counselor education at the Citadel, where he also serves as the coordinator of school counseling field experiences. He earned his doctorate in counselor education and supervision from the University of Tennessee, Knoxville. Oberman's experiences include work as a career counselor, as well as a counselor educator with an emphasis in school and career counseling. His research interests focus on teaching career counseling, the supervision of school counselors-in-training, and the implementation of the ASCA National Model.

⑤SAGE research**methods**

The essential online tool for researchers from the world's leading methods publisher

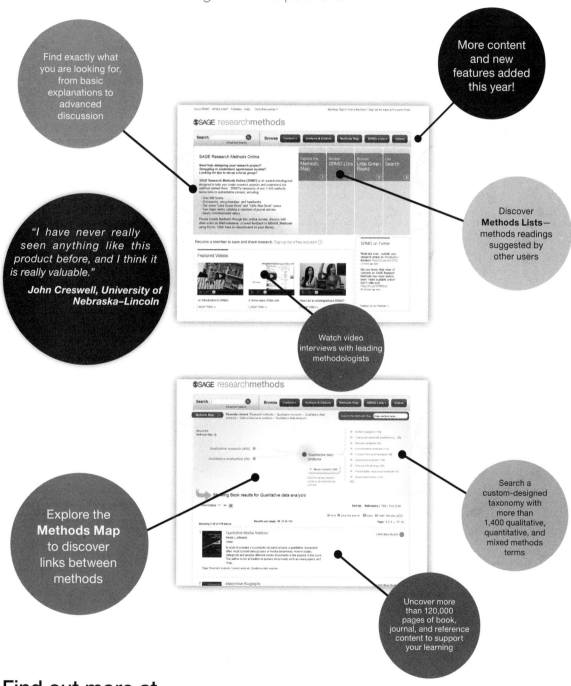

Find exactly what you are looking for, from basic explanations to advanced discussion

More content and new features added this year!

"I have never really seen anything like this product before, and I think it is really valuable."

John Creswell, University of Nebraska–Lincoln

Discover **Methods Lists**— methods readings suggested by other users

Watch video interviews with leading methodologists

Explore the **Methods Map** to discover links between methods

Search a custom-designed taxonomy with more than 1,400 qualitative, quantitative, and mixed methods terms

Uncover more than 120,000 pages of book, journal, and reference content to support your learning

Find out more at
www.sageresearchmethods.com